The
Education of
Henry
Adams

II

The Education of Henry Adams

An Autobiography

TIME *Reading Program Special Edition*
TIME INCORPORATED, NEW YORK

TIME INC. BOOK DIVISION
EDITOR *Norman P. Ross*
COPY DIRECTOR *William Jay Gold*
ART DIRECTOR *Edward A. Hamilton*
CHIEF OF RESEARCH *Beatrice T. Dobie*
EDITOR, TIME READING PROGRAM *Max Gissen*
ASSISTANT EDITOR *Jerry Korn*
RESEARCHER *Ann S. Lang*
DESIGNER *Lore Levenberg*

PUBLISHER *Jerome S. Hardy*
GENERAL MANAGER *John A. Watters*

TIME MAGAZINE
EDITOR *Roy Alexander*
MANAGING EDITOR *Otto Fuerbringer*
PUBLISHER *Bernhard M. Auer*

COVER DESIGN *Hank Brennan*

Contents

16

The Press

(1868)

At ten o'clock of a July night, in heat that made the tropical rain-shower simmer, the Adams family and the Motley family clambered down the side of their Cunard steamer into the government tugboat, which set them ashore in black darkness at the end of some North River pier. Had they been Tyrian traders of the year B.C. 1000, landing from a galley fresh from Gibraltar, they could hardly have been stranger on the shore of a world, so changed from what it had been ten years before. The historian of the Dutch, no longer historian but diplomatist, started up an unknown street, in company with the private secretary who had become private citizen, in search of carriages to convey the two parties to the Brevoort House. The pursuit was arduous but successful. Towards midnight they found shelter once more in their native land.

How much its character had changed or was changing, they could not wholly know, and they could but partly feel. For that matter, the land itself knew no more than they. Society in America was always trying, almost as blindly as an earthworm, to realize and understand itself;

to catch up with its own head, and to twist about in search of its tail. Society offered the profile of a long, straggling caravan, stretching loosely towards the prairies, its few score of leaders far in advance and its millions of immigrants, negroes, and Indians far in the rear, somewhere in archaic time. It enjoyed the vast advantage over Europe that all seemed, for the moment, to move in one direction, while Europe wasted most of its energy in trying several contradictory movements at once; but whenever Europe or Asia should be polarized or oriented towards the same point, America might easily lose her lead. Meanwhile each newcomer needed to slip into a place as near the head of the caravan as possible, and needed most to know where the leaders could be found.

One could divine pretty nearly where the force lay, since the last ten years had given to the great mechanical energies — coal, iron, steam — a distinct superiority in power over the old industrial elements — agriculture, handwork, and learning; but the result of this revolution on a survivor from the fifties resembled the action of the earthworm; he twisted about, in vain, to recover his starting-point; he could no longer see his own trail; he had become an estray; a flotsam or jetsam of wreckage; a belated reveller, or a scholar-gipsy like Matthew Arnold's. His world was dead. Not a Polish Jew fresh from Warsaw or Cracow — not a furtive Yacoob or Ysaac still reeking of the Ghetto, snarling a weird Yiddish to the officers of the customs — but had a keener instinct, an intenser energy, and a freer hand than he — American of Americans, with Heaven knew how many Puritans and Patriots behind him, and an education that had cost a civil war. He made no complaint and found no fault with his time; he was no worse off than the Indians or the buffalo who had been ejected from their heritage by his own people; but he vehemently insisted that he was not himself at fault.

The defeat was not due to him, nor yet to any superiority of his rivals. He had been unfairly forced out of the track, and must get back into it as best he could.

One comfort he could enjoy to the full. Little as he might be fitted for the work that was before him, he had only to look at his father and Motley to see figures less fitted for it than he. All were equally survivals from the forties — bric-à-brac from the time of Louis Philippe; stylists; doctrinaires; ornaments that had been more or less suited to the colonial architecture, but which never had much value in Desbrosses Street or Fifth Avenue. They could scarcely have earned five dollars a day in any modern industry. The men who commanded high pay were as a rule not ornamental. Even Commodore Vanderbilt and Jay Gould lacked social charm. Doubtless the country needed ornament — needed it very badly indeed — but it needed energy still more, and capital most of all, for its supply was ridiculously out of proportion to its wants. On the new scale of power, merely to make the continent habitable for civilized people would require an immediate outlay that would have bankrupted the world. As yet, no portion of the world except a few narrow stretches of western Europe had ever been tolerably provided with the essentials of comfort and convenience; to fit out an entire continent with roads and the decencies of life would exhaust the credit of the entire planet. Such an estimate seemed outrageous to a Texan member of Congress who loved the simplicity of nature's noblemen; but the mere suggestion that a sun existed above him would outrage the self-respect of a deep-sea fish that carried a lantern on the end of its nose. From the moment that railways were introduced, life took on extravagance.

Thus the belated reveller who landed in the dark at the Desbrosses Street ferry, found his energies exhausted in the effort to see his own length. The new Americans, of

whom he was to be one, must, whether they were fit or
unfit, create a world of their own, a science, a society, a
philosophy, a universe, where they had not yet created
a road or even learned to dig their own iron. They had
no time for thought; they saw, and could see, nothing
beyond their day's work; their attitude to the universe
outside them was that of the deep-sea fish. Above all, they
naturally and intensely disliked to be told what to do, and
how to do it, by men who took their ideas and their methods from the abstract theories of history, philosophy, or
theology. They knew enough to know that their world
was one of energies quite new.

All this, the newcomer understood and accepted, since
he could not help himself and saw that the American
could help himself as little as the newcomer; but the fact
remained that the more he knew, the less he was educated.
Society knew as much as this, and seemed rather inclined
to boast of it, at least on the stump; but the leaders of
industry betrayed no sentiment, popular or other. They
used, without qualm, whatever instruments they found at
hand. They had been obliged, in 1861, to turn aside and
waste immense energy in settling what had been settled
a thousand years before, and should never have been revived. At prodigious expense, by sheer force, they broke
resistance down, leaving everything but the mere fact of
power untouched, since nothing else had a solution. Race
and thought were beyond reach. Having cleared its path
so far, society went back to its work, and threw itself
on that which stood first — its roads. The field was vast;
altogether beyond its power to control offhand; and society dropped every thought of dealing with anything
more than the single fraction called a railway system. This
relatively small part of its task was still so big as to need
the energies of a generation, for it required all the new
machinery to be created — capital, banks, mines, furnaces,

shops, power-houses, technical knowledge, mechanical population, together with a steady remodelling of social and political habits, ideas, and institutions to fit the new scale and suit the new conditions. The generation between 1865 and 1895 was already mortgaged to the railways, and no one knew it better than the generation itself.

Whether Henry Adams knew it or not, he knew enough to act as though he did. He reached Quincy once more, ready for the new start. His brother Charles had determined to strike for the railroads; Henry was to strike for the press; and they hoped to play into each other's hands. They had great need, for they found no one else to play with. After discovering the worthlessness of a so-called education, they had still to discover the worthlessness of so-called social connection. No young man had a larger acquaintance and relationship than Henry Adams, yet he knew no one who could help him. He was for sale, in the open market. So were many of his friends. All the world knew it, and knew too that they were cheap; to be bought at the price of a mechanic. There was no concealment, no delicacy, and no illusion about it. Neither he nor his friends complained; but he felt sometimes a little surprised that, as far as he knew, no one, seeking in the labor market, ever so much as inquired about their fitness. The want of solidarity between old and young seemed American. The young man was required to impose himself, by the usual business methods, as a necessity on his elders, in order to compel them to buy him as an investment. As Adams felt it, he was in a manner expected to blackmail. Many a young man complained to him in after life of the same experience, which became a matter of curious reflection as he grew old. The labor market of good society was ill-organized.

Boston seemed to offer no market for educated labor. A peculiar and perplexing amalgam Boston always was, and although it had changed much in ten years, it was not less perplexing. One no longer dined at two o'clock; one could no longer skate on Back Bay; one heard talk of Bostonians worth five millions or more as something not incredible. Yet the place seemed still simple, and less rest-less-minded than ever before. In the line that Adams had chosen to follow, he needed more than all else the help of the press, but any shadow of hope on that side vanished instantly. The less one meddled with the Boston press, the better. All the newspapermen were clear on that point. The same was true of politics. Boston meant business. The Bostonians were building railways. Adams would have liked to help in building railways, but had no education. He was not fit.

He passed three or four months thus, visiting relations, renewing friendships, and studying the situation. At thirty years old, the man who has not yet got further than to study the situation, is lost, or near it. He could see nothing in the situation that could be of use to him. His friends had won no more from it than he. His brother Charles, after three years of civil life, was no better off than him-self, except for being married and in greater need of in-come. His brother John had become a brilliant political leader on the wrong side. No one had yet regained the lost ground of the war.

He went to Newport and tried to be fashionable, but even in the simple life of 1868, he failed as fashion. All the style he had learned so painfully in London was worse than useless in America where every standard was differ-ent. Newport was charming, but it asked for no education and gave none. What it gave was much gayer and pleas-anter, and one enjoyed it amazingly; but friendships in that society were a kind of social partnership, like the classes at college; not education but the subjects of education. All were doing the same thing, and asking the same question of the future. None could help. Society seemed founded on the law that all was for the best New Yorkers in the best of Newports, and that all young people were rich if they could waltz. It was a new version of the Ant and Grasshopper.

At the end of three months, the only person, among the hundreds he had met, who had offered him a word of encouragement or had shown a sign of acquaintance with his doings, was Edward Atkinson. Boston was cool towards sons, whether prodigals or other, and needed much time to make up its mind what to do for them — time which Adams, at thirty years old, could hardly spare. He had not the courage or self-confidence to hire an office in State Street, as so many of his friends did, and doze there alone, vacuity within and a snowstorm outside, waiting for Fortune to knock at the door, or hoping to find her asleep in the elevator; or on the staircase, since elevators were not yet in use. Whether this course would have offered his best chance he never knew; it was one of the points in practical education which most needed a clear understanding, and he could never reach it. His father and mother would have been glad to see him stay with them and begin reading Blackstone again, and he showed no very filial tenderness by abruptly breaking the tie that had lasted so long. After all, perhaps Beacon Street was as good as any other street for his objects in life; possibly his easiest and surest path was from Beacon Street to State Street and back again, all the days of his years. Who could tell? Even after life was over, the doubt could not be determined.

In thus sacrificing his heritage, he only followed the path that had led him from the beginning. Boston was full of his brothers. He had reckoned from childhood on

outlawry as his peculiar birthright. The mere thought of
beginning life again in Mount Vernon Street lowered the
pulsations of his heart. This is a story of education — not
a mere lesson of life — and, with education, temperament
has in strictness nothing to do, although in practice they
run close together. Neither by temperament nor by education was he fitted for Boston. He had drifted far away
and behind his companions there; no one trusted his temperament or education; he had to go.

Since no other path seemed to offer itself, he stuck to
his plan of joining the press, and selected Washington as
the shortest road to New York, but, in 1868, Washington
stood outside the social pale. No Bostonian had ever gone
there. One announced one's self as an adventurer and an
office-seeker, a person of deplorably bad judgment, and
the charges were true. The chances of ending in the gutter
were, at best, even. The risk was the greater in Adams's
case, because he had no very clear idea what to do when
he got there. That he must educate himself over again,
for objects quite new, in an air altogether hostile to his
old educations, was the only certainty; but how he was
to do it — how he was to convert the idler in Rotten Row
into the lobbyist of the Capital — he had not an idea, and
no one to teach him. The question of money is rarely
serious for a young American unless he is married, and
money never troubled Adams more than others; not because he had it, but because he could do without it, like
most people in Washington who all lived on the income
of bricklayers; but with or without money he met the
difficulty that, after getting to Washington in order to
go on the press, it was necessary to seek a press to go on.
For large work he could count on the *North American
Review*, but this was scarcely a press. For current discussion and correspondence, he could depend on the New

York *Nation;* but what he needed was a New York daily, and no New York daily needed him. He lost his one chance by the death of Henry J. Raymond. The *Tribune* under Horace Greeley was out of the question both for political and personal reasons, and because Whitelaw Reid had already undertaken that singularly venturesome position, amid difficulties that would have swamped Adams in four-and-twenty hours. Charles A. Dana had made the *Sun* a very successful as well as a very amusing paper, but had hurt his own social position in doing it; and Adams knew himself well enough to know that he could never please himself and Dana too; with the best intentions, he must always fail as a blackguard, and at that time a strong dash of blackguardism was life to the *Sun.* As for the *New York Herald*, it was a despotic empire admitting no personality but that of Bennett. Thus, for the moment, the New York daily press offered no field except the free-trade Holy Land of the *Evening Post* under William Cullen Bryant, while beside it lay only the elevated plateau of the New Jerusalem occupied by Godkin and the *Nation.* Much as Adams liked Godkin, and glad as he was to creep under the shelter of the *Evening Post* and the *Nation*, he was well aware that he should find there only the same circle of readers that he reached in the *North American Review.*

The outlook was dim, but it was all he had, and at Washington, except for the personal friendship of Mr. Evarts who was then Attorney-General and living there, he would stand in solitude much like that of London in 1861. Evarts did what no one in Boston seemed to care for doing; he held out a hand to the young man. Whether Boston, like Salem, really shunned strangers, or whether Evarts was an exception even in New York, he had the social instinct which Boston had not. Generous by nature, prodigal in hospitality, fond of young people, and a born man-of-the-world, Evarts gave and took liberally, without scruple, and accepted the world without fearing or abusing it. His wit was the least part of his social attraction. His talk was broad and free. He laughed where he could; he joked if a joke was possible; he was true to his friends, and never lost his temper or became ill-natured. Like all New Yorkers he was decidedly not a Bostonian; but he was what one might call a transplanted New Englander, like General Sherman; a variety, grown in ranker soil. In the course of life, and in widely different countries, Adams incurred heavy debts of gratitude to persons on whom he had no claim and to whom he could seldom make return; perhaps half-a-dozen such debts remained unpaid at last, although six is a large number as lives go; but kindness seldom came more happily than when Mr. Evarts took him to Washington in October, 1868.

Adams accepted the hospitality of the sleeper, with deep gratitude, the more because his first struggle with a sleeping-car made him doubt the value — to him — of a Pullman civilization; but he was even more grateful for the shelter of Mr. Evarts's house in H Street at the corner of Fourteenth, where he abode in safety and content till he found rooms in the roomless village. To him the village seemed unchanged. Had he not known that a great war and eight years of astonishing movement had passed over it, he would have noticed nothing that betrayed growth. As of old, houses were few; rooms fewer; even the men were the same. No one seemed to miss the usual comforts of civilization, and Adams was glad to get rid of them, for his best chance lay in the eighteenth century.

The first step, of course, was the making of acquaintance, and the first acquaintance was naturally the President, to whom an aspirant to the press officially paid respect. Evarts immediately took him to the White House and presented him to President Andrew Johnson. The interview was brief and consisted in the stock remark common to monarchs and valets, that the young man looked even younger than he was. The younger man felt even younger than he looked. He never saw the President again, and never felt a wish to see him, for Andrew Johnson was not the sort of man whom a young reformer of thirty, with two or three foreign educations, was likely to see with enthusiasm; yet, musing over the interview as a matter of education, long years afterwards, he could not help recalling the President's figure with a distinctness that surprised him. The old-fashioned Southern Senator and statesman sat in his chair at his desk with a look of self-esteem that had its value. None doubted. All were great men; some, no doubt, were greater than others; but all were statesmen and all were supported, lifted, inspired by the moral certainty of rightness. To them the universe was serious, even solemn, but it was their universe, a Southern conception of right. Lamar used to say that he never entertained a doubt of the soundness of the Southern system until he found that slavery could not stand a war. Slavery was only a part of the Southern system, and the life of it all — the vigor — the poetry — was its moral certainty of self. The Southerner could not doubt; and this self-assurance not only gave Andrew Johnson the look of a true President, but actually made him one. When Adams came to look back on it afterwards, he was surprised to realize how strong the Executive was in 1868 — perhaps the strongest he was ever to see. Certainly he never again found himself so well satisfied, or so much at home.

Seward was still Secretary of State. Hardly yet an old man, though showing marks of time and violence, Mr. Seward seemed little changed in these eight years. He was the same — with a difference. Perhaps he — unlike

Henry Adams — had at last got an education, and all he wanted. Perhaps he had resigned himself to doing without it. Whatever the reason, although his manner was as roughly kind as ever, and his talk as free, he appeared to have closed his account with the public; he no longer seemed to care; he asked nothing, gave nothing, and invited no support; he talked little of himself or of others, and waited only for his discharge. Adams was well pleased to be near him in these last days of his power and fame, and went much to his house in the evenings when he was sure to be at his whist. At last, as the end drew near, wanting to feel that the great man — the only chief he ever served even as a volunteer — recognized some personal relation, he asked Mr. Seward to dine with him one evening in his rooms, and play his game of whist there, as he did every night in his own house. Mr. Seward came and had his whist, and Adams remembered his rough parting speech: "A very sensible entertainment!" It was the only favor he ever asked of Mr. Seward, and the only one he ever accepted.

Thus, as a teacher of wisdom, after twenty years of example, Governor Seward passed out of one's life, and Adams lost what should have been his firmest ally; but in truth the State Department had ceased to be the centre of his interest, and the Treasury had taken its place. The Secretary of the Treasury was a man new to politics — Hugh McCulloch — not a person of much importance in the eyes of practical politicians such as young members of the press meant themselves to become, but they all liked Mr. McCulloch, though they thought him a stop-gap rather than a force. Had they known what sort of forces the Treasury was to offer them for support in the generation to come, they might have reflected a long while on their estimate of McCulloch. Adams was fated to watch the flittings of many more Secretaries than he ever cared to know, and he rather came back in the end to the idea that McCulloch was the best of them, although he seemed to represent everything that one liked least. He was no politician, he had no party, and no power. He was not fashionable or decorative. He was a banker, and towards bankers Adams felt the narrow prejudice which the serf feels to his overseer; for he knew he must obey, and he knew that the helpless showed only their helplessness when they tempered obedience by mockery. The world, after 1865, became a bankers' world, and no banker would ever trust one who had deserted State Street, and had gone to Washington with purposes of doubtful credit, or of no credit at all, for he could not have put up enough collateral to borrow five thousand dollars of any bank in America. The banker never would trust him, and he would never trust the banker. To him, the banking mind was obnoxious; and this antipathy caused him the more surprise at finding McCulloch the broadest, most liberal, most genial, and most practical public man in Washington.

There could be no doubt of it. The burden of the Treasury at that time was very great. The whole financial system was in chaos; every part of it required reform; the utmost experience, tact, and skill could not make the machine work smoothly. No one knew how well Mc-Culloch did it until his successor took it in charge, and tried to correct his methods. Adams did not know enough to appreciate McCulloch's technical skill, but he was struck at his open and generous treatment of young men. Of all rare qualities, this was, in Adams's experience, the rarest. As a rule, officials dread interference. The strongest often resent it most. Any official who admits equality in discussion of his official course, feels it to be an act of virtue; after a few months or years he tires of the effort.

Every friend in power is a friend lost. This rule is so nearly absolute that it may be taken in practice as admitting no exception. Apparent exceptions exist, and McCulloch was one of them.

McCulloch had been spared the gluttonous selfishness and infantile jealousy which are the commoner results of early political education. He had neither past nor future, and could afford to be careless of his company. Adams found him surrounded by all the active and intelligent young men in the country. Full of faith, greedy for work, eager for reform, energetic, confident, capable, quick of study, charmed with a fight, equally ready to defend or attack, they were unselfish, and even — as young men went — honest. They came mostly from the army, with the spirit of the volunteers. Frank Walker, Frank Barlow, Frank Bartlett were types of the generation. Most of the press, and much of the public, especially in the West, shared their ideas. No one denied the need for reform. The whole government, from top to bottom, was rotten with the senility of what was antiquated and the instability of what was improvised. The currency was only one example; the tariff was another; but the whole fabric required reconstruction as much as in 1789, for the Constitution had become as antiquated as the Confederation. Sooner or later a shock must come, the more dangerous the longer postponed. The Civil War had made a new system in fact; the country would have to reorganize the machinery in practice and theory.

One might discuss indefinitely the question which branch of government needed reform most urgently; all needed it enough, but no one denied that the finances were a scandal, and a constant, universal nuisance. The tariff was worse, though more interests upheld it. McCulloch had the singular merit of facing reform with large good-nature and willing sympathy — outside of parties, jobs, bargains, corporations or intrigues — which Adams never was to meet again.

Chaos often breeds life, when order breeds habit. The Civil War had bred life. The army bred courage. Young men of the volunteer type were not always docile under control, but they were handy in a fight. Adams was greatly pleased to be admitted as one of them. He found himself much at home with them — more at home than he ever had been before, or was ever to be again — in the atmosphere of the Treasury. He had no strong party passion, and he felt as though he and his friends owned this administration, which, in its dying days, had neither friends nor future except in them.

These were not the only allies; the whole government in all its branches was alive with them. Just at that moment the Supreme Court was about to take up the Legal Tender cases where Judge Curtis had been employed to argue against the constitutional power of the Government to make an artificial standard of value in time of peace. Evarts was anxious to fix on a line of argument that should have a chance of standing up against that of Judge Curtis, and was puzzled to do it. He did not know which foot to put forward. About to deal with Judge Curtis, the last of the strong jurists of Marshall's school, he could risk no chances. In doubt, the quickest way to clear one's mind is to discuss, and Evarts deliberately forced discussion. Day after day, driving, dining, walking he provoked Adams to dispute his positions. He needed an anvil, he said, to hammer his ideas on.

Adams was flattered at being an anvil, which is, after all, more solid than the hammer; and he did not feel called on to treat Mr. Evarts's arguments with more respect than Mr. Evarts himself expressed for them; so he contradicted with freedom. Like most young men, he was much of a doctrinaire, and the question was, in any event, rather historical or political than legal. He could easily maintain, by way of argument, that the required power had never been given, and that no sound constitutional reason could possibly exist for authorizing the Government to over- throw the standard of value without necessity, in time of peace. The dispute itself had not much value for him, even as education, but it led to his seeking light from the Chief Justice himself. Following up the subject for his letters to the *Nation* and his articles in the *North Ameri- can Review*, Adams grew to be intimate with the Chief Justice, who, as one of the oldest and strongest leaders of the Free Soil Party, had claims to his personal regard; for the old Free Soilers were becoming few. Like all strong- willed and self-asserting men, Mr. Chase had the faults of his qualities. He was never easy to drive in harness, or light in hand. He saw vividly what was wrong, and did not always allow for what was relatively right. He loved power as though he were still a Senator. His position to- wards Legal Tender was awkward. As Secretary of the Treasury he had been its author; as Chief Justice he be- came its enemy. Legal Tender caused no great pleasure or pain in the sum of life to a newspaper correspondent, but it served as a subject for letters, and the Chief Justice was very willing to win an ally in the press who would tell his story as he wished it to be read. The intimacy in Mr. Chase's house grew rapidly, and the alliance was no small help to the comforts of a struggling newspaper adven- turer in Washington. No matter what one might think of his politics or temper, Mr. Chase was a dramatic figure, of high senatorial rank, if also of certain senatorial faults; a valuable ally.

As was sure, sooner or later, to happen, Adams one day met Charles Sumner on the street, and instantly stopped to greet him. As though eight years of broken ties were the natural course of friendship, Sumner at once, after an exclamation of surprise, dropped back into the relation of hero to the school boy. Adams enjoyed accepting it. He was then thirty years old and Sumner was fifty-seven; he had seen more of the world than Sumner ever dreamed of, and he felt a sort of amused curiosity to be treated once more as a child. At best, the renewal of broken relations is a nervous matter, and in this case it bristled with thorns, for Sumner's quarrel with Mr. Adams had not been the most delicate of his ruptured relations, and he was liable to be sensitive in many ways that even Bostonians could hardly keep in constant mind; yet it interested and fascinated Henry Adams as a new study of political humanity. The younger man knew that the meeting would have to come, and was ready for it, if only as a newspaper need; but to Sumner it came as a surprise and a disagreeable one, as Adams conceived. He learned something — a piece of practical education worth the effort — by watching Sumner's behavior. He could see that many thoughts — mostly unpleasant — were passing through his mind, since he made no inquiry about any of Adams's family, or allusion to any of his friends or his residence abroad. He talked only of the present. To him, Adams in Washington should have seemed more or less of a critic, perhaps a spy, certainly an intriguer or adventurer like scores of others; a politician without party; a writer without principles; an office-seeker certain to beg for support. All this was, for his purposes, true. Adams could do him no good, and would be likely to do him all the harm in his power. Adams accepted it all; expected to be kept at arm's length; admitted that the reasons were just. He was the more surprised to see that Sumner invited a renewal of old relations. He found himself treated almost confidentially. Not only was he asked to make a fourth at Sumner's pleasant little dinners in the house on La Fayette Square, but he found himself admitted to the Senator's study and informed of his views, policy and purposes, which were sometimes even more astounding than his curious gaps or lapses of omniscience.

On the whole, the relation was the queerest that Henry Adams ever kept up. He liked and admired Sumner, but thought his mind a pathological study. At times he inclined to think that Sumner felt his solitude, and, in the political wilderness, craved educated society; but this hardly told the whole story. Sumner's mind had reached the calm of water which receives and reflects images without absorbing them; it contained nothing but itself. The images from without, the objects mechanically perceived by the senses, existed by courtesy until the mental surface was ruffled, but never became part of the thought. Henry Adams roused no emotion; if he had roused a disagreeable one, he would have ceased to exist. The mind would have mechanically rejected, as it had mechanically admitted him. Not that Sumner was more aggressively egoistic than other Senators — Conkling, for instance — but that with him the disease had affected the whole mind; it was chronic and absolute; while, with other Senators for the most part, it was still acute.

Perhaps for this very reason, Sumner was the more valuable acquaintance for a newspaper-man. Adams found him most useful; perhaps quite the most useful of all these great authorities who were the stock-in-trade of the newspaper business; the accumulated capital of a Silurian age. A few months or years more, and they were gone. In 1868, they were like the town itself, changing but not changed. La Fayette Square was society. Within a few hundred yards of Mr. Clark Mills's nursery monument to the equestrian seat of Andrew Jackson, one found all one's acquaintance as well as hotels, banks, markets and national government. Beyond the Square the country began. No rich or fashionable stranger had yet discovered

the town. No literary or scientific man, no artist, no
gentleman without office or employment, had ever lived
there. It was rural, and its society was primitive. Scarcely
a person in it had ever known life in a great city. Mr.
Evarts, Mr. Sam Hooper, of Boston, and perhaps one or
two of the diplomatists had alone mixed in that sort of
world. The happy village was innocent of a club. The
one-horse tram on F Street to the Capitol was ample for
traffic. Every pleasant spring morning at the Pennsylvania
Station, society met to bid good-bye to its friends going
off on the single express. The State Department was
lodged in an infant asylum far out on Fourteenth Street
while Mr. Mullett was constructing his architectural infant asylum next the White House. The value of real
estate had not increased since 1800, and the pavements
were more impassable than the mud. All this favored a
young man who had come to make a name. In four-and-
twenty hours he could know everybody; in two days
everybody knew him.

After seven years' arduous and unsuccessful effort to
explore the outskirts of London society, the Washington
world offered an easy and delightful repose. When he
looked round him, from the safe shelter of Mr. Evarts's
roof, on the men he was to work with — or against — he
had to admit that nine-tenths of his acquired education
was useless, and the other tenth harmful. He would have
to begin again from the beginning. He must learn to talk
to the Western Congressman, and to hide his own ante-
cedents. The task was amusing. He could see nothing to
prevent him from enjoying it, with immoral unconcern
for all that had gone before and for anything that might
follow. The lobby offered a spectacle almost picturesque.
Few figures on the Paris stage were more entertaining
and dramatic than old Sam Ward, who knew more of
life than all the departments of the Government together,

including the Senate and the Smithsonian. Society had not much to give, but what it had, it gave with an open hand. For the moment, politics had ceased to disturb social relations. All parties were mixed up and jumbled together in a sort of tidal slack-water. The Government resembled Adams himself in the matter of education. All that had gone before was useless, and some of it was worse.

17

President
Grant

(1869)

The first effect of this leap into the unknown was a fit of low spirits new to the young man's education; due in part to the overpowering beauty and sweetness of the Maryland autumn, almost unendurable for its strain on one who had toned his life down to the November grays and browns of northern Europe. Life could not go on so beautiful and so sad. Luckily, no one else felt it or knew it. He bore it as well as he could, and when he picked himself up, winter had come, and he was settled in bachelor's quarters, as modest as those of a clerk in the Departments far out on G Street, towards Georgetown, where an old Finn named Dohna, who had come out with the Russian Minister Stoeckel long before, had bought or built a new house. Congress had met. Two or three months remained to the old administration, but all interest centered in the new one. The town began to swarm with office-seekers, among whom a young writer was lost. He drifted among them, unnoticed, glad to learn his work under cover of the confusion. He never aspired to

become a regular reporter; he knew he should fail in trying a career so ambitious and energetic; but he picked up
friends on the press — Nordhoff, Murat Halstead, Henry
Watterson, Sam Bowles — all reformers, and all mixed
and jumbled together in a tidal wave of expectation,
waiting for General Grant to give orders. No one seemed
to know much about it. Even Senators had nothing to say.
One could only make notes and study finance.

In waiting, he amused himself as he could. In the amusements of Washington, education had no part, but the
simplicity of the amusements proved the simplicity of
everything else, ambitions, interests, thoughts, and knowledge. Proverbially Washington was a poor place for education, and of course young diplomats avoided or disliked
it, but, as a rule, diplomats disliked every place except
Paris, and the world contained only one Paris. They
abused London more violently than Washington; they
praised no post under the sun; and they were merely describing three-fourths of their stations when they complained that there were no theatres, no restaurants, no
monde, no *demi-monde*, no drives, no splendor, and, as
Mme. de Struve used to say, no *grandezza*. This was all
true; Washington was a mere political camp, as transient
and temporary as a camp-meeting for religious revival,
but the diplomats had least reason to complain, since they
were more sought for there than they would ever be elsewhere. For young men Washington was in one way paradise, since they were few, and greatly in demand. After
watching the abject unimportance of the young diplomat
in London society, Adams found himself a young duke in
Washington. He had ten years of youth to make up,
and a ravenous appetite. Washington was the easiest society he had ever seen, and even the Bostonian became
simple, good-natured, almost genial, in the softness of a

Washington spring. Society went on excellently well without houses, or carriages, or jewels, or toilettes, or pavements, or shops, or *grandezza* of any sort; and the market was excellent as well as cheap. One could not stay there a month without loving the shabby town. Even the Washington girl, who was neither rich nor well-dressed nor well-educated nor clever, had singular charm, and used it. According to Mr. Adams the father, this charm dated back as far as Monroe's administration, to his personal knowledge.

Therefore, behind all the processes of political or financial or newspaper training, the social side of Washington was to be taken for granted as three-fourths of existence. Its details matter nothing. Life ceased to be strenuous, and the victim thanked God for it. Politics and reform became the detail, and waltzing the profession. Adams was not alone. Senator Sumner had as private secretary a young man named Moorfield Storey, who became a dangerous example of frivolity. The new Attorney-General, E. R. Hoar, brought with him from Concord a son, Sam Hoar, whose example rivalled that of Storey. Another impenitent was named Dewey, a young naval officer. Adams came far down in the list. He wished he had been higher. He could have spared a world of superannuated history, science, or politics, to have reversed better in waltzing.

He had no adequate notion how little he knew, especially of women, and Washington offered no standard of comparison. All were profoundly ignorant together, and as indifferent as children to education. No one needed knowledge. Washington was happier without style. Certainly Adams was happier without it; happier than he had ever been before; happier than any one in the harsh world of strenuousness could dream of. This must be taken as background for such little education as he gained; but the life belonged to the eighteenth century, and in no way concerned education for the twentieth.

In such an atmosphere, one made no great pretence of hard work. If the world wants hard work, the world must pay for it; and, if it will not pay, it has no fault to find with the worker. Thus far, no one had made a suggestion of pay for any work that Adams had done or could do; if he worked at all, it was for social consideration, and social pleasure was his pay. For this he was willing to go on working, as an artist goes on painting when no one buys his pictures. Artists have done it from the beginning of time, and will do it after time has expired, since they cannot help themselves, and they find their return in the pride of their social superiority as they feel it. Society commonly abets them and encourages their attitude of contempt. The society of Washington was too simple and Southern as yet, to feel anarchistic longings, and it never read or saw what artists produced elsewhere, but it good-naturedly abetted them when it had the chance, and respected itself the more for the frailty. Adams found even the Government at his service, and every one willing to answer his questions. He worked, after a fashion; not very hard, but as much as the Government would have required of him for nine hundred dollars a year; and his work defied frivolity. He got more pleasure from writing than the world ever got from reading him, for his work was not amusing, nor was he. One must not try to amuse money-lenders or investors, and this was the class to which he began by appealing. He gave three months to an article on the finances of the United States, just then a subject greatly needing treatment; and when he had finished it, he sent it to London to his friend Henry Reeve, the ponderous editor of the *Edinburgh Review*. Reeve probably thought it good; at all events, he said so; and he printed it in April. Of course it was reprinted in

America, but in England such articles were still anonymous, and the author remained unknown.

The author was not then asking for advertisement, and made no claim for credit. His object was literary. He wanted to win a place on the staff of the *Edinburgh Review*, under the vast shadow of Lord Macaulay; and, to a young American in 1868, such rank seemed colossal — the highest in the literary world — as it had been only five-and-twenty years before. Time and tide had flowed since then, but the position still flattered vanity, though it brought no other flattery or reward except the regular thirty pounds of pay — fifty dollars a month, measured in time and labor.

The Edinburgh article finished, he set himself to work on a scheme for the *North American Review*. In England, Lord Robert Cecil had invented for the *London Quarterly* an annual review of politics which he called the "Session." Adams stole the idea and the name — he thought he had been enough in Lord Robert's house, in days of his struggle with adversity, to excuse the theft — and began what he meant for a permanent series of annual political reviews which he hoped to make, in time, a political authority. With his sources of information, and his social intimacies at Washington, he could not help saying something that would command attention. He had the field to himself, and he meant to give himself a free hand, as he went on. Whether the newspapers liked it or not, they would have to reckon with him; for such a power, once established, was more effective than all the speeches in Congress or reports to the President that could be crammed into the Government presses.

The first of these "Sessions" appeared in April, but it could not be condensed into a single article, and had to be supplemented in October by another which bore the title of "Civil Service Reform," and was really a part of

the same review. A good deal of authentic history slipped
into these papers. Whether any one except his press associates ever read them, he never knew and never greatly
cared. The difference is slight, to the influence of an
author, whether he is read by five hundred readers, or by
five hundred thousand; if he can select the five hundred,
he reaches the five hundred thousand. The fateful year
1870 was near at hand, which was to mark the close of
the literary epoch, when quarterlies gave way to month-
lies; letter-press to illustration; volumes to pages. The
outburst was brilliant. Bret Harte led, and Robert Louis
Stevenson followed. Guy de Maupassant and Rudyard
Kipling brought up the rear, and dazzled the world. As
usual, Adams found himself fifty years behind his time,
but a number of belated wanderers kept him company,
and they produced on each other the effect or illusion of
a public opinion. They straggled apart, at longer and
longer intervals, through the procession, but they were
still within hearing distance of each other. The drift was
still superficially conservative. Just as the Church spoke
with apparent authority, so the quarterlies laid down an
apparent law, and no one could surely say where the real
authority, or the real law, lay. Science did not know.
Truths *a priori* held their own against truths purely relative. According to Lowell, Right was forever on the
Scaffold, Wrong was forever on the Throne; and most
people still thought they believed it. Adams was not the
only relic of the eighteenth century, and he could still
depend on a certain number of listeners — mostly respectable, and some rich.

Want of audience did not trouble him; he was well
enough off in that respect, and would have succeeded in
all his calculations if this had been his only hazard. Where
he broke down was at a point where he always suffered
wreck and where nine adventurers out of ten make their

errors. One may be more or less certain of organized forces; one can never be certain of men. He belonged to the eighteenth century, and the eighteenth century upset all his plans. For the moment, America was more eighteenth century than himself; it reverted to the stone age.

As education -- of a certain sort -- the story had probably a certain value, though he could never see it. One seldom can see much education in the buck of a broncho; even less in the kick of a mule. The lesson it teaches is only that of getting out of the animal's way. This was the lesson that Henry Adams had learned over and over again in politics since 1860.

At least four-fifths of the American people -- Adams among the rest -- had united in the election of General Grant to the Presidency, and probably had been more or less affected in their choice by the parallel they felt between Grant and Washington. Nothing could be more obvious. Grant represented order. He was a great soldier, and the soldier always represented order. He might be as partisan as he pleased, but a general who had organized and commanded half a million or a million men in the field, must know how to administer. Even Washington, who was, in education and experience, a mere cave-dweller, had known how to organize a government, and had found Jeffersons and Hamiltons to organize his departments. The task of bringing the Government back to regular practices, and of restoring moral and mechanical order to administration, was not very difficult; it was ready to do it itself, with a little encouragement. No doubt the confusion, especially in the old slave States and in the currency, was considerable, but the general disposition was good, and every one had echoed the famous phrase: "Let us have peace."

Adams was young and easily deceived, in spite of his diplomatic adventures, but even at twice his age he could

not see that this reliance on Grant was unreasonable. Had
Grant been a Congressman one would have been on one's
guard, for one knew the type. One never expected from
a Congressman more than good intentions and public
spirit. Newspaper-men as a rule had no great respect for
the lower House; Senators had less; and Cabinet officers
had none at all. Indeed, one day when Adams was pleading with a Cabinet officer for patience and tact in dealing
with Representatives, the Secretary impatiently broke out:
"You can't use tact with a Congressman! A Congressman
is a hog! You must take a stick and hit him on the snout!"
Adams knew far too little, compared with the Secretary,
to contradict him, though he thought the phrase somewhat harsh even as applied to the average Congressman of
1869 — he saw little or nothing of later ones — but he
knew a shorter way of silencing criticism. He had but to
ask: "If a Congressman is a hog, what is a Senator?" This
innocent question, put in a candid spirit, petrified any
executive officer that ever sat a week in his office. Even
Adams admitted that Senators passed belief. The comic
side of their egotism partly disguised its extravagance,
but faction had gone so far under Andrew Johnson that
at times the whole Senate seemed to catch hysterics of
nervous bucking without apparent reason. Great leaders,
like Sumner and Conkling, could not be burlesqued; they
were more grotesque than ridicule could make them; even
Grant, who rarely sparkled in epigram, became witty on
their account; but their egotism and factiousness were no
laughing matter. They did permanent and terrible mischief, as Garfield and Blaine, and even McKinley and
John Hay, were to feel. The most troublesome task of a
reform President was that of bringing the Senate back to
decency.

Therefore no one, and Henry Adams less than most,

felt hope that any President chosen from the ranks of politics or politicians would raise the character of government; and by instinct if not by reason, all the world united on Grant. The Senate understood what the world expected, and waited in silence for a struggle with Grant more serious than that with Andrew Johnson. Newspaper-men were alive with eagerness to support the President against the Senate. The newspaper-man is, more than most men, a double personality; and his person feels best satisfied in its double instinct when writing in one sense and thinking in another. All newspaper-men, whatever they wrote, felt alike about the Senate. Adams floated with the stream. He was eager to join in the fight which he foresaw as sooner or later inevitable. He meant to support the executive in attacking the Senate and taking away its two-thirds vote and power of confirmation, nor did he much care how it should be done, for he thought it safer to effect the revolution in 1870 than to wait till 1920.

With this thought in mind, he went to the Capitol to hear the names announced which should reveal the carefully guarded secret of Grant's Cabinet. To the end of his life, he wondered at the suddenness of the revolution which actually, within five minutes, changed his intended future into an absurdity so laughable as to make him ashamed of it. He was to hear a long list of Cabinet announcements not much weaker or more futile than that of Grant, and none of them made him blush, while Grant's nominations had the singular effect of making the hearer ashamed, not so much of Grant, as of himself. He had made another total misconception of life — another inconceivable false start. Yet, unlikely as it seemed, he had missed his motive narrowly, and his intention had been more than sound, for the Senators made no secret of saying with senatorial frankness that Grant's nominations

betrayed his intent as plainly as they betrayed his incompetence. A great soldier might be a baby politician.

Adams left the Capitol, much in the same misty mental
condition that he recalled as marking his railway journey
to London on May 13, 1861; he felt in himself what Gladstone bewailed so sadly, "the incapacity of viewing things
all round." He knew, without absolutely saying it, that
Grant had cut short the life which Adams had laid out
for himself in the future. After such a miscarriage, no
thought of effectual reform could revive for at least one
generation, and he had no fancy for ineffectual politics.
What course could he sail next? He had tried so many,
and society had barred them all! For the moment, he saw
no hope but in following the stream on which he had
launched himself. The new Cabinet, as individuals, were
not hostile. Subsequently Grant made changes in the list
which were mostly welcome to a Bostonian — or should
have been — although fatal to Adams. The name of Hamilton Fish, as Secretary of State, suggested extreme con-
servatism and probable deference to Sumner. The name
of George S. Boutwell, as Secretary of the Treasury,
suggested only a somewhat lugubrious joke; Mr. Boutwell
could be described only as the opposite of Mr. McCulloch,
and meant inertia; or, in plain words, total extinction for
any one resembling Henry Adams. On the other hand,
the name of Jacob D. Cox, as Secretary of the Interior,
suggested help and comfort; while that of Judge Hoar,
as Attorney-General, promised friendship. On the whole,
the personal outlook, merely for literary purposes, seemed
fairly cheerful, and the political outlook, though hazy,
still depended on Grant himself. No one doubted that
Grant's intention had been one of reform; that his aim
had been to place his administration above politics; and
until he should actually drive his supporters away, one

might hope to support him. One's little lantern must therefore be turned on Grant. One seemed to know him so well, and really knew so little.

By chance it happened that Adam Badeau took the lower suite of rooms at Dohna's, and, as it was convenient to have one table, the two men dined together and became intimate. Badeau was exceedingly social, though not in appearance imposing. He was stout; his face was red, and his habits were regularly irregular; but he was very intelligent, a good newspaper-man, and an excellent military historian. His life of Grant was no ordinary book. Unlike most newspaper-men, he was a friendly critic of Grant, as suited an officer who had been on the General's staff. As a rule, the newspaper correspondents in Washington were unfriendly, and the lobby sceptical. From that side one heard tales that made one's hair stand on end, and the old West Point army officers were no more flattering. All described him as vicious, narrow, dull, and vindictive. Badeau, who had come to Washington for a consulate which was slow to reach him, resorted more or less to whiskey for encouragement, and became irritable, besides being loquacious. He talked much about Grant, and showed a certain artistic feeling for analysis of character, as a true literary critic would naturally do. Loyal to Grant, and still more so to Mrs. Grant, who acted as his patroness, he said nothing, even when far gone, that was offensive about either, but he held that no one except himself and Rawlins understood the General. To him, Grant appeared as an intermittent energy, immensely powerful when awake, but passive and plastic in repose. He said that neither he nor the rest of the staff knew why Grant succeeded; they believed in him because of his success. For stretches of time, his mind seemed torpid. Rawlins and the others would systematically talk their ideas into it, for weeks, not directly, but by discussion among themselves, in his presence. In the end, he would announce the idea as his own, without seeming conscious of the discussion; and would give the orders to carry it out with all the energy that belonged to his nature. They could never measure his character or be sure when he would act. They could never follow a mental process in his thought. They were not sure that he did think.

In all this, Adams took deep interest, for although he was not, like Badeau, waiting for Mrs. Grant's power of suggestion to act on the General's mind in order to germinate in a consulate or a legation, his portrait gallery of great men was becoming large, and it amused him to add an authentic likeness of the greatest general the world had seen since Napoleon. Badeau's analysis was rather delicate; infinitely superior to that of Sam Ward or Charles Nordhoff.

Badeau took Adams to the White House one evening and introduced him to the President and Mrs. Grant. First and last, he saw a dozen Presidents at the White House, and the most famous were by no means the most agreeable, but he found Grant the most curious object of study among them all. About no one did opinions differ so widely. Adams had no opinion, or occasion to make one. A single word with Grant satisfied him that, for his own good, the fewer words he risked, the better. Thus far in life he had met with but one man of the same intellectual or unintellectual type — Garibaldi. Of the two, Garibaldi seemed to him a trifle the more intellectual, but, in both, the intellect counted for nothing; only the energy counted. The type was pre-intellectual, archaic, and would have seemed so even to the cave-dwellers. Adam, according to legend, was such a man.

In time one came to recognize the type in other men, with differences and variations, as normal; men whose energies were the greater, the less they wasted on thought; men who sprang from the soil to power; apt to be distrustful of themselves and of others; shy; jealous; sometimes vindictive; more or less dull in outward appearance; always needing stimulants; but for whom action was the highest stimulant — the instinct of fight. Such men were forces of nature, energies of the prime, like the *Pteraspis*, but they made short work of scholars. They had commanded thousands of such and saw no more in them than in others. The fact was certain; it crushed argument and intellect at once.

Adams did not feel Grant as a hostile force; like Badeau he saw only an uncertain one. When in action he was superb and safe to follow; only when torpid he was dangerous. To deal with him one must stand near, like Rawlins, and practice more or less sympathetic habits. Simple-minded beyond the experience of Wall Street or State Street, he resorted, like most men of the same intellectual calibre, to commonplaces when at a loss for expression: "Let us have peace!" or, "The best way to treat a bad law is to execute it"; or a score of such reversible sentences generally to be gauged by their sententiousness; but sometimes he made one doubt his good faith; as when he seriously remarked to a particularly bright young woman that Venice would be a fine city if it were drained. In Mark Twain, this suggestion would have taken rank among his best witticisms; in Grant it was a measure of simplicity not singular. Robert E. Lee betrayed the same intellectual commonplace, in a Virginian form, not to the same degree, but quite distinctly enough for one who knew the American. What worried Adams was not the commonplace; it was, as usual, his own education. Grant fretted and irritated him, like the *Terebratula*, as a defiance of first principles. He had no right to exist. He should have been extinct for ages. The idea that, as society grew

older, it grew one-sided, upset evolution, and made of
education a fraud. That, two thousand years after Alexander the Great and Julius Cæsar, a man like Grant should
be called — and should actually and truly be — the highest
product of the most advanced evolution, made evolution
ludicrous. One must be as commonplace as Grant's own
commonplaces to maintain such an absurdity. The progress of evolution from President Washington to President
Grant, was alone evidence enough to upset Darwin.

Education became more perplexing at every phase. No
theory was worth the pen that wrote it. America had no
use for Adams because he was eighteenth-century, and
yet it worshipped Grant because he was archaic and
should have lived in a cave and worn skins. Darwinists
ought to conclude that America was reverting to the stone
age, but the theory of reversion was more absurd than
that of evolution. Grant's administration reverted to nothing. One could not catch a trait of the past, still less of
the future. It was not even sensibly American. Not an
official in it, except perhaps Rawlins whom Adams never
met, and who died in September, suggested an American
idea.

Yet this administration, which upset Adams's whole
life, was not unfriendly; it was made up largely of friends.
Secretary Fish was almost kind; he kept the tradition of
New York social values; he was human and took no
pleasure in giving pain. Adams felt no prejudice whatever in his favor, and he had nothing in mind or person
to attract regard; his social gifts were not remarkable;
he was not in the least magnetic; he was far from young;
but he won confidence from the start and remained a
friend to the finish. As far as concerned Mr. Fish, one
felt rather happily suited, and one was still better off in
the Interior Department with J. D. Cox. Indeed, if Cox
had been in the Treasury and Boutwell in the Interior,

one would have been quite satisfied as far as personal relations went, while, in the Attorney-General's Office, Judge Hoar seemed to fill every possible ideal, both personal and political.

The difficulty was not the want of friends, and had the whole government been filled with them, it would have helped little without the President and the Treasury. Grant avowed from the start a policy of drift; and a policy of drift attaches only barnacles. At thirty, one has no interest in becoming a barnacle, but even in that character Henry Adams would have been ill-seen. His friends were reformers, critics, doubtful in party allegiance, and he was himself an object of suspicion. Grant had no objects, wanted no help, wished for no champions. The Executive asked only to be let alone. This was his meaning when he said: "Let us have peace!"

No one wanted to go into opposition. As for Adams, all his hopes of success in life turned on his finding an administration to support. He knew well enough the rules of self-interest. He was for sale. He wanted to be bought. His price was excessively cheap, for he did not even ask an office, and had his eye, not on the Government, but on New York. All he wanted was something to support; something that would let itself be supported. Luck went dead against him. For once, he was fifty years in advance of his time.

18

Free Fight

(1869–1870)

The old New Englander was apt to be a solitary animal, but the young New Englander was sometimes human. Judge Hoar brought his son Sam to Washington, and Sam Hoar loved largely and well. He taught Adams the charm of Washington spring. Education for education, none ever compared with the delight of this. The Potomac and its tributaries squandered beauty. Rock Creek was as wild as the Rocky Mountains. Here and there a negro log cabin alone disturbed the dogwood and the judas-tree, the azalea and the laurel. The tulip and the chestnut gave no sense of struggle against a stingy nature. The soft, full outlines of the landscape carried no hidden horror of glaciers in its bosom. The brooding heat of the profligate vegetation; the cool charm of the running water; the terrific splendor of the June thunder-gust in the deep and solitary woods, were all sensual, animal, elemental. No European spring had shown him the same intermixture of delicate grace and passionate depravity that marked the Maryland May. He loved it too much, as though it were Greek and half human. He could not leave it, but loitered on into July, falling into the Southern ways of the summer village about La Fayette Square, as one whose rights of inheritance could not be questioned. Few Americans were so poor as to question them.

In spite of the fatal deception — or undeception — about Grant's political character, Adams's first winter in Washington had so much amused him that he had not a thought of change. He loved it too much to question its value. What did he know about its value, or what did any one know? His father knew more about it than any one else in Boston, and he was amused to find that his father, whose recollections went back to 1820, betrayed for Washington much the same sentimental weakness, and described the society about President Monroe much as his son felt the society about President Johnson. He feared its effect on young men, with some justice, since it had been fatal to two of his brothers; but he understood the charm, and he knew that a life in Quincy or Boston was not likely to deaden it.

Henry was in a savage humor on the subject of Boston. He saw Boutwells at every counter. He found a personal grief in every tree. Fifteen or twenty years afterwards, Clarence King used to amuse him by mourning over the narrow escape that nature had made in attaining perfection. Except for two mistakes, the earth would have been a success. One of these errors was the inclination of the ecliptic; the other was the differentiation of the sexes, and the saddest thought about the last was that it should have been so modern. Adams, in his splenetic temper, held that both these unnecessary evils had wreaked their worst on Boston. The climate made eternal war on society, and sex was a species of crime. The ecliptic had inclined itself beyond recovery till life was as thin as the elm trees. Of course he was in the wrong. The thinness was in himself, not in Boston; but this is a story of education, and Adams was struggling to shape himself to his time. Boston was trying to do the same thing. Everywhere, except in Washington, Americans were toiling for the same object. Every one complained of surroundings, except where, as at Washington, there were no surroundings to complain of. Boston kept its head better than its neighbors did, and very little time was needed to prove it, even to Adams's confusion.

Before he got back to Quincy, the summer was already half over, and in another six weeks the effects of President Grant's character showed themselves. They were startling — astounding — terrifying. The mystery that shrouded the famous, classical attempt of Jay Gould to corner gold in September, 1869, has never been cleared up — at least so far as to make it intelligible to Adams. Gould was led, by the change at Washington, into the belief that he could safely corner gold without interference from the Government. He took a number of precautions, which he admitted; and he spent a large sum of money, as he also testified, to obtain assurances which were not sufficient to have satisfied so astute a gambler; yet he made the venture. Any criminal lawyer must have begun investigation by insisting, rigorously, that no such man, in such a position, could be permitted to plead that he had taken, and pursued, such a course, without assurances which did satisfy him. The plea was professionally inadmissible.

This meant that any criminal lawyer would have been bound to start an investigation by insisting that Gould had assurances from the White House or the Treasury, since none other could have satisfied him. To young men wasting their summer at Quincy for want of some one to hire their services at three dollars a day, such a dramatic scandal was Heaven-sent. Charles and Henry Adams jumped at it like salmon at a fly, with as much voracity as Jay

Gould, or his *âme damnée* Jim Fisk, had ever shown for Erie; and with as little fear of consequences. They risked something; no one could say what; but the people about the Erie office were not regarded as lambs.

The unravelling a skein so tangled as that of the Erie Railway was a task that might have given months of labor to the most efficient District Attorney, with all his official tools to work with. Charles took the railway history; Henry took the so-called Gold Conspiracy; and they went to New York to work it up. The surface was in full view. They had no trouble in Wall Street, and they paid their respects in person to the famous Jim Fisk in his Opera-House Palace; but the New York side of the story helped Henry little. He needed to penetrate the political mystery, and for this purpose he had to wait for Congress to meet. At first he feared that Congress would suppress the scandal, but the Congressional Investigation was ordered and took place. He soon knew all that was to be known; the material for his essay was furnished by the Government.

Material furnished by a government seldom satisfies critics or historians, for it lies always under suspicion. Here was a mystery, and as usual, the chief mystery was the means of making sure that any mystery existed. All Adams's great friends — Fish, Cox, Hoar, Evarts, Sumner, and their surroundings — were precisely the persons most mystified. They knew less than Adams did; they sought information, and frankly admitted that their relations with the White House and the Treasury were not confidential. No one volunteered advice. No one offered suggestion. One got no light, even from the press, although press agents expressed in private the most damning convictions with their usual cynical frankness. The Congressional Committee took a quantity of evidence which it dared not probe, and refused to analyze. Although the fault lay somewhere on the Administration, and could lie nowhere else, the trail always faded and died out at the point where any member of the Administration became visible. Every one dreaded to press inquiry. Adams himself feared finding out too much. He found out too much already, when he saw in evidence that Jay Gould had actually succeeded in stretching his net over Grant's closest surroundings, and that Boutwell's incompetence was the bottom of Gould's calculation. With the conventional air of assumed confidence, every one in public assured every one else that the President himself was the savior of the situation, and in private assured each other that if the President had not been caught this time, he was sure to be trapped the next, for the ways of Wall Street were dark and double. All this was wildly exciting to Adams. That Grant should have fallen, within six months, into such a morass — or should have let Boutwell drop him into it — rendered the outlook for the next four years — probably eight — possibly twelve — mysterious, or frankly opaque, to a young man who had hitched his wagon, as Emerson told him, to the star of reform. The country might outlive it, but not he. The worst scandals of the eighteenth century were relatively harmless by the side of this, which smirched executive, judiciary, banks, corporate systems, professions, and people, all the great active forces of society, in one dirty cesspool of vulgar corruption. Only six months before, this innocent young man, fresh from the cynicism of European diplomacy, had expected to enter an honorable career in the press as the champion and confidant of a new Washington, and already he foresaw a life of wasted energy, sweeping the stables of American society clean of the endless corruption which his second Washington was quite certain to breed.

By vigorously shutting one's eyes, as though one were an Assistant Secretary, a writer for the press might ignore the Erie scandal, and still help his friends or allies in the Government who were doing their best to give it an air of decency; but a few weeks showed that the Erie scandal was a mere incident, a rather vulgar Wall Street trap, into which, according to one's point of view, Grant had been drawn by Jay Gould, or Jay Gould had been misled by Grant. One could hardly doubt that both of them were astonished and disgusted by the result; but neither Jay Gould nor any other astute American mind — still less the complex Jew — could ever have accustomed itself to the incredible and inexplicable lapses of Grant's intelligence; and perhaps, on the whole, Gould was the less mischievous victim, if victims they both were. The same laxity that led Gould into a trap which might easily have become the penitentiary, led the United States Senate, the Executive departments and the Judiciary into confusion, cross-purposes, and ill-temper that would have been scandalous in a boarding-school of girls. For satirists or comedians, the study was rich and endless, and they exploited its corners with happy results, but a young man fresh from the rustic simplicity of London noticed with horror that the grossest satires on the American Senator and politician never failed to excite the laughter and applause of every audience. Rich and poor joined in throwing contempt on their own representatives. Society laughed a vacant and meaningless derision over its own failure. Nothing remained for a young man without position or power except to laugh too.

Yet the spectacle was no laughing matter to him, whatever it might be to the public. Society is immoral and immortal; it can afford to commit any kind of folly, and indulge in any sort of vice; it cannot be killed, and the fragments that survive can always laugh at the dead; but a young man has only one chance, and brief time to seize it. Any one in power above him can extinguish the chance.

He is horribly at the mercy of fools and cowards. One dull administration can rapidly drive out every active subordinate. At Washington, in 1869–70, every intelligent man about the Government prepared to go. The people would have liked to go too, for they stood helpless before the chaos; some laughed and some raved; all were disgusted; but they had to content themselves by turning their backs and going to work harder than ever on their railroads and foundries. They were strong enough to carry even their politics. Only the helpless remained stranded in Washington.

The shrewdest statesman of all was Mr. Boutwell, who showed how he understood the situation by turning out of the Treasury every one who could interfere with his repose, and then locking himself up in it, alone. What he did there, no one knew. His colleagues asked him in vain. Not a word could they get from him, either in the Cabinet or out of it, of suggestion or information on matters even of vital interest. The Treasury as an active influence ceased to exist. Mr. Boutwell waited with confidence for society to drag his department out of the mire, as it was sure to do if he waited long enough.

Warned by his friends in the Cabinet as well as in the Treasury that Mr. Boutwell meant to invite no support, and cared to receive none, Adams had only the State and Interior Departments left to serve. He wanted no better than to serve them. Opposition was his horror; pure waste of energy; a union with Northern Democrats and Southern rebels who never had much in common with any Adams, and had never shown any warm interest about them except to drive them from public life. If Mr. Boutwell turned him out of the Treasury with the indifference or contempt that made even a beetle helpless, Mr. Fish opened the State Department freely, and seemed to talk with as much openness as any newspaper-man could ask. At all events, Adams could cling to this last plank of salvation, and make himself perhaps the recognized champion of Mr. Fish in the New York press. He never once thought of his disaster between Seward and Sumner in 1861. Such an accident could not occur again. Fish and Sumner were inseparable, and their policy was sure to be safe enough for support. No mosquito could be so unlucky as to be caught a second time between a Secretary and a Senator who were both his friends.

This dream of security lasted hardly longer than that of 1861. Adams saw Sumner take possession of the Department, and he approved; he saw Sumner seize the British mission for Motley, and he was delighted; but when he renewed his relations with Sumner in the winter of 1869–70, he began slowly to grasp the idea that Sumner had a foreign policy of his own which he proposed also to force on the Department. This was not all. Secretary Fish seemed to have vanished. Besides the Department of State over which he nominally presided in the Infant Asylum on Fourteenth Street, there had risen a Department of Foreign Relations over which Senator Sumner ruled with a high hand at the Capitol; and, finally, one clearly made out a third Foreign Office in the War Department, with President Grant himself for chief, pressing a policy of extension in the West Indies which no Northeastern man ever approved. For his life, Adams could not learn where to place himself among all these forces. Officially he would have followed the responsible Secretary of State, but he could not find the Secretary. Fish seemed to be friendly towards Sumner, and docile towards Grant, but he asserted as yet no policy of his own. As for Grant's policy, Adams never had a chance to know fully what it was, but, as far as he did know, he was ready to give it ardent support. The difficulty came only when he heard Sumner's views, which, as he had reason to know, were always commands, to be disregarded only by traitors.

Little by little, Sumner unfolded his foreign policy, and Adams gasped with fresh astonishment at every new article of the creed. To his profound regret he heard Sumner begin by imposing his veto on all extension within the tropics; which cost the island of St. Thomas to the United States, besides the Bay of Samana as an alternative, and ruined Grant's policy. Then he listened with incredulous stupor while Sumner unfolded his plan for concentrating and pressing every possible American claim against England, with a view of compelling the cession of Canada to the United States.

Adams did not then know — in fact, he never knew, or could find any one to tell him — what was going on behind the doors of the White House. He doubted whether Mr. Fish or Bancroft Davis knew much more than he. The game of cross-purposes was as impenetrable in Foreign Affairs as in the Gold Conspiracy. President Grant let every one go on, but whom he supported, Adams could not be expected to divine. One point alone seemed clear to a man — no longer so very young — who had lately come from a seven years' residence in London. He thought he knew as much as any one in Washington about England, and he listened with the more perplexity to Mr. Sumner's talk, because it opened the gravest doubts of Sumner's sanity. If war was his object, and Canada were worth it, Sumner's scheme showed genius, and Adams was ready to treat it seriously; but if he thought he could obtain Canada from England as a voluntary set-off to the Alabama Claims, he drivelled. On the point of fact, Adams was as peremptory as Sumner on the point of policy, but he could only wonder whether Mr. Fish would dare say it. When at last Mr. Fish did say it, a year later, Sumner publicly cut his acquaintance.

Adams was the more puzzled because he could not believe Sumner so mad as to quarrel both with Fish and with Grant. A quarrel with Seward and Andrew Johnson was bad enough, and had profited no one; but a quarrel with General Grant was lunacy. Grant might be whatever one liked, as far as morals or temper or intellect were concerned, but he was not a man whom a lightweight cared to challenge for a fight; and Sumner, whether he knew it or not, was a very light weight in the Republican Party, if separated from his Committee of Foreign Relations. As a party manager he had not the weight of half-a-dozen men whose very names were unknown to him.

Between these great forces, where was the Administration and how was one to support it? One must first find it, and even then it was not easily caught. Grant's simplicity was more disconcerting than the complexity of a Talleyrand. Mr. Fish afterwards told Adams, with the rather grim humor he sometimes indulged in, that Grant took a dislike to Motley because he parted his hair in the middle. Adams repeated the story to Godkin, who made much play with it in the *Nation*, till it was denied. Adams saw no reason why it should be denied. Grant had as good a right to dislike the hair as the head, if the hair seemed to him a part of it. Very shrewd men have formed very sound judgments on less material than hair — on clothes, for example, according to Mr. Carlyle, or on a pen, according to Cardinal de Retz — and nine men in ten could hardly give as good a reason as hair for their likes or dislikes. In truth, Grant disliked Motley at sight, because they had nothing in common; and for the same reason he disliked Sumner. For the same reason he would be sure to dislike Adams if Adams gave him a chance. Even Fish could not be quite sure of Grant, except for the powerful effect which wealth had, or appeared to have, on Grant's imagination.

The quarrel that lowered over the State Department did not break in storm till July, 1870, after Adams had vanished, but another quarrel, almost as fatal to Adams as that between Fish and Sumner, worried him even more. Of all members of the Cabinet, the one whom he had most personal interest in cultivating was Attorney-General Hoar. The Legal Tender decision, which had been the first stumbling-block to Adams at Washington, grew in interest till it threatened to become something more serious than a block; it fell on one's head like a plaster ceiling, and could not be escaped. The impending battle between Fish and Sumner was nothing like so serious as the outbreak between Hoar and Chief Justice Chase. Adams had come to Washington hoping to support the Executive in a policy of breaking down the Senate, but he never dreamed that he would be required to help in breaking down the Supreme Court. Although, step by step, he had been driven, like the rest of the world, to admit that American society had outgrown most of its institutions, he still clung to the Supreme Court, much as a churchman clings to his bishops, because they are his only symbol of unity; his last rag of Right. Between the Executive and the Legislature, citizens could have no Rights; they were at the mercy of Power. They had created the Court to protect them from unlimited Power, and it was little enough protection at best. Adams wanted to save the independence of the Court at least for his lifetime, and could not conceive that the Executive should wish to overthrow it.

Frank Walker shared this feeling, and, by way of helping the Court, he had promised Adams for the *North American Review* an article on the history of the Legal

Tender Act, founded on a volume just then published by Spaulding, the putative father of the legal-tender clause in 1861. Secretary Jacob D. Cox, who alone sympathized with reform, saved from Boutwell's decree of banishment such reformers as he could find place for, and he saved Walker for a time by giving him the Census of 1870. Walker was obliged to abandon his article for the *North American* in order to devote himself to the Census. He gave Adams his notes, and Adams completed the article.

He had not toiled in vain over the Bank of England Restriction. He knew enough about Legal Tender to leave it alone. If the banks and bankers wanted fiat money, fiat money was good enough for a newspaper-man; and if they changed about and wanted "intrinsic" value, gold and silver came equally welcome to a writer who was paid half the wages of an ordinary mechanic. He had no notion of attacking or defending Legal Tender; his object was to defend the Chief Justice and the Court. Walker argued that, whatever might afterwards have been the necessity for legal tender, there was no necessity for it at the time the Act was passed. With the help of the Chief Justice's recollections, Adams completed the article, which appeared in the April number of the *North American*. Its ferocity was Walker's, for Adams never cared to abandon the knife for the hatchet, but Walker reeked of the army and the *Springfield Republican*, and his energy ran away with Adams's restraint. The unfortunate Spaulding complained loudly of this treatment, not without justice, but the article itself had serious historical value, for Walker demolished every shred of Spaulding's contention that legal tender was necessary at the time; and the Chief Justice told his part of the story with conviction. The Chief Justice seemed to be pleased. The Attorney-General, pleased or not, made no sign. The article had enough historical interest to induce Adams to reprint it in a volume of Essays twenty years afterwards; but its historical value was not its point in education. The point was that, in spite of the best intentions, the plainest self-interest, and the strongest wish to escape further trouble, the article threw Adams into opposition. Judge Hoar, like Boutwell, was implacable.

Hoar went on to demolish the Chief Justice; while Henry Adams went on, drifting further and further from the Administration. He did this in common with all the world, including Hoar himself. Scarcely a newspaper in the country kept discipline. The *New York Tribune* was one of the most criminal. Dissolution of ties in every direction marked the dissolution of temper, and the Senate Chamber became again a scene of irritated egotism that passed ridicule. Senators quarrelled with each other, and no one objected, but they picked quarrels also with the Executive and threw every Department into confusion. Among others they quarrelled with Hoar, and drove him from office.

That Sumner and Hoar, the two New Englanders in great position who happened to be the two persons most necessary for his success at Washington, should be the first victims of Grant's lax rule, must have had some meaning for Adams's education, if Adams could only have understood what it was. He studied, but failed. Sympathy with him was not their weakness. Directly, in the form of help, he knew he could hope as little from them as from Boutwell. So far from inviting attachment they, like other New Englanders, blushed to own a friend. Not one of the whole delegation would ever, of his own accord, try to help Adams or any other young man who did not beg for it, although they would always accept whatever services they had not to pay for. The lesson of education was not there. The selfishness of politics was the earliest of all political education, and Adams had nothing to learn from its study; but the situation struck him as curious — so curious that he devoted years to reflecting upon it. His four most powerful friends had matched themselves, two and two, and were fighting in pairs to a finish; Sumner-Fish; Chase-Hoar; with foreign affairs and the judiciary as prizes! What value had the fight in education?

Adams was puzzled, and was not the only puzzled bystander. The stage-type of statesman was amusing, whether as Roscoe Conkling or Colonel Mulberry Sellers, but what was his value? The statesmen of the old type, whether Sumners or Conklings or Hoars or Lamars, were personally as honest as human nature could produce. They trod with lofty contempt on other people's jobs, especially when there was good in them. Yet the public thought that Sumner and Conkling cost the country a hundred times more than all the jobs they ever trod on; just as Lamar and the old Southern statesmen, who were also honest in money-matters, cost the country a civil war. This painful moral doubt worried Adams less than it worried his friends and the public, but it affected the whole field of politics for twenty years. The newspapers discussed little else than the alleged moral laxity of Grant, Garfield, and Blaine. If the press were taken seriously, politics turned on jobs, and some of Adams's best friends, like Godkin, ruined their influence by their insistence on points of morals. Society hesitated, wavered, oscillated between harshness and laxity, pitilessly sacrificing the weak, and deferentially following the strong. In spite of all such criticism, the public nominated Grant, Garfield, and Blaine for the Presidency, and voted for them afterwards, not seeming to care for the question; until young men were forced to see that either some new standard must be created, or none could be upheld. The moral law had expired — like the Constitution.

Grant's administration outraged every rule of ordinary

decency, but scores of promising men, whom the country could not well spare, were ruined in saying so. The world cared little for decency. What it wanted, it did not know; probably a system that would work, and men who could work it; but it found neither. Adams had tried his own little hands on it, and had failed. His friends had been driven out of Washington or had taken to fisticuffs. He himself sat down and stared helplessly into the future.

The result was a review of the Session for the July *North American* into which he crammed and condensed everything he thought he had observed and all he had been told. He thought it good history then, and he thought it better twenty years afterwards; he thought it even good enough to reprint. As it happened, in the process of his devious education, this "Session" of 1869–70 proved to be his last study in current politics, and his last dying testament as a humble member of the press. As such, he stood by it. He could have said no more, had he gone on reviewing every session in the rest of the century. The political dilemma was as clear in 1870 as it was likely to be in 1970. The system of 1789 had broken down, and with it the eighteenth-century fabric of *a priori*, or moral, principles. Politicians had tacitly given it up. Grant's administration marked the avowal. Nine-tenths of men's political energies must henceforth be wasted on expedients to piece out — to patch — or, in vulgar language, to tinker — the political machine as often as it broke down. Such a system, or want of system, might last centuries, if tempered by an occasional revolution or civil war; but as a machine, it was, or soon would be, the poorest in the world — the clumsiest — the most inefficient.

Here again was an education, but what it was worth he could not guess. Indeed, when he raised his eyes to the loftiest and most triumphant results of politics — to Mr.

Boutwell, Mr. Conkling or even Mr. Sumner — he could not honestly say that such an education, even when it carried one up to these unattainable heights, was worth anything. There were men, as yet standing on lower levels — clever and amusing men like Garfield and Blaine — who took no little pleasure in making fun of the senatorial demi-gods, and who used language about Grant himself which the *North American Review* would not have admitted. One asked doubtfully what was likely to become of these men in their turn. What kind of political ambition was to result from this destructive political education?

Yet the sum of political life was, or should have been, the attainment of a working political system. Society needed to reach it. If moral standards broke down, and machinery stopped working, new morals and machinery of some sort had to be invented. An eternity of Grants, or even of Garfields or of Conklings or of Jay Goulds, refused to be conceived as possible. Practical Americans laughed, and went their way. Society paid them to be practical. Whenever society cared to pay Adams, he too would be practical, take his pay, and hold his tongue; but meanwhile he was driven to associate with Democratic Congressmen and educate them. He served David Wells as an active assistant professor of revenue reform, and turned his rooms into a college. The Administration drove him, and thousands of other young men, into active enmity, not only to Grant, but to the system or want of system, which took possession of the President. Every hope or thought which had brought Adams to Washington proved to be absurd. No one wanted him; no one wanted any of his friends in reform; the blackmailer alone was the normal product of politics as of business.

All this was excessively amusing. Adams never had been so busy, so interested, so much in the thick of the crowd.

He knew Congressmen by scores and newspaper-men by the dozen. He wrote for his various organs all sorts of attacks and defences. He enjoyed the life enormously, and found himself as happy as Sam Ward or Sunset Cox; much happier than his friends Fish or J. D. Cox, or Chief Justice Chase or Attorney-General Hoar or Charles Sumner. When spring came, he took to the woods, which were best of all, for after the first of April, what Maurice de Guérin called "the vast maternity" of nature showed charms more voluptuous than the vast paternity of the United States Senate. Senators were less ornamental than the dogwood or even the judas-tree. They were, as a rule, less good company. Adams astonished himself by remarking what a purified charm was lent to the Capitol by the greatest possible distance, as one caught glimpses of the dome over miles of forest foliage. At such moments he pondered on the distant beauty of St. Peter's and the steps of Ara Cœli.

Yet he shortened his spring, for he needed to get back to London for the season. He had finished his New York "Gold Conspiracy," which he meant for his friend Henry Reeve and the *Edinburgh Review*. It was the best piece of work he had done, but this was not his reason for publishing it in England. The Erie scandal had provoked a sort of revolt among respectable New Yorkers, as well as among some who were not so respectable; and the attack on Erie was beginning to promise success. London was a sensitive spot for the Erie management, and it was thought well to strike them there, where they were socially and financially exposed. The tactics suited him in another way, for any expression about America in an English review attracted ten times the attention in America that the same article would attract in the *North American*. Habitually the American dailies reprinted such articles in full. Adams wanted to escape the terrors of copyright; his highest ambition was to be pirated and advertised free of charge, since, in any case, his pay was nothing. Under the excitement of chase, he was becoming a pirate himself, and liked it.

19

Chaos

(1870)

One fine May afternoon in 1870 Adams drove again up St. James's Street wondering more than ever at the marvels of life. Nine years had passed since the historic entrance of May, 1861. Outwardly London was the same. Outwardly Europe showed no great change. Palmerston and Russell were forgotten; but Disraeli and Gladstone were still much alive. One's friends were more than ever prominent. John Bright was in the Cabinet; W. E. Forster was about to enter it; reform ran riot. Never had the sun of progress shone so fair. Evolution from lower to higher raged like an epidemic. Darwin was the greatest of prophets in the most evolutionary of worlds. Gladstone had overthrown the Irish Church; was overthrowing the Irish landlords; was trying to pass an Education Act. Improvement, prosperity, power, were leaping and bounding over every country road. Even America, with her Erie scandals and Alabama Claims, hardly made a discordant note.

At the Legation, Motley ruled; the long Adams reign was forgotten; the rebellion had passed into history. In society no one cared to recall the years before the Prince of Wales. The smart set had come to their own. Half the houses that Adams had frequented, from 1861 to 1865, were closed or closing in 1870. Death had ravaged one's circle of friends. Mrs. Milnes Gaskell and her sister Miss Charlotte Wynn were both dead, and Mr. James Milnes Gaskell was no longer in Parliament. That field of education seemed closed too.

One found one's self in a singular frame of mind — more eighteenth-century than ever — almost rococo — and unable to catch anywhere the cog-wheels of evolution. Experience ceased to educate. London taught less freely than of old. That one bad style was leading to another — that the older men were more amusing than the younger — that Lord Houghton's breakfast-table showed gaps hard to fill — that there were fewer men one wanted to meet — these, and a hundred more such remarks, helped little towards a quicker and more intelligent activity. For English reforms, Adams cared nothing. The reforms were themselves mediæval. The Education Bill of his friend W. E. Forster seemed to him a guaranty against all education he had use for. He resented change. He would have kept the Pope in the Vatican and the Queen at Windsor Castle as historical monuments. He did not care to Americanize Europe. The Bastille or the Ghetto was a curiosity worth a great deal of money, if preserved; and so was a Bishop; so was Napoleon III. The tourist was the great conservative who hated novelty and adored dirt. Adams came back to London without a thought of revolution or restlessness or reform. He wanted amusement, quiet, and gaiety.

Had he not been born in 1838 under the shadow of Boston State House, and been brought up in the Early Victorian epoch, he would have cast off his old skin, and made his court to Marlborough House, in partnership with the American woman and the Jew banker. Commonsense dictated it; but Adams and his friends were unfashionable by some law of Anglo-Saxon custom — some

innate atrophy of mind. Figuring himself as already a man
of action, and rather far up towards the front, he had no
idea of making a new effort or catching up with a new
world. He saw nothing ahead of him. The world was
never more calm. He wanted to talk with Ministers about
the Alabama Claims, because he looked on the Claims as
his own special creation, discussed between him and his
father long before they had been discussed by Government; he wanted to make notes for his next year's articles;
but he had not a thought that, within three months, his
world was to be upset, and he under it. Frank Palgrave
came one day, more contentious, contemptuous, and paradoxical than ever, because Napoleon III seemed to be
threatening war with Germany. Palgrave said that "Germany would beat France into scraps" if there was war.
Adams thought not. The chances were always against
catastrophes. No one else expected great changes in
Europe. Palgrave was always extreme; his language was
incautious — violent!

In this year of all years, Adams lost sight of education.
Things began smoothly, and London glowed with the
pleasant sense of familiarity and dinners. He sniffed with
voluptuous delight the coal-smoke of Cheapside and revelled in the architecture of Oxford Street. May Fair
never shone so fair to Arthur Pendennis as it did to the
returned American. The country never smiled its velvet
smile of trained and easy hostess as it did when he was so
lucky as to be asked on a country visit. He loved it all —
everything — had always loved it! He felt almost attached
to the Royal Exchange. He thought he owned the St.
James's Club. He patronized the Legation.

The first shock came lightly, as though Nature were
playing tricks on her spoiled child, though she had thus
far not exerted herself to spoil him. Reeve refused the
Gold Conspiracy. Adams had become used to the idea

that he was free of the Quarterlies, and that his writing would be printed of course; but he was stunned by the reason of refusal. Reeve said it would bring half-a-dozen libel suits on him. One knew that the power of Erie was almost as great in England as in America, but one was hardly prepared to find it controlling the Quarterlies. The English press professed to be shocked in 1870 by the Erie scandal, as it had professed in 1860 to be shocked by the scandal of slavery, but when invited to support those who were trying to abate these scandals, the English press said it was afraid. To Adams, Reeve's refusal seemed portentous. He and his brother and the *North American Review* were running greater risks every day, and no one thought of fear. That a notorious story, taken bodily from an official document, should scare the *Edinburgh Review* into silence for fear of Jay Gould and Jim Fisk, passed even Adams's experience of English eccentricity, though it was large.

He gladly set down Reeve's refusal of the Gold Conspiracy to respectability and editorial law, but when he sent the manuscript on to the *Quarterly*, the editor of the *Quarterly* also refused it. The literary standard of the two Quarterlies was not so high as to suggest that the article was illiterate beyond the power of an active and willing editor to redeem it. Adams had no choice but to realize that he had to deal in 1870 with the same old English character of 1860, and the same inability in himself to understand it. As usual, when an ally was needed, the American was driven into the arms of the radicals. Respectability, everywhere and always, turned its back the moment one asked to do it a favor. Called suddenly away from England, he despatched the article, at the last moment, to the *Westminster Review* and heard no more about it for nearly six months.

He had been some weeks in London when he received

a telegram from his brother-in-law at the Bagni di Lucca telling him that his sister had been thrown from a cab and injured, and that he had better come on. He started that night, and reached the Bagni di Lucca on the second day. Tetanus had already set in.

The last lesson — the sum and term of education — began then. He had passed through thirty years of rather varied experience without having once felt the shell of custom broken. He had never seen Nature — only her surface — the sugar-coating that she shows to youth. Flung suddenly in his face, with the harsh brutality of chance, the terror of the blow stayed by him thenceforth for life, until repetition made it more than the will could struggle with; more than he could call on himself to bear. He found his sister, a woman of forty, as gay and brilliant in the terrors of lockjaw as she had been in the careless fun of 1859, lying in bed in consequence of a miserable cab-accident that had bruised her foot. Hour by hour the muscles grew rigid, while the mind remained bright, until after ten days of fiendish torture she died in convulsions.

One had heard and read a great deal about death, and even seen a little of it, and knew by heart the thousand commonplaces of religion and poetry which seemed to deaden one's senses and veil the horror. Society being immortal, could put on immortality at will. Adams being mortal, felt only the mortality. Death took features altogether new to him, in these rich and sensuous surroundings. Nature enjoyed it, played with it, the horror added to her charm, she liked the torture, and smothered her victim with caresses. Never had one seen her so winning. The hot Italian summer brooded outside, over the market-place and the picturesque peasants, and, in the singular color of the Tuscan atmosphere, the hills and vineyards of the Apennines seemed bursting with mid-summer blood. The sick-room itself glowed with the Italian joy of life; friends filled it; no harsh northern lights pierced the soft shadows; even the dying woman shared the sense of the Italian summer, the soft, velvet air, the humor, the courage, the sensual fulness of Nature and man. She faced death, as women mostly do, bravely and even gaily, racked slowly to unconsciousness, but yielding only to violence, as a soldier sabred in battle. For many thousands of years, on these hills and plains, Nature had gone on sabring men and women with the same air of sensual pleasure.

Impressions like these are not reasoned or catalogued in the mind; they are felt as part of violent emotion; and the mind that feels them is a different one from that which reasons; it is thought of a different power and a different person. The first serious consciousness of Nature's gesture — her attitude towards life — took form then as a phantasm, a nightmare, an insanity of force. For the first time, the stage-scenery of the senses collapsed; the human mind felt itself stripped naked, vibrating in a void of shapeless energies, with resistless mass, colliding, crushing, wasting, and destroying what these same energies had created and labored from eternity to perfect. Society became fantastic, a vision of pantomime with a mechanical motion; and its so-called thought merged in the mere sense of life, and pleasure in the sense. The usual anodynes of social medicine became evident artifice. Stoicism was perhaps the best; religion was the most human; but the idea that any personal deity could find pleasure or profit in torturing a poor woman, by accident, with a fiendish cruelty known to man only in perverted and insane temperaments, could not be held for a moment. For pure blasphemy, it made pure atheism a comfort. God might be, as the Church said, a Substance, but He could not be a Person.

With nerves strained for the first time beyond their

power of tension, he slowly travelled northwards with his friends, and stopped for a few days at Ouchy to recover his balance in a new world; for the fantastic mystery of coincidences had made the world, which he thought real, mimic and reproduce the distorted nightmare of his personal horror. He did not yet know it, and he was twenty years in finding it out; but he had need of all the beauty of the Lake below and of the Alps above, to restore the finite to its place. For the first time in his life, Mont Blanc for a moment looked to him what it was — a chaos of anarchic and purposeless forces — and he needed days of repose to see it clothe itself again with the illusions of his senses, the white purity of its snows, the splendor of its light, and the infinity of its heavenly peace. Nature was kind; Lake Geneva was beautiful beyond itself, and the Alps put on charms real as terrors; but man became chaotic, and before the illusions of Nature were wholly restored, the illusions of Europe suddenly vanished, leaving a new world to learn.

On July 4, all Europe had been in peace; on July 14, Europe was in full chaos of war. One felt helpless and ignorant, but one might have been king or kaiser without feeling stronger to deal with the chaos. Mr. Gladstone was as much astounded as Adams; the Emperor Napoleon was nearly as stupefied as either, and Bismarck himself hardly knew how he did it. As education, the outbreak of the war was wholly lost on a man dealing with death hand-to-hand, who could not throw it aside to look at it across the Rhine. Only when he got up to Paris, he began to feel the approach of catastrophe. Providence set up no *affiches* to announce the tragedy. Under one's eyes France cut herself adrift, and floated off, on an unknown stream, towards a less known ocean. Standing on the curb of the Boulevard, one could see as much as though one stood by the side of the Emperor or in command of an army corps. The effect was lurid. The public seemed to look on the war, as it had looked on the wars of Louis XIV and Francis I, as a branch of decorative art. The French, like true artists, always regarded war as one of the fine arts. Louis XIV practised it; Napoleon I perfected it; and Napoleon III had till then pursued it in the same spirit with singular success. In Paris, in July, 1870, the war was brought out like an opera of Meyerbeer. One felt one's self a supernumerary hired to fill the scene. Every evening at the theatre the comedy was interrupted by order, and one stood up by order, to join in singing the *Marseillaise* to order. For nearly twenty years one had been forbidden to sing the *Marseillaise* under any circumstances, but at last regiment after regiment marched through the streets shouting "Marchons!" while the by-standers cared not enough to join. Patriotism seemed to have been brought out of the Government stores, and distributed by grammes *per capita*. One had seen one's own people dragged unwillingly into a war, and had watched one's own regiments march to the front without sign of enthusiasm; on the contrary, most serious, anxious, and conscious of the whole weight of the crisis; but in Paris every one conspired to ignore the crisis, which every one felt at hand. Here was education for the million, but the lesson was intricate. Superficially Napoleon and his Ministers and marshals were playing a game against Thiers and Gambetta. A bystander knew almost as little as they did about the result. How could Adams prophesy that in another year or two, when he spoke of *his* Paris and its tastes, people would smile at his dotage?

As soon as he could, he fled to England and once more took refuge in the profound peace of Wenlock Abbey. Only the few remaining monks, undisturbed by the brutalities of Henry VIII — three or four young Englishmen

— survived there, with Milnes Gaskell acting as Prior.
The August sun was warm; the calm of the Abbey was ten
times secular; not a discordant sound — hardly a sound of
any sort except the cawing of the ancient rookery at sunset — broke the stillness; and, after the excitement of the
last month, one felt a palpable haze of peace brooding over
the Edge and the Welsh Marches. Since the reign of
Pteraspis, nothing had greatly changed; nothing except the
monks. Lying on the turf, the ground littered with newspapers, the monks studied the war correspondence. In one
respect Adams had succeeded in educating himself; he had
learned to follow a campaign.

   While at Wenlock, he received a letter from President
Eliot inviting him to take an Assistant Professorship of History, to be created shortly at Harvard College. After waiting ten or a dozen years for some one to show consciousness of his existence, even a *Terebratula* would be pleased
and grateful for a compliment which implied that the new
President of Harvard College wanted his help; but Adams
knew nothing about history, and much less about teaching,
while he knew more than enough about Harvard College;
and wrote at once to thank President Eliot, with much
regret that the honor should be above his powers. His mind
was full of other matters. The summer, from which he
had expected only amusement and social relations with
new people, had ended in the most intimate personal tragedy, and the most terrific political convulsion he had ever
known or was likely to know. He had failed in every object of his trip. The Quarterlies had refused his best essay.
He had made no acquaintances and hardly picked up the
old ones. He sailed from Liverpool, on September 1, to
begin again where he had started two years before, but
with no longer a hope of attaching himself to a President
or a party or a press. He was a free lance and no other

career stood in sight or mind. To that point education had brought him.

Yet he found, on reaching home, that he had not done quite so badly as he feared. His article on the Session in the July *North American* had made a success. Though he could not quite see what partisan object it served, he heard with flattered astonishment that it had been reprinted by the Democratic National Committee and circulated as a campaign document by the hundred thousand copies. He was henceforth in opposition, do what he might; and a Massachusetts Democrat, say what he pleased; while his only reward or return for this partisan service consisted in being formally answered by Senator Timothy Howe, of Wisconsin, in a Republican campaign document, presumed to be also freely circulated, in which the Senator, besides refuting his opinions, did him the honor — most unusual and picturesque in a Senator's rhetoric — of likening him to a begonia.

The begonia is, or then was, a plant of such senatorial qualities as to make the simile, in intention, most flattering. Far from charming in its refinement, the begonia was remarkable for curious and showy foliage; it was conspicuous; it seemed to have no useful purpose; and it insisted on standing always in the most prominent positions. Adams would have greatly liked to be a begonia in Washington, for this was rather his ideal of the successful statesman, and he thought about it still more when the *Westminster Review* for October brought him his article on the Gold Conspiracy, which was also instantly pirated on a great scale. Piratical he was himself henceforth driven to be, and he asked only to be pirated, for he was sure not to be paid; but the honors of piracy resemble the colors of the begonia; they are showy but not useful. Here was a *tour de force* he had never dreamed himself equal to performing:

two long, dry, quarterly, thirty or forty page articles, appearing in quick succession, and pirated for audiences running well into the hundred thousands; and not one person, man or woman, offering him so much as a congratulation, except to call him a begonia.

Had this been all, life might have gone on very happily as before, but the ways of America to a young person of literary and political tastes were such as the so-called evolution of civilized man had not before evolved. No sooner had Adams made at Washington what he modestly hoped was a sufficient success, than his whole family set on him to drag him away. For the first time since 1861 his father interposed; his mother entreated; and his brother Charles argued and urged that he should come to Harvard College. Charles had views of further joint operations in a new field. He said that Henry had done at Washington all he could possibly do; that his position there wanted solidity; that he was, after all, an adventurer; that a few years in Cambridge would give him personal weight; that his chief function was not to be that of teacher, but that of editing the *North American Review* which was to be coupled with the professorship, and would lead to the daily press. In short, that he needed the university more than the university needed him.

Henry knew the university well enough to know that the department of history was controlled by one of the most astute and ideal administrators in the world — Professor Gurney — and that it was Gurney who had established the new professorship, and had cast his net over Adams to carry the double load of mediæval history and the *Review*. He could see no relation whatever between himself and a professorship. He sought education; he did not sell it. He knew no history; he knew only a few historians; his ignorance was mischievous because it was literary, accidental, indifferent. On the other hand he knew

Gurney, and felt much influenced by his advice. One cannot take one's self quite seriously in such matters; it could not much affect the sum of solar energies whether one went on dancing with girls in Washington, or began talking to boys at Cambridge. The good people who thought it did matter had a sort of right to guide. One could not reject their advice; still less disregard their wishes.

The sum of the matter was that Henry went out to Cambridge and had a few words with President Eliot which seemed to him almost as American as the talk about diplomacy with his father ten years before. "But, Mr. President," urged Adams, "I know nothing about Mediæval History." With the courteous manner and bland smile so familiar for the next generation of Americans, Mr. Eliot mildly but firmly replied, "If you will point out to me any one who knows more, Mr. Adams, I will appoint him." The answer was neither logical nor convincing, but Adams could not meet it without overstepping his privileges. He could not say that, under the circumstances, the appointment of any professor at all seemed to him unnecessary.

So, at twenty-four hours' notice, he broke his life in halves again in order to begin a new education, on lines he had not chosen, in subjects for which he cared less than nothing; in a place he did not love, and before a future which repelled. Thousands of men have to do the same thing, but his case was peculiar because he had no need to do it. He did it because his best and wisest friends urged it, and he never could make up his mind whether they were right or not. To him this kind of education was always false. For himself he had no doubts. He thought it a mistake; but his opinion did not prove that it was one, since, in all probability, whatever he did would be more or less a mistake. He had reached cross-roads of education which all led astray. What he could gain at Harvard College he did not know, but in any case it was nothing he wanted. What he lost at Washington he could partly see, but in any case it was not fortune. Grant's administration wrecked men by thousands, but profited few. Perhaps Mr. Fish was the solitary exception. One might search the whole list of Congress, Judiciary, and Executives during the twenty-five years 1870 to 1895, and find little but damaged reputation. The period was poor in purpose and barren in results.

Henry Adams, if not the rose, lived as near it as any politician, and knew, more or less, all the men in any way prominent at Washington, or knew all about them. Among them, in his opinion, the best equipped, the most active-minded, and most industrious was Abram Hewitt, who sat in Congress for a dozen years, between 1874 and 1886, sometimes leading the House and always wielding influence second to none. With nobody did Adams form closer or longer relations than with Mr. Hewitt, whom he regarded as the most useful public man in Washington; and he was the more struck by Hewitt's saying, at the end of his laborious career as legislator, that he left behind him no permanent result except the Act consolidating the Surveys. Adams knew no other man who had done so much, unless Mr. Sherman's legislation is accepted as an instance of success. Hewitt's nearest rival would probably have been Senator Pendleton who stood father to civil service reform in 1882, an attempt to correct a vice that should never have been allowed to be born. These were the men who succeeded.

The press stood in much the same light. No editor, no political writer, and no public administrator achieved enough good reputation to preserve his memory for twenty years. A number of them achieved bad reputations, or damaged good ones that had been gained in the Civil

War. On the whole, even for Senators, diplomats, and Cabinet officers, the period was wearisome and stale.

None of Adams's generation profited by public activity unless it were William C. Whitney, and even he could not be induced to return to it. Such ambitions as these were out of one's reach, but supposing one tried for what was feasible, attached one's self closely to the Garfields, Arthurs, Frelinghuysens, Blaines, Bayards, or Whitneys, who happened to hold office; and supposing one asked for the mission to Belgium or Portugal, and obtained it; supposing one served a term as Assistant Secretary or Chief of Bureau; or, finally, supposing one had gone as sub-editor on the *New York Tribune* or *Times* — how much more education would one have gained than by going to Harvard College? These questions seemed better worth an answer than most of the questions on examination papers at college or in the civil service; all the more because one never found an answer to them, then or afterwards, and because, to his mind, the value of American society altogether was mixed up with the value of Washington.

At first, the simple beginner, struggling with principles, wanted to throw off responsibility on the American people, whose bare and toiling shoulders had to carry the load of every social or political stupidity; but the American people had no more to do with it than with the customs of Peking. American character might perhaps account for it, but what accounted for American character? All Boston, all New England, and all respectable New York, including Charles Francis Adams the father and Charles Francis Adams the son, agreed that Washington was no place for a respectable young man. All Washington, including Presidents, Cabinet officers, Judiciary, Senators, Congressmen, and clerks, expressed the same opinion, and conspired to drive away every young man who happened to be there,

or tried to approach. Not one young man of promise remained in the Government service. All drifted into opposition. The Government did not want them in Washington. Adams's case was perhaps the strongest because he
thought he had done well. He was forced to guess it, since
he knew no one who would have risked so extravagant a
step as that of encouraging a young man in a literary
career, or even in a political one; society forbade it, as well
as residence in a political capital; but Harvard College must
have seen some hope for him, since it made him professor
against his will; even the publishers and editors of the
North American Review must have felt a certain amount
of confidence in him, since they put the *Review* in his
hands. After all, the *Review* was the first literary power in
America, even though it paid almost as little in gold as the
United States Treasury. The degree of Harvard College
might bear a value as ephemeral as the commission of a
President of the United States; but the government of the
college, measured by money alone, and patronage, was a
matter of more importance than that of some branches of
the national service. In social position, the college was the
superior of them all put together. In knowledge, she could
assert no superiority, since the Government made no
claims, and prided itself on ignorance. The service of Harvard College was distinctly honorable; perhaps the most
honorable in America; and if Harvard College thought
Henry Adams worth employing at four dollars a day, why
should Washington decline his services when he asked
nothing? Why should he be dragged from a career he
liked in a place he loved, into a career he detested, in a
place and climate he shunned? Was it enough to satisfy
him, that all America should call Washington barren and
dangerous? What made Washington more dangerous than
New York?

The American character showed singular limitations

which sometimes drove the student of civilized man to despair. Crushed by his own ignorance — lost in the darkness of his own gropings — the scholar finds himself jostled of a sudden by a crowd of men who seem to him ignorant that there is a thing called ignorance; who have forgotten how to amuse themselves; who cannot even understand that they are bored. The American thought of himself as a restless, pushing, energetic, ingenious person, always awake and trying to get ahead of his neighbors. Perhaps this idea of the national character might be correct for New York or Chicago; it was not correct for Washington. There the American showed himself, four times in five, as a quiet, peaceful, shy figure, rather in the mould of Abraham Lincoln, somewhat sad, sometimes pathetic, once tragic; or like Grant, inarticulate, uncertain, distrustful of himself, still more distrustful of others, and awed by money. That the American, by temperament, worked to excess, was true; work and whiskey were his stimulants; work was a form of vice; but he never cared much for money or power after he earned them. The amusement of the pursuit was all the amusement he got from it; he had no use for wealth. Jim Fisk alone seemed to know what he wanted; Jay Gould never did. At Washington one met mostly such true Americans, but if one wanted to know them better, one went to study them in Europe. Bored, patient, helpless; pathetically dependent on his wife and daughters; indulgent to excess; mostly a modest, decent, excellent, valuable citizen; the American was to be met at every railway station in Europe, carefully explaining to every listener that the happiest day of his life would be the day he should land on the pier at New York. He was ashamed to be amused; his mind no longer answered to the stimulus of variety; he could not face a new thought. All his immense strength, his intense nervous energy, his keen analytic perceptions, were oriented in one direction, and he could not change it. Congress was full of such men; in the Senate, Sumner was almost the only exception; in the Executive, Grant and Boutwell were varieties of the type — political specimens — pathetic in their helplessness to do anything with power when it came to them. They knew not how to amuse themselves; they could not conceive how other people were amused. Work, whiskey, and cards were life. The atmosphere of political Washington was theirs — or was supposed by the outside world to be in their control — and this was the reason why the outside world judged that Washington was fatal even for a young man of thirty-two, who had passed through the whole variety of temptations, in every capital of Europe, for a dozen years; who never played cards, and who loathed whiskey.

20

Failure

(1871)

Far back in childhood, among its earliest memories, Henry Adams could recall his first visit to Harvard College. He must have been nine years old when on one of the singularly gloomy winter afternoons which beguiled Cambridgeport, his mother drove him out to visit his aunt, Mrs. Everett. Edward Everett was then President of the college and lived in the old President's House on Harvard Square. The boy remembered the drawing-room, on the left of the hall door, in which Mrs. Everett received them. He remembered a marble greyhound in the corner. The house had an air of colonial self-respect that impressed even a nine-year-old child.

When Adams closed his interview with President Eliot, he asked the Bursar about his aunt's old drawing-room, for the house had been turned to base uses. The room and the deserted kitchen adjacent to it were to let. He took them. Above him, his brother Brooks, then a law student, had rooms, with a private staircase. Opposite was J. R. Dennett, a young instructor almost as literary as Adams himself, and more rebellious to conventions. Inquiry revealed a boarding-table, somewhere in the neighborhood, also supposed to be superior in its class. Chauncey Wright,

Francis Wharton, Dennett, John Fiske, or their equivalents in learning and lecture, were seen there, among three
or four law students like Brooks Adams. With these primitive arrangements, all of them had to be satisfied. The
standard was below that of Washington, but it was, for the
moment, the best.

For the next nine months the Assistant Professor had no
time to waste on comforts or amusements. He exhausted all
his strength in trying to keep one day ahead of his duties.
Often the stint ran on, till night and sleep ran short. He
could not stop to think whether he were doing the work
rightly. He could not get it done to please him, rightly or
wrongly, for he never could satisfy himself what to do.

The fault he had found with Harvard College as an
undergraduate must have been more or less just, for the
college was making a great effort to meet these self-
criticisms, and had elected President Eliot in 1869 to carry
out its reforms. Professor Gurney was one of the leading
reformers, and had tried his hand on his own department
of History. The two full Professors of History — Torrey
and Gurney, charming men both — could not cover the
ground. Between Gurney's classical courses and Torrey's
modern ones, lay a gap of a thousand years, which Adams
was expected to fill. The students had already elected
courses numbered 1, 2, and 3, without knowing what was
to be taught or who was to teach. If their new professor
had asked what idea was in their minds, they must have replied that nothing at all was in their minds, since their professor had nothing in his, and down to the moment he took
his chair and looked his scholars in the face, he had given,
as far as he could remember, an hour, more or less, to the
Middle Ages.

Not that his ignorance troubled him! He knew enough
to be ignorant. His course had led him through oceans of
ignorance; he had tumbled from one ocean into another

till he had learned to swim; but even to him education was a serious thing. A parent gives life, but as parent, gives no more. A murderer takes life, but his deed stops there. A teacher affects eternity; he can never tell where his influence stops. A teacher is expected to teach truth, and may perhaps flatter himself that he does so, if he stops with the alphabet or the multiplication table, as a mother teaches truth by making her child eat with a spoon; but morals are quite another truth and philosophy is more complex still. A teacher must either treat history as a catalogue, a record, a romance, or as an evolution; and whether he affirms or denies evolution, he falls into all the burning faggots of the pit. He makes of his scholars either priests or atheists, plutocrats or socialists, judges or anarchists, almost in spite of himself. In essence incoherent and immoral, history had either to be taught as such — or falsified.

Adams wanted to do neither. He had no theory of evolution to teach, and could not make the facts fit one. He had no fancy for telling agreeable tales to amuse sluggish-minded boys, in order to publish them afterwards as lectures. He could still less compel his students to learn the Anglo-Saxon Chronicle and the Venerable Bede by heart. He saw no relation whatever between his students and the Middle Ages unless it were the Church, and there the ground was particularly dangerous. He knew better than though he were a professional historian that the man who should solve the riddle of the Middle Ages and bring them into the line of evolution from past to present, would be a greater man than Lamarck or Linnæus; but history had nowhere broken down so pitiably, or avowed itself so hopelessly bankrupt, as there. Since Gibbon, the spectacle was almost a scandal. History had lost even the sense of shame. It was a hundred years behind the experimental sciences. For all serious purpose, it was less instructive than Walter Scott and Alexandre Dumas.

All this was without offence to Sir Henry Maine, Tylor, McLennan, Buckle, Auguste Comte, and the various philosophers who, from time to time, stirred the scandal, and made it more scandalous. No doubt, a teacher might make some use of these writers or their theories; but Adams could fit them into no theory of his own. The college expected him to pass at least half his time in teaching the boys a few elementary dates and relations, that they might not be a disgrace to the university. This was formal; and he could frankly tell the boys that, provided they passed their examinations, they might get their facts where they liked, and use the teacher only for questions. The only privilege a student had that was worth his claiming, was that of talking to the professor, and the professor was bound to encourage it. His only difficulty on that side was to get them to talk at all. He had to devise schemes to find what they were thinking about, and induce them to risk criticism from their fellows. Any large body of students stifles the student. No man can instruct more than half-a-dozen students at once. The whole problem of education is one of its cost in money.

The lecture system to classes of hundreds, which was very much that of the twelfth century, suited Adams not at all. Barred from philosophy and bored by facts, he wanted to teach his students something not wholly useless. The number of students whose minds were of an order above the average was, in his experience, barely one in ten; the rest could not be much stimulated by any inducements a teacher could suggest. All were respectable, and in seven years of contact, Adams never had cause to complain of one; but nine minds in ten take polish passively, like a hard surface; only the tenth sensibly reacts.

Adams thought that, as no one seemed to care what he did, he would try to cultivate this tenth mind, though necessarily at the expense of the other nine. He frankly acted on the rule that a teacher, who knew nothing of his subject, should not pretend to teach his scholars what he did not know, but should join them in trying to find the best way of learning it. The rather pretentious name of historical method was sometimes given to this process of instruction, but the name smacked of German pedagogy, and a young professor who respected neither history nor method, and whose sole object of interest was his students' minds, fell into trouble enough without adding to it a German parentage.

The task was doomed to failure for a reason which he could not control. Nothing is easier than to teach historical method, but, when learned, it has little use. History is a tangled skein that one may take up at any point, and break when one has unravelled enough; but complexity precedes evolution. The *Pteraspis* grins horribly from the closed entrance. One may not begin at the beginning, and one has but the loosest relative truths to follow up. Adams found himself obliged to force his material into some shape to which a method could be applied. He could think only of law as subject; the Law School as end; and he took, as victims of his experiment, half-a-dozen highly intelligent young men who seemed willing to work. The course began with the beginning, as far as the books showed a beginning in primitive man, and came down through the Salic Franks to the Norman English. Since no textbooks existed, the professor refused to profess, knowing no more than his students, and the students read what they pleased and compared their results. As pedagogy, nothing could be more triumphant. The boys worked like rabbits, and dug holes all over the field of archaic society; no difficulty stopped them; unknown languages yielded before their attack, and customary law became familiar as the police court; undoubtedly they learned, after a fashion, to chase an idea, like a hare, through as dense a thicket of obscure facts as they were likely to meet at the bar; but their teacher knew from his own experience that his wonderful method led nowhere, and they would have to exert themselves to get rid of it in the Law School even more than they exerted themselves to acquire it in the college. Their science had no system, and could have none, since its subject was merely antiquarian. Try as hard as he might, the professor could not make it actual.

What was the use of training an active mind to waste its energy? The experiments might in time train Adams as a professor, but this result was still less to his taste. He wanted to help the boys to a career, but not one of his many devices to stimulate the intellectual reaction of the student's mind satisfied either him or the students. For himself he was clear that the fault lay in the system, which could lead only to inertia. Such little knowledge of himself as he possessed warranted him in affirming that his mind required conflict, competition, contradiction even more than that of the student. He too wanted a rank-list to set his name upon. His reform of the system would have begun in the lecture-room at his own desk. He would have seated a rival assistant professor opposite him, whose business should be strictly limited to expressing opposite views. Nothing short of this would ever interest either the professor or the student; but of all university freaks, no irregularity shocked the intellectual atmosphere so much as contradiction or competition between teachers. In that respect the thirteenth-century university system was worth the whole teaching of the modern school.

All his pretty efforts to create conflicts of thought among his students failed for want of system. None met the needs of instruction. In spite of President Eliot's reforms and his steady, generous, liberal support, the system remained costly, clumsy and futile. The university — as far as it was represented by Henry Adams — produced at great waste of time and money results not worth reaching.

He made use of his lost two years of German schooling to inflict their results on his students, and by a happy chance he was in the full tide of fashion. The Germans were crowning their new emperor at Versailles, and surrounding his head with a halo of Pepins and Merwigs, Othos and Barbarossas. James Bryce had even discovered the Holy Roman Empire. Germany was never so powerful, and the Assistant Professor of History had nothing else as his stock in trade. He imposed Germany on his scholars with a heavy hand. He was rejoiced; but he sometimes doubted whether they should be grateful. On the whole, he was content neither with what he had taught nor with the way he had taught it. The seven years he passed in teaching seemed to him lost.

The uses of adversity are beyond measure strange. As a professor, he regarded himself as a failure. Without false modesty he thought he knew what he meant. He had tried a great many experiments, and wholly succeeded in none. He had succumbed to the weight of the system. He had accomplished nothing that he tried to do. He regarded the system as wrong; more mischievous to the teachers than to the students; fallacious from the beginning to end. He quitted the university at last, in 1877, with a feeling, that, if it had not been for the invariable courtesy and kindness shown by every one in it, from the President to the injured students, he should be sore at his failure.

These were his own feelings, but they seemed not to be felt in the college. With the same perplexing impartiality that had so much disconcerted him in his undergraduate days, the college insisted on expressing an opposite view. John Fiske went so far in his notice of the family in "Appleton's Cyclopedia," as to say that Henry had left a great reputation at Harvard College; which was a proof of John Fiske's personal regard that Adams heartily returned; and set the kind expression down to *camaraderie*. The case was different when President Eliot himself hinted that Adams's services merited recognition. Adams could have wept on his shoulder in hysterics, so grateful was he for the rare good-will that inspired the compliment; but he could not allow the college to think that he esteemed himself entitled to distinction. He knew better, and his was among the failures which were respectable enough to deserve self-respect. Yet nothing in the vanity of life struck him as more humiliating than that Harvard College, which he had persistently criticised, abused, abandoned, and neglected, should alone have offered him a dollar, an office, an encouragement, or a kindness. Harvard College might have its faults, but at least it redeemed America, since it was true to its own.

The only part of education that the professor thought a success was the students. He found them excellent company. Cast more or less in the same mould, without violent emotions or sentiment, and, except for the veneer of American habits, ignorant of all that man had ever thought or hoped, their minds burst open like flowers at the sunlight of a suggestion. They were quick to respond; plastic to a mould; and incapable of fatigue. Their faith in education was so full of pathos that one dared not ask them what they thought they could do with education when they got it. Adams did put the question to one of them, and was surprised at the answer: "The degree of Harvard College is worth money to me in Chicago." This reply upset his experience; for the degree of Harvard College had been rather a drawback to a young man in Boston and Washington. So far as it went, the answer was good, and settled one's doubts. Adams knew no better, although he had given twenty years to pursuing the same education, and was no nearer a result than they. He still had to take for granted many things that they need not — among the rest, that his teaching did them more good than harm. In his own opinion the greatest good he could do them was to hold his tongue. They needed much faith then; they were likely to need more if they lived long.

He never knew whether his colleagues shared his doubts about their own utility. Unlike himself, they knew more or less their business. He could not tell his scholars that history glowed with social virtue; the Professor of Chemistry cared not a chemical atom whether society was virtuous or not. Adams could not pretend that mediæval society proved evolution; the Professor of Physics smiled at evolution. Adams was glad to dwell on the virtues of the Church and the triumphs of its art: the Professor of Political Economy had to treat them as waste of force. They knew what they had to teach; he did not. They might perhaps be frauds without knowing it; but he knew certainly nothing else of himself. He could teach his students nothing; he was only educating himself at their cost.

Education, like politics, is a rough affair, and every instructor has to shut his eyes and hold his tongue as though he were a priest. The students alone satisfied. They thought they gained something. Perhaps they did, for even in America and in the twentieth century, life could not be wholly industrial. Adams fervently hoped that they might remain content; but supposing twenty years more to pass, and they should turn on him as fiercely as he had turned on his old instructors — what answer could he make? The college had pleaded guilty, and tried to reform. He had pleaded guilty from the start, and his reforms had failed before those of the college.

The lecture-room was futile enough, but the faculty-room was worse. American society feared total wreck in the maelstrom of political and corporate administration,

but it could not look for help to college dons. Adams
knew, in that capacity, both Congressmen and professors,
and he preferred Congressmen. The same failure marked
the society of a college. Several score of the best-educated,
most agreeable, and personally the most sociable people in
America united in Cambridge to make a social desert that
would have starved a polar bear. The liveliest and most
agreeable of men — James Russell Lowell, Francis J.
Child, Louis Agassiz, his son Alexander, Gurney, John
Fiske, William James and a dozen others, who would have
made the joy of London or Paris — tried their best to
break out and be like other men in Cambridge and Boston,
but society called them professors, and professors they
had to be. While all these brilliant men were greedy for
companionship, all were famished for want of it. Society
was a faculty-meeting without business. The elements
were there; but society cannot be made up of elements —
people who are expected to be silent unless they have
observations to make — and all the elements are bound to
remain apart if required to make observations.

Thus it turned out that of all his many educations,
Adams thought that of school-teacher the thinnest. Yet he
was forced to admit that the education of an editor, in
some ways, was thinner still. The editor had barely time
to edit; he had none to write. If copy fell short, he was
obliged to scribble a book-review on the virtues of the
Anglo-Saxons or the vices of the Popes; for he knew
more about Edward the Confessor or Boniface VIII than
he did about President Grant. For seven years he wrote
nothing; the *Review* lived on his brother Charles's railway
articles. The editor could help others, but could do nothing for himself. As a writer, he was totally forgotten by
the time he had been an editor for twelve months. As editor he could find no writer to take his place for politics
and affairs of current concern. The *Review* became

chiefly historical. Russell Lowell and Frank Palgrave helped him to keep it literary. The editor was a helpless drudge whose successes, if he made any, belonged to his writers; but whose failures might easily bankrupt himself. Such a Review may be made a sink of money with captivating ease. The secrets of success as an editor were easily learned; the highest was that of getting advertisements. Ten pages of advertising made an editor a success; five marked him as a failure. The merits or demerits of his literature had little to do with his results except when they led to adversity.

A year or two of education as editor satiated most of his appetite for that career as a profession. After a very slight experience, he said no more on the subject. He felt willing to let any one edit, if he himself might write. Vulgarly speaking, it was a dog's life when it did not succeed, and little better when it did. A professor had at least the pleasure of associating with his students; an editor lived the life of an owl. A professor commonly became a pedagogue or a pedant; an editor became an authority on advertising. On the whole, Adams preferred his attic in Washington. He was educated enough. Ignorance paid better, for at least it earned fifty dollars a month.

With this result Henry Adams's education, at his entry into life, stopped, and his life began. He had to take that life as he best could, with such accidental education as luck had given him; but he held that it was wrong, and that, if he were to begin again, he would do it on a better system. He thought he knew nearly what system to pursue. At that time Alexander Agassiz had not yet got his head above water so far as to serve for a model, as he did twenty or thirty years afterwards; but the editorship of the *North American Review* had one solitary merit; it made the editor acquainted at a distance with almost every one in the country who could write or who could be the cause of writing. Adams was vastly pleased to be received among these clever people as one of themselves, and felt always a little surprised at their treating him as an equal, for they all had education; but among them, only one stood out in extraordinary prominence as the type and model of what Adams would have liked to be, and of what the American, as he conceived, should have been and was not.

Thanks to the article on Sir Charles Lyell, Adams passed for a friend of geologists, and the extent of his knowledge mattered much less to them than the extent of his friendship, for geologists were as a class not much better off than himself, and friends were sorely few. One of his friends from earliest childhood, and nearest neighbor in Quincy, Frank Emmons, had become a geologist and joined the Fortieth Parallel Survey under Government. At Washington in the winter of 1869–70 Emmons had invited Adams to go out with him on one of the field-parties in summer. Of course when Adams took the *Review* he put it at the service of the Survey, and regretted only that he could not do more. When the first year of professing and editing was at last over, and his July *North American* appeared, he drew a long breath of relief, and took the next train for the West. Of his year's work he was no judge. He had become a small spring in a large mechanism, and his work counted only in the sum; but he had been treated civilly by everybody, and he felt at home even in Boston. Putting in his pocket the July number of the *North American*, with a notice of the Fortieth Parallel Survey by Professor J. D. Whitney, he started for the plains and the Rocky Mountains.

In the year 1871, the West was still fresh, and the Union Pacific was young. Beyond the Missouri River, one felt the atmosphere of Indians and buffaloes. One saw the last vestiges of an old education, worth studying if one would; but it was not that which Adams sought; rather, he came out to spy upon the land of the future. The Survey occasionally borrowed troopers from the nearest station in case of happening on hostile Indians, but otherwise the topographers and geologists thought more about minerals than about Sioux. They held under their hammers a thousand miles of mineral country with all its riddles to solve, and its stores of possible wealth to mark. They felt the future in their hands.

Emmons's party was out of reach in the Uintahs, but Arnold Hague's had come in to Laramie for supplies, and they took charge of Adams for a time. Their wanderings or adventures matter nothing to the story of education. They were all hardened mountaineers and surveyors who took everything for granted, and spared each other the most wearisome bore of English and Scotch life, the stories of the big game they killed. A bear was an occasional amusement; a wapiti was a constant necessity; but the only wild animal dangerous to man was a rattlesnake or a skunk. One shot for amusement, but one had other matters to talk about.

Adams enjoyed killing big game, but loathed the labor of cutting it up; so that he rarely unslung the little carbine he was in a manner required to carry. On the other hand, he liked to wander off alone on his mule, and pass the day fishing a mountain stream or exploring a valley. One morning when the party was camped high above Estes Park, on the flank of Long's Peak, he borrowed a rod, and rode down over a rough trail into Estes Park, for some trout. The day was fine, and hazy with the smoke of forest fires a thousand miles away; the park stretched its English beauties off to the base of its bordering mountains in natural landscape and archaic peace; the stream was just fishy enough to tempt lingering along its banks. Hour after hour the sun moved westward and the fish moved eastward, or disappeared altogether, until at last when the fisherman cinched his mule, sunset was nearer than he thought. Darkness caught him before he could catch his trail. Not caring to tumble into some fifty-foot hole, he "allowed" he was lost, and turned back. In half-an-hour he was out of the hills, and under the stars of Estes Park, but he saw no prospect of supper or of bed.

Estes Park was large enough to serve for a bed on a summer night for an army of professors, but the supper question offered difficulties. There was but one cabin in the Park, near its entrance, and he felt no great confidence in finding it, but he thought his mule cleverer than himself, and the dim lines of mountain crest against the stars fenced his range of error. The patient mule plodded on without other road than the gentle slope of the ground, and some two hours must have passed before a light showed in the distance. As the mule came up to the cabin door, two or three men came out to see the stranger.

One of these men was Clarence King on his way up to the camp. Adams fell into his arms. As with most friendships, it was never a matter of growth or doubt. Friends are born in archaic horizons; they were shaped with the *Pteraspis* in Siluria; they have nothing to do with the accident of space. King had come up that day from Greeley in a light four-wheeled buggy, over a trail hardly fit for a commissariat mule, as Adams had reason to know since he went back in the buggy. In the cabin, luxury provided a room and one bed for guests. They shared the room and the bed, and talked till far towards dawn.

King had everything to interest and delight Adams. He knew more than Adams did of art and poetry; he knew America, especially west of the hundredth meridian, better than any one; he knew the professor by heart, and he knew the Congressman better than he did the professor. He knew even women; even the American woman; even the New York woman, which is saying much. Incidentally he knew more practical geology than was good for him, and saw ahead at least one generation further than the text-books. That he saw right was a different matter. Since the beginning of time no man has lived who is known to have seen right; the charm of King was that he saw what others did and a great deal more. His wit and humor; his bub-bling energy which swept every one into the current of his interest; his personal charm of youth and manners; his faculty of giving and taking, profusely, lavishly, whether in thought or in money as though he were Na-ture herself, marked him almost alone among Americans. He had in him something of the Greek — a touch of Alcibiades or Alexander. One Clarence King only existed in the world.

A new friend is always a miracle, but at thirty-three years old, such a bird of paradise rising in the sage-brush was an avatar. One friend in a lifetime is much; two are many; three are hardly possible. Friendship needs a cer-tain parallelism of life, a community of thought, a rivalry of aim. King, like Adams, and all their generation, was at that moment passing the critical point of his career. The one, coming from the west, saturated with the sunshine of the Sierras, met the other, drifting from the east, drenched in the fogs of London, and both had the same problems to handle — the same stock of implements — the same field to work in; above all, the same obstacles to overcome.

As a companion, King's charm was great, but this was not the quality that so much attracted Adams, nor could he affect even distant rivalry on this ground. Adams could never tell a story, chiefly because he always forgot it; and he was never guilty of a witticism, unless by accident. King and the Fortieth Parallel influenced him in a way far more vital. The lines of their lives converged, but King had moulded and directed his life logically, scientifically, as Adams thought American life should be directed. He had given himself education all of a piece, yet broad. Standing in the middle of his career, where their paths at last came together, he could look back and look forward on a straight line, with scientific knowledge for its base. Adams's life, past or future, was a succession of violent breaks or waves, with no base at all. King's abnormal energy had already won him great success. None of his contemporaries had done so much, single-handed, or were likely to leave so deep a trail. He had managed to induce Congress to adopt almost its first modern act of legislation. He had organized, as a civil — not military — measure, a Government Survey. He had paralleled the Continental Railway in Geology; a feat as yet unequalled by other governments which had as a rule no continents to survey. He was creating one of the classic scientific works of the century. The chances were great that he could, whenever he chose to quit the Government service, take the pick of the gold and silver, copper or coal, and build up his fortune as he pleased. Whatever prize he wanted lay ready for him — scientific, social, literary, political — and he knew how to take them in turn. With ordinary luck he would die at eighty the richest and most many-sided genius of his day.

So little egoistic he was that none of his friends felt envy of his extraordinary superiority, but rather grovelled before it, so that women were jealous of the power he had over men; but women were many and Kings were one. The men worshipped not so much their friend, as the ideal American they all wanted to be. The women were jealous because, at heart, King had no faith in the American woman; he loved types more robust.

The young men of the Fortieth Parallel had Californian instincts; they were brothers of Bret Harte. They felt no leanings towards the simple uniformities of Lyell and Darwin; they saw little proof of slight and imperceptible changes; to them, catastrophe was the law of change; they cared little for simplicity and much for complexity; but it was the complexity of Nature, not of New York or even of the Mississippi Valley. King loved paradox; he started them like rabbits, and cared for them no longer, when caught or lost; but they delighted Adams, for they helped, among other things, to persuade him that history was more amusing than science. The only question left open to doubt was their relative money value.

In Emmons's camp, far up in the Uintahs, these talks were continued till the frosts became sharp in the mountains. History and science spread out in personal horizons towards goals no longer far away. No more education was possible for either man. Such as they were, they had got to stand the chances of the world they lived in; and when Adams started back to Cambridge, to take up again the humble tasks of schoolmaster and editor he was harnessed to his cart. Education, systematic or accidental, had done its worst. Henceforth, he went on, submissive.

21

Twenty Years After

(1892)

Once more! this is a story of education, not of adventure!
It is meant to help young men — or such as have intelligence enough to seek help — but it is not meant to amuse
them. What one did — or did not do — with one's education, after getting it, need trouble the inquirer in no way;
it is a personal matter only which would confuse him.
Perhaps Henry Adams was not worth educating; most
keen judges incline to think that barely one man in a hundred owns a mind capable of reacting to any purpose on
the forces that surround him, and fully half of these react
wrongly. The object of education for that mind should
be the teaching itself how to react with vigor and economy. No doubt the world at large will always lag so far
behind the active mind as to make a soft cushion of inertia
to drop upon, as it did for Henry Adams; but education
should try to lessen the obstacles, diminish the friction,
invigorate the energy, and should train minds to react, not

at haphazard, but by choice, on the lines of force that attract their world. What one knows is, in youth, of little moment; they know enough who know how to learn. Throughout human history the waste of mind has been appalling, and, as this story is meant to show, society has conspired to promote it. No doubt the teacher is the worst criminal, but the world stands behind him and drags the student from his course. The moral is stentorian. Only the most energetic, the most highly fitted, and the most favored have overcome the friction or the viscosity of inertia, and these were compelled to waste three-fourths of their energy in doing it.

Fit or unfit, Henry Adams stopped his own education in 1871, and began to apply it for practical uses, like his neighbors. At the end of twenty years, he found that he had finished, and could sum up the result. He had no complaint to make against man or woman. They had all treated him kindly; he had never met with ill-will, ill-temper, or even ill-manners, or known a quarrel. He had never seen serious dishonesty or ingratitude. He had found a readiness in the young to respond to suggestion that seemed to him far beyond all he had reason to expect. Considering the stock complaints against the world, he could not understand why he had nothing to complain of.

During these twenty years he had done as much work, in quantity, as his neighbors wanted; more than they would ever stop to look at, and more than his share. Merely in print, he thought altogether ridiculous the number of volumes he counted on the shelves of public libraries. He had no notion whether they served a useful purpose; he had worked in the dark; but so had most of his friends, even the artists, none of whom held any lofty opinion of their success in raising the standards of society, or felt profound respect for the methods or manners of their time, at home or abroad, but all of whom had tried, in a way, to hold the standard up. The effort had been, for the older generation, exhausting, as one could see in the Hunts; but the generation after 1870 made more figure, not in proportion to public wealth or in the census, but in their own self-assertion. A fair number of the men who were born in the thirties had won names — Phillips Brooks; Bret Harte; Henry James; H. H. Richardson; John La Farge; and the list might be made fairly long if it were worth while; but from their school had sprung others, like Augustus St. Gaudens, McKim, Stanford White, and scores born in the forties, who counted as force even in the mental inertia of sixty or eighty million people. Among all these Clarence King, John Hay, and Henry Adams had led modest existences, trying to fill in the social gaps of a class which, as yet, showed but thin ranks and little cohesion. The combination offered no very glittering prizes, but they pursued it for twenty years with as much patience and effort as though it led to fame or power, until, at last, Henry Adams thought his own duties sufficiently performed and his account with society settled. He had enjoyed his life amazingly, and would not have exchanged it for any other that came in his way; he was, or thought he was, perfectly satisfied with it; but for reasons that had nothing to do with education, he was tired; his nervous energy ran low; and, like a horse that wears out, he quitted the race-course, left the stable, and sought pastures as far as possible from the old. Education had ended in 1871; life was complete in 1890; the rest mattered so little!

As had happened so often, he found himself in London when the question of return imposed its verdict on him after much fruitless effort to rest elsewhere. The time was the month of January, 1892; he was alone, in hospital, in the gloom of midwinter. He was close on his fifty-fourth birthday, and Pall Mall had forgotten him as completely as it had forgotten his elders. He had not seen London for a dozen years, and was rather amused to have only a bed for a world and a familiar black fog for horizon. The coal-fire smelt homelike; the fog had a fruity taste of youth; anything was better than being turned out into the wastes of Wigmore Street. He could always amuse himself by living over his youth, and driving once more down Oxford Street in 1858, with life before him to imagine far less amusing than it had turned out to be.

The future attracted him less. Lying there for a week he reflected on what he could do next. He had just come up from the South Seas with John La Farge, who had reluctantly crawled away towards New York to resume the grinding routine of studio-work at an age when life runs low. Adams would rather, as choice, have gone back to the east, if it were only to sleep forever in the trade-winds under the southern stars, wandering over the dark purple ocean, with its purple sense of solitude and void. Not that he liked the sensation, but that it was the most unearthly he had felt. He had not yet happened on Rudyard Kipling's "Mandalay," but he knew the poetry before he knew the poem, like millions of wanderers, who have perhaps alone felt the world exactly as it is. Nothing attracted him less than the idea of beginning a new education. The old one had been poor enough; any new one could only add to its faults. Life had been cut in halves, and the old half had passed away, education and all, leaving no stock to graft on.

The new world he faced in Paris and London seemed to him fantastic. Willing to admit it real in the sense of having some kind of existence outside his own mind, he could not admit it reasonable. In Paris, his heart sank to mere pulp before the dismal ballets at the Grand Opera and the eternal vaudeville at the old Palais Royal; but, except for them, his own Paris of the Second Empire was as extinct as that of the first Napoleon. At the galleries and exhibitions, he was racked by the effort of art to be original, and when one day, after much reflection, John La Farge asked whether there might not still be room for something simple in art, Adams shook his head. As he saw the world, it was no longer simple and could not express itself simply. It should express what it was; and this was something that neither Adams nor La Farge understood.

Under the first blast of this furnace-heat, the lights seemed fairly to go out. He felt nothing in common with the world as it promised to be. He was ready to quit it, and the easiest path led back to the east; but he could not venture alone, and the rarest of animals is a companion. He must return to America to get one. Perhaps, while waiting, he might write more history, and on the chance as a last resource, he gave orders for copying everything he could reach in archives, but this was mere habit. He went home as a horse goes back to his stable, because he knew nowhere else to go.

Home was Washington. As soon as Grant's administration ended, in 1877, and Evarts became Secretary of State, Adams went back there, partly to write history, but chiefly because his seven years of laborious banishment, in Boston, convinced him that, as far as he had a function in life, it was as stable-companion to statesmen, whether they liked it or not. At about the same time, old George Bancroft did the same thing, and presently John Hay came on to be Assistant Secretary of State for Mr. Evarts, and stayed there to write the "Life" of Lincoln. In 1884 Adams joined him in employing Richardson to build them adjoining houses on La Fayette Square. As far as Adams had a home this was it. To the house on La

Fayette Square he must turn, for he had no other status — no position in the world.

Never did he make a decision more reluctantly than this of going back to his manger. His father and mother were dead. All his family led settled lives of their own. Except for two or three friends in Washington, who were themselves uncertain of stay, no one cared whether he came or went, and he cared least. There was nothing to care about. Every one was busy; nearly every one seemed contented. Since 1871 nothing had ruffled the surface of the American world, and even the progress of Europe in her sideway track to dis-Europeaning herself had ceased to be violent.

After a dreary January in Paris, at last when no excuse could be persuaded to offer itself for further delay, he crossed the channel and passed a week with his old friend, Milnes Gaskell, at Thornes, in Yorkshire, while the westerly gales raved a warning against going home. Yorkshire in January is not an island in the South Seas. It has few points of resemblance to Tahiti; not many to Fiji or Samoa; but, as so often before, it was a rest between past and future, and Adams was grateful for it.

At last, on February 3, he drove, after a fashion, down the Irish Channel, on board the Teutonic. He had not crossed the Atlantic for a dozen years, and had never seen an ocean steamer of the new type. He had seen nothing new of any sort, or much changed in France or England. The railways made quicker time, but were no more comfortable. The scale was the same. The Channel service was hardly improved since 1858, or so little as to make no impression. Europe seemed to have been stationary for twenty years. To a man who had been stationary like Europe, the Teutonic was a marvel. That he should be able to eat his dinner through a week of howling winter gales was a miracle. That he should have a deck stateroom, with fresh air, and read all night, if he chose, by electric light, was matter for more wonder than life had yet supplied, in its old forms. Wonder may be double — even treble. Adams's wonder ran off into figures. As the Niagara was to the Teutonic — as 1860 was to 1890 — so the Teutonic and 1890 must be to the next term — and then? Apparently the question concerned only America. Western Europe offered no such conundrum. There one might double scale and speed indefinitely without passing bounds.

Fate was kind on that voyage. Rudyard Kipling, on his wedding trip to America, thanks to the mediation of Henry James, dashed over the passenger his exuberant fountain of gaiety and wit — as though playing a garden hose on a thirsty and faded begonia. Kipling could never know what peace of mind he gave, for he could hardly ever need it himself so much; and yet, in the full delight of his endless fun and variety, one felt the old conundrum repeat itself. Somehow, somewhere, Kipling and the American were not one, but two, and could not be glued together. The American felt that the defect, if defect it were, was in himself; he had felt it when he was with Swinburne, and, again, with Robert Louis Stevenson, even under the palms of Vailima; but he did not carry self-abasement to the point of thinking himself singular. Whatever the defect might be, it was American; it belonged to the type; it lived in the blood. Whatever the quality might be that held him apart, it was English; it lived also in the blood; one felt it little if at all, with Celts, and one yearned reciprocally among Fiji cannibals. Clarence King used to say that it was due to discord between the wave-lengths of the man-atoms; but the theory offered difficulties in measurement. Perhaps, after all, it was only that genius soars; but this theory, too, had its dark corners. All through life, one had seen the American on his literary knees to the European; and all through many lives back for some two centuries, one had seen the European snub or patronize the American; not always intentionally, but effectually. It was in the nature of things. Kipling neither snubbed nor patronized; he was all gaiety and good-nature; but he would have been first to feel what one meant. Genius has to pay itself that unwilling self-respect.

Towards the middle of February, 1892, Adams found himself again in Washington. In Paris and London he had seen nothing to make a return to life worth while; in Washington he saw plenty of reasons for staying dead. Changes had taken place there; improvements had been made; with time — much time — the city might become habitable according to some fashionable standard; but all one's friends had died or disappeared several times over, leaving one almost as strange as in Boston or London. Slowly, a certain society had built itself up about the Government; houses had been opened and there was much dining; much calling; much leaving of cards; but a solitary man counted for less than in 1868. Society seemed hardly more at home than he. Both Executive and Congress held it aloof. No one in society seemed to have the ear of anybody in Government. No one in Government knew any reason for consulting any one in society. The world had ceased to be wholly political, but politics had become less social. A survivor of the Civil War — like George Bancroft, or John Hay — tried to keep footing, but without brilliant success. They were free to say or do what they liked, but no one took much notice of anything said or done.

A presidential election was to take place in November, and no one showed much interest in the result. The two candidates were singular persons, of whom it was the common saying that one of them had no friends; the other, only enemies. Calvin Brice, who was at that time altogether the wittiest and cleverest member of the Senate, was in the habit of describing Mr. Cleveland in glowing terms and at great length, as one of the loftiest natures and noblest characters of ancient or modern time; "but," he concluded, "in future I prefer to look on at his proceedings from the safe summit of some neighboring hill." The same remark applied to Mr. Harrison. In this respect, they were the greatest of Presidents, for, whatever harm they might do their enemies, was as nothing when compared to the mortality they inflicted on their friends. Men fled them as though they had the evil eye. To the American people, the two candidates and the two parties were so evenly balanced that the scales showed hardly a perceptible difference. Mr. Harrison was an excellent President, a man of ability and force; perhaps the best President the Republican Party had put forward since Lincoln's death; yet, on the whole, Adams felt a shade of preference for President Cleveland, not so much personally as because the Democrats represented to him the last remnants of the eighteenth century; the survivors of Hosea Biglow's Cornwallis; the sole remaining protestants against a banker's Olympus which had become, for five-and-twenty years, more and more despotic over Esop's frog-empire. One might no longer croak except to vote for King Log, or — failing storks — for Grover Cleveland; and even then could not be sure where King Banker lurked behind. The costly education in politics had led to political torpor. Every one did not share it. Clarence King and John Hay were loyal Republicans who never for a moment conceived that there could be merit in other ideals. With King, the feeling was chiefly love of archaic races; sympathy with the negro and Indian and corresponding dislike of their enemies; but with Hay, party loyalty became a phase of being, a little like the loyalty of a highly cultivated churchman to his Church. He saw all the failings of the party, and still more keenly those of the partisans; but he could not live outside. To Adams a Western Democrat or a Western Republican, a city Democrat or a city Republican, a W. C. Whitney or a J. G. Blaine, were actually the same man, as far as their usefulness to the objects of King, Hay, or Adams was concerned. They graded themselves as friends or enemies, not as Republicans or Democrats. To Hay, the difference was that of being respectable or not.

Since 1879, King, Hay and Adams had been inseparable. Step by step, they had gone on in the closest sympathy, rather shunning than inviting public position, until, in 1892, none of them held any post at all. With great effort, in Hayes's administration, all King's friends, including Abram Hewitt and Carl Schurz, had carried the bill for uniting the Surveys and had placed King at the head of the Bureau; but King waited only to organize the service, and then resigned, in order to seek his private fortune in the West. Hay, after serving as Assistant Secretary of State under Secretary Evarts during a part of Hayes's administration, then also insisted on going out, in order to write with Nicolay the "Life" of Lincoln. Adams had held no office, and when his friends asked the reason, he could not go into long explanations, but preferred to answer simply that no President had ever invited him to fill one. The reason was good, and was also conveniently true, but left open an awkward doubt of his morals or capacity. Why had no President ever cared to employ him? The question needed a volume of intricate explanation. There never was a day when he would have refused to perform any duty that the Government imposed on him, but the American Government never to his knowledge imposed duties. The point was never raised with regard to him, or to any one else. The Government required candidates to offer; the business of the Executive began and ended with the consent or refusal to confer. The social formula carried this passive attitude a shade further. Any public man who may for years have used some other man's house as his own, when promoted to a position of patronage commonly feels himself obliged to inquire, directly or indirectly, whether his friend wants anything; which is equivalent to a civil act of divorce, since he feels awkward in the old relation. The handsomest formula, in an impartial choice, was the grandly courteous Southern phrase of Lamar: "Of course Mr. Adams knows that anything in my power is at his service." *A la disposicion de Usted!* The form must have been correct since it released both parties. He was right; Mr. Adams did know all about it; a bow and a conventional smile closed the subject forever, and every one felt flattered.

Such an intimate, promoted to power, was always lost. His duties and cares absorbed him and affected his balance of mind. Unless his friend served some political purpose, friendship was an effort. Men who neither wrote for newspapers nor made campaign speeches, who rarely subscribed to the campaign fund, and who entered the White House as seldom as possible, placed themselves outside the sphere of usefulness, and did so with entirely adequate knowledge of what they were doing. They never expected the President to ask for their services, and saw no reason why he should do so. As for Henry Adams, in fifty years that he knew Washington, no one would have been more surprised than himself had any President ever asked him to perform so much of a service as to cross the square. Only Texan Congressmen imagined that the

President needed their services in some remote consulate after worrying him for months to find one.

In Washington this law or custom is universally understood, and no one's character necessarily suffered because he held no office. No one took office unless he wanted it; and in turn the outsider was never asked to do work or subscribe money. Adams saw no office that he wanted, and he gravely thought that, from his point of view, in the long run, he was likely to be a more useful citizen without office. He could at least act as audience, and, in those days, a Washington audience seldom filled even a small theatre. He felt quite well satisfied to look on, and from time to time he thought he might risk a criticism of the players; but though he found his own position regular, he never quite understood that of John Hay. The Republican leaders treated Hay as one of themselves; they asked his services and took his money with a freedom that staggered even a hardened observer; but they never needed him in equivalent office. In Washington Hay was the only competent man in the party for diplomatic work. He corresponded in his powers of usefulness exactly with Lord Granville in London, who had been for forty years the saving grace of every Liberal administration in turn. Had usefulness to the public service been ever a question, Hay should have had a first-class mission under Hayes; should have been placed in the Cabinet by Garfield, and should have been restored to it by Harrison. These gentlemen were always using him; always invited his services, and always took his money.

Adams's opinion of politics and politicians, as he frankly admitted, lacked enthusiasm, although never, in his severest temper, did he apply to them the terms they freely applied to each other; and he explained everything by his old explanation of Grant's character as more or less a general type; but what roused in his mind more rebellion was the patience and good-nature with which Hay allowed himself to be used. The trait was not confined to politics. Hay seemed to like to be used, and this was one of his many charms; but in politics this sort of good-nature demands supernatural patience. Whatever astonishing lapses of social convention the politicians betrayed, Hay laughed equally heartily, and told the stories with constant amusement, at his own expense. Like most Americans, he liked to play at making Presidents, but, unlike most, he laughed not only at the Presidents he helped to make, but also at himself for laughing.

One must be rich, and come from Ohio or New York, to gratify an expensive taste like this. Other men, on both political flanks, did the same thing, and did it well, less for selfish objects than for the amusement of the game; but Hay alone lived in Washington and in the centre of the Ohio influences that ruled the Republican Party during thirty years. On the whole, these influences were respectable, and although Adams could not, under any circumstances, have had any value, even financially, for Ohio politicians, Hay might have much, as he showed, if they only knew enough to appreciate him. The American politician was occasionally an amusing object; Hay laughed, and, for want of other resource, Adams laughed too; but perhaps it was partly irritation at seeing how President Harrison dealt his cards that made Adams welcome President Cleveland back to the White House.

At all events, neither Hay nor King nor Adams had much to gain by reëlecting Mr. Harrison in 1892, or by defeating him, as far as he was concerned; and as far as concerned Mr. Cleveland, they seemed to have even less personal concern. The whole country, to outward appearance, stood in much the same frame of mind. Everywhere was slack-water. Hay himself was almost as languid and indifferent as Adams. Neither had occupation. Both had finished their literary work. The "Life" of Lincoln had been begun, completed, and published hand in hand with the "History" of Jefferson and Madison, so that between them they had written nearly all the American history there was to write. The intermediate period needed intermediate treatment; the gap between James Madison and Abraham Lincoln could not be judicially filled by either of them. Both were heartily tired of the subject, and America seemed as tired as they. What was worse, the redeeming energy of Americans which had generally served as the resource of minds otherwise vacant, the creation of new force, the application of expanding power, showed signs of check. Even the year before, in 1891, far off in the Pacific, one had met everywhere in the East a sort of stagnation — a creeping paralysis — complaints of shipping and producers — that spread throughout the whole southern hemisphere. Questions of exchange and silver-production loomed large. Credit was shaken, and a change of party government might shake it even in Washington. The matter did not concern Adams, who had no credit, and was always richest when the rich were poor; but it helped to dull the vibration of society.

However they studied it, the balance of profit and loss, on the last twenty years, for the three friends, King, Hay, and Adams, was exceedingly obscure in 1892. They had lost twenty years, but what had they gained? They often discussed the question. Hay had a singular faculty for remembering faces, and would break off suddenly the thread of his talk, as he looked out of the window on La Fayette Square, to notice an old corps commander or admiral of the Civil War, tottering along to the club for his cards or his cocktail: "There is old Dash who broke the rebel lines at Blankburg! Think of his having been a thunderbolt of war!" Or what drew Adams's closer attention:

"There goes old Boutwell gambolling like the gambolling kid!" There they went! Men who had swayed the course of empire as well as the course of Hay, King, and Adams, less valued than the ephemeral Congressman behind them, who could not have told whether the general was a Boutwell or Boutwell a general. Theirs was the highest known success, and one asked what it was worth to them. Apart from personal vanity, what would they sell it for? Would any one of them, from President downwards, refuse ten thousand a year in place of all the consideration he received from the world on account of his success?

Yet consideration had value, and at that time Adams enjoyed lecturing Augustus St. Gaudens, in hours of depression, on its economics: "Honestly you must admit that even if you don't pay your expenses you get a certain amount of advantage from doing the best work. Very likely some of the really successful Americans would be willing you should come to dinner sometimes, if you did not come too often, while they would think twice about Hay, and would never stand me." The forgotten statesman had no value at all; the general and admiral not much; the historian but little; on the whole, the artist stood best, and of course, wealth rested outside the question, since it was acting as judge; but, in the last resort, the judge certainly admitted that consideration had some value as an asset, though hardly as much as ten — or five — thousand a year.

Hay and Adams had the advantage of looking out of their windows on the antiquities of La Fayette Square, with the sense of having all that any one had; all that the world had to offer; all that they wanted in life, including their names on scores of title-pages and in one or two biographical dictionaries; but this had nothing to do with consideration, and they knew no more than Boutwell or St. Gaudens whether to call it success. Hay had passed ten years in writing the "Life" of Lincoln, and perhaps President Lincoln was the better for it, but what Hay got from it was not so easy to see, except the privilege of seeing popular bookmakers steal from his book and cover the theft by abusing the author. Adams had given ten or a dozen years to Jefferson and Madison, with expenses which, in any mercantile business, could hardly have been reckoned at less than a hundred thousand dollars, on a salary of five thousand a year; and when he asked what return he got from this expenditure, rather more extravagant in proportion to his means than a racing-stable, he could see none whatever. Such works never return money. Even Frank Parkman never printed a first edition of his relatively cheap and popular volumes, numbering more than seven hundred copies, until quite at the end of his life. A thousand copies of a book that cost twenty dollars or more was as much as any author could expect; two thousand copies was a visionary estimate unless it were canvassed for subscription. As far as Adams knew, he had but three serious readers — Abram Hewitt, Wayne McVeagh, and Hay himself. He was amply satisfied with their consideration, and could dispense with that of the other fifty-nine million, nine hundred and ninety-nine thousand, nine hundred and ninety-seven; but neither he nor Hay was better off in any other respect, and their chief title to consideration was their right to look out of their windows on great men, alive or dead, in La Fayette Square, a privilege which had nothing to do with their writings.

The world was always good-natured; civil; glad to be amused; open-armed to any one who amused it; patient with every one who did not insist on putting himself in its way, or costing it money; but this was not consideration, still less power in any of its concrete forms, and applied as well or better to a comic actor. Certainly a rare soprano or tenor voice earned infinitely more applause as it gave infinitely more pleasure, even in America; but one does what one can with one's means, and casting up one's balance sheet, one expects only a reasonable return on one's capital. Hay and Adams had risked nothing and never played for high stakes. King had followed the ambitious course. He had played for many millions. He had more than once come close to a great success, but the result was still in doubt, and meanwhile he was passing the best years of his life underground. For companionship he was mostly lost.

Thus, in 1892, neither Hay, King, nor Adams knew whether they had attained success, or how to estimate it, or what to call it; and the American people seemed to have no clearer idea than they. Indeed, the American people had no idea at all; they were wandering in a wilderness much more sandy than the Hebrews had ever trodden about Sinai; they had neither serpents nor golden calves to worship. They had lost the sense of worship; for the idea that they worshipped money seemed a delusion. Worship of money was an old-world trait; a healthy appetite akin to worship of the Gods, or to worship of power in any concrete shape; but the American wasted money more recklessly than any one ever did before; he spent more to less purpose than any extravagant court aristocracy; he had no sense of relative values, and knew not what to do with his money when he got it, except use it to make more, or throw it away. Probably, since human society began, it had seen no such curious spectacle as the houses of the San Francisco millionaires on Nob Hill. Except for the railway system, the enormous wealth taken out of the ground since 1840, had disappeared. West of the Alleghenies, the whole country might have been swept clean, and could have been replaced in better form within one or two years. The American mind had less respect for money than the European or Asiatic mind, and bore its loss more easily; but it had been deflected by its pursuit till it could turn in no other direction. It shunned, distrusted, disliked, the dangerous attraction of ideals, and stood alone in history for its ignorance of the past.

Personal contact brought this American trait close to Adams's notice. His first step, on returning to Washington, took him out to the cemetery known as Rock Creek, to see the bronze figure which St. Gaudens had made for him in his absence. Naturally every detail interested him; every line; every touch of the artist; every change of light and shade; every point of relation; every possible doubt of St. Gaudens's correctness of taste or feeling; so that, as the spring approached, he was apt to stop there often to see what the figure had to tell him that was new; but, in all that it had to say, he never once thought of questioning what it meant. He supposed its meaning to be the one commonplace about it — the oldest idea known to human thought. He knew that if he asked an Asiatic its meaning, not a man, woman, or child from Cairo to Kamtchatka would have needed more than a glance to reply. From the Egyptian Sphinx to the Kamakura Daibuts; from Prometheus to Christ; from Michael Angelo to Shelley, art had wrought on this eternal figure almost as though it had nothing else to say. The interest of the figure was not in its meaning, but in the response of the observer. As Adams sat there, numbers of people came, for the figure seemed to have become a tourist fashion, and all wanted to know its meaning. Most took it for a portrait-statue, and the remnant were vacant-minded in the absence of a personal guide. None felt what would have been a nursery-instinct to a Hindu baby or a Japanese jinricksha-runner. The only exceptions were the clergy, who taught a lesson even deeper. One after another brought companions there, and, apparently fascinated by their own reflection, broke out passionately against the expression they felt in the figure of despair, of atheism, of denial. Like the others, the priest saw only what he brought. Like all great artists, St. Gaudens held up the mirror and no more. The American layman had lost sight of ideals; the American priest had lost sight of faith. Both were more American than the old, half-witted soldiers who denounced the wasting, on a mere grave, of money which should have been given for drink.

Landed, lost, and forgotten, in the centre of this vast plain of self-content, Adams could see but one active interest, to which all others were subservient, and which absorbed the energies of some sixty million people to the exclusion of every other force, real or imaginary. The power of the railway system had enormously increased since 1870. Already the coal output of 160,000,000 tons closely approached the 180,000,000 of the British Empire, and one held one's breath at the nearness of what one had never expected to see, the crossing of courses, and the lead of American energies. The moment was deeply exciting to a historian, but the railway system itself interested one less than in 1868, since it offered less chance for future profit. Adams had been born with the railway system; had grown up with it; had been over pretty nearly every mile of it with curious eyes, and knew as much about it as his neighbors; but not there could he look for a new education. Incomplete though it was, the system seemed on the whole to satisfy the wants of society better than any other part of the social machine, and society was content with its creation, for the time, and with itself for creating it. Nothing new was to be done or learned there, and the world hurried on to its telephones, bicycles, and electric trams. At past fifty, Adams solemnly and painfully learned to ride the bicycle.

Nothing else occurred to him as a means of new life. Nothing else offered itself, however carefully he sought. He looked for no change. He lingered in Washington till near July without noticing a new idea. Then he went back to England to pass his summer on the Deeside. In October he returned to Washington and there awaited the re-election of Mr. Cleveland, which led to no deeper thought than that of taking up some small notes that happened to be outstanding. He had seen enough of the world to be a coward, and above all he had an uneasy distrust of bankers. Even dead men allow themselves a few narrow prejudices.

22

Chicago

(1893)

Drifting in the dead-water of the *fin-de-siècle* — and during this last decade every one talked, and seemed to feel *fin-de-siècle* — where not a breath stirred the idle air of education or fretted the mental torpor of self-content, one lived alone. Adams had long ceased going into society. For years he had not dined out of his own house, and in public his face was as unknown as that of an extinct statesman. He had often noticed that six months' oblivion amounts to newspaper-death, and that resurrection is rare. Nothing is easier, if a man wants it, than rest, profound as the grave.

His friends sometimes took pity on him, and came to share a meal or pass a night on their passage south or northwards, but existence was, on the whole, exceedingly solitary, or seemed so to him. Of the society favorites who made the life of every dinner-table and of the halls of Congress — Tom Reed, Bourke Cockran, Edward Wolcott — he knew not one. Although Calvin Brice was his next neighbor for six years, entertaining lavishly as no one had ever entertained before in Washington, Adams never entered his house. W. C. Whitney rivalled Senator

Brice in hospitality, and was besides an old acquaintance of the reforming era, but Adams saw him as little as he saw his chief, President Cleveland, or President Harrison or Secretary Bayard or Blaine or Olney. One has no choice but to go everywhere or nowhere. No one may pick and choose between houses, or accept hospitality without returning it. He loved solitude as little as others did; but he was unfit for social work, and he sank under the surface.

Luckily for such helpless animals as solitary men, the world is not only good-natured but even friendly and generous; it loves to pardon if pardon is not demanded as a right. Adams's social offences were many, and no one was more sensitive to it than himself; but a few houses always remained which he could enter without being asked, and quit without being noticed. One was John Hay's; another was Cabot Lodge's; a third led to an intimacy which had the singular effect of educating him in knowledge of the very class of American politician who had done most to block his intended path in life. Senator Cameron of Pennsylvania had married in 1880 a young niece of Senator John Sherman of Ohio, thus making an alliance of dynastic importance in politics, and in society a reign of sixteen years, during which Mrs. Cameron and Mrs. Lodge led a career, without precedent and without succession, as the dispensers of sunshine over Washington. Both of them had been kind to Adams, and a dozen years of this intimacy had made him one of their habitual household, as he was of Hay's. In a small society, such ties between houses become political and social force. Without intention or consciousness, they fix one's status in the world. Whatever one's preferences in politics might be, one's house was bound to the Republican interest when sandwiched between Senator Cameron, John Hay, and

Cabot Lodge, with Theodore Roosevelt equally at home in them all, and Cecil Spring-Rice to unite them by impartial variety. The relation was daily, and the alliance undisturbed by power or patronage, since Mr. Harrison, in those respects, showed little more taste than Mr. Cleveland for the society and interests of this particular band of followers, whose relations with the White House were sometimes comic, but never intimate.

In February, 1893, Senator Cameron took his family to South Carolina, where he had bought an old plantation at Coffin's Point on St. Helena Island, and Adams, as one of the family, was taken, with the rest, to open the new experience. From there he went on to Havana, and came back to Coffin's Point to linger till near April. In May the Senator took his family to Chicago to see the Exposition, and Adams went with them. Early in June, all sailed for England together, and at last, in the middle of July, all found themselves in Switzerland, at Prangins, Chamounix, and Zermatt. On July 22 they drove across the Furka Pass and went down by rail to Lucerne.

Months of close contact teach character, if character has interest; and to Adams the Cameron type had keen interest, ever since it had shipwrecked his career in the person of President Grant. Perhaps it owed life to Scotch blood; perhaps to the blood of Adam and Eve, the primitive strain of man; perhaps only to the blood of the cottager working against the blood of the townsman; but whatever it was, one liked it for its simplicity. The Pennsylvania mind, as minds go, was not complex; it reasoned little and never talked; but in practical matters it was the steadiest of all American types; perhaps the most efficient; certainly the safest.

Adams had printed as much as this in his books, but had never been able to find a type to describe, the two great historical Pennsylvanians having been, as every one had so often heard, Benjamin Franklin of Boston and Albert Gallatin of Geneva. Of Albert Gallatin, indeed, he had made a voluminous study and an elaborate picture, only to show that he was, if American at all, a New Yorker, with a Calvinistic strain — rather Connecticut than Pennsylvanian. The true Pennsylvanian was a narrower type; as narrow as the kirk; as shy of other people's narrowness as a Yankee; as self-limited as a Puritan farmer. To him, none but Pennsylvanians were white. Chinaman, negro, Dago, Italian, Englishman, Yankee — all was one in the depths of Pennsylvanian consciousness. The mental machine could run only on what it took for American lines. This was familiar, ever since one's study of President Grant in 1869; but in 1893, as then, the type was admirably strong and useful if one wanted only to run on the same lines. Practically the Pennsylvanian forgot his prejudices when he allied his interests. He then became supple in action and large in motive, whatever he thought of his colleagues. When he happened to be right — which was, of course, whenever one agreed with him — he was the strongest American in America. As an ally he was worth all the rest, because he understood his own class, who were always a majority; and knew how to deal with them as no New Englander could. If one wanted work done in Congress, one did wisely to avoid asking a New Englander to do it. A Pennsylvanian not only could do it, but did it willingly, practically, and intelligently.

Never in the range of human possibilities had a Cameron believed in an Adams — or an Adams in a Cameron — but they had, curiously enough, almost always worked together. The Camerons had what the Adamses thought the political vice of reaching their objects without much regard to their methods. The loftiest virtue of the Pennsylvania machine had never been its scrupulous purity or sparkling professions. The machine worked by coarse

means on coarse interests; but its practical success had
been the most curious subject of study in American history. When one summed up the results of Pennsylvanian
influence, one inclined to think that Pennsylvania set up
the Government in 1789; saved it in 1861; created the
American system; developed its iron and coal power; and
invented its great railways. Following up the same line,
in his studies of American character, Adams reached the
result — to him altogether paradoxical — that Cameron's
qualities and defects united in equal share to make him
the most useful member of the Senate.

In the interest of studying, at last, a perfect and favor-
able specimen of this American type which had so persistently suppressed his own, Adams was slow to notice
that Cameron strongly influenced him, but he could not
see a trace of any influence which he exercised on Cameron. Not an opinion or a view of his on any subject was
ever reflected back on him from Cameron's mind; not
even an expression or a fact. Yet the difference in age was
trifling, and in education slight. On the other hand, Cameron made deep impression on Adams, and in nothing so
much as on the great subject of discussion that year — the
question of silver.

Adams had taken no interest in the matter, and knew
nothing about it, except as a very tedious hobby of his
friend Dana Horton; but inevitably, from the moment he
was forced to choose sides, he was sure to choose silver.
Every political idea and personal prejudice he ever dallied
with held him to the silver standard, and made a barrier
between him and gold. He knew well enough all that was
to be said for the gold standard as economy, but he had
never in his life taken politics for a pursuit of economy.
One might have a political or an economical policy; one
could not have both at the same time. This was heresy
in the English school, but it had always been law in the

American. Equally he knew all that was to be said on the moral side of the question, and he admitted that his interests were, as Boston maintained, wholly on the side of gold; but, had they been ten times as great as they were, he could not have helped his bankers or croupiers to load the dice and pack the cards to make sure his winning the stakes. At least he was bound to profess disapproval — or thought he was. From early childhood his moral principles had struggled blindly with his interests, but he was certain of one law that ruled all others — masses of men invariably follow interests in deciding morals. Morality is a private and costly luxury. The morality of the silver or gold standards was to be decided by popular vote, and the popular vote would be decided by interests; but on which side lay the larger interest? To him the interest was political; he thought it probably his last chance of standing up for his eighteenth-century principles, strict construction, limited powers, George Washington, John Adams, and the rest. He had, in a half-hearted way, struggled all his life against State Street, banks, capitalism altogether, as he knew it in old England or new England, and he was fated to make his last resistance behind the silver standard.

For him this result was clear, and if he erred, he erred in company with nine men out of ten in Washington, for there was little difference on the merits. Adams was sure to learn backwards, but the case seemed entirely different with Cameron, a typical Pennsylvanian, a practical politician, whom all the reformers, including all the Adamses, had abused for a lifetime for subservience to moneyed interests and political jobbery. He was sure to go with the banks and corporations which had made and sustained him. On the contrary, he stood out obstinately as the leading champion of silver in the East. The reformers, represented by the *Evening Post* and Godkin,

whose personal interests lay with the gold standard, at
once assumed that Senator Cameron had a personal interest in silver, and denounced his corruption as hotly as
though he had been convicted of taking a bribe.

More than silver and gold, the moral standard interested Adams. His own interests were with gold, but he
supported silver; the *Evening Post's* and Godkin's interests were with gold, and they frankly said so, yet they
avowedly pursued their interests even into politics; Cameron's interests had always been with the corporations,
yet he supported silver. Thus morality required that
Adams should be condemned for going against his interests; that Godkin was virtuous in following his interests;
and that Cameron was a scoundrel whatever he did.

Granting that one of the three was a moral idiot, which
was it: — Adams or Godkin or Cameron? Until a Council
or a Pope or a Congress or the newspapers or a popular
election has decided a question of doubtful morality, individuals are apt to err, especially when putting money
into their own pockets; but in democracies, the majority
alone gives law. To any one who knew the relative popularity of Cameron and Godkin, the idea of a popular vote
between them seemed excessively humorous; yet the
popular vote in the end did decide against Cameron, for
Godkin.

The Boston moralist and reformer went on, as always,
like Dr. Johnson, impatiently stamping his foot and following his interests, or his antipathies; but the true American, slow to grasp new and complicated ideas, groped in
the dark to discover where his greater interest lay. As
usual, the banks taught him. In the course of fifty years
the banks taught one many wise lessons for which an insect had to be grateful whether it liked them or not; but
of all the lessons Adams learned from them, none compared in dramatic effect with that of July 22, 1893, when,

after talking silver all the morning with Senator Cameron on the top of their travelling-carriage crossing the Furka Pass, they reached Lucerne in the afternoon, where Adams found letters from his brothers requesting his immediate return to Boston because the community was bankrupt and he was probably a beggar.

If he wanted education, he knew no quicker mode of learning a lesson than that of being struck on the head by it; and yet he was himself surprised at his own slowness to understand what had struck him. For several years a sufferer from insomnia, his first thought was of beggary of nerves, and he made ready to face a sleepless night, but although his mind tried to wrestle with the problem how any man could be ruined who had, months before, paid off every dollar of debt he knew himself to owe, he gave up that insoluble riddle in order to fall back on the larger principle that beggary could be no more for him than it was for others who were more valuable members of society, and, with that, he went to sleep like a good citizen, and the next day started for Quincy where he arrived August 7.

As a starting-point for a new education at fifty-five years old, the shock of finding one's self suspended, for several months, over the edge of bankruptcy, without knowing how one got there, or how to get away, is to be strongly recommended. By slow degrees the situation dawned on him that the banks had lent him, among others, some money — thousands of millions were — as bankruptcy — the same — for which he, among others, was responsible and of which he knew no more than they. The humor of this situation seemed to him so much more pointed than the terror, as to make him laugh at himself with a sincerity he had been long strange to. As far as he could comprehend, he had nothing to lose that he cared about, but the banks stood to lose their existence. Money mattered as little to him as to anybody, but money was their life. For the first time he had the banks in his power; he could afford to laugh; and the whole community was in the same position, though few laughed. All sat down on the banks and asked what the banks were going to do about it. To Adams the situation seemed farcical, but the more he saw of it, the less he understood it. He was quite sure that nobody understood it much better. Blindly some very powerful energy was at work, doing something that nobody wanted done. When Adams went to his bank to draw a hundred dollars of his own money on deposit, the cashier refused to let him have more than fifty, and Adams accepted the fifty without complaint because he was himself refusing to let the banks have some hundreds or thousands that belonged to them. Each wanted to help the other, yet both refused to pay their debts, and he could find no answer to the question which was responsible for getting the other into the situation, since lenders and borrowers were the same interest and socially the same person. Evidently the force was one; its operation was mechanical; its effect must be proportional to its power; but no one knew what it meant, and most people dismissed it as an emotion — a panic — that meant nothing.

Men died like flies under the strain, and Boston grew suddenly old, haggard, and thin. Adams alone waxed fat and was happy, for at last he had got hold of his world and could finish his education, interrupted for twenty years. He cared not whether it were worth finishing, if only it amused; but he seemed, for the first time since 1870, to feel that something new and curious was about to happen to the world. Great changes had taken place since 1870 in the forces at work; the old machine ran far behind its duty; somewhere — somehow — it was bound to break down, and if it happened to break precisely over one's head, it gave the better chance for study.

For the first time in several years he saw much of his brother Brooks in Quincy, and was surprised to find him absorbed in the same perplexities. Brooks was then a man of forty-five years old; a strong writer and a vigorous thinker who irritated too many Boston conventions ever to suit the atmosphere; but the two brothers could talk to each other without atmosphere and were used to audiences of one. Brooks had discovered or developed a law of history that civilization followed the exchanges, and having worked it out for the Mediterranean was working it out for the Atlantic. Everything American, as well as most things European and Asiatic, became unstable by this law, seeking new equilibrium and compelled to find it. Loving paradox, Brooks, with the advantages of ten years' study, had swept away much rubbish in the effort to build up a new line of thought for himself, but he found that no paradox compared with that of daily events. The facts were constantly outrunning his thoughts. The instability was greater than he calculated; the speed of acceleration passed bounds. Among other general rules he laid down the paradox that, in the social disequilibrium between capital and labor, the logical outcome was not collectivism, but anarchism; and Henry made note of it for study.

By the time he got back to Washington on September 19, the storm having partly blown over, life had taken on a new face, and one so interesting that he set off to Chicago to study the Exposition again, and stayed there a fortnight absorbed in it. He found matter of study to fill a hundred years, and his education spread over chaos. Indeed, it seemed to him as though, this year, education went mad. The silver question, thorny as it was, fell into relations as simple as words of one syllable, compared with the problems of credit and exchange that came to complicate it; and when one sought rest at Chicago, educational game started like rabbits from every building, and ran out of sight among thousands of its kind before one could mark its burrow. The Exposition itself defied philosophy. One might find fault till the last gate closed, one could still explain nothing that needed explanation. As a scenic display, Paris had never approached it, but the inconceivable scenic display consisted in its being there at all — more surprising, as it was, than anything else on the continent, Niagara Falls, the Yellowstone Geysers, and the whole railway system thrown in, since these were all natural products in their place; while, since Noah's Ark, no such Babel of loose and ill-joined, such vague and ill-defined and unrelated thoughts and half-thoughts and experimental outcries as the Exposition, had ever ruffled the surface of the Lakes.

The first astonishment became greater every day. That the Exposition should be a natural growth and product of the Northwest offered a step in evolution to startle Darwin; but that it should be anything else seemed an idea more startling still; and even granting it were not — admitting it to be a sort of industrial, speculative growth and product of the Beaux Arts artistically induced to pass the summer on the shore of Lake Michigan — could it be made to seem at home there? Was the American made to seem at home in it? Honestly, he had the air of enjoying it as though it were all his own; he felt it was good; he was proud of it; for the most part, he acted as though he had passed his life in landscape gardening and architectural decoration. If he had not done it himself, he had known how to get it done to suit him, as he knew how to get his wives and daughters dressed at Worth's or Paquin's. Perhaps he could not do it again; the next time he would want to do it himself and would show his own faults; but for the moment he seemed to have leaped directly from Corinth and Syracuse and Venice, over the heads of London and New York, to impose classical standards on plastic Chicago. Critics had no trouble in criticising the classicism, but all trading cities had always shown traders' taste, and, to the stern purist of religious faith, no art was thinner than Venetian Gothic. All trader's taste smelt of bric-à-brac; Chicago tried at least to give her taste a look of unity.

One sat down to ponder on the steps beneath Richard Hunt's dome almost as deeply as on the steps of Ara Cœli, and much to the same purpose. Here was a breach of continuity — a rupture in historical sequence! Was it real, or only apparent? One's personal universe hung on the answer, for, if the rupture was real and the new American world could take this sharp and conscious twist towards ideals, one's personal friends would come in, at last, as winners in the great American chariot-race for fame. If the people of the Northwest actually knew what was good when they saw it, they would some day talk about Hunt and Richardson, La Farge and St. Gaudens, Burnham and McKim, and Stanford White when their politicians and millionaires were otherwise forgotten. The artists and architects who had done the work offered little encouragement to hope it; they talked freely enough, but not in terms that one cared to quote; and to them the Northwest refused to look artistic. They talked as though they worked only for themselves; as though art, to the Western people, was a stage decoration; a diamond shirt-stud; a paper collar; but possibly the architects of Pæstum and Girgenti had talked in the same way, and the Greek had said the same thing of Semitic Carthage two thousand years ago.

Jostled by these hopes and doubts, one turned to the exhibits for help, and found it. The industrial schools tried to teach so much and so quickly that the instruction ran to waste. Some millions of other people felt the same helplessness, but few of them were seeking education, and to them helplessness seemed natural and normal, for they had grown up in the habit of thinking a steam-engine or a dynamo as natural as the sun, and expected to understand one as little as the other. For the historian alone the Exposition made a serious effort. Historical exhibits were common, but they never went far enough; none were thoroughly worked out. One of the best was that of the Cunard steamers, but still a student hungry for results found himself obliged to waste a pencil and several sheets of paper trying to calculate exactly when, according to the given increase of power, tonnage, and speed, the growth of the ocean steamer would reach its limits. His figures brought him, he thought, to the year 1927; another generation to spare before force, space, and time should meet. The ocean steamer ran the surest line of triangulation into the future, because it was the nearest of man's products to a unity; railroads taught less because they seemed already finished except for mere increase in number; explosives taught most, but needed a tribe of chemists, physicists, and mathematicians to explain; the dynamo taught least because it had barely reached infancy, and, if its progress was to be constant at the rate of the last ten years, it would result in infinite costly energy within a generation. One lingered long among the dynamos, for they were new, and they gave to history a new phase. Men of science could never understand the ignorance and naïveté of the historian, who, when he came suddenly on a new power, asked naturally what it was; did it pull or did it push? Was it a screw or thrust? Did it flow or vibrate? Was it a wire or a mathematical line? And a score of such questions to which he expected answers and was astonished to get none.

Education ran riot at Chicago, at least for retarded

minds which had never faced in concrete form so many matters of which they were ignorant. Men who knew nothing whatever — who had never run a steam-engine, the simplest of forces — who had never put their hands on a lever — had never touched an electric battery — never talked through a telephone, and had not the shadow of a notion what amount of force was meant by a *watt* or an *ampère* or an *erg*, or any other term of measurement introduced within a hundred years — had no choice but to sit down on the steps and brood as they had never brooded on the benches of Harvard College, either as student or professor, aghast at what they had said and done in all these years, and still more ashamed of the childlike ignorance and babbling futility of the society that let them say and do it. The historical mind can think only in historical processes, and probably this was the first time since historians existed, that any of them had sat down helpless before a mechanical sequence. Before a metaphysical or a theological or a political sequence, most historians had felt helpless, but the single clue to which they had hitherto trusted was the unity of natural force.

Did he himself quite know what he meant? Certainly not! If he had known enough to state his problem, his education would have been complete at once. Chicago asked in 1893 for the first time the question whether the American people knew where they were driving. Adams answered, for one, that he did not know, but would try to find out. On reflecting sufficiently deeply, under the shadow of Richard Hunt's architecture, he decided that the American people probably knew no more than he did; but that they might still be driving or drifting unconsciously to some point in thought, as their solar system was said to be drifting towards some point in space; and that, possibly, if relations enough could be observed, this point might be fixed. Chicago was the first expression of American thought as a unity; one must start there.

Washington was the second. When he got back there, he fell headlong into the extra session of Congress called to repeal the Silver Act. The silver minority made an obstinate attempt to prevent it, and most of the majority had little heart in the creation of a single gold standard. The banks alone, and the dealers in exchange, insisted upon it; the political parties divided according to capitalistic geographical lines, Senator Cameron offering almost the only exception; but they mixed with unusual good-temper, and made liberal allowance for each others' actions and motives. The struggle was rather less irritable than such struggles generally were, and it ended like a comedy. On the evening of the final vote, Senator Cameron came back from the Capitol with Senator Brice, Senator Jones, Senator Lodge, and Moreton Frewen, all in the gayest of humors as though they were rid of a heavy responsibility. Adams, too, in a bystander's spirit, felt light in mind. He had stood up for his eighteenth century, his Constitution of 1789, his George Washington, his Harvard College, his Quincy, and his Plymouth Pilgrims, as long as any one would stand up with him. He had said it was hopeless twenty years before, but he had kept on, in the same old attitude, by habit and taste, until he found himself altogether alone. He had hugged his antiquated dislike of bankers and capitalistic society until he had become little better than a crank. He had known for years that he must accept the régime, but he had known a great many other disagreeable certainties — like age, senility, and death — against which one made what little resistance one could. The matter was settled at last by the people. For a hundred years, between 1793 and 1893, the American people had hesitated, vacillated, swayed forward and back, between two forces, one simply industrial, the other capitalistic, centralizing, and mechanical. In 1893, the issue came on the single gold standard, and the majority at last declared itself, once for all, in favor of the capitalistic system with all its necessary machinery. All one's friends, all one's best citizens, reformers, churches, colleges, educated classes, had joined the banks to force submission to capitalism; a submission long foreseen by the mere law of mass. Of all forms of society or government, this was the one he liked least, but his likes or dislikes were as antiquated as the rebel doctrine of State rights. A capitalistic system had been adopted, and if it were to be run at all, it must be run by capital and by capitalistic methods; for nothing could surpass the nonsensity of trying to run so complex and so concentrated a machine by Southern and Western farmers in grotesque alliance with city day-laborers, as had been tried in 1800 and 1828, and had failed even under simple conditions.

There, education in domestic politics stopped. The rest was question of gear; of running machinery; of economy; and involved no disputed principle. Once admitted that the machine must be efficient, society might dispute in what social interest it should be run, but in any case it must work concentration. Such great revolutions commonly leave some bitterness behind, but nothing in politics ever surprised Henry Adams more than the ease with which he and his silver friends slipped across the chasm, and alighted on the single gold standard and the capitalistic system with its methods; the protective tariff; the corporations and trusts; the trades-unions and socialistic paternalism which necessarily made their complement; the whole mechanical consolidation of force, which ruthlessly stamped out the life of the class into which Adams was born, but created monopolies capable of controlling the new energies that America adored.

Society rested, after sweeping into the ash-heap these cinders of a misdirected education. After this vigorous impulse, nothing remained for a historian but to ask — how long and how far!

23

Silence

(1894–1898)

The convulsion of 1893 left its victims in dead-water, and closed much education. While the country braced itself up to an effort such as no one had thought within its powers, the individual crawled as he best could, through the wreck, and found many values of life upset. But for connecting the nineteenth and twentieth centuries, the four years, 1893 to 1897, had no value in the drama of education, and might be left out. Much that had made life pleasant between 1870 and 1890 perished in the ruin, and among the earliest wreckage had been the fortunes of Clarence King. The lesson taught whatever the bystander chose to read in it; but to Adams it seemed singularly full of moral, if he could but understand it. In 1871 he had thought King's education ideal, and his personal fitness unrivalled. No other young American approached him for the combination of chances — physical energy, social standing, mental scope and training, wit, geniality, and science, that seemed superlatively American and irresistibly strong. His nearest rival was Alexander Agassiz, and, as far as their friends knew, no one else could be classed with them in the running. The result of twenty years' effort proved that the theory of scientific education failed where most theory fails — for want of money. Even Henry Adams, who kept himself, as he thought, quite outside of every possible financial risk, had been caught in the cogs, and held for months over the gulf of bankruptcy, saved only by the chance that the whole class of millionaires were more or less bankrupt too, and the banks were forced to let the mice escape with the rats; but, in sum, education without capital could always be taken by the throat and forced to disgorge its gains, nor was it helped by the knowledge that no one intended it, but that all alike suffered. Whether voluntary or mechanical the result for education was the same. The failure of the scientific scheme, without money to back it, was flagrant.

The scientific scheme in theory was alone sound, for science should be equivalent to money; in practice science was helpless without money. The weak holder was, in his own language, sure to be frozen out. Education must fit the complex conditions of a new society, always accelerating its movement, and its fitness could be known only from success. One looked about for examples of success among the educated of one's time — the men born in the thirties, and trained to professions. Within one's immediate acquaintance, three were typical: John Hay, Whitelaw Reid, and William C. Whitney; all of whom owed their free hand to marriage, education serving only for ornament, but among whom, in 1893, William C. Whitney was far and away the most popular type.

Newspapers might prate about wealth till commonplace print was exhausted, but as matter of habit, few Americans envied the very rich for anything the most of them got out of money. New York might occasionally fear them, but more often laughed or sneered at them, and never showed them respect. Scarcely one of the very rich men held any position in society by virtue of his wealth, or could have been elected to an office, or even into a good club. Setting aside the few, like Pierpont Morgan, whose social position had little to do with greater or less wealth, riches were in New York no object of envy on account of the joys they brought in their train, and Whitney was not even one of the very rich; yet in his case the envy was palpable. There was reason for it. Already in 1893 Whitney had finished with politics after having gratified every ambition, and swung the country almost at his will; he had thrown away the usual objects of political ambition like the ashes of smoked cigarettes; had turned to other amusements, satiated every taste, gorged every appetite, won every object that New York afforded, and, not yet satisfied, had carried his field of activity abroad, until New York no longer knew what most to envy, his horses or his houses. He had succeeded precisely where Clarence King had failed.

Barely forty years had passed since all these men started in a bunch to race for power, and the results were fixed beyond reversal; but one knew no better in 1894 than in 1854 what an American education ought to be in order to count as success. Even granting that it counted as money, its value could not be called general. America contained scores of men worth five millions or upwards, whose lives were no more worth living than those of their cooks, and to whom the task of making money equivalent to education offered more difficulties than to Adams the task of making education equivalent to money. Social position seemed to have value still, while education counted for nothing. A mathematician, linguist, chemist, electrician, engineer, if fortunate, might average a value of ten dollars a day in the open market. An administrator, organizer, manager, with mediæval qualities of energy and will, but no education beyond his special branch, would probably be worth at least ten times as much.

Society had failed to discover what sort of education suited it best. Wealth valued social position and classical education as highly as either of these valued wealth, and the women still tended to keep the scales even. For anything Adams could see he was himself as contented as though he had been educated; while Clarence King, whose education was exactly suited to theory, had failed; and Whitney, who was not better educated than Adams, had achieved phenomenal success.

Had Adams in 1894 been starting in life as he did in 1854, he must have repeated that all he asked of education was the facile use of the four old tools: Mathematics, French, German, and Spanish. With these he could still make his way to any object within his vision, and would have a decisive advantage over nine rivals in ten. Statesman or lawyer, chemist or electrician, priest or professor, native or foreign, he would fear none.

King's breakdown, physical as well as financial, brought the indirect gain to Adams that, on recovering strength, King induced him to go to Cuba, where, in January, 1894, they drifted into the little town of Santiago. The picturesque Cuban society, which King knew well, was more amusing than any other that one had yet discovered in the whole broad world, but made no profession of teaching anything unless it were Cuban Spanish or the *danza;* and neither on his own nor on King's account did the visitor ask any loftier study than that of the buzzards floating on the trade-wind down the valley to Dos Bocas, or the colors of sea and shore at sunrise from the height of the Gran Piedra; but, as though they were still twenty years old and revolution were as young as they, the decaying fabric, which had never been solid, fell on their heads and drew them with it into an ocean of mischief. In the half-century between 1850 and 1900, empires were always falling on one's head, and, of all lessons, these constant political convulsions taught least. Since the time of Rameses, revolutions have raised more doubts than they solved, but they have sometimes the merit of changing one's point of view, and the Cuban rebellion served to sever the last tie that attached Adams to a Democratic administration. He thought that President Cleveland could have settled the Cuban question, without war, had he chosen to do his duty, and this feeling, generally held by the Democratic Party, joined with the stress of economical needs and the gold standard to break into bits the old organization and to leave no choice between parties. The new American, whether consciously or not, had turned his back on the nineteenth century before he was done with it; the gold standard, the protective system, and the laws of mass could have no other outcome, and, as so often before, the movement, once accelerated by attempting to impede it, had the additional, brutal consequence of crushing equally the good and the bad that stood in its way.

The lesson was old — so old that it became tedious. One had studied nothing else since childhood, and wearied of it. For yet another year Adams lingered on these outskirts of the vortex, among the picturesque, primitive types of a world which had never been fairly involved in the general motion, and were the more amusing for their torpor. After passing the winter with King in the West Indies, he passed the summer with Hay in the Yellowstone, and found there little to study. The Geysers were an old story; the Snake River posed no vital statistics except in its fordings; even the Tetons were as calm as they were lovely; while the wapiti and bear, innocent of strikes and corners, laid no traps. In return the party treated them with affection. Never did a band less bloody or bloodthirsty wander over the roof of the continent. Hay loved as little as Adams did, the labor of skinning and butchering big game; he had even outgrown the sedate, middle-aged, meditative joy of duck-shooting, and found the trout of the Yellowstone too easy a prey. Hallett Phillips himself, who managed the party, loved to play Indian hunter without hunting so much as a field-mouse; Iddings the geologist was reduced to shooting only for the table, and the guileless prattle of Billy Hofer alone taught the simple life. Compared with the Rockies of 1871, the sense of wildness had vanished; one saw no possible adventures except to break one's neck as in chasing an aniseed fox. Only the more intelligent ponies scented an occasional friendly and sociable bear.

When the party came out of the Yellowstone, Adams went on alone to Seattle and Vancouver to inspect the last American railway systems yet untried. They, too, offered little new learning, and no sooner had he finished this debauch of Northwestern geography than with desperate thirst for exhausting the American field, he set out for Mexico and the Gulf, making a sweep of the Caribbean and clearing up, in these six or eight months, at least twenty thousand miles of American land and water.

He was beginning to think, when he got back to Washington in April, 1895, that he knew enough about the edges of life — tropical islands, mountain solitudes, archaic law, and retrograde types. Infinitely more amusing and incomparably more picturesque than civilization, they educated only artists, and, as one's sixtieth year approached, the artist began to die; only a certain intense cerebral restlessness survived which no longer responded to sensual stimulants; one was driven from beauty to beauty as though art were a trotting-match. For this, one was in some degree prepared, for the old man had been a stage-type since drama began; but one felt some perplexity to account for failure on the opposite or mechanical side, where nothing but cerebral action was needed.

Taking for granted that the alternative to art was arithmetic, he plunged deep into statistics, fancying that education would find the surest bottom there; and the study proved the easiest he had ever approached. Even the Government volunteered unlimited statistics, endless columns of figures, bottomless averages merely for the asking. At the Statistical Bureau, Worthington Ford supplied any material that curiosity could imagine for filling the vast gaps of ignorance, and methods for applying the plasters of fact. One seemed for a while to be winning ground, and one's averages projected themselves as laws into the future. Perhaps the most perplexing part of the study lay in the attitude of the statisticians, who showed no enthusiastic confidence in their own figures. They should have reached certainty, but they talked like other men who knew less. The method did not result in faith. Indeed, every increase of mass — of volume and velocity — seemed to bring in new elements, and, at last, a scholar, fresh in arithmetic and ignorant of algebra, fell into a superstitious terror of complexity as the sink of facts. Nothing came out as it should. In principle, according to figures, any one could set up or pull down a society. One could frame no sort of satisfactory answer to the constructive doctrines of Adam Smith, or to the destructive criticisms of Karl Marx or to the anarchistic imprecations of Élisée Reclus. One revelled at will in the ruin of every society in the past, and rejoiced in proving the prospective overthrow of every society that seemed possible in the future; but meanwhile these societies which violated every law, moral, arithmetical, and economical, not only propagated each other, but produced also fresh complexities with every propagation and developed mass with every complexity.

The human factor was worse still. Since the stupefying discovery of *Pteraspis* in 1867, nothing had so confused the student as the conduct of mankind in the *fin-de-siècle*. No one seemed very much concerned about this world or the future, unless it might be the anarchists, and they only because they disliked the present. Adams disliked the present as much as they did, and his interest in future society was becoming slight, yet he was kept alive by irritation at finding his life so thin and fruitless. Meanwhile he watched mankind march on, like a train of pack-horses on the Snake River, tumbling from one morass into another, and at short intervals, for no reason but temper, falling to butchery, like Cain. Since 1850, massacres had become so common that society scarcely noticed them unless they summed up hundreds of thousands, as in Armenia; wars had been almost continuous, and were beginning again in Cuba, threatening in South Africa, and possible in Manchuria; yet impartial judges thought them all not merely unnecessary, but foolish — induced by greed of the coarsest class, as though the Pharaohs or the Romans were still robbing their neighbors. The robbery might be natural and inevitable, but the murder seemed altogether archaic.

At one moment of perplexity to account for this trait of *Pteraspis*, or shark, which seemed to have survived every moral improvement of society, he took to study of the religious press. Possibly growth in human nature might show itself there. He found no need to speak unkindly of it; but, as an agent of motion, he preferred on the whole the vigor of the shark, with its chances of betterment; and he very gravely doubted, from his aching consciousness of religious void, whether any large fraction of society cared for a future life, or even for the present one, thirty years hence. Not an act, or an expression, or an image, showed depth of faith or hope.

The object of education, therefore, was changed. For many years it had lost itself in studying what the world had ceased to care for; if it were to begin again, it must try to find out what the mass of mankind did care for, and why. Religion, politics, statistics, travel had thus far led to nothing. Even the Chicago Fair had only confused the roads. Accidental education could go no further, for one's mind was already littered and stuffed beyond hope with the millions of chance images stored away without order in the memory. One might as well try to educate a gravel-pit. The task was futile, which disturbed a student less than the discovery that, in pursuing it, he was becoming himself ridiculous. Nothing is more tiresome than a super-annuated pedagogue.

For the moment he was rescued, as often before, by a woman. Towards midsummer, 1895, Mrs. Cabot Lodge bade him follow her to Europe with the Senator and her two sons. The study of history is useful to the historian by teaching him his ignorance of women; and the mass of this ignorance crushes one who is familiar enough with what are called historical sources to realize how few women have ever been known. The woman who is known only through a man is known wrong, and excepting one or two like Mme. de Sévigné, no woman has pictured herself. The American woman of the nineteenth century will live only as the man saw her; probably she will be less known than the woman of the eighteenth; none of the female descendants of Abigail Adams can ever be nearly so familiar as her letters have made her; and all this is pure loss to history, for the American woman of the nineteenth century was much better company than the American man; she was probably much better company than her grand-mothers. With Mrs. Lodge and her husband, Senator since 1893, Adams's relations had been those of elder brother or uncle since 1871 when Cabot Lodge had left his examination-papers on Assistant Professor Adams's desk, and crossed the street to Christ Church in Cambridge to get married. With Lodge himself, as scholar, fellow in-structor, co-editor of the *North American Review,* and political reformer from 1873 to 1878, he had worked intimately, but with him afterwards as politician he had not much relation; and since Lodge had suffered what Adams thought the misfortune of becoming not only a Senator but a Senator from Massachusetts — a singular social relation which Adams had known only as fatal to friends — a superstitious student, intimate with the laws of historical fatality, would rather have recognized him only as an enemy; but apart from this accident he valued Lodge highly, and in the waste places of average humanity had been greatly dependent on his house. Senators can never be approached with safety, but a Senator who has a very superior wife and several superior children who feel no deference for Senators as such, may be approached at times with relative impunity while they keep him under restraint.

Where Mrs. Lodge summoned, one followed with gratitude, and so it chanced that in August one found one's self for the first time at Caen, Coutances, and Mont-Saint-Michel in Normandy. If history had a chapter with which he thought himself familiar, it was the twelfth and thirteenth centuries; yet so little has labor to do with knowledge that these bare playgrounds of the lecture system turned into green and verdurous virgin forests merely through the medium of younger eyes and fresher minds. His German bias must have given his youth a terrible twist, for the Lodges saw at a glance what he had thought unessential because un-German. They breathed native air in the Normandy of 1200, a compliment which would have seemed to the Senator lacking in taste or even in sense when addressed to one of a class of men who passed life in trying to persuade themselves and the public that they breathed nothing less American than a blizzard; but this atmosphere, in the touch of a real emotion, betrayed the unconscious humor of the senatorial mind. In the thir-

teenth century, by an unusual chance, even a Senator became natural, simple, interested, cultivated, artistic, liberal
— genial.

Through the Lodge eyes the old problem became new
and personal; it threw off all association with the German
lecture-room. One could not at first see what this novelty
meant; it had the air of mere antiquarian emotion like
Wenlock Abbey and *Pteraspis;* but it expelled archaic
law and antiquarianism once for all, without seeming conscious of it; and Adams drifted back to Washington with a
new sense of history. Again he wandered south, and in
April returned to Mexico with the Camerons to study the
charms of *pulque* and Churriguerresque architecture. In
May he ran through Europe again with Hay, as far south
as Ravenna. There came the end of the passage. After thus
covering once more, in 1896, many thousand miles of
the old trails, Adams went home in October, with every
one else, to elect McKinley President and to start the
world anew.

For the old world of public men and measures since
1870, Adams wept no tears. Within or without, during or
after it, as partisan or historian, he never saw anything to
admire in it, or anything he wanted to save; and in this
respect he reflected only the public mind which balanced
itself so exactly between the unpopularity of both parties
as to express no sympathy with either. Even among the
most powerful men of that generation he knew none who
had a good word to say for it. No period so thoroughly
ordinary had been known in American politics since
Christopher Columbus first disturbed the balance of
American society; but the natural result of such lack
of interest in public affairs, in a small society like that of
Washington, led an idle bystander to depend abjectly on
intimacy of private relation. One dragged one's self down
the long vista of Pennsylvania Avenue, by leaning heavily

on one's friends, and avoiding to look at anything else.
Thus life had grown narrow with years, more and more
concentrated on the circle of houses round La Fayette
Square, which had no direct or personal share in power
except in the case of Mr. Blaine, whose tumultuous struggle for existence held him apart. Suddenly Mr. McKinley
entered the White House and laid his hand heavily on this
special group. In a moment the whole nest so slowly constructed, was torn to pieces and scattered over the world.
Adams found himself alone. John Hay took his orders
for London. Rockhill departed to Athens. Cecil Spring-
Rice had been buried in Persia. Cameron refused to remain in public life either at home or abroad, and broke up
his house on the Square. Only the Lodges and Roosevelts
remained, but even they were at once absorbed in the interests of power. Since 1861, no such social convulsion had
occurred.

Even this was not quite the worst. To one whose interests lay chiefly in foreign affairs, and who, at this moment,
felt most strongly the nightmare of Cuban, Hawaiian, and
Nicaraguan chaos, the man in the State Department
seemed more important than the man in the White House.
Adams knew no one in the United States fit to manage
these matters in the face of a hostile Europe, and had no
candidate to propose; but he was shocked beyond all re-
straints of expression to learn that the President meant to
put Senator John Sherman in the State Department in
order to make a place for Mr. Hanna in the Senate. Grant
himself had done nothing that seemed so bad as this to one
who had lived long enough to distinguish between the
ways of presidential jobbery, if not between the jobs. John
Sherman, otherwise admirably fitted for the place, a
friendly influence for nearly forty years, was notoriously
feeble and quite senile, so that the intrigue seemed to
Adams the betrayal of an old friend as well as of the State

Department. One might have shrugged one's shoulders had the President named Mr. Hanna his Secretary of State, for Mr. Hanna was a man of force if not of experience, and selections much worse than this had often turned out well enough; but John Sherman must inevitably and tragically break down.

The prospect for once was not less vile than the men. One can bear coldly the jobbery of enemies, but not that of friends, and to Adams this kind of jobbery seemed always infinitely worse than all the petty money bribes ever exploited by the newspapers. Nor was the matter improved by hints that the President might call John Hay to the Department whenever John Sherman should retire. Indeed, had Hay been even unconsciously party to such an intrigue, he would have put an end, once for all, to further concern in public affairs on his friend's part; but even without this last disaster, one felt that Washington had become no longer habitable. Nothing was left there but solitary contemplation of Mr. McKinley's ways which were not likely to be more amusing than the ways of his predecessors; or of senatorial ways, which offered no novelty of what the French language expressively calls *embêtement;* or of poor Mr. Sherman's ways which would surely cause anguish to his friends. Once more, one must go!

Nothing was easier! On and off, one had done the same thing since the year 1858, at frequent intervals, and had now reached the month of March, 1897; yet, as the whole result of six years' dogged effort to begin a new education, one could not recommend it to the young. The outlook lacked hope. The object of travel had become more and more dim, ever since the gibbering ghost of the Civil Law had been locked in its dark closet, as far back as 1860. Noah's dove had not searched the earth for resting-places so carefully, or with so little success. Any spot on land or water satisfies a dove who wants and finds rest; but no perch suits a dove of sixty years old, alone and uneducated, who has lost his taste even for olives. To this, also, the young may be driven, as education, and the lesson fails in humor; but it may be worth knowing to some of them that the planet offers hardly a dozen places where an elderly man can pass a week alone without ennui, and none at all where he can pass a year.

Irritated by such complaints, the world naturally answers that no man of sixty should live, which is doubtless true, though not original. The man of sixty, with a certain irritability proper to his years, retorts that the world has no business to throw on him the task of removing its carrion, and that while he remains he has a right to require amusement — or at least education, since this costs nothing to any one — and that a world which cannot educate, will not amuse, and is ugly besides, has even less right to exist than he. Both views seem sound; but the world wearily objects to be called by epithets what society always admits in practice; for no one likes to be told that he is a bore, or ignorant, or even ugly; and having nothing to say in its defence, it rejoins that, whatever license is pardonable in youth, the man of sixty who wishes consideration had better hold his tongue. This truth also has the defect of being too true. The rule holds equally for men of half that age. Only the very young have the right to betray their ignorance or ill-breeding. Elderly people commonly know enough not to betray themselves.

Exceptions are plenty on both sides, as the Senate knew to its acute suffering; but young or old, women or men, seemed agreed on one point with singular unanimity; each praised silence in others. Of all characteristics in human nature, this has been one of the most abiding. Mere superficial gleaning of what, in the long history of human expression, has been said by the fool or unsaid by the wise, shows that, for once, no difference of opinion has ever existed on this. "Even a fool," said the wisest of men, "when he holdeth his peace, is counted wise," and still more often, the wisest of men, when he spoke the highest wisdom, has been counted a fool. They agreed only on the merits of silence in others. Socrates made remarks in its favor, which should have struck the Athenians as new to them; but of late the repetition had grown tiresome. Thomas Carlyle vociferated his admiration of it. Matthew Arnold thought it the best form of expression; and Adams thought Matthew Arnold the best form of expression in his time. Algernon Swinburne called it the most noble to the end. Alfred de Vigny's dying wolf remarked: —

> "A voir ce que l'on fut sur terre et ce qu'on laisse,
> Seul le silence est grand; tout le reste est faiblesse."

> "When one thinks what one leaves in the world when
> one dies,
> Only silence is strong,—all the rest is but lies."

Even Byron, whom a more brilliant era of genius seemed to have decided to be but an indifferent poet, had ventured to affirm that —

> "The Alp's snow summit nearer heaven is seen
> Than the volcano's fierce eruptive crest;"

with other verses, to the effect that words are but a "temporary torturing flame"; of which no one knew more than himself. The evidence of the poets could not be more emphatic: —

> "Silent, while years engrave the brow!
> Silent,—the best are silent now!"

Although none of these great geniuses had shown faith in silence as a cure for their own ills or ignorance, all of them, and all philosophy after them, affirmed that no man, even at sixty, had ever been known to attain knowledge; but that a very few were believed to have attained ignorance, which was in result the same. More than this, in every society worth the name, the man of sixty had been encouraged to ride this hobby — the Pursuit of Ignorance in Silence — as though it were the easiest way to get rid of him. In America the silence was more oppressive than the ignorance; but perhaps elsewhere the world might still hide some haunt of *futilitarian* silence where content reigned — although long search had not revealed it — and so the pilgrimage began anew!

The first step led to London where John Hay was to be established. One had seen so many American Ministers received in London that the Lord Chamberlain himself scarcely knew more about it; education could not be expected there; but there Adams arrived, April 21, 1897, as though thirty-six years were so many days, for Queen Victoria still reigned and one saw little change in St. James's Street. True, Carlton House Terrace, like the streets of Rome, actually squeaked and gibbered with ghosts, till one felt like Odysseus before the press of shadows, daunted by a "bloodless fear"; but in spring London is pleasant, and it was more cheery than ever in May, 1897, when every one was welcoming the return of life after the long winter since 1893. One's fortunes, or one's friends' fortunes, were again in flood.

This amusement could not be prolonged, for one found one's self the oldest Englishman in England, much too familiar with family jars better forgotten, and old traditions better unknown. No wrinkled Tannhäuser, returning to the Wartburg, needed a wrinkled Venus to show him that he was no longer at home, and that even penitence was a sort of impertinence. He slipped away to Paris, and set up a household at St. Germain where he taught and learned French history for nieces who swarmed under the venerable cedars of the Pavillon d'Angoulême, and rode about the green forest-alleys of St. Germain and Marly. From time to time Hay wrote humorous laments, but nothing occurred to break the summer-peace of the stranded Tannhäuser, who slowly began to feel at home in France as in other countries he had thought more homelike. At length, like other dead Americans, he went to Paris because he could go nowhere else, and lingered there till the Hays came by, in January, 1898; and Mrs. Hay, who had been a stanch and strong ally for twenty years, bade him go with them to Egypt.

Adams cared little to see Egypt again, but he was glad to see Hay, and readily drifted after him to the Nile. What they saw and what they said had as little to do with education as possible, until one evening, as they were looking at the sun set across the Nile from Assouan, Spencer Eddy brought them a telegram to announce the sinking of the Maine in Havana Harbor. This was the greatest stride in education since 1865, but what did it teach? One leant on a fragment of column in the great hall at Karnak and watched a jackal creep down the débris of ruin. The jackal's ancestors had surely crept up the same wall when it was building. What was his view about the value of silence? One lay in the sands and watched the expression of the Sphinx. Brooks Adams had taught him that the relation between civilizations was that of trade. Henry wandered, or was storm-driven, down the coast. He tried to trace out the ancient harbor of Ephesus. He went over to Athens, picked up Rockhill, and searched for the harbor of Tiryns; together they went on to Constantinople and studied the great walls of Constantine and the greater domes of Justinian. His hobby had turned into a camel, and he hoped, if he rode long enough in silence, that at last he might come on a city of thought along the great highways of exchange.

24

Indian Summer

(1898–1899)

The summer of the Spanish War began the Indian summer of life to one who had reached sixty years of age, and cared only to reap in peace such harvest as these sixty years had yielded. He had reason to be more than content with it. Since 1864 he had felt no such sense of power and momentum, and had seen no such number of personal friends wielding it. The sense of solidarity counts for much in one's contentment, but the sense of winning one's game counts for more; and in London, in 1898, the scene was singularly interesting to the last survivor of the Legation of 1861. He thought himself perhaps the only person living who could get full enjoyment of the drama. He carried every scene of it, in a century and a half since the Stamp Act, quite alive in his mind — all the interminable disputes of his disputatious ancestors as far back as the year 1750 — as well as his own insignificance in the Civil War, every step in which had the object of bringing England into an American system. For this they had written libraries of argument and remonstrance, and had piled war on war, losing their tempers for life, and souring the gentle and patient Puritan nature of their descendants, until even their private secretaries at times used language almost intemperate; and suddenly, by pure chance, the blessing fell on Hay. After two hundred years of stupid and greedy blundering, which no argument and no violence affected, the people of England learned their lesson just at the moment when Hay would otherwise have faced a flood of the old anxieties. Hay himself scarcely knew how grateful he should be, for to him the change came almost of course. He saw only the necessary stages that had led to it, and to him they seemed natural; but to Adams, still living in the atmosphere of Palmerston and John Russell, the sudden appearance of Germany as the grizzly terror which in twenty years effected what Adamses had tried for two hundred in vain — frightened England into America's arms — seemed as melodramatic as any plot of Napoleon the Great. He could feel only the sense of satisfaction at seeing the diplomatic triumph of all his family, since the breed existed, at last realized under his own eyes for the advantage of his oldest and closest ally.

This was history, not education, yet it taught something exceedingly serious, if not ultimate, could one trust the lesson. For the first time in his life, he felt a sense of possible purpose working itself out in history. Probably no one else on this earthly planet — not even Hay — could have come out on precisely such extreme personal satisfaction, but as he sat at Hay's table, listening to any member of the British Cabinet, for all were alike now, discuss the Philippines as a question of balance of power in the East, he could see that the family work of a hundred and fifty years fell at once into the grand perspective of true empire-building, which Hay's work set off with artistic skill. The roughness of the archaic foundations looked stronger and larger in scale for the refinement and certainty of the arcade. In the long list of famous American Ministers in

London, none could have given the work quite the completeness, the harmony, the perfect ease of Hay.

Never before had Adams been able to discern the working of law in history, which was the reason of his failure in teaching it, for chaos cannot be taught; but he thought he had a personal property by inheritance in this proof of sequence and intelligence in the affairs of man — a property which no one else had right to dispute; and this personal triumph left him a little cold towards the other diplomatic results of the war. He knew that Porto Rico must be taken, but he would have been glad to escape the Philippines. Apart from too intimate an acquaintance with the value of islands in the South Seas, he knew the West Indies well enough to be assured that, whatever the American people might think or say about it, they would sooner or later have to police those islands, not against Europe, but for Europe, and America too. Education on the outskirts of civilized life teaches not very much, but it taught this; and one felt no call to shoulder the load of archipelagoes in the antipodes when one was trying painfully to pluck up courage to face the labor of shouldering archipelagoes at home. The country decided otherwise, and one acquiesced readily enough, since the matter concerned only the public willingness to carry loads; in London, the balance of power in the East came alone into discussion; and in every point of view one had as much reason to be gratified with the result as though one had shared in the danger, instead of being vigorously employed in looking on from a great distance. After all, friends had done the work, if not one's self, and he too serves a certain purpose who only stands and cheers.

In June, at the crisis of interest, the Camerons came over, and took the fine old house of Surrenden Dering in Kent which they made a sort of country house to the Embassy. Kent has charms rivalling those of Shropshire,

and, even compared with the many beautiful places scattered along the Welsh border, few are nobler or more
genial than Surrenden with its unbroken descent from the
Saxons, its avenues, its terraces, its deer-park, its large repose on the Kentish hillside, and its broad outlook over
what was once the forest of Anderida. Filled with a constant stream of guests, the house seemed to wait for the
chance to show its charms to the American, with whose
activity the whole world was resounding; and never since
the battle of Hastings could the little telegraph office of
the Kentish village have done such work. There, on a hot
July 4, 1898, to an expectant group under the shady trees,
came the telegram announcing the destruction of the
Spanish Armada, as it might have come to Queen Eliza-
beth in 1588; and there, later in the season, came the order
summoning Hay to the State Department.

Hay had no wish to be Secretary of State. He much
preferred to remain Ambassador, and his friends were
quite as cold about it as he. No one knew so well what
sort of strain falls on Secretaries of State, or how little
strength he had in reserve against it. Even at Surrenden
he showed none too much endurance, and he would
gladly have found a valid excuse for refusing. The discussion on both sides was earnest, but the decided voice of the
conclave was that, though if he were a mere office-seeker
he might certainly decline promotion, if he were a member of the Government he could not. No serious statesman
could accept a favor and refuse a service. Doubtless he
might refuse, but in that case he must resign. The amusement of making Presidents has keen fascination for idle
American hands, but these black arts have the old drawback of all deviltry; one must serve the spirit one evokes,
even though the service were perdition to body and soul.
For him, no doubt, the service, though hard, might bring
some share of profit, but for the friends who gave this

unselfish decision, all would prove loss. For one, Adams on that subject had become a little daft. No one in his experience had ever passed unscathed through that malarious marsh. In his fancy, office was poison; it killed — body and soul — physically and socially. Office was more poisonous than priestcraft or pedagogy in proportion as it held more power; but the poison he complained of was not ambition; he shared none of Cardinal Wolsey's belated penitence for that healthy stimulant, as he had shared none of the fruits; his poison was that of the will — the distortion of sight — the warping of mind — the degradation of tissue — the coarsening of taste — the narrowing of sympathy to the emotions of a caged rat. Hay needed no office in order to wield influence. For him, influence lay about the streets, waiting for him to stoop to it; he enjoyed more than enough power without office; no one of his position, wealth, and political experience, living at the centre of politics in contact with the active party managers, could escape influence. His only ambition was to escape annoyance, and no one knew better than he that, at sixty years of age, sensitive to physical strain, still more sensitive to brutality, vindictiveness, or betrayal, he took office at cost of life.

Neither he nor any of the Surrenden circle made pretence of gladness at the new dignity for, with all his gaiety of manner and lightness of wit, he took dark views of himself, none the lighter for their humor, and his obedience to the President's order was the gloomiest acquiescence he had ever smiled. Adams took dark views, too, not so much on Hay's account as on his own, for, while Hay had at least the honors of office, his friends would share only the ennuis of it; but, as usual with Hay, nothing was gained by taking such matters solemnly, and old habits of the Civil War left their mark of military drill on every one who lived through it. He shouldered his pack and started for home. Adams had no mind to lose his friend without a struggle, though he had never known such sort of struggle to avail. The chance was desperate, but he could not afford to throw it away; so, as soon as the Surrenden establishment broke up, on October 17, he prepared for return home, and on November 13, none too gladly, found himself again gazing into La Fayette Square.

He had made another false start and lost two years more of education; nor had he excuse; for, this time, neither politics nor society drew him away from his trail. He had nothing to do with Hay's politics at home or abroad, and never affected agreement with his views or his methods, nor did Hay care whether his friends agreed or disagreed. They all united in trying to help each other to get along the best way they could, and all they tried to save was the personal relation. Even there, Adams would have been beaten had he not been helped by Mrs. Hay, who saw the necessity of distraction, and led her husband into the habit of stopping every afternoon to take his friend off for an hour's walk, followed by a cup of tea with Mrs. Hay afterwards, and a chat with any one who called.

For the moment, therefore, the situation was saved, at least in outward appearance, and Adams could go back to his own pursuits which were slowly taking a direction. Perhaps they had no right to be called pursuits, for in truth one consciously pursued nothing, but drifted as attraction offered itself. The short session broke up the Washington circle, so that, on March 22, Adams was able to sail with the Lodges for Europe and to pass April in Sicily and Rome.

With the Lodges, education always began afresh. Forty years had left little of the Palermo that Garibaldi had shown to the boy of 1860, but Sicily in all ages seems to have taught only catastrophe and violence, running riot on that theme ever since Ulysses began its study on the

eye of Cyclops. For a lesson in anarchy, without a shade
of sequence, Sicily stands alone and defies evolution. Syracuse teaches more than Rome. Yet even Rome was not
mute, and the church of Ara Cœli seemed more and more
to draw all the threads of thought to a centre, for every
new journey led back to its steps — Karnak, Ephesus, Del-
phi, Mycenæ, Constantinople, Syracuse — all lying on the
road to the Capitol. What they had to bring by way of
intellectual riches could not yet be discerned, but they
carried camel-loads of moral; and New York sent most
of all, for in forty years, America had made so vast a stride
to empire that the world of 1860 stood already on a distant
horizon somewhere on the same plane with the republic of
Brutus and Cato, while schoolboys read of Abraham Lincoln as they did of Julius Cæsar. Vast swarms of Americans knew the Civil War only by school history, as they
knew the story of Cromwell or Cicero, and were as familiar with political assassination as though they had lived
under Nero. The climax of empire could be seen approaching, year after year, as though Sulla were a President or McKinley a Consul.

Nothing annoyed Americans more than to be told this
simple and obvious — in no way unpleasant — truth; therefore one sat silent as ever on the Capitol; but, by way of
completing the lesson, the Lodges added a pilgrimage to
Assisi and an interview with St. Francis, whose solution
of historical riddles seemed the most satisfactory — or sufficient — ever offered; worth fully forty years' more
study, and better worth it than Gibbon himself, or even
St. Augustine, St. Ambrose, or St. Jerome. The most bewildering effect of all these fresh cross-lights on the old
Assistant Professor of 1874 was due to the astonishing
contrast between what he had taught then and what he
found himself confusedly trying to learn five-and-twenty
years afterwards — between the twelfth century of his

thirtieth and that of his sixtieth years. At Harvard College, weary of spirit in the wastes of Anglo-Saxon law, he had occasionally given way to outbursts of derision at shedding his life-blood for the sublime truths of Sac and Soc: —

HIC JACET
HOMUNCULUS SCRIPTOR
DOCTOR BARBARICUS
HENRICUS ADAMS
ADAE FILIUS ET EVAE
PRIMO EXPLICUIT
SOCNAM

The Latin was as twelfth-century as the law, and he meant as satire the claim that he had been first to explain the legal meaning of Sac and Soc, although any German professor would have scorned it as a shameless and presumptuous bid for immortality; but the whole point of view had vanished in 1900. Not he, but Sir Henry Maine and Rudolph Sohm, were the parents or creators of Sac and Soc. Convinced that the clue of religion led to nothing, and that politics led to chaos, one had turned to the law, as one's scholars turned to the Law School, because one could see no other path to a profession.

The law had proved as futile as politics or religion, or any other single thread spun by the human spider; it offered no more continuity than architecture or coinage, and no more force of its own. St. Francis expressed supreme contempt for them all, and solved the whole problem by rejecting it altogether. Adams returned to Paris with a broken and contrite spirit, prepared to admit that his life had no meaning, and conscious that in any case it no longer mattered. He passed a summer of solitude contrasting sadly with the last at Surrenden; but the solitude did what the society did not — it forced and drove

him into the study of his ignorance in silence. Here at last
he entered the practice of his final profession. Hunted by
ennui, he could no longer escape, and, by way of a summer school, he began a methodical survey — a triangulation — of the twelfth century. The pursuit had a singular
French charm which France had long lost — a calmness,
lucidity, simplicity of expression, vigor of action, complexity of local color, that made Paris flat. In the long summer days one found a sort of saturated green pleasure in
the forests, and gray infinity of rest in the little twelfth-
century churches that lined them, as unassuming as their
own mosses, and as sure of their purpose as their round
arches; but churches were many and summer was short,
so that he was at last driven back to the quays and photographs. For weeks he lived in silence.

His solitude was broken in November by the chance
arrival of John La Farge. At that moment, contact with
La Farge had a new value. Of all the men who had deeply
affected their friends since 1850 John La Farge was certainly the foremost, and for Henry Adams, who had sat
at his feet since 1872, the question how much he owed to
La Farge could be answered only by admitting that he had
no standard to measure it by. Of all his friends La Farge
alone owned a mind complex enough to contrast against
the commonplaces of American uniformity, and in the
process had vastly perplexed most Americans who came
in contact with it. The American mind — the Bostonian as
well as the Southern or Western — likes to walk straight
up to its object, and assert or deny something that it takes
for a fact; it has a conventional approach, a conventional
analysis, and a conventional conclusion, as well as a conventional expression, all the time loudly asserting its un-
conventionality. The most disconcerting trait of John La
Farge was his reversal of the process. His approach was
quiet and indirect; he moved round an object, and never

separated it from its surroundings; he prided himself on faithfulness to tradition and convention; he was never abrupt and abhorred dispute. His manners and attitude towards the universe were the same, whether tossing in the middle of the Pacific Ocean sketching the trade-wind from a whale-boat in the blast of sea-sickness, or drinking the *cha-no-yu* in the formal rites of Japan, or sipping his cocoanut cup of kava in the ceremonial of Samoan chiefs, or reflecting under the sacred bo-tree at Anaradjpura.

One was never quite sure of his whole meaning until too late to respond, for he had no difficulty in carrying different shades of contradiction in his mind. As he said of his friend Okakura, his thought ran as a stream runs through grass, hidden perhaps but always there; and one felt often uncertain in what direction it flowed, for even a contradiction was to him only a shade of difference, a complementary color, about which no intelligent artist would dispute. Constantly he repulsed argument: "Adams, you reason too much!" was one of his standing reproaches even in the mild discussion of rice and mangoes in the warm night of Tahiti dinners. He should have blamed Adams for being born in Boston. The mind resorts to reason for want of training, and Adams had never met a perfectly trained mind.

To La Farge, eccentricity meant convention; a mind really eccentric never betrayed it. True eccentricity was a tone — a shade — a *nuance* — and the finer the tone, the truer the eccentricity. Of course all artists hold more or less the same point of view in their art, but few carry it into daily life, and often the contrast is excessive between their art and their talk. One evening Humphreys Johnston, who was devoted to La Farge, asked him to meet Whistler at dinner. La Farge was ill — more ill than usual even for him — but he admired and liked Whistler, and insisted on going. By chance, Adams was so placed as to overhear the conversation of both, and had no choice but to hear that of Whistler, which engrossed the table. At that moment the Boer War was raging, and, as every one knows, on that subject Whistler raged worse than the Boers. For two hours he declaimed against England — witty, declamatory, extravagant, bitter, amusing, and noisy; but in substance what he said was not merely commonplace — it was true! That is to say, his hearers, including Adams and, as far as he knew, La Farge, agreed with it all, and mostly as a matter of course; yet La Farge was silent, and this difference of expression was a difference of art. Whistler in his art carried the sense of *nuance* and tone far beyond any point reached by La Farge, or even attempted; but in talk he showed, above or below his color-instinct, a willingness to seem eccentric where no real eccentricity, unless perhaps of temper, existed.

This vehemence, which Whistler never betrayed in his painting, La Farge seemed to lavish on his glass. With the relative value of La Farge's glass in the history of glass-decoration, Adams was too ignorant to meddle, and as a rule artists were if possible more ignorant than he; but whatever it was, it led him back to the twelfth century and to Chartres where La Farge not only felt at home, but felt a sort of ownership. No other American had a right there, unless he too were a member of the Church and worked in glass. Adams himself was an interloper, but long habit led La Farge to resign himself to Adams as one who meant well, though deplorably Bostonian; while Adams, though near sixty years old before he knew anything either of glass or of Chartres, asked no better than to learn, and only La Farge could help him, for he knew enough at least to see that La Farge alone could use glass like a thirteenth-century artist. In Europe the art had been dead for centuries, and modern glass was pitiable. Even La Farge felt the early glass rather as a document than as a historical emotion, and in hundreds of windows at Chartres and Bourges and Paris, Adams knew barely one or two that were meant to hold their own against a color-scheme so strong as his. In conversation La Farge's mind was opaline with infinite shades and refractions of light, and with color toned down to the finest gradations. In glass it was insubordinate; it was renaissance; it asserted his personal force with depth and vehemence of tone never before seen. He seemed bent on crushing rivalry.

Even the gloom of a Paris December at the Elysée Palace Hotel was somewhat relieved by this companionship, and education made a step backwards towards Chartres, but La Farge's health became more and more alarming, and Adams was glad to get him safely back to New York, January 15, 1900, while he himself went at once to Washington to find out what had become of Hay. Nothing good could be hoped, for Hay's troubles had begun, and were quite as great as he had foreseen. Adams saw as little encouragement as Hay himself did, though he dared not say so. He doubted Hay's endurance, the President's firmness in supporting him, and the loyalty of his party friends; but all this worry on Hay's account fretted him not nearly so much as the Boer War did on his own. Here was a problem in his political education that passed all experience since the Treason winter of 1860–61! Much to his astonishment, very few Americans seemed to share his point of view; their hostility to England seemed mere temper; but to Adams the war became almost a personal outrage. He had been taught from childhood, even in England, that his forbears and their associates in 1776 had settled, once for all, the liberties of the British free colonies, and he very strongly objected to being thrown on the defensive again, and forced to sit down, a hundred and fifty years after John Adams had begun the task, to prove, by appeal to law and fact, that George Washington was not a felon, whatever might be the case with George III. For reasons still more personal, he declined peremptorily to entertain question of the felony of John Adams. He felt obliged to go even further, and avow the opinion that if at any time England should take towards Canada the position she took towards her Boer colonies, the United States would be bound, by their record, to interpose, and to insist on the application of the principles of 1776. To him the attitude of Mr. Chamberlain and his colleagues seemed exceedingly un-American, and terribly embarrassing to Hay.

Trained early, in the stress of civil war, to hold his tongue, and to help make the political machine run somehow, since it could never be made to run well, he would not bother Hay with theoretical objections which were every day fretting him in practical forms. Hay's chance lay in patience and good-temper till the luck should turn, and to him the only object was time; but as political education the point seemed vital to Adams, who never liked shutting his eyes or denying an evident fact. Practical politics consists in ignoring facts, but education and politics are two different and often contradictory things. In this case, the contradiction seemed crude.

With Hay's politics, at home or abroad, Adams had nothing whatever to do. Hay belonged to the New York school, like Abram Hewitt, Evarts, W. C. Whitney, Samuel J. Tilden — men who played the game for ambition or amusement, and played it, as a rule, much better than the professionals, but whose aims were considerably larger than those of the usual player, and who felt no great love for the cheap drudgery of the work. In return, the professionals felt no great love for them, and set them aside when they could. Only their control of money made them inevitable, and even this did not always carry their points. The story of Abram Hewitt would offer one type of this statesman series, and that of Hay another. President Cleveland set aside the one; President Harrison set aside the other. "There is no politics in it," was his comment on Hay's appointment to office. Hay held a different opinion and turned to McKinley whose judgment of men was finer than common in Presidents. Mr. McKinley brought to the problem of American government a solution which lay very far outside of Henry Adams's education, but which seemed to be at least practical and American. He undertook to pool interests in a general trust into which every interest should be taken, more or less at its own valuation, and whose mass should, under his management, create efficiency. He achieved very remarkable results. How much they cost was another matter; if the public is ever driven to its last resources and the usual remedies of chaos, the result will probably cost more.

Himself a marvellous manager of men, McKinley found several manipulators to help him, almost as remarkable as himself, one of whom was Hay; but unfortunately Hay's strength was weakest and his task hardest. At home, interests could be easily combined by simply paying their price; but abroad whatever helped on one side, hurt him on another. Hay thought England must be brought first into the combine; but at that time Germany, Russia, and France were all combining against England, and the Boer War helped them. For the moment Hay had no ally, abroad or at home, except Pauncefote, and Adams always maintained that Pauncefote alone pulled him through.

Yet the difficulty abroad was far less troublesome than the obstacles at home. The Senate had grown more and more unmanageable, even since the time of Andrew Johnson, and this was less the fault of the Senate than of the system. "A treaty of peace, in any normal state of things," said Hay, "ought to be ratified with unanimity in twenty-four hours. They wasted six weeks in wrangling over this one, and ratified it with one vote to spare. We have five or six matters now demanding settlement. I can settle them all, honorably and advantageously to our own side; and I am assured by leading men in the Senate that not one of these treaties, if negotiated, will pass the Senate. I should have a majority in every case, but a malcontent third would certainly dish every one of them. To such monstrous shape has the original mistake of the Constitution grown in the evolution of our politics. You must understand, it is not merely *my* solution the Senate will reject. They will reject, for instance, any treaty, whatever, on any subject, with England. I doubt if they would accept any treaty of consequence with Russia or Germany. The recalcitrant third would be differently composed, but it would be on hand. So that the real duties of a Secretary of State seem to be three: to fight claims upon us by other States; to press more or less fraudulent claims of our own citizens upon other countries; to find offices for the friends of Senators when there are none. Is it worth while — for me — to keep up this useless labor?"

To Adams, who, like Hay, had seen a dozen acquaintances struggling with the same enemies, the question had scarcely the interest of a new study. He had said all he had to say about it in a dozen or more volumes relating to the politics of a hundred years before. To him, the spectacle was so familiar as to be humorous. The intrigue was too open to be interesting. The interference of the German and Russian legations, and of the Clan-na-Gael, with the press and the Senate was innocently undisguised. The charming Russian Minister, Count Cassini, the ideal of diplomatic manners and training, let few days pass without appealing through the press to the public against the government. The German Minister, Von Holleben, more cautiously did the same thing, and of course every whisper of theirs was brought instantly to the Department. These three forces, acting with the regular opposition and the natural obstructionists, could always stop action in the Senate. The fathers had intended to neutralize the energy of government and had succeeded, but their machine was never meant to do the work of a twenty-million horse-power society in the twentieth century, where much work needed to be quickly and efficiently done. The only defence of the system was that, as Government did nothing well, it had best do nothing; but the Government, in truth, did perfectly well all it was given to do; and even if the charge were true, it applied equally to human society altogether, if one chose to treat mankind from that point of view. As a matter of mechanics, so much work must be done; bad machinery merely added to friction.

Always unselfish, generous, easy, patient, and loyal, Hay had treated the world as something to be taken in block without pulling it to pieces to get rid of its defects; he liked it all: he laughed and accepted; he had never known unhappiness and would have gladly lived his entire life over again exactly as it happened. In the whole New York school, one met a similar dash of humor and cynicism more or less pronounced but seldom bitter. Yet even the gayest of tempers succumbs at last to constant friction. The old friend was rapidly fading. The habit remained, but the easy intimacy, the careless gaiety, the casual humor, the equality of indifference, were sinking into the routine of office; the mind lingered in the Department; the thought failed to react; the wit and humor shrank within the blank walls of politics, and the irritations multiplied. To a head of bureau, the result seemed ennobling.

Although, as education, this branch of study was more familiar and older than the twelfth century, the task of bringing the two periods into a common relation was new. Ignorance required that these political and social and sci-

entific values of the twelfth and twentieth centuries should
be correlated in some relation of movement that could be
expressed in mathematics, nor did one care in the least that
all the world said it could not be done, or that one knew
not enough mathematics even to figure a formula beyond
the schoolboy $s = \dfrac{gt^2}{2}$. If Kepler and Newton could take
liberties with the sun and moon, an obscure person in a
remote wilderness like La Fayette Square could take liberties with Congress, and venture to multiply half its attraction into the square of its time. He had only to find a value,
even infinitesimal, for its attraction at any given time. A
historical formula that should satisfy the conditions of the
stellar universe weighed heavily on his mind; but a trifling
matter like this was one in which he could look for no help
from anybody — he could look only for derision at best.

All his associates in history condemned such an attempt
as futile and almost immoral — certainly hostile to sound
historical system. Adams tried it only because of its hostility to all that he had taught for history, since he started
afresh from the new point that, whatever was right, all he
had ever taught was wrong. He had pursued ignorance
thus far with success, and had swept his mind clear of
knowledge. In beginning again, from the starting-point of
Sir Isaac Newton, he looked about him in vain for a
teacher. Few men in Washington cared to overstep the
school conventions, and the most distinguished of them,
Simon Newcomb, was too sound a mathematician to treat
such a scheme seriously. The greatest of Americans, judged
by his rank in science, Willard Gibbs, never came to
Washington, and Adams never enjoyed a chance to meet
him. After Gibbs, one of the most distinguished was
Langley, of the Smithsonian, who was more accessible, to
whom Adams had been much in the habit of turning
whenever he wanted an outlet for his vast reservoirs of

ignorance. Langley listened with outward patience to his disputatious questionings; but he too nourished a scientific passion for doubt, and sentimental attachment for its avowal. He had the physicist's heinous fault of professing to know nothing between flashes of intense perception. Like so many other great observers, Langley was not a mathematician, and like most physicists, he believed in physics. Rigidly denying himself the amusement of philosophy, which consists chiefly in suggesting unintelligible answers to insoluble problems, he still knew the problems, and liked to wander past them in a courteous temper, even bowing to them distantly as though recognizing their existence, while doubting their respectability. He generously let others doubt what he felt obliged to affirm; and early put into Adams's hands the "Concepts of Modern Science," a volume by Judge Stallo, which had been treated for a dozen years by the schools with a conspiracy of silence such as inevitably meets every revolutionary work that upsets the stock and machinery of instruction. Adams read and failed to understand; then he asked questions and failed to get answers.

Probably this was education. Perhaps it was the only scientific education open to a student sixty-odd years old, who asked to be as ignorant as an astronomer. For him the details of science meant nothing: he wanted to know its mass. Solar heat was not enough, or was too much. Kinetic atoms led only to motion; never to direction or progress. History had no use for multiplicity; it needed unity; it could study only motion, direction, attraction, relation. Everything must be made to move together; one must seek new worlds to measure; and so, like Rasselas, Adams set out once more, and found himself on May 12 settled in rooms at the very door of the Trocadero.

25

The Dynamo and the Virgin

(1900)

Until the Great Exposition of 1900 closed its doors in November, Adams haunted it, aching to absorb knowledge, and helpless to find it. He would have liked to know how much of it could have been grasped by the best-informed man in the world. While he was thus meditating chaos, Langley came by, and showed it to him. At Langley's behest, the Exhibition dropped its superfluous rags and stripped itself to the skin, for Langley knew what to study, and why, and how; while Adams might as well have stood outside in the night, staring at the Milky Way. Yet Langley said nothing new, and taught nothing that one might not have learned from Lord Bacon, three hundred years before; but though one should have known the "Advancement of Science" as well as one knew the "Comedy of Errors," the literary knowledge counted for nothing until some teacher should show how to apply it.

Bacon took a vast deal of trouble in teaching King James I and his subjects, American or other, towards the year 1620, that true science was the development or economy of forces; yet an elderly American in 1900 knew neither the formula nor the forces; or even so much as to say to himself that his historical business in the Exposition concerned only the economies or developments of force since 1893, when he began the study at Chicago.

Nothing in education is so astonishing as the amount of ignorance it accumulates in the form of inert facts. Adams had looked at most of the accumulations of art in the storehouses called Art Museums; yet he did not know how to look at the art exhibits of 1900. He had studied Karl Marx and his doctrines of history with profound attention, yet he could not apply them at Paris. Langley, with the ease of a great master of experiment, threw out of the field every exhibit that did not reveal a new application of force, and naturally threw out, to begin with, almost the whole art exhibit. Equally, he ignored almost the whole industrial exhibit. He led his pupil directly to the forces. His chief interest was in new motors to make his airship feasible, and he taught Adams the astonishing complexities of the new Daimler motor, and of the automobile, which, since 1893, had become a nightmare at a hundred kilometres an hour, almost as destructive as the electric tram which was only ten years older; and threatening to become as terrible as the locomotive steam-engine itself, which was almost exactly Adams's own age.

Then he showed his scholar the great hall of dynamos, and explained how little he knew about electricity or force of any kind, even of his own special sun, which spouted heat in inconceivable volume, but which, as far as he knew, might spout less or more, at any time, for all the certainty he felt in it. To him, the dynamo itself was but an ingenious channel for conveying somewhere the heat latent in a few tons of poor coal hidden in a dirty engine-house carefully kept out of sight; but to Adams the dynamo became a symbol of infinity. As he grew accustomed to the great gallery of machines, he began to feel the forty-foot dynamos as a moral force, much as the early Christians felt the Cross. The planet itself seemed less impressive, in its old-fashioned, deliberate, annual or daily revolution, than this huge wheel, revolving within arm's-length at some vertiginous speed, and barely murmuring — scarcely humming an audible warning to stand a hair's-breadth further for respect of power — while it would not wake the baby lying close against its frame. Before the end, one began to pray to it; inherited instinct taught the natural expression of man before silent and infinite force. Among the thousand symbols of ultimate energy, the dynamo was not so human as some, but it was the most expressive.

Yet the dynamo, next to the steam-engine, was the most familiar of exhibits. For Adams's objects its value lay chiefly in its occult mechanism. Between the dynamo in the gallery of machines and the engine-house outside, the break of continuity amounted to abysmal fracture for a historian's objects. No more relation could he discover between the steam and the electric current than between the Cross and the cathedral. The forces were interchangeable if not reversible, but he could see only an absolute *fiat* in electricity as in faith. Langley could not help him. Indeed, Langley seemed to be worried by the same trouble, for he constantly repeated that the new forces were anarchical, and specially that he was not responsible for the new rays, that were little short of parricidal in their wicked spirit towards science. His own rays, with which he had doubled the solar spectrum, were altogether harmless and beneficent; but Radium denied its God — or, what was to Langley the same thing, denied the truths of his Science. The force was wholly new.

A historian who asked only to learn enough to be as futile as Langley or Kelvin, made rapid progress under this teaching, and mixed himself up in the tangle of ideas until he achieved a sort of Paradise of ignorance vastly consoling to his fatigued senses. He wrapped himself in vibrations and rays which were new, and he would have hugged Marconi and Branly had he met them, as he hugged the dynamo; while he lost his arithmetic in trying to figure out the equation between the discoveries and the economies of force. The economies, like the discoveries, were absolute, supersensual, occult; incapable of expression in horse-power. What mathematical equivalent could he suggest as the value of a Branly coherer? Frozen air, or the electric furnace, had some scale of measurement, no doubt, if somebody could invent a thermometer adequate to the purpose; but X-rays had played no part whatever in man's consciousness, and the atom itself had figured only as a fiction of thought. In these seven years man had translated himself into a new universe which had no common scale of measurement with the old. He had entered a supersensual world, in which he could measure nothing except by chance collisions of movements imperceptible to his senses, perhaps even imperceptible to his instruments, but perceptible to each other, and so to some known ray at the end of the scale. Langley seemed prepared for anything, even for an indeterminable number of universes interfused — physics stark mad in metaphysics.

Historians undertake to arrange sequences, — called stories, or histories — assuming in silence a relation of cause and effect. These assumptions, hidden in the depths of dusty libraries, have been astounding, but commonly unconscious and childlike; so much so, that if any captious critic were to drag them to light, historians would probably reply, with one voice, that they had never supposed themselves required to know what they were talking about. Adams, for one, had toiled in vain to find out what he meant. He had even published a dozen volumes of American history for no other purpose than to satisfy himself whether, by the severest process of stating, with the least possible comment, such facts as seemed sure, in such order as seemed rigorously consequent, he could fix for a familiar moment a necessary sequence of human movement. The result had satisfied him as little as at Harvard College. Where he saw sequence, other men saw something quite different, and no one saw the same unit of measure. He cared little about his experiments and less about his statesmen, who seemed to him quite as ignorant as himself and, as a rule, no more honest; but he insisted on a relation of sequence, and if he could not reach it by one method, he would try as many methods as science knew. Satisfied that the sequence of men led to nothing and that the sequence of their society could lead no further, while the mere sequence of time was artificial, and the sequence of thought was chaos, he turned at last to the sequence of force; and thus it happened that, after ten years' pursuit, he found himself lying in the Gallery of Machines at the Great Exposition of 1900, his historical neck broken by the sudden irruption of forces totally new.

Since no one else showed much concern, an elderly person without other cares had no need to betray alarm. The year 1900 was not the first to upset schoolmasters. Copernicus and Galileo had broken many professorial necks about 1600; Columbus had stood the world on its head towards 1500; but the nearest approach to the revolution of 1900 was that of 310, when Constantine set up the Cross. The rays that Langley disowned, as well as those which he fathered, were occult, supersensual, irrational; they were a revelation of mysterious energy like that of the Cross; they were what, in terms of mediæval science, were called immediate modes of the divine substance.

The historian was thus reduced to his last resources. Clearly if he was bound to reduce all these forces to a common value, this common value could have no measure but that of their attraction on his own mind. He must treat them as they had been felt; as convertible, reversible, interchangeable attractions on thought. He made up his mind to venture it; he would risk translating rays into faith. Such a reversible process would vastly amuse a chemist, but the chemist could not deny that he, or some of his fellow physicists, could feel the force of both. When Adams was a boy in Boston, the best chemist in the place had probably never heard of Venus except by way of scandal, or of the Virgin except as idolatry; neither had he heard of dynamos or automobiles or radium; yet his mind was ready to feel the force of all, though the rays were unborn and the women were dead.

Here opened another totally new education, which promised to be by far the most hazardous of all. The knife-edge along which he must crawl, like Sir Lancelot in the twelfth century, divided two kingdoms of force which had nothing in common but attraction. They were as different as a magnet is from gravitation, supposing one knew what a magnet was, or gravitation, or love. The force of the Virgin was still felt at Lourdes, and seemed to be as potent as X-rays; but in America neither Venus nor Virgin ever had value as force — at most as sentiment. No American had ever been truly afraid of either.

This problem in dynamics gravely perplexed an American historian. The Woman had once been supreme; in

France she still seemed potent, not merely as a sentiment, but as a force. Why was she unknown in America? For evidently America was ashamed of her, and she was ashamed of herself, otherwise they would not have strewn fig-leaves so profusely all over her. When she was a true force, she was ignorant of fig-leaves, but the monthly-magazine-made American female had not a feature that would have been recognized by Adam. The trait was notorious, and often humorous, but any one brought up among Puritans knew that sex was sin. In any previous age, sex was strength. Neither art nor beauty was needed. Every one, even among Puritans, knew that neither Diana of the Ephesians nor any of the Oriental goddesses was worshipped for her beauty. She was goddess because of her force; she was the animated dynamo; she was reproduction — the greatest and most mysterious of all energies; all she needed was to be fecund. Singularly enough, not one of Adams's many schools of education had ever drawn his attention to the opening lines of Lucretius, though they were perhaps the finest in all Latin literature, where the poet invoked Venus exactly as Dante invoked the Virgin: —

"Quae quoniam rerum naturam *sola* gubernas."

The Venus of Epicurean philosophy survived in the Virgin of the Schools: —

> "Donna, sei tanto grande, e tanto vali,
> Che qual vuol grazia, e a te non ricorre,
> Sua disianza vuol volar senz' ali."

All this was to American thought as though it had never existed. The true American knew something of the facts, but nothing of the feelings; he read the letter, but he never felt the law. Before this historical chasm, a mind like that of Adams felt itself helpless; he turned from the Virgin to the Dynamo as though he were a Branly coherer. On one side, at the Louvre and at Chartres, as he knew by the record of work actually done and still before his eyes, was the highest energy ever known to man, the creator of four-fifths of his noblest art, exercising vastly more attraction over the human mind than all the steam-engines and dynamos ever dreamed of; and yet this energy was unknown to the American mind. An American Virgin would never dare command; an American Venus would never dare exist.

The question, which to any plain American of the nineteenth century seemed as remote as it did to Adams, drew him almost violently to study, once it was posed; and on this point Langleys were as useless as though they were Herbert Spencers or dynamos. The idea survived only as art. There one turned as naturally as though the artist were himself a woman. Adams began to ponder, asking himself whether he knew of any American artist who had ever insisted on the power of sex, as every classic had always done; but he could think only of Walt Whitman; Bret Harte, as far as the magazines would let him venture; and one or two painters, for the flesh-tones. All the rest had used sex for sentiment, never for force; to them, Eve was a tender flower, and Herodias an unfeminine horror. American art, like the American language and American education, was as far as possible sexless. Society regarded this victory over sex as its greatest triumph, and the historian readily admitted it, since the moral issue, for the moment, did not concern one who was studying the relations of unmoral force. He cared nothing for the sex of the dynamo until he could measure its energy.

Vaguely seeking a clue, he wandered through the art

exhibit, and, in his stroll, stopped almost every day before St. Gaudens's General Sherman, which had been given the central post of honor. St. Gaudens himself was in Paris, putting on the work his usual interminable last touches, and listening to the usual contradictory suggestions of brother sculptors. Of all the American artists who gave to American art whatever life it breathed in the seventies, St. Gaudens was perhaps the most sympathetic, but certainly the most inarticulate. General Grant or Don Cameron had scarcely less instinct of rhetoric than he. All the others — the Hunts, Richardson, John La Farge, Stanford White — were exuberant; only St. Gaudens could never discuss or dilate on an emotion, or suggest artistic arguments for giving to his work the forms that he felt. He never laid down the law, or affected the despot, or became brutalized like Whistler by the brutalities of his world. He required no incense; he was no egoist; his simplicity of thought was excessive; he could not imitate, or give any form but his own to the creations of his hand. No one felt more strongly than he the strength of other men, but the idea that they could affect him never stirred an image in his mind.

This summer his health was poor and his spirits were low. For such a temper, Adams was not the best companion, since his own gaiety was not *folle;* but he risked going now and then to the studio on Mont Parnasse to draw him out for a stroll in the Bois de Boulogne, or dinner as pleased his moods, and in return St. Gaudens sometimes let Adams go about in his company.

Once St. Gaudens took him down to Amiens, with a party of Frenchmen, to see the cathedral. Not until they found themselves actually studying the sculpture of the western portal, did it dawn on Adams's mind that, for his purposes, St. Gaudens on that spot had more interest to him than the cathedral itself. Great men before great monuments express great truths, provided they are not taken too solemnly. Adams never tired of quoting the supreme phrase of his idol Gibbon, before the Gothic cathedrals: "I darted a contemptuous look on the stately monuments of superstition." Even in the footnotes of his history, Gibbon had never inserted a bit of humor more human than this, and one would have paid largely for a photograph of the fat little historian, on the background of Notre Dame of Amiens, trying to persuade his readers — perhaps himself — that he was darting a contemptuous look on the stately monument, for which he felt in fact the respect which every man of his vast study and active mind always feels before objects worthy of it; but besides the humor, one felt also the relation. Gibbon ignored the Virgin, because in 1789 religious monuments were out of fashion. In 1900 his remark sounded fresh and simple as the green fields to ears that had heard a hundred years of other remarks, mostly no more fresh and certainly less simple. Without malice, one might find it more instructive than a whole lecture of Ruskin. One sees what one brings, and at that moment Gibbon brought the French Revolution. Ruskin brought reaction against the Revolution. St. Gaudens had passed beyond all. He liked the stately monuments much more than he liked Gibbon or Ruskin; he loved their dignity; their unity; their scale; their lines; their lights and shadows; their decorative sculpture; but he was even less conscious than they of the force that created it all — the Virgin, the Woman — by whose genius "the stately monuments of superstition" were built, through which she was expressed. He would have seen more meaning in Isis with the cow's horns, at Edfoo, who expressed the same thought. The art remained, but the energy was lost even upon the artist.

Yet in mind and person St. Gaudens was a survival of

the 1500; he bore the stamp of the Renaissance, and should have carried an image of the Virgin round his neck, or stuck in his hat, like Louis XI. In mere time he was a lost soul that had strayed by chance into the twentieth century, and forgotten where it came from. He writhed and cursed at his ignorance, much as Adams did at his own, but in the opposite sense. St. Gaudens was a child of Benvenuto Cellini, smothered in an American cradle. Adams was a quintessence of Boston, devoured by curiosity to think like Benvenuto. St. Gaudens's art was starved from birth, and Adams's instinct was blighted from babyhood. Each had but half of a nature, and when they came together before the Virgin of Amiens they ought both to have felt in her the force that made them one; but it was not so. To Adams she became more than ever a channel of force; to St. Gaudens she remained as before a channel of taste.

For a symbol of power, St. Gaudens instinctively preferred the horse, as was plain in his horse and Victory of the Sherman monument. Doubtless Sherman also felt it so. The attitude was so American that, for at least forty years, Adams had never realized that any other could be in sound taste. How many years had he taken to admit a notion of what Michael Angelo and Rubens were driving at? He could not say; but he knew that only since 1895 had he begun to feel the Virgin or Venus as force, and not everywhere even so. At Chartres — perhaps at Lourdes — possibly at Cnidos if one could still find there the divinely naked Aphrodite of Praxiteles — but otherwise one must look for force to the goddesses of Indian mythology. The idea died out long ago in the German and English stock. St. Gaudens at Amiens was hardly less sensitive to the force of the female energy than Matthew Arnold at the Grande Chartreuse. Neither of them felt goddesses as power — only as reflected emotion, human expression, beauty, purity, taste, scarcely even as sympathy. They felt a railway train as power; yet they, and all other artists, constantly complained that the power embodied in a railway train could never be embodied in art. All the steam in the world could not, like the Virgin, build Chartres.

Yet in mechanics, whatever the mechanicians might think, both energies acted as interchangeable forces on man, and by action on man all known force may be measured. Indeed, few men of science measured force in any other way. After once admitting that a straight line was the shortest distance between two points, no serious mathematician cared to deny anything that suited his convenience, and rejected no symbol, unproved or unproveable, that helped him to accomplish work. The symbol was force, as a compass-needle or a triangle was force, as the mechanist might prove by losing it, and nothing could be gained by ignoring their value. Symbol or energy, the Virgin had acted as the greatest force the Western world ever felt, and had drawn man's activities to herself more strongly than any other power, natural or supernatural, had ever done; the historian's business was to follow the track of the energy; to find where it came from and where it went to; its complex source and shifting channels; its values, equivalents, conversions. It could scarcely be more complex than radium; it could hardly be deflected, diverted, polarized, absorbed more perplexingly than other radiant matter. Adams knew nothing about any of them, but as a mathematical problem of influence on human progress, though all were occult, all reacted on his mind, and he rather inclined to think the Virgin easiest to handle.

The pursuit turned out to be long and tortuous, leading at last into the vast forests of scholastic science. From Zeno to Descartes, hand in hand with Thomas Aquinas, Montaigne, and Pascal, one stumbled as stupidly as though one were still a German student of 1860. Only with the instinct of despair could one force one's self into this old thicket of ignorance after having been repulsed at a score of entrances more promising and more popular. Thus far, no path had led anywhere, unless perhaps to an exceedingly modest living. Forty-five years of study had proved to be quite futile for the pursuit of power; one controlled no more force in 1900 than in 1850, although the amount of force controlled by society had enormously increased. The secret of education still hid itself somewhere behind ignorance, and one fumbled over it as feebly as ever. In such labyrinths, the staff is a force almost more necessary than the legs; the pen becomes a sort of blind-man's dog, to keep him from falling into the gutters. The pen works for itself, and acts like a hand, modelling the plastic material over and over again to the form that suits it best. The form is never arbitrary, but is a sort of growth like crystallization, as any artist knows too well; for often the pencil or pen runs into side-paths and shapelessness, loses its relations, stops or is bogged. Then it has to return on its trail, and recover, if it can, its line of force. The result of a year's work depends more on what is struck out than on what is left in; on the sequence of the main lines of thought, than on their play or variety. Compelled once more to lean heavily on this support, Adams covered more thousands of pages with figures as formal as though they were algebra, laboriously striking out, altering, burning, experimenting, until the year had expired, the Exposition had long been closed, and winter drawing to its end, before he sailed from Cherbourg, on January 19, 1901, for home.

26

Twilight

(1901)

While the world that thought itself frivolous, and submitted meekly to hearing itself decried as vain, fluttered through the Paris Exposition, jogging the futilities of St. Gaudens, Rodin, and Besnard, the world that thought itself serious, and showed other infallible marks of coming mental paroxysm, was engaged in weird doings at Peking and elsewhere such as startled even itself. Of all branches of education, the science of gauging people and events by their relative importance defies study most insolently. For three or four generations, society has united in withering with contempt and opprobrium the shameless futility of Mme. de Pompadour and Mme. du Barry; yet, if one bid at an auction for some object that had been approved by the taste of either lady, one quickly found that it were better to buy half-a-dozen Napoleons or Frederics, or Maria Theresas, or all the philosophy and science of their time, than to bid for a cane-bottomed chair that either of these two ladies had adorned. The same thing might be said, in a different sense, of Voltaire; while, as every one knows, the money-value of any hand-stroke of Watteau or Hogarth, Nattier or Sir Joshua, is out of all proportion to the importance of the men. Society seemed to delight in talking with solemn conviction about serious values, and in paying fantastic prices for nothing but the most futile. The drama acted at Peking, in the summer of 1900, was, in the eyes of a student, the most serious that could be offered for his study, since it brought him suddenly to the inevitable struggle for the control of China, which, in his view, must decide the control of the world; yet, as a money-value, the fall of China was chiefly studied in Paris and London as a calamity to Chinese porcelain. The value of a Ming vase was more serious than universal war.

The drama of the Legations interested the public much as though it were a novel of Alexandre Dumas, but the bearing of the drama on future history offered an interest vastly greater. Adams knew no more about it than though he were the best-informed statesman in Europe. Like them all, he took for granted that the Legations were massacred, and that John Hay, who alone championed China's "administrative entity," would be massacred too, since he must henceforth look on, in impotence, while Russia and Germany dismembered China, and shut up America at home. Nine statesmen out of ten, in Europe, accepted this result in advance, seeing no way to prevent it. Adams saw none, and laughed at Hay for his helplessness.

When Hay suddenly ignored European leadership, took the lead himself, rescued the Legations and saved China, Adams looked on, as incredulous as Europe, though not quite so stupid, since, on that branch of education, he knew enough for his purpose. Nothing so meteoric had ever been done in American diplomacy. On returning to Washington, January 30, 1901, he found most of the world as astonished as himself, but less stupid than usual. For a moment, indeed, the world had been struck dumb at seeing Hay put Europe aside and set the Washington

Government at the head of civilization so quietly that civilization submitted, by mere instinct of docility, to receive and obey his orders; but, after the first shock of silence, society felt the force of the stroke through its fineness, and burst into almost tumultuous applause. Instantly the diplomacy of the nineteenth century, with all its painful scuffles and struggles, was forgotten, and the American blushed to be told of his submissions in the past. History broke in halves.

Hay was too good an artist not to feel the artistic skill of his own work, and the success reacted on his health, giving him fresh life, for with him as with most men, success was a tonic, and depression a specific poison; but as usual, his troubles nested at home. Success doubles strain. President McKinley's diplomatic court had become the largest in the world, and the diplomatic relations required far more work than ever before, while the staff of the Department was little more efficient, and the friction in the Senate had become coagulated. Hay took to studying the "Diary" of John Quincy Adams eighty years before, and calculated that the resistance had increased about ten times, as measured by waste of days and increase of effort, although Secretary of State J. Q. Adams thought himself very hardly treated. Hay cheerfully noted that it was killing him, and proved it, for the effort of the afternoon walk became sometimes painful.

For the moment, things were going fairly well, and Hay's unruly team were less fidgety, but Pauncefote still pulled the whole load and turned the dangerous corners safely, while Cassini and Holleben helped the Senate to make what trouble they could, without serious offence, and the Irish, after the genial Celtic nature, obstructed even themselves. The fortunate Irish, thanks to their sympathetic qualities, never made lasting enmities; but the

Germans seemed in a fair way to rouse ill-will and even ugly temper in the spirit of politics, which was by no means a part of Hay's plans. He had as much as he could do to overcome domestic friction, and felt no wish to alienate foreign powers. Yet so much could be said in favor of the foreigners that they commonly knew why they made trouble, and were steady to a motive. Cassini had for years pursued, in Peking as in Washington, a policy of his own, never disguised, and as little in harmony with his chief as with Hay; he made his opposition on fixed lines for notorious objects; but Senators could seldom give a reason for obstruction. In every hundred men, a certain number obstruct by instinct, and try to invent reasons to explain it afterwards. The Senate was no worse than the board of a university; but incorporators as a rule have not made this class of men dictators on purpose to prevent action. In the Senate, a single vote commonly stopped legislation, or, in committee, stifled discussion.

Hay's policy of removing, one after another, all irritations, and closing all discussions with foreign countries, roused incessant obstruction, which could be overcome only by patience and bargaining in executive patronage, if indeed it could be overcome at all. The price actually paid was not very great except in the physical exhaustion of Hay and Pauncefote, Root and McKinley. No serious bargaining of equivalents could be attempted; Senators would not sacrifice five dollars in their own States to gain five hundred thousand in another; but whenever a foreign country was willing to surrender an advantage without an equivalent, Hay had a chance to offer the Senate a treaty. In all such cases the price paid for the treaty was paid wholly to the Senate, and amounted to nothing very serious except in waste of time and wear of strength. "Life is so gay and horrid!" laughed Hay; "the Major will have promised all the consulates in the service; the Senators will all come to me and refuse to believe me disconsulate; I shall see all my treaties slaughtered, one by one, by the thirty-four per cent of kickers and strikers; the only mitigation I can foresee is being sick a good part of the time; I am nearing my grand climacteric, and the great *culbute* is approaching."

He was thinking of his friend Blaine, and might have thought of all his predecessors, for all had suffered alike, and to Adams as historian their sufferings had been a long delight — the solitary picturesque and tragic element in politics — incidentally requiring character-studies like Aaron Burr and William B. Giles, Calhoun and Webster and Sumner, with Sir Forcible Feebles like James M. Mason and stage exaggerations like Roscoe Conkling. The Senate took the place of Shakespeare, and offered real Brutuses and Bolingbrokes, Jack Cades, Falstaffs, and Malvolios — endless varieties of human nature nowhere else to be studied, and none the less amusing because they killed, or because they were like schoolboys in their simplicity. "Life is so gay and horrid!" Hay still felt the humor, though more and more rarely, but what he felt most was the enormous complexity and friction of the vast mass he was trying to guide. He bitterly complained that it had made him a bore — of all things the most senatorial, and to him the most obnoxious. The old friend was lost, and only the teacher remained, driven to madness by the complexities and multiplicities of his new world.

To one who, at past sixty years old, is still passionately seeking education, these small, or large, annoyances had no great value except as measures of mass and motion. For him the practical interest and the practical man were such as looked forward to the next election, or perhaps, in corporations, five or ten years. Scarcely half-a-dozen men in America could be named who were known to have looked a dozen years ahead; while any historian who means to keep his alignment with past and future must cover a horizon of two generations at least. If he seeks to align himself with the future, he must assume a condition of some sort for a world fifty years beyond his own. Every historian — sometimes unconsciously, but always inevitably — must have put to himself the question: How long could such-or-such an outworn system last? He can never give himself less than one generation to show the full effects of a changed condition. His object is to triangulate from the widest possible base to the furthest point he thinks he can see, which is always far beyond the curvature of the horizon.

To the practical man, such an attempt is idiotic, and probably the practical man is in the right to-day; but, whichever is right — if the question of right or wrong enters at all into the matter — the historian has no choice but to go on alone. Even in his own profession few companions offer help, and his walk soon becomes solitary, leading further and further into a wilderness where twilight is short and the shadows are dense. Already Hay literally staggered in his tracks for weariness. More worn than he, Clarence King dropped. One day in the spring he stopped an hour in Washington to bid good-bye, cheerily and simply telling how his doctors had condemned him to Arizona for his lungs. All three friends knew that they were nearing the end, and that if it were not the one it would be the other; but the affectation of readiness for death is a stage rôle, and stoicism is a stupid resource, though the only one. *Non dolet, Paete!* One is ashamed of it even in the acting.

The sunshine of life had not been so dazzling of late but that a share of it flickered out for Adams and Hay when King disappeared from their lives; but Hay had still his family and ambition, while Adams could only blunder back alone, helplessly, wearily, his eyes rather dim with tears, to his vague trail across the darkening prairie of education, without a motive, big or small, except curiosity to reach, before he too should drop, some point that would give him a far look ahead. He was morbidly curious to see some light at the end of the passage, as though thirty years were a shadow, and he were again to fall into King's arms at the door of the last and only log cabin left in life. Time had become terribly short, and the sense of knowing so little when others knew so much, crushed out hope.

He knew not in what new direction to turn, and sat at his desk, idly pulling threads out of the tangled skein of science, to see whether or why they aligned themselves. The commonest and oldest toy he knew was the child's magnet, with which he had played since babyhood, the most familiar of puzzles. He covered his desk with magnets, and mapped out their lines of force by compass. Then he read all the books he could find, and tried in vain to make his lines of force agree with theirs. The books confounded him. He could not credit his own understanding. Here was literally the most concrete fact in nature, next to gravitation which it defied; a force which must have radiated lines of energy without stop, since time began, if not longer, and which might probably go on radiating after the sun should fall into the earth, since no one knew why — or how — or what it radiated — or even whether it radiated at all. Perhaps the earliest known of all natural forces after the solar energies, it seemed to have suggested no idea to any one until some mariner bethought himself that it might serve for a pointer. Another thousand years passed when it taught some other intelligent man to use it as a pump, supply-pipe, sieve, or reservoir for collecting electricity, still without knowing how it worked or what it was. For a historian, the story of Faraday's

experiments and the invention of the dynamo passed belief; it revealed a condition of human ignorance and helplessness before the commonest forces, such as his mind
refused to credit. He could not conceive but that some
one, somewhere, could tell him all about the magnet, if one
could but find the book — although he had been forced
to admit the same helplessness in the face of gravitation,
phosphorescence, and odors; and he could imagine no
reason why society should treat radium as revolutionary
in science when every infant, for ages past, had seen the
magnet doing what radium did; for surely the kind of
radiation mattered nothing compared with the energy
that radiated and the matter supplied for radiation. He
dared not venture into the complexities of chemistry, or
microbes, so long as this child's toy offered complexities
that befogged his mind beyond X-rays, and turned the
atom into an endless variety of pumps endlessly pumping
an endless variety of ethers. He wanted to ask Mme. Curie
to invent a motor attachable to her salt of radium, and
pump its forces through it, as Faraday did with a magnet.
He figured the human mind itself as another radiating
matter through which man had always pumped a subtler
fluid.

In all this futility, it was not the magnet or the rays
or the microbes that troubled him, or even his helplessness
before the forces. To that he was used from childhood.
The magnet in its new relation staggered his new education by its evidence of growing complexity, and multiplicity, and even contradiction, in life. He could not
escape it; politics or science, the lesson was the same, and
at every step it blocked his path whichever way he turned.
He found it in politics; he ran against it in science; he
struck it in everyday life, as though he were still Adam
in the Garden of Eden between God who was unity, and

Satan who was complexity, with no means of deciding which was truth. The problem was the same for McKinley as for Adam, and for the Senate as for Satan. Hay was going to wreck on it, like King and Adams.

All one's life, one had struggled for unity, and unity had always won. The National Government and the national unity had overcome every resistance, and the Darwinian evolutionists were triumphant over all the curates; yet the greater the unity and the momentum, the worse became the complexity and the friction. One had in vain bowed one's neck to railways, banks, corporations, trusts, and even to the popular will as far as one could understand it — or even further; the multiplicity of unity had steadily increased, was increasing, and threatened to increase beyond reason. He had surrendered all his favorite prejudices, and foresworn even the forms of criticism — except for his pet amusement, the Senate, which was a tonic or stimulant necessary to healthy life; he had accepted uniformity and *Pteraspis* and ice age and tramways and telephones; and now — just when he was ready to hang the crowning garland on the brow of a completed education — science itself warned him to begin it again from the beginning.

Maundering among the magnets he bethought himself that once, a full generation earlier, he had begun active life by writing a confession of geological faith at the bidding of Sir Charles Lyell, and that it might be worth looking at if only to steady his vision. He read it again, and thought it better than he could do at sixty-three; but elderly minds always work loose. He saw his doubts grown larger, and became curious to know what had been said about them since 1870. The Geological Survey supplied stacks of volumes, and reading for steady months; while, the longer he read, the more he wondered, pondered, doubted what his delightful old friend Sir Charles Lyell would have said about it.

Truly the animal that is to be trained to unity must be caught young. Unity is vision; it must have been part of the process of learning to see. The older the mind, the older its complexities, and the further it looks, the more it sees, until even the stars resolve themselves into multiples; yet the child will always see but one. Adams asked whether geology since 1867 had drifted towards unity or multiplicity, and he felt that the drift would depend on the age of the man who drifted.

Seeking some impersonal point for measure, he turned to see what had happened to his oldest friend and cousin the ganoid fish, the *Pteraspis* of Ludlow and Wenlock, with whom he had sported when geological life was young; as though they had all remained together in time to act the Mask of Comus at Ludlow Castle, and repeat "how charming is divine philosophy!" He felt almost aggrieved to find Walcott so vigorously acting the part of Comus as to have flung the ganoid all the way off to Colorado and far back into the Lower Trenton limestone, making the *Pteraspis* as modern as a Mississippi gar-pike by spawning an ancestry for him, indefinitely more remote, in the dawn of known organic life. A few thousand feet, more or less, of limestone were the liveliest amusement to the ganoid, but they buried the uniformitarian alive, under the weight of his own uniformity. Not for all the ganoid fish that ever swam, would a discreet historian dare to hazard even in secret an opinion about the value of Natural Selection by Minute Changes under Uniform Conditions, for he could know no more about it than most of his neighbors who knew nothing; but natural selection that did not select — evolution finished before it began — minute changes that refused to change anything during the whole geological record — survival of the highest order in a fauna which had no origin — uniformity under conditions which had disturbed everything else in creation — to an honest-meaning though ignorant student who needed to prove Natural Selection and not assume it, such sequence brought no peace. He wished to be shown that changes in form caused evolution in force; that chemical or mechanical energy had by natural selection and minute changes, under uniform conditions, converted itself into thought. The ganoid fish seemed to prove — to him — that it had selected neither new form nor new force, but that the curates were right in thinking that force could be increased in volume or raised in intensity only by help of outside force. To him, the ganoid was a huge perplexity, none the less because neither he nor the ganoid troubled Darwinians, but the more because it helped to reveal that Darwinism seemed to survive only in England. In vain he asked what sort of evolution had taken its place. Almost any doctrine seemed orthodox. Even sudden conversions due to mere vital force acting on its own lines quite beyond mechanical explanation, had cropped up again. A little more, and he would be driven back on the old independence of species.

What the ontologist thought about it was his own affair, like the theologist's view on theology, for complexity was nothing to them; but to the historian who sought only the direction of thought and had begun as the confident child of Darwin and Lyell in 1867, the matter of direction seemed vital. Then he had entered gaily the door of the glacial epoch, and had surveyed a universe of unities and uniformities. In 1900 he entered a far vaster universe, where all the old roads ran about in every direction, overrunning, dividing, subdividing, stopping abruptly, vanishing slowly, with side-paths that led nowhere, and sequences that could not be proved. The active geologists had mostly become specialists dealing with complexities far too technical for an amateur, but the old formulas still seemed to serve for beginners, as they had served when new.

So the cause of the glacial epoch remained at the mercy of Lyell and Croll, although Geikie had split up the period into half-a-dozen intermittent chills in recent geology and in the northern hemisphere alone, while no geologist had ventured to assert that the glaciation of the southern hemisphere could possibly be referred to a horizon more remote. Continents still rose wildly and wildly sank, though Professor Suess of Vienna had written an epoch-making work, showing that continents were anchored like crystals, and only oceans rose and sank. Lyell's genial uniformity seemed genial still, for nothing had taken its place, though, in the interval, granite had grown young, nothing had been explained, and a bewildering system of huge overthrusts had upset geological mechanics. The textbooks refused even to discuss theories, frankly throwing up their hands and avowing that progress depended on studying each rock as a law to itself.

Adams had no more to do with the correctness of the science than the gar-pike or the Port Jackson shark, for its correctness in no way concerned him, and only impertinence could lead him to dispute or discuss the principles of any science; but the history of the mind concerned the historian alone, and the historian had no vital concern in anything else, for he found no change to record in the body. In thought the Schools, like the Church, raised ignorance to a faith and degraded dogma to heresy. Evolution survived like the trilobites without evolving, and yet the evolutionists held the whole field, and had even plucked up courage to rebel against the Cossack ukase of Lord Kelvin forbidding them to ask more than twenty million years for their experiments.

No doubt the geologists had always submitted sadly to this last and utmost violence inflicted on them by the Pontiff of Physical Religion in the effort to force unification of the universe; they had protested with mild conviction that they could not state the geological record in terms of time; they had murmured *Ignoramus* under their breath; but they had never dared to assert the *Ignorabimus* that lay on the tips of their tongues.

Yet the admission seemed close at hand. Evolution was becoming change of form broken by freaks of force, and warped at times by attractions affecting intelligence, twisted and tortured at other times by sheer violence, cosmic, chemical, solar, supersensual, electrolytic — who knew what? — defying science, if not denying known law; and the wisest of men could but imitate the Church, and invoke a "larger synthesis" to unify the anarchy again. Historians have got into far too much trouble by following schools of theology in their efforts to enlarge their synthesis, that they should willingly repeat the process in science. For human purposes a point must always be soon reached where larger synthesis is suicide.

Politics and geology pointed alike to the larger synthesis of rapidly increasing complexity; but still an elderly man knew that the change might be only in himself. The admission cost nothing. Any student, of any age, thinking only of a thought and not of his thought, should delight in turning about and trying the opposite motion, as he delights in the spring which brings even to a tired and irritated statesman the larger synthesis of peach-blooms, cherry-blossoms, and dogwood, to prove the folly of fret. Every schoolboy knows that this sum of all knowledge never saved him from whipping; mere years help nothing; King and Hay and Adams could neither of them escape floundering through the corridors of chaos that opened as they passed to the end; but they could at least float with the stream if they only knew which way the current ran. Adams would have liked to begin afresh with the *Limulus* and *Lepidosteus* in the waters of Braintree, side by side with Adamses and Quincys and Harvard College, all unchanged and unchangeable since archaic time; but what purpose would it serve? A seeker of truth — or illusion — would be none the less restless, though a shark!

27

Teufelsdröckh

(1901)

Inevitable Paris beckoned, and resistance became more and more futile as the store of years grew less; for the world contains no other spot than Paris where education can be pursued from every side. Even more vigorously than in the twelfth century, Paris taught in the twentieth, with no other school approaching it for variety of direction and energy of mind. Of the teaching in detail, a man who knew only what accident had taught him in the nineteenth century, could know next to nothing, since science had got quite beyond his horizon, and mathematics had become the only necessary language of thought; but one could play with the toys of childhood, including Ming porcelain, salons of painting, operas and theatres, beaux-arts and Gothic architecture, theology and anarchy, in any jumble of time; or totter about with Joe Stickney, talking Greek philosophy or recent poetry, or studying "Louise" at the Opéra Comique, or discussing the charm of youth and the Seine with Bay Lodge and his exquisite young wife. Paris remained Parisian in spite of change, mistress of herself though China fell. Scores of artists — sculptors and painters, poets and dramatists,

workers in gems and metals, designers in stuffs and furniture — hundreds of chemists, physicists, even philosophers, philologists, physicians, and historians — were at
work, a thousand times as actively as ever before, and
the mass and originality of their product would have
swamped any previous age, as it very nearly swamped its
own; but the effect was one of chaos, and Adams stood as
helpless before it as before the chaos of New York. His
single thought was to keep in front of the movement, and,
if necessary, lead it to chaos, but never fall behind. Only
the young have time to linger in the rear.

The amusements of youth had to be abandoned, for not
even pugilism needs more staying-power than the labors
of the pale-faced student of the Latin Quarter in the
haunts of Montparnasse or Montmartre, where one must
feel no fatigue at two o'clock in the morning in a beer-
garden even after four hours of Mounet Sully at the
Théatre Français. In those branches, education might be
called closed. Fashion, too, could no longer teach anything
worth knowing to a man who, holding open the door into
the next world, regarded himself as merely looking round
to take a last glance of this. The glance was more amusing
than any he had known in his active life, but it was more —
infinitely more — chaotic and complex.

Still something remained to be done for education beyond the chaos, and as usual the woman helped. For thirty
years or thereabouts, he had been repeating that he really
must go to Baireuth. Suddenly Mrs. Lodge appeared on
the horizon and bade him come. He joined them, parents
and children, alert and eager and appreciative as ever, at
the little old town of Rothenburg-on-the-Taube, and they
went on to the Baireuth festival together.

Thirty years earlier, a Baireuth festival would have
made an immense stride in education, and the spirit of the

master would have opened a vast new world. In 1901 the effect was altogether different from the spirit of the master. In 1876 the rococo setting of Baireuth seemed the correct atmosphere for Siegfried and Brünhilde, perhaps even for Parsifal. Baireuth was out of the world, calm, contemplative, and remote. In 1901 the world had altogether changed, and Wagner had become a part of it, as familiar as Shakespeare or Bret Harte. The rococo element jarred. Even the Hudson and the Susquehanna — perhaps the Potomac itself — had often risen to drown out the gods of Walhalla, and one could hardly listen to the "Götterdämmerung" in New York, among throngs of intense young enthusiasts, without paroxysms of nervous excitement that toned down to musical philistinism at Baireuth, as though the gods were Bavarian composers. New York or Paris might be whatever one pleased— venal, sordid, vulgar — but society nursed there, in the rottenness of its decay, certain anarchistic ferments, and thought them proof of art. Perhaps they were; and at all events, Wagner was chiefly responsible for them as artistic emotion. New York knew better than Baireuth what Wagner meant, and the frivolities of Paris had more than once included the rising of the Seine to drown out the Étoile or Montmartre, as well as the sorcery of ambition that casts spells of enchantment on the hero. Paris still felt a subtle flattery in the thought that the last great tragedy of gods and men would surely happen there, while no one could conceive of its happening at Baireuth, or would care if it did. Paris coquetted with catastrophe as though it were an old mistress — faced it almost gaily as she had done so often, for they were acquainted since Rome began to ravage Europe; while New York met it with a glow of fascinated horror, like an inevitable earthquake, and heard Ternina announce it with conviction that made nerves quiver and thrill as they had long ceased to do under the accents of popular oratory proclaiming popular virtue. Flattery had lost its charm, but the *Fluch-motif* went home.

Adams had been carried with the tide till Brünhilde had become a habit and Ternina an ally. He too had played with anarchy; though not with socialism, which, to young men who nourished artistic emotions under the dome of the Pantheon, seemed hopelessly bourgeois, and lowest middle-class. Bay Lodge and Joe Stickney had given birth to the wholly new and original party of Conservative Christian Anarchists, to restore true poetry under the inspiration of the "Götterdämmerung." Such a party saw no inspiration in Baireuth, where landscape, history, and audience were — relatively — stodgy, and where the only emotion was a musical dilettantism that the master had abhorred.

Yet Baireuth still amused even a conservative Christian anarchist who cared as little as "Grane, mein Ross," whether the singers sang false, and who came only to learn what Wagner had supposed himself to mean. This end attained as pleased Frau Wagner and the Heiliger Geist, he was ready to go on; and the Senator, yearning for sterner study, pointed to a haven at Moscow. For years Adams had taught American youth never to travel without a Senator who was useful even in America at times, but indispensable in Russia where, in 1901, anarchists, even though conservative and Christian, were ill-seen.

This wing of the anarchistic party consisted rigorously of but two members, Adams and Bay Lodge. The conservative Christian anarchist, as a party, drew life from Hegel and Schopenhauer rightly understood. By the necessity of their philosophical descent, each member of the fraternity denounced the other as unequal to his lofty task and inadequate to grasp it. Of course, no third member could be so much as considered, since the great principle of contradiction could be expressed only by opposites;

and no agreement could be conceived, because anarchy, by definition, must be chaos and collision, as in the kinetic theory of a perfect gas. Doubtless this law of contradiction was itself agreement, a restriction of personal liberty inconsistent with freedom; but the "larger synthesis" admitted a limited agreement provided it were strictly confined to the end of larger contradiction. Thus the great end of all philosophy — the "larger synthesis" — was attained, but the process was arduous, and while Adams, as the older member, assumed to declare the principle, Bay Lodge necessarily denied both the assumption and the principle in order to assure its truth.

Adams proclaimed that in the last synthesis, order and anarchy were one, but that the unity was chaos. As anarchist, conservative and Christian, he had no motive or duty but to attain the end; and, to hasten it, he was bound to accelerate progress; to concentrate energy; to accumulate power; to multiply and intensify forces; to reduce friction, increase velocity and magnify momentum, partly because this was the mechanical law of the universe as science explained it; but partly also in order to get done with the present which artists and some others complained of; and finally — and chiefly — because a rigorous philosophy required it, in order to penetrate the beyond, and satisfy man's destiny by reaching the largest synthesis in its ultimate contradiction.

Of course the untaught critic instantly objected that this scheme was neither conservative, Christian, nor anarchic, but such objection meant only that the critic should begin his education in any infant school in order to learn that anarchy which should be logical would cease to be anarchic. To the conservative Christian anarchist, the amiable doctrines of Kropotkin were sentimental ideas of Russian mental inertia covered with the name of anarchy merely to disguise their innocence; and the outpourings of

Elisée Reclus were ideals of the French *ouvrier*, diluted with absinthe, resulting in a bourgeois dream of order and inertia. Neither made a pretence of anarchy except as a momentary stage towards order and unity. Neither of them had formed any other conception of the universe than what they had inherited from the priestly class to which their minds obviously belonged. With them, as with the socialist, communist, or collectivist, the mind that followed nature had no relation; if anarchists needed order, they must go back to the twelfth century where their thought had enjoyed its thousand years of reign. The conservative Christian anarchist could have no associate, no object, no faith except the nature of nature itself; and his "larger synthesis" had only the fault of being so supremely true that even the highest obligation of duty could scarcely oblige Bay Lodge to deny it in order to prove it. Only the self-evident truth that no philosophy of order — except the Church — had ever satisfied the philosopher reconciled the conservative Christian anarchist to prove his own.

Naturally these ideas were so far in advance of the age that hardly more people could understand them than understood Wagner or Hegel; for that matter, since the time of Socrates, wise men have been mostly shy of claiming to understand anything; but such refinements were Greek or German, and affected the practical American but little. He admitted that, for the moment, the darkness was dense. He could not affirm with confidence, even to himself, that his "largest synthesis" would certainly turn out to be chaos, since he would be equally obliged to deny the chaos. The poet groped blindly for an emotion. The play of thought for thought's sake had mostly ceased. The throb of fifty or a hundred million steam horse-power, doubling every ten years, and already more despotic than all the horses that ever lived, and all the riders they ever carried, drowned rhyme and reason. No one was to blame, for all were equally servants of the power, and worked merely to increase it; but the conservative Christian anarchist saw light.

Thus the student of Hegel prepared himself for a visit to Russia in order to enlarge his "synthesis" — and much he needed it! In America all were conservative Christian anarchists; the faith was national, racial, geographic. The true American had never seen such supreme virtue in any of the innumerable shades between social anarchy and social order as to mark it for exclusively human and his own. He never had known a complete union either in Church or State or thought, and had never seen any need for it. The freedom gave him courage to meet any contradiction, and intelligence enough to ignore it. Exactly the opposite condition had marked Russian growth. The Czar's empire was a phase of conservative Christian anarchy more interesting to history than all the complex variety of American newspapers, schools, trusts, sects, frauds, and Congressmen. These were Nature — pure and anarchic as the conservative Christian anarchist saw Nature — active, vibrating, mostly unconscious, and quickly reacting on force; but, from the first glimpse one caught from the sleeping-car window, in the early morning, of the Polish Jew at the accidental railway station, in all his weird horror, to the last vision of the Russian peasant, lighting his candle and kissing his ikon before the railway Virgin in the station at St. Petersburg, all was logical, conservative, Christian and anarchic. Russia had nothing in common with any ancient or modern world that history knew; she had been the oldest source of all civilization in Europe, and had kept none for herself; neither Europe nor Asia had ever known such a phase, which seemed to fall into no line of evolution whatever, and was as wonderful to the student of Gothic architecture in the twelfth century, as to the student of the dynamo in the twentieth. Studied in the dry light of conservative Christian anarchy, Russia became luminous like the salt of radium; but with a negative luminosity as though she were a substance whose energies had been sucked out — an inert residuum — with movement of pure inertia. From the car window one seemed to float past undulations of nomad life — herders deserted by their leaders and herds — wandering waves stopped in their wanderings — waiting for their winds or warriors to return and lead them westward; tribes that had camped, like Khirgis, for the season, and had lost the means of motion without acquiring the habit of permanence. They waited and suffered. As they stood they were out of place, and could never have been normal. Their country acted as a sink of energy like the Caspian Sea, and its surface kept the uniformity of ice and snow. One Russian peasant kissing an ikon on a saint's day, in the Kremlin, served for a hundred million. The student had no need to study Wallace, or re-read Tolstoy or Tourguenieff or Dostoiewski to refresh his memory of the most poignant analysis of human inertia ever put in words; Gorky was more than enough: Kropotkin answered every purpose.

The Russian people could never have changed — could they ever be changed? Could inertia of race, on such a scale, be broken up, or take new form? Even in America, on an infinitely smaller scale, the question was old and unanswered. All the so-called primitive races, and some nearer survivals, had raised doubts which persisted against the most obstinate convictions of evolution. The Senator himself shook his head, and after surveying Warsaw and Moscow to his content, went on to St. Petersburg to ask questions of Mr. de Witte and Prince Khilkoff. Their conversation added new doubts; for their efforts had been immense, their expenditure enormous, and their results on the people seemed to be uncertain as yet, even to themselves. Ten or fifteen years of violent stimulus seemed resulting in nothing, for, since 1898, Russia lagged.

The tourist-student, having duly reflected, asked the Senator whether he should allow three generations, or more, to swing the Russian people into the Western movement. The Senator seemed disposed to ask for more. The student had nothing to say. For him, all opinion founded on fact must be error, because the facts can never be complete, and their relations must be always infinite. Very likely, Russia would instantly become the most brilliant constellation of human progress through all the ordered stages of good; but meanwhile one might give a value as movement of inertia to the mass, and assume a slow acceleration that would, at the end of a generation, leave the gap between east and west relatively the same.

This result reached, the Lodges thought their moral improvement required a visit to Berlin; but forty years of varied emotions had not deadened Adams's memories of Berlin, and he preferred, at any cost, to escape new ones. When the Lodges started for Germany, Adams took steamer for Sweden and landed happily, in a day or two, at Stockholm.

Until the student is fairly sure that his problem is soluble, he gains little by obstinately insisting on solving it. One might doubt whether Mr. de Witte himself, or Prince Khilkoff, or any Grand Duke, or the Emperor, knew much more about it than their neighbors; and Adams was quite sure that, even in America, he should listen with uncertain confidence to the views of any Secretary of the Treasury, or railway president, or President of the United States whom he had ever known, that should concern the America of the next generation. The mere fact that any man should dare to offer them would prove his incompetence to judge. Yet Russia was too vast a force to be treated as an object of unconcern. As inertia, if in no other way, she represented three-fourths of the human race, and her movement might be the true movement of the future, against the hasty and unsure acceleration of America. No one could yet know what would best suit humanity, and the tourist who carried his La Fontaine in mind, caught himself talking as bear or as monkey according to the mirror he held before him. "Am I satisfied?" he asked: —

> "Moi? pourquoi non?
> N'ai-je pas quatre pieds aussi bien que les autres?
> Mon portrait jusqu'ici ne m'a rien reproché;
> Mais pour mon frère l'ours, on ne l'a qu'ébauché;
> Jamais, s'il me veut croire, il ne se fera peindre."

Granting that his brother the bear lacked perfection in details, his own figure as monkey was not necessarily ideal or decorative, nor was he in the least sure what form it might take even in one generation. He had himself never ventured to dream of three. No man could guess what the Daimler motor and X-rays would do to him; but so much was sure; the monkey and motor were terribly afraid of the bear; how much, only a man close to their foreign departments knew. As the monkey looked back across the Baltic from the safe battlements of Stockholm, Russia looked more portentous than from the Kremlin.

The image was that of the retreating ice-cap — a wall of archaic glacier, as fixed, as ancient, as eternal, as the wall of archaic ice that blocked the ocean a few hundred miles to the northward, and more likely to advance. Scandinavia had been ever at its mercy. Europe had never changed. The imaginary line that crossed the level continent from the Baltic to the Black Sea, merely extended the northern barrier-line. The Hungarians and Poles on one side still struggled against the Russian inertia of race, and retained their own energies under the same conditions that caused inertia across the frontier. Race ruled the conditions; conditions hardly affected race; and yet no one could tell the patient tourist what race was, or how it should be known. History offered a feeble and delusive smile at the sound of the word; evolutionists and ethnologists disputed its very existence; no one knew what to make of it; yet, without the clue, history was a nursery tale.

The Germans, Scandinavians, Poles and Hungarians, energetic as they were, had never held their own against the heterogeneous mass of inertia called Russia, and trembled with terror whenever Russia moved. From Stockholm one looked back on it as t ıough it were an ice-sheet, and so had Stockholm watched it for centuries. In contrast with the dreary forests of Russia and the stern streets of St. Petersburg, Stockholm seemed a southern vision, and Sweden lured the tourist on. Through a cheerful New England landscape and bright autumn, he rambled northwards till he found himself at Trondhjem and discovered Norway. Education crowded upon him in immense masses as he triangulated these vast surfaces of history about which he had lectured and read for a life-time. When the historian fully realizes his ignorance — which sometimes happens to Americans — he becomes even more tiresome to himself than to others, because his *naïveté* is irrepressible. Adams could not get over his astonishment, though he had preached the Norse doctrine all his life against the stupid and beer-swilling Saxon boors whom Freeman loved, and who, to the despair of science, produced Shakespeare. Mere contact with Norway started voyages of thought, and, under their illusions, he took the mail-steamer to the north, and on September 14, reached Hammerfest.

Frivolous amusement was hardly what one saw, through the equinoctial twilight, peering at the flying tourist, down the deep fiords, from dim patches of snow, where the last Laps and reindeer were watching the mail-steamer thread the intricate channels outside, as their ancestors had watched the first Norse fishermen learn them in the succession of time; but it was not the Laps, or the snow, or the arctic gloom, that impressed the tourist, so much as the lights of an electro-magnetic civilization and the stupefying contrast with Russia, which more and more insisted on taking the first place in historical interest. Nowhere had the new forces so vigorously corrected the errors of the old, or so effectively redressed the balance of the ecliptic. As one approached the end — the spot where, seventy years before a futile Carlylean Teufelsdröckh had stopped to ask futile questions of the silent infinite — the infinite seemed to have become loquacious, not to say familiar, chattering gossip in one's ear. An installation of electric lighting and telephones led tourists close up to the polar ice-cap, beyond the level of the magnetic pole; and there the newer Teufelsdröckh sat dumb with surprise, and glared at the permanent electric lights of Hammerfest.

He had good reason — better than the Teufelsdröckh of 1830, in his liveliest Scotch imagination, ever dreamed, or mortal man had ever told. At best, a week in these dim Northern seas, without means of speech, within the Arctic circle, at the equinox, lent itself to gravity if not to gloom; but only a week before, breakfasting in the restaurant at Stockholm, his eye had caught, across the neighboring table, a headline in a Swedish newspaper, announcing an attempt on the life of President McKinley, and from Stockholm to Trondhjem, and so up the coast to Hammerfest, day after day the news came, telling of the President's condition, and the doings and sayings of Hay and Roosevelt, until at last a little journal was cried on reaching some dim haven, announcing the President's death a few hours before. To Adams the death of McKinley and the advent of Roosevelt were not wholly void of personal emotion, but this was little in comparison with his depth of wonder at hearing hourly reports from his most intimate friends, sent to him far within the realm of night, not to please him, but to correct the faults of the solar system. The electro-dynamo-social universe worked better than the sun.

No such strange chance had ever happened to a historian before, and it upset for the moment his whole philosophy of conservative anarchy. The acceleration was marvellous, and wholly in the lines of unity. To recover his grasp of chaos, he must look back across the gulf to Russia, and the gap seemed to have suddenly become an abyss. Russia was infinitely distant. Yet the nightmare of the glacial ice-cap still pressed down on him from the hills, in full vision, and no one could look out on the dusky and oily sea that lapped these spectral islands without consciousness that only a day's steaming to the northward would bring him to the ice-barrier, ready at any moment to advance, which obliged tourists to stop where Laps and reindeer and Norse fishermen had stopped so long ago that memory of their very origin was lost. Adams had never before met a *ne plus ultra*, and knew not what to make of it; but he felt at least the emotion of his Norwegian fisherman ancestors, doubtless numbering hundreds of thousands, jammed with their faces to the sea, the ice on the north, the ice-cap of Russian inertia pressing from behind, and the ice a trifling danger compared with the inertia. From the day they first followed the retreating ice-cap round the North Cape, down to the present moment, their problem was the same.

The new Teufelsdröckh, though considerably older than the old one, saw no clearer into past or future, but he was fully as much perplexed. From the archaic ice-barrier to the Caspian Sea, a long line of division, permanent since ice and inertia first took possession, divided his lines of force, with no relation to climate or geography or soil.

The less a tourist knows, the fewer mistakes he need make, for he will not expect himself to explain ignorance. A century ago he carried letters and sought knowledge; to-day he knows that no one knows; he needs too much and ignorance is learning. He wandered south again, and came out at Kiel, Hamburg, Bremen, and Cologne. A mere glance showed him that here was a Germany new to mankind. Hamburg was almost as American as St. Louis. In forty years, the green rusticity of Düsseldorf had taken on the sooty grime of Birmingham. The Rhine in 1900 resembled the Rhine of 1858 much as it resembled the Rhine of the Salic Franks. Cologne was a railway centre that had completed its cathedral which bore an absent-minded air of a cathedral of Chicago. The thirteenth century, carefully strained-off, catalogued, and locked up, was visible to tourists as a kind of Neanderthal, cave-dwelling, curiosity. The Rhine was more modern than the Hudson, as might well be, since it produced far more coal; but all this counted for little beside the radical change in the lines of force.

In 1858 the whole plain of northern Europe, as well as the Danube in the south, bore evident marks of being still the prehistoric highway between Asia and the Ocean. The trade-route followed the old routes of invasion, and Cologne was a resting-place between Warsaw and Flanders. Throughout northern Germany, Russia was felt even more powerfully than France. In 1901 Russia had vanished, and not even France was felt; hardly England or America. Coal alone was felt — its stamp alone pervaded the Rhine district and persisted to Picardy — and the stamp was the same as that of Birmingham and Pittsburgh. The Rhine produced the same power, and the power produced the same people — the same mind — the same impulse. For a man sixty-three years old who had no hope of earning a living, these three months of education were the most arduous he ever attempted, and Russia was the most indigestible morsel he ever met; but the sum of it, viewed from Cologne, seemed reasonable. From Hammerfest to Cherbourg on one shore of the ocean — from Halifax to Norfolk on the other — one great empire was ruled by one great emperor — Coal. Political and human jealousies might tear it apart or divide it, but the power and the empire were one. Unity had gained that ground. Beyond lay Russia, and there an older, perhaps a surer, power, resting on the eternal law of inertia, held its own.

As a personal matter, the relative value of the two powers became more interesting every year; for the mass of Russian inertia was moving irresistibly over China, and John Hay stood in its path. As long as de Witte ruled, Hay was safe. Should de Witte fall, Hay would totter. One could only sit down and watch the doings of Mr. de Witte and Mr. de Plehve.

28

The Height of Knowledge

(1902)

America has always taken tragedy lightly. Too busy to stop the activity of their twenty-million-horse-power society, Americans ignore tragic motives that would have overshadowed the Middle Ages; and the world learns to regard assassination as a form of hysteria, and death as neurosis, to be treated by a rest-cure. Three hideous political murders, that would have fattened the Eumenides with horror, have thrown scarcely a shadow on the White House.

The year 1901 was a year of tragedy that seemed to Hay to centre on himself. First came, in summer, the accidental death of his son, Del Hay. Close on the tragedy of his son, followed that of his chief, "all the more hideous that we were so sure of his recovery." The world turned suddenly into a graveyard. "I have acquired the funeral habit." "Nicolay is dying. I went to see him yesterday, and he did not know me." Among the letters of condolence showered upon him was one from Clarence King at Pasadena, "heart-breaking in grace and tenderness — the old King manner"; and King himself "simply waiting till nature and the foe have done their struggle." The tragedy of King impressed him intensely: "There you have it in the face!" he said — "the best and brightest man of his generation, with talents immeasurably beyond any of his contemporaries; with industry that has often sickened me to witness it; with everything in his favor but blind luck; hounded by disaster from his cradle, with none of the joy of life to which he was entitled, dying at last, with nameless suffering, alone and uncared-for, in a California tavern. *Ca vous amuse, la vie?*"

The first summons that met Adams, before he had even landed on the pier at New York, December 29, was to Clarence King's funeral, and from the funeral service he had no gayer road to travel than that which led to Washington, where a revolution had occurred that must in any case have made the men of his age instantly old, but which, besides hurrying to the front the generation that till then he had regarded as boys, could not fail to break the social ties that had till then held them all together.

Ca vous amuse, la vie? Honestly, the lessons of education were becoming too trite. Hay himself, probably for the first time, felt half glad that Roosevelt should want him to stay in office, if only to save himself the trouble of quitting; but to Adams all was pure loss. On that side, his education had been finished at school. His friends in power were lost, and he knew life too well to risk total wreck by trying to save them.

As far as concerned Roosevelt, the chance was hopeless. To them at sixty-three, Roosevelt at forty-three could not be taken seriously in his old character, and could not be recovered in his new one. Power when wielded by abnormal energy is the most serious of facts, and all Roosevelt's friends know that his restless and combative energy was more than abnormal. Roosevelt, more than any other man living within the range of notoriety, showed the singular primitive quality that belongs to ultimate matter — the quality that mediæval theology assigned to God — he was pure act. With him wielding unmeasured power with immeasurable energy, in the White House, the relation of age to youth — of teacher to pupil — was altogether out of place; and no other was possible. Even Hay's relation was a false one, while Adams's ceased of itself. History's truths are little valuable now; but human nature retains a few of its archaic, proverbial laws, and the wisest courtier that ever lived — Lucius Seneca himself — must have remained in some shade of doubt what advantage he should get from the power of his friend and pupil Nero Claudius, until, as a gentleman past sixty, he received Nero's filial invitation to kill himself. Seneca closed the vast circle of his knowledge by learning that a friend in power was a friend lost — a fact very much worth insisting upon — while the gray-headed moth that had fluttered through many moth-administrations and had singed his wings more or less in them all, though he now slept nine months out of the twelve, acquired an instinct of self-preservation that kept him to the north side of La Fayette Square, and, after a sufficient habitude of Presidents and Senators, deterred him from hovering between them.

Those who seek education in the paths of duty are always deceived by the illusion that power in the hands of friends is an advantage to them. As far as Adams could teach experience, he was bound to warn them that he had found it an invariable disaster. Power is poison. Its effect on Presidents had been always tragic, chiefly as an almost insane excitement at first, and a worse reaction afterwards;

but also because no mind is so well balanced as to bear the strain of seizing unlimited force without habit or knowledge of it; and finding it disputed with him by hungry packs of wolves and hounds whose lives depend on snatching the carrion. Roosevelt enjoyed a singularly direct nature and honest intent, but he lived naturally in restless agitation that would have worn out most tempers in a month, and his first year of Presidency showed chronic excitement that made a friend tremble. The effect of unlimited power on limited mind is worth noting in Presidents because it must represent the same process in society, and the power of self-control must have limit somewhere in face of the control of the infinite.

Here, education seemed to see its first and last lesson, but this is a matter of psychology which lies far down in the depths of history and of science; it will recur in other forms. The personal lesson is different. Roosevelt was lost, but this seemed no reason why Hay and Lodge should also be lost, yet the result was mathematically certain. With Hay, it was only the steady decline of strength, and the necessary economy of force; but with Lodge it was law of politics. He could not help himself, for his position as the President's friend and independent statesman at once was false, and he must be unsure in both relations.

To a student, the importance of Cabot Lodge was great — much greater than that of the usual Senator — but it hung on his position in Massachusetts rather than on his control of Executive patronage; and his standing in Massachusetts was highly insecure. Nowhere in America was society so complex or change so rapid. No doubt the Bostonian had always been noted for a certain chronic irritability — a sort of Bostonitis — which, in its primitive Puritan forms, seemed due to knowing too much of his neighbors, and thinking too much of himself. Many years earlier William M. Evarts had pointed out to Adams the impossibility of uniting New England behind a New England leader. The trait led to good ends — such as admiration of Abraham Lincoln and George Washington — but the virtue was exacting; for New England standards were various, scarcely reconcilable with each other, and constantly multiplying in number, until balance between them threatened to become impossible. The old ones were quite difficult enough — State Street and the banks exacted one stamp; the old Congregational clergy another; Harvard College, poor in votes, but rich in social influence, a third; the foreign element, especially the Irish, held aloof, and seldom consented to approve any one; the new socialist class, rapidly growing, promised to become more exclusive than the Irish. New power was disintegrating society, and setting independent centres of force to work, until money had all it could do to hold the machine together. No one could represent it faithfully as a whole.

Naturally, Adams's sympathies lay strongly with Lodge, but the task of appreciation was much more difficult in his case than in that of his chief friend and scholar, the President. As a type for study, or a standard for education, Lodge was the more interesting of the two. Roosevelts are born and never can be taught; but Lodge was a creature of teaching — Boston incarnate — the child of his local parentage; and while his ambition led him to be more, the intent, though virtuous, was — as Adams admitted in his own case — restless. An excellent talker, a voracious reader, a ready wit, an accomplished orator, with a clear mind and a powerful memory, he could never feel perfectly at ease whatever leg he stood on, but shifted, sometimes with painful strain of temper, from one sensitive muscle to another, uncertain whether to pose as an uncompromising Yankee; or a pure American; or a patriot in the still purer atmosphere of Irish, Germans, or Jews; or a scholar and historian of Harvard College. English to the

last fibre of his thought — saturated with English literature, English tradition, English taste — revolted by every
vice and by most virtues of Frenchmen and Germans, or
any other Continental standards, but at home and happy
among the vices and extravagances of Shakespeare —
standing first on the social, then on the political foot; now
worshipping, now banning; shocked by the wanton display of immorality, but practising the license of political
usage; sometimes bitter, often genial, always intelligent —
Lodge had the singular merit of interesting. The usual
statesmen flocked in swarms like crows, black and monot-
onous. Lodge's plumage was varied, and, like his flight,
harked back to race. He betrayed the consciousness that
he and his people had a past, if they dared but avow it,
and might have a future, if they could but divine it.

Adams, too, was Bostonian, and the Bostonian's uncertainty of attitude was as natural to him as to Lodge. Only
Bostonians can understand Bostonians and thoroughly
sympathize with the inconsequences of the Boston mind.
His theory and practice were also at variance. He professed in theory equal distrust of English thought, and
called it a huge rag-bag of bric-à-brac, sometimes precious
but never sure. For him, only the Greek, the Italian or
the French standards had claims to respect, and the bar-
barism of Shakespeare was as flagrant as to Voltaire; but
his theory never affected his practice. He knew that his
artistic standard was the illusion of his own mind; that
English disorder approached nearer to truth, if truth existed, than French measure or Italian line, or German
logic; he read his Shakespeare as the Evangel of conservative Christian anarchy, neither very conservative nor very
Christian, but stupendously anarchistic. He loved the
atrocities of English art and society, as he loved Charles
Dickens and Miss Austen, not because of their example,
but because of their humor. He made no scruple of defy-

ing sequence and denying consistency — but he was not a Senator.

Double standards are inspiration to men of letters, but they are apt to be fatal to politicians. Adams had no reason to care whether his standards were popular or not, and no one else cared more than he; but Roosevelt and Lodge were playing a game in which they were always liable to find the shifty sands of American opinion yield suddenly under their feet. With this game an elderly friend had long before carried acquaintance as far as he wished. There was nothing in it for him but the amusement of the pugilist or acrobat. The larger study was lost in the division of interests and the ambitions of fifth-rate men; but foreign affairs dealt only with large units, and made personal relation possible with Hay which could not be maintained with Roosevelt or Lodge. As an affair of pure education the point is worth notice from young men who are drawn into politics. The work of domestic progress is done by masses of mechanical power — steam, electric, furnace, or other — which have to be controlled by a score or two of individuals who have shown capacity to manage it. The work of internal government has become the task of controlling these men, who are socially as remote as heathen gods, alone worth knowing, but never known, and who could tell nothing of political value if one skinned them alive. Most of them have nothing to tell, but are forces as dumb as their dynamos, absorbed in the development or economy of power. They are trustees for the public, and whenever society assumes the property, it must confer on them that title; but the power will remain as before, whoever manages it, and will then control society without appeal, as it controls its stokers and pit-men. Modern politics is, at bottom, a struggle not of men but of forces. The men become every year more and more creatures of force, massed about central power-houses. The conflict is no longer between the men, but between the motors that drive the men, and the men tend to succumb to their own motive forces.

This is a moral that man strongly objects to admit, especially in mediæval pursuits like politics and poetry, nor is it worth while for a teacher to insist upon it. What he insists upon is only that, in domestic politics, every one works for an immediate object, commonly for some private job, and invariably in a near horizon, while in foreign affairs the outlook is far ahead, over a field as wide as the world. There the merest scholar could see what he was doing. For history, international relations are the only sure standards of movement; the only foundation for a map. For this reason, Adams had always insisted that international relation was the only sure base for a chart of history.

He cared little to convince any one of the correctness of his view, but as teacher he was bound to explain it, and as friend he found it convenient. The Secretary of State has always stood as much alone as the historian. Required to look far ahead and round him, he measures forces unknown to party managers, and has found Congress more or less hostile ever since Congress first sat. The Secretary of State exists only to recognize the existence of a world which Congress would rather ignore; of obligations which Congress repudiates whenever it can; of bargains which Congress distrusts and tries to turn to its advantage or to reject. Since the first day the Senate existed, it has always intrigued against the Secretary of State whenever the Secretary has been obliged to extend his functions beyond the appointment of Consuls in Senators' service.

This is a matter of history which any one may approve or dispute as he will; but as education it gave new resources to an old scholar, for it made of Hay the best schoolmaster since 1865. Hay had become the most imposing figure ever known in the office. He had an influence that no other

Secretary of State ever possessed, as he had a nation behind him such as history had never imagined. He needed to write no state papers; he wanted no help, and he stood far above counsel or advice; but he could instruct an attentive scholar as no other teacher in the world could do; and Adams sought only instruction — wanted only to chart the international channel for fifty years to come; to triangulate the future; to obtain his dimension, and fix the acceleration of movement in politics since the year 1200, as he was trying to fix it in philosophy and physics; in finance and force.

Hay had been so long at the head of foreign affairs that at last the stream of events favored him. With infinite effort he had achieved the astonishing diplomatic feat of inducing the Senate, with only six negative votes, to permit Great Britain to renounce, without equivalent, treaty rights which she had for fifty years defended tooth and nail. This unprecedented triumph in his negotiations with the Senate enabled him to carry one step further his measures for general peace. About England the Senate could make no further effective opposition, for England was won, and Canada alone could give trouble. The next difficulty was with France, and there the Senate blocked advance, but England assumed the task, and, owing to political changes in France, effected the object — a combination which, as late as 1901, had been visionary. The next, and far more difficult step, was to bring Germany into the combine; while, at the end of the vista, most unmanageable of all, Russia remained to be satisfied and disarmed. This was the instinct of what might be named McKinleyism; the system of combinations, consolidations, trusts, realized at home, and realizable abroad.

With the system, a student nurtured in ideas of the eighteenth century had nothing to do, and made not the least pretence of meddling; but nothing forbade him to study, and he noticed to his astonishment that this capitalistic scheme of combining governments, like railways or furnaces, was in effect precisely the socialist scheme of Jaurès and Bebel. That John Hay, of all men, should adopt a socialist policy seemed an idea more absurd than conservative Christian anarchy, but paradox had become the only orthodoxy in politics as in science. When one saw the field, one realized that Hay could not help himself, nor could Bebel. Either Germany must destroy England and France to create the next inevitable unification as a system of continent against continent — or she must pool interests. Both schemes in turn were attributed to the Kaiser; one or the other he would have to choose; opinion was balanced doubtfully on their merits; but, granting both to be feasible, Hay's and McKinley's statesmanship turned on the point of persuading the Kaiser to join what might be called the Coal-power combination, rather than build up the only possible alternative, a Gun-power combination by merging Germany in Russia. Thus Bebel and Jaurès, McKinley and Hay, were partners.

The problem was pretty — even fascinating — and, to an old Civil-War private soldier in diplomacy, as rigorous as a geometrical demonstration. As the last possible lesson in life, it had all sorts of ultimate values. Unless education marches on both feet — theory and practice — it risks going astray; and Hay was probably the most accomplished master of both then living. He knew not only the forces but also the men, and he had no other thought than his policy.

Probably this was the moment of highest knowledge that a scholar could ever reach. He had under his eyes the whole educational staff of the Government at a time when the Government had just reached the heights of highest activity and influence. Since 1860, education had done its worst, under the greatest masters and at enormous expense to the world, to train these two minds to catch and comprehend every spring of international action, not to speak of personal influence; and the entire machinery of politics in several great countries had little to do but supply the last and best information. Education could be carried no further.

With its effects on Hay, Adams had nothing to do; but its effects on himself were grotesque. Never had the proportions of his ignorance looked so appalling. He seemed to know nothing — to be groping in darkness — to be falling forever in space; and the worst depth consisted in the assurance, incredible as it seemed, that no one knew more. He had, at least, the mechanical assurance of certain values to guide him — like the relative intensities of his Coal-powers, and relative inertia of his Gun-powers — but he conceived that had he known, besides the mechanics, every relative value of persons, as well as he knew the inmost thoughts of his own Government — had the Czar and the Kaiser and the Mikado turned schoolmasters, like Hay, and taught him all they knew, he would still have known nothing. They knew nothing themselves. Only by comparison of their ignorance could the student measure his own.

29

The Abyss of Ignorance

(1902)

The years hurried past, and gave hardly time to note their work. Three or four months, though big with change, come to an end before the mind can catch up with it. Winter vanished; spring burst into flower; and again Paris opened its arms, though not for long. Mr. Cameron came over, and took the castle of Inverlochy for three months, which he summoned his friends to garrison. Lochaber seldom laughs, except for its children, such as Camerons, McDonalds, Campbells and other products of the mist; but in the summer of 1902 Scotland put on fewer airs of coquetry than usual. Since the terrible harvest of 1879 which one had watched sprouting on its stalks on the Shropshire hillsides, nothing had equalled the gloom. Even when the victims fled to Switzerland, they found the Lake of Geneva and the Rhine not much gayer, and Carlsruhe no more restful than Paris; until at last, in desperation, one drifted back to the Avenue of the Bois de Boulogne, and, like the Cuckoo, dropped into the nest of a better citizen. Diplomacy has its uses. Reynolds Hitt, transferred to Berlin, abandoned his attic to Adams, and there, for long summers to come, he hid in ignorance and silence.

Life at last managed of its own accord to settle itself into a working arrangement. After so many years of effort to find one's drift, the drift found the seeker, and slowly swept him forward and back, with a steady progress oceanwards. Such lessons as summer taught, winter tested, and one had only to watch the apparent movement of the stars in order to guess one's declination. The process is possible only for men who have exhausted auto-motion. Adams never knew why, knowing nothing of Faraday, he began to mimic Faraday's trick of seeing lines of force all about him, where he had always seen lines of will. Perhaps the effect of knowing no mathematics is to leave the mind to imagine figures — images — phantoms; one's mind is a watery mirror at best; but, once conceived, the image became rapidly simple, and the lines of force presented themselves as lines of attraction. Repulsions counted only as battle of attractions. By this path, the mind stepped into the mechanical theory of the universe before knowing it, and entered a distinct new phase of education.

This was the work of the dynamo and the Virgin of Chartres. Like his masters, since thought began, he was handicapped by the eternal mystery of Force — the sink of all science. For thousands of years in history, he found that Force had been felt as occult attraction — love of God and lust for power in a future life. After 1500, when this attraction began to decline, philosophers fell back on some *vis a tergo* — instinct of danger from behind, like Darwin's survival of the fittest; and one of the greatest

minds, between Descartes and Newton — Pascal — saw
the master-motor of man in *ennui*, which was also scientific: "I have often said that all the troubles of man come
from his not knowing how to sit still." Mere restlessness
forces action. "So passes the whole of life. We combat
obstacles in order to get repose, and, when got, the repose
is insupportable; for we think either of the troubles we
have, or of those that threaten us; and even if we felt safe
on every side, *ennui* would of its own accord spring up
from the depths of the heart where it is rooted by nature,
and would fill the mind with its venom."

> "If goodness lead him not, yet weariness
>   May toss him to My breast."

Ennui, like Natural Selection, accounted for change,
but failed to account for direction of change. For that,
an attractive force was essential; a force from outside; a
shaping influence. Pascal and all the old philosophies
called this outside force God or Gods. Caring but little
for the name, and fixed only on tracing the Force, Adams
had gone straight to the Virgin at Chartres, and asked her
to show him God, face to face, as she did for St. Bernard.
She replied, kindly as ever, as though she were still the
young mother of to-day, with a sort of patient pity for
masculine dulness: "My dear outcast, what is it you seek?
This is the Church of Christ! If you seek him through
me, you are welcome, sinner or saint; but he and I are
one. We are Love! We have little or nothing to do with
God's other energies which are infinite, and concern us
the less because our interest is only in man, and the infinite
is not knowable to man. Yet if you are troubled by your
ignorance, you see how I am surrounded by the masters
of the schools! Ask them!"

The answer sounded singularly like the usual answer

of British science which had repeated since Bacon that one must not try to know the unknowable, though one was quite powerless to ignore it; but the Virgin carried more conviction, for her feminine lack of interest in all perfections except her own was honester than the formal phrase of science; since nothing was easier than to follow her advice, and turn to Thomas Aquinas, who, unlike modern physicists, answered at once and plainly: "To me," said St. Thomas, "Christ and the Mother are one Force — Love — simple, single, and sufficient for all human wants; but Love is a human interest which acts even on man so partially that you and I, as philosophers, need expect no share in it. Therefore we turn to Christ and the Schools who represent all other Force. We deal with Multiplicity and call it God. After the Virgin has redeemed by her personal Force as Love all that is redeemable in man, the Schools embrace the rest, and give it Form, Unity, and Motive."

This chart of Force was more easily studied than any other possible scheme, for one had but to do what the Church was always promising to do— abolish in one flash of lightning not only man, but also the Church itself, the earth, the other planets, and the sun, in order to clear the air; without affecting mediæval science. The student felt warranted in doing what the Church threatened — abolishing his solar system altogether — in order to look at God as actual; continuous movement, universal cause, and interchangeable force. This was pantheism, but the Schools were pantheist; at least as pantheistic as the *Energetik* of the Germans; and their duty was the ultimate energy, whose thought and act were one.

Rid of man and his mind, the universe of Thomas Aquinas seemed rather more scientific than that of Haeckel or Ernst Mach. Contradiction for contradiction, Attraction for attraction, Energy for energy, St.

Thomas's idea of God had merits. Modern science offered not a vestige of proof, or a theory of connection between its forces, or any scheme of reconciliation between thought and mechanics; while St. Thomas at least linked together the joints of his machine. As far as a superficial student could follow, the thirteenth century supposed mind to be a mode of force directly derived from the intelligent prime motor, and the cause of all form and sequence in the universe — therefore the only proof of unity. Without thought in the unit, there could be no unity; without unity no orderly sequence or ordered society. Thought alone was Form. Mind and Unity flourished or perished together.

This education startled even a man who had dabbled in fifty educations all over the world; for, if he were obliged to insist on a Universe, he seemed driven to the Church. Modern science guaranteed no unity. The student seemed to feel himself, like all his predecessors, caught, trapped, meshed in this eternal drag-net of religion.

In practice the student escapes this dilemma in two ways: the first is that of ignoring it, as one escapes most dilemmas; the second is that the Church rejects pantheism as worse than atheism, and will have nothing to do with the pantheist at any price. In wandering through the forests of ignorance, one necessarily fell upon the famous old bear that scared children at play; but, even had the animal shown more logic than its victim, one had learned from Socrates to distrust, above all other traps, the trap of logic — the mirror of the mind. Yet the search for a unit of force led into catacombs of thought where hundreds of thousands of educations had found their end. Generation after generation of painful and honest-minded scholars had been content to stay in these labyrinths forever, pursuing ignorance in silence, in company with the most famous teachers of all time. Not one of them had ever found a logical highroad of escape.

Adams cared little whether he escaped or not, but he felt clear that he could not stop there, even to enjoy the society of Spinoza and Thomas Aquinas. True, the Church alone had asserted unity with any conviction, and the historian alone knew what oceans of blood and treasure the assertion had cost; but the only honest alternative to affirming unity was to deny it; and the denial would require a new education. At sixty-five years old a new education promised hardly more than the old.

Possibly the modern legislator or magistrate might no longer know enough to treat as the Church did the man who denied unity, unless the denial took the form of a bomb; but no teacher would know how to explain what he thought he meant by denying unity. Society would certainly punish the denial if ever any one learned enough to understand it. Philosophers, as a rule, cared little what principles society affirmed or denied, since the philosopher commonly held that though he might sometimes be right by good luck on some one point, no complex of individual opinions could possibly be anything but wrong; yet, supposing society to be ignored, the philosopher was no further forward. Nihilism had no bottom. For thousands of years every philosopher had stood on the shore of this sunless sea, diving for pearls and never finding them. All had seen that, since they could not find bottom, they must assume it. The Church claimed to have found it, but, since 1450, motives for agreeing on some new assumption of Unity, broader and deeper than that of the Church, had doubled in force until even the universities and schools, like the Church and State, seemed about to be driven into an attempt to educate, though specially forbidden to do it.

Like most of his generation, Adams had taken the word

of science that the new unit was as good as found. It would not be an intelligence — probably not even a consciousness — but it would serve. He passed sixty years waiting for it, and at the end of that time, on reviewing the ground, he was led to think that the final synthesis of science and its ultimate triumph was the kinetic theory of gases; which seemed to cover all motion in space, and to furnish the measure of time. So far as he understood it, the theory asserted that any portion of space is occupied by molecules of gas, flying in right lines at velocities varying up to a mile in a second, and colliding with each other at intervals varying up to 17,750,000 times in a second. To this analysis — if one understood it right — all matter whatever was reducible, and the only difference of opinion in science regarded the doubt whether a still deeper analysis would reduce the atom of gas to pure motion.

Thus, unless one mistook the meaning of motion, which might well be, the scientific synthesis commonly called Unity was the scientific analysis commonly called Multiplicity. The two things were the same, all forms being shifting phases of motion. Granting this ocean of colliding atoms, the last hope of humanity, what happened if one dropped the sounder into the abyss — let it go — frankly gave up Unity altogether? What was Unity? Why was one to be forced to affirm it?

Here everybody flatly refused help. Science seemed content with its old phrase of "larger synthesis," which was well enough for science, but meant chaos for man. One would have been glad to stop and ask no more, but the anarchist bomb bade one go on, and the bomb is a powerful persuader. One could not stop, even to enjoy the charms of a perfect gas colliding seventeen million times in a second, much like an automobile in Paris. Science itself had been crowded so close to the edge of the abyss that its attempts to escape were as metaphysical as the leap, while an ignorant old man felt no motive for trying to escape, seeing that the only escape possible lay in the form of *vis a tergo* commonly called Death. He got out his Descartes again; dipped into his Hume and Berkeley; wrestled anew with his Kant; pondered solemnly over his Hegel and Schopenhauer and Hartmann; strayed gaily away with his Greeks — all merely to ask what Unity meant, and what happened when one denied it.

Apparently one never denied it. Every philosopher, whether sane or insane, naturally affirmed it. The utmost flight of anarchy seemed to have stopped with the assertion of two principles, and even these fitted into each other, like good and evil, light and darkness. Pessimism itself, black as it might be painted, had been content to turn the universe of contradictions into the human thought as one Will, and treat it as representation. Metaphysics insisted on treating the universe as one thought or treating thought as one universe; and philosophers agreed, like kinetic gas, that the universe could be known only as motion of mind, and therefore as unity. One could know it only as one's self; it was psychology.

Of all forms of pessimism, the metaphysical form was, for a historian, the least enticing. Of all studies, the one he would rather have avoided was that of his own mind. He knew no tragedy so heartrending as introspection, and the more, because — as Mephistopheles said of Marguerite — he was not the first. Nearly all the highest intelligence known to history had drowned itself in the reflection of its own thought, and the bovine survivors had rudely told the truth about it, without affecting the intelligent. One's own time had not been exempt. Even since 1870 friends by scores had fallen victims to it. Within five-and-twenty years, a new library had grown out of it. Harvard College was a focus of the study; France supported hospitals for it; England published magazines of it. Nothing was easier than to take one's mind in one's hand, and ask one's psychological friends what they made of it, and the more because it mattered so little to either party, since their minds, whatever they were, had pretty nearly ceased to reflect, and let them do what they liked with the small remnant, they could scarcely do anything very new with it. All one asked was to learn what they hoped to do.

Unfortunately the pursuit of ignorance in silence had, by this time, led the weary pilgrim into such mountains of ignorance that he could no longer see any path whatever, and could not even understand a signpost. He failed to fathom the depths of the new psychology, which proved to him that, on that side as on the mathematical side, his power of thought was atrophied, if, indeed, it ever existed. Since he could not fathom the science, he could only ask the simplest of questions: Did the new psychology hold that the ψυχή — soul or mind — was or was not a unit? He gathered from the books that the psychologists had, in a few cases, distinguished several personalities in the same mind, each conscious and constant, individual and exclusive. The fact seemed scarcely surprising, since it had been a habit of mind from earliest recorded time, and equally familiar to the last acquaintance who had taken a drug or caught a fever, or eaten a Welsh rarebit before bed; for surely no one could follow the action of a vivid dream, and still need to be told that the actors evoked by his mind were not himself, but quite unknown to all he had ever recognized as self. The new psychology went further, and seemed convinced that it had actually split personality not only into dualism, but also into complex groups, like telephonic centres and systems, that might be isolated and called up at will, and whose physical action might be occult in the sense of strangeness to any known form of force. Dualism seemed to have become as common as binary stars. Alternating personalities turned up constantly, even among one's friends. The facts seemed certain, or at least as certain as other facts; all they needed was explanation.

This was not the business of the searcher of ignorance, who felt himself in no way responsible for causes. To his mind, the compound $\nu\chi\acute{\eta}$ took at once the form of a bicycle-rider, mechanically balancing himself by inhibiting all his inferior personalities, and sure to fall into the sub-conscious chaos below, if one of his inferior personalities got on top. The only absolute truth was the sub-conscious chaos below, which every one could feel when he sought it.

Whether the psychologists admitted it or not, mattered little to the student who, by the law of his profession, was engaged in studying his own mind. On him, the effect was surprising. He woke up with a shudder as though he had himself fallen off his bicycle. If his mind were really this sort of magnet, mechanically dispersing its lines of force when it went to sleep, and mechanically orienting them when it woke up — which was normal, the dispersion or orientation? The mind, like the body, kept its unity unless it happened to lose balance, but the professor of physics, who slipped on a pavement and hurt himself, knew no more than an idiot what knocked him down, though he did know — what the idiot could hardly do — that his normal condition was idiocy, or want of balance, and that his sanity was unstable artifice. His normal thought was dispersion, sleep, dream, inconsequence; the simultaneous action of different thought-centres without central control. His artificial balance was acquired habit. He was an acrobat, with a dwarf on his back, crossing a chasm on a slack-rope, and commonly breaking his neck.

By that path of newest science, one saw no unity ahead

— nothing but a dissolving mind — and the historian felt himself driven back on thought as one continuous Force, without Race, Sex, School, Country, or Church. This has been always the fate of rigorous thinkers, and has always succeeded in making them famous, as it did Gibbon, Buckle, and Auguste Comte. Their method made what progress the science of history knew, which was little enough, but they did at last fix the law that, if history ever meant to correct the errors she made in detail, she must agree on a scale for the whole. Every local historian might defy this law till history ended, but its necessity would be the same for man as for space or time or force, and without it the historian would always remain a child in science.

Any schoolboy could see that man as a force must be measured by motion, from a fixed point. Psychology helped here by suggesting a unit — the point of history when man held the highest idea of himself as a unit in a unified universe. Eight or ten years of study had led Adams to think he might use the century 1150–1250, expressed in Amiens Cathedral and the Works of Thomas Aquinas, as the unit from which he might measure motion down to his own time, without assuming anything as true or untrue, except relation. The movement might be studied at once in philosophy and mechanics. Setting himself to the task, he began a volume which he mentally knew as "Mont-Saint-Michel and Chartres: a Study of Thirteenth-Century Unity." From that point he proposed to fix a position for himself, which he could label: "The Education of Henry Adams: a Study of Twentieth-Century Multiplicity." With the help of these two points of relation, he hoped to project his lines forward and backward indefinitely, subject to correction from any one who should know better. Thereupon, he sailed for home.

30

Vis
Inertiae

(1903)

Washington was always amusing, but in 1900, as in 1800, its chief interest lay in its distance from New York. The movement of New York had become planetary — beyond control — while the task of Washington, in 1900 as in 1800, was to control it. The success of Washington in the past century promised ill for its success in the next.

To a student who had passed the best years of his life in pondering over the political philosophy of Jefferson, Gallatin, and Madison, the problem that Roosevelt took in hand seemed alive with historical interest, but it would need at least another half-century to show its results. As yet, one could not measure the forces or their arrangement; the forces had not even aligned themselves except in foreign affairs; and there one turned to seek the channel of wisdom as naturally as though Washington did not exist. The President could do nothing effectual in foreign affairs, but at least he could see something of the field.

Hay had reached the summit of his career, and saw himself on the edge of wreck. Committed to the task of keeping China "open," he saw China about to be shut.

Almost alone in the world, he represented the "open door," and could not escape being crushed by it. Yet luck had been with him in full tide. Though Sir Julian Paunce-fote had died in May, 1902, after carrying out tasks that filled an ex-private secretary of 1861 with open-mouthed astonishment, Hay had been helped by the appointment of Michael Herbert as his successor, who counted for double the value of an ordinary diplomat. To reduce fric-tion is the chief use of friendship, and in politics the loss by friction is outrageous. To Herbert and his wife, the small knot of houses that seemed to give a vague unity to foreign affairs opened their doors and their hearts, for the Herberts were already at home there; and this personal sympathy prolonged Hay's life, for it not only eased the effort of endurance, but it also led directly to a revolution in Germany. Down to that moment, the Kaiser, rightly or wrongly, had counted as the ally of the Czar in all matters relating to the East. Holleben and Cassini were taken to be a single force in Eastern affairs, and this supposed alliance gave Hay no little anxiety and some trouble. Suddenly Holleben, who seemed to have had no thought but to obey with almost agonized anxiety the least hint of the Kaiser's will, received a telegram ordering him to pretext illness and come home, which he obeyed within four-and-twenty hours. The ways of the German Foreign Office had been always abrupt, not to say ruthless, to-wards its agents, and yet commonly some discontent had been shown as excuse; but, in this case, no cause was guessed for Holleben's disgrace except the Kaiser's wish to have a personal representative at Washington. Breaking down all precedent, he sent Speck von Sternburg to coun-terbalance Herbert.

Welcome as Speck was in the same social intimacy, and valuable as his presence was to Hay, the personal gain was trifling compared with the political. Of Hay's official tasks, one knew no more than any newspaper reporter did, but of one's own diplomatic education the successive steps had become strides. The scholar was studying, not on Hay's account, but on his own. He had seen Hay, in 1898, bring England into his combine; he had seen the steady movement which was to bring France back into an Atlantic system; and now he saw suddenly the dramatic swing of Germany towards the west — the movement of all others nearest mathematical certainty. Whether the Kaiser meant it or not, he gave the effect of meaning to assert his independence of Russia, and to Hay this change of front had enormous value. The least was that it seemed to isolate Cassini, and unmask the Russian movement which became more threatening every month as the Manchurian scheme had to be revealed.

Of course the student saw whole continents of study opened to him by the Kaiser's *coup d'état*. Carefully as he had tried to follow the Kaiser's career, he had never suspected such refinement of policy, which raised his opinion of the Kaiser's ability to the highest point, and altogether upset the centre of statesmanship. That Germany could be so quickly detached from separate objects and brought into an Atlantic system seemed a paradox more paradoxical than any that one's education had yet offered, though it had offered little but paradox. If Germany could be held there, a century of friction would be saved. No price would be too great for such an object; although no price could probably be wrung out of Congress as equivalent for it. The Kaiser, by one personal act of energy, freed Hay's hands so completely that he saw his problems simplified to Russia alone.

Naturally Russia was a problem ten times as difficult. The history of Europe for two hundred years had accomplished little but to state one or two sides of the Russian problem. One's year of Berlin in youth, though it taught no Civil Law, had opened one's eyes to the Russian enigma, and both German and French historians had labored over its proportions with a sort of fascinated horror. Germany, of all countries, was most vitally concerned in it; but even a cave-dweller in La Fayette Square, seeking only a measure of motion since the Crusades, saw before his eyes, in the spring of 1903, a survey of future order or anarchy that would exhaust the power of his telescopes and defy the accuracy of his theodolites.

The drama had become passionately interesting and grew every day more Byzantine; for the Russian Government itself showed clear signs of dislocation, and the orders of Lamsdorf and de Witte were reversed when applied in Manchuria. Historians and students should have no sympathies or antipathies, but Adams had private reasons for wishing well to the Czar and his people. At much length, in several labored chapters of history, he had told how the personal friendliness of the Czar Alexander I, in 1810, saved the fortunes of J. Q. Adams, and opened to him the brilliant diplomatic career that ended in the White House. Even in his own effaced existence he had reasons, not altogether trivial, for gratitude to the Czar Alexander II, whose firm neutrality had saved him some terribly anxious days and nights in 1862; while he had seen enough of Russia to sympathize warmly with Prince Khilkoff's railways and de Witte's industries. The last and highest triumph of history would, to his mind, be the bringing of Russia into the Atlantic combine, and the just and fair allotment of the whole world among the regulated activities of the universe. At the rate of unification since 1840, this end should be possible within another sixty years; and, in foresight of that point, Adams could already finish — provisionally — his chart of international unity; but, for the moment, the gravest doubts and ignorance covered the whole field. No one — Czar or diplomat,

Kaiser or Mikado — seemed to know anything. Through individual Russians one could always see with ease, for their diplomacy never suggested depth; and perhaps Hay protected Cassini for the very reason that Cassini could not disguise an emotion, and never failed to betray that, in setting the enormous bulk of Russian inertia to roll over China, he regretted infinitely that he should have to roll it over Hay too. He would almost rather have rolled it over de Witte and Lamsdorf. His political philosophy, like that of all Russians, seemed fixed in the single idea that Russia must fatally roll — must, by her irresistible inertia, crush whatever stood in her way.

For Hay and his pooling policy, inherited from Mc-Kinley, the fatalism of Russian inertia meant the failure of American intensity. When Russia rolled over a neighboring people, she absorbed their energies in her own movement of custom and race which neither Czar nor peasant could convert, or wished to convert, into any Western equivalent. In 1903 Hay saw Russia knocking away the last blocks that held back the launch of this huge mass into the China Sea. The vast force of inertia known as China was to be united with the huge bulk of Russia in a single mass which no amount of new force could henceforward deflect. Had the Russian Government, with the sharpest sense of enlightenment, employed scores of de Wittes and Khilkoffs, and borrowed all the resources of Europe, it could not have lifted such a weight; and had no idea of trying.

These were the positions charted on the map of political unity by an insect in Washington in the spring of 1903; and they seemed to him fixed. Russia held Europe and America in her grasp, and Cassini held Hay in his. The Siberian Railway offered checkmate to all possible opposition. Japan must make the best terms she could; England must go on receding; America and Germany

would look on at the avalanche. The wall of Russian
inertia that barred Europe across the Baltic, would bar
America across the Pacific; and Hay's policy of the open
door would infallibly fail.

Thus the game seemed lost, in spite of the Kaiser's
brilliant stroke, and the movement of Russia eastward
must drag Germany after it by its mere mass. To the humble student, the loss of Hay's game affected only Hay;
for himself, the game — not the stakes — was the chief
interest; and though want of habit made him object to
read his newspapers blackened — since he liked to blacken
them himself — he was in any case condemned to pass but
a short space of time either in Siberia or in Paris, and could
balance his endless columns of calculation equally in either
place. The figures, not the facts, concerned his chart, and
he mused deeply over his next equation. The Atlantic
would have to deal with a vast continental mass of inert
motion, like a glacier, which moved, and consciously
moved, by mechanical gravitation alone. Russia saw herself so, and so must an American see her; he had no more
to do than measure, if he could, the mass. Was volume or
intensity the stronger? What and where was the *vis nova*
that could hold its own before this prodigious ice-cap of
vis inertiae? What was movement of inertia, and what its
laws?

Naturally a student knew nothing about mechanical
laws, but he took for granted that he could learn, and went
to his books to ask. He found that the force of inertia
had troubled wiser men than he. The dictionary said that
inertia was a property of matter, by which matter tends,
when at rest, to remain so, and, when in motion, to move
on in a straight line. Finding that his mind refused to
imagine itself at rest or in a straight line, he was forced,
as usual, to let it imagine something else; and since the
question concerned the mind, and not matter, he decided

from personal experience that his mind was never at rest, but moved — when normal — about something it called a motive, and never moved without motives to move it. So long as these motives were habitual, and their attraction regular, the consequent result might, for convenience, be called movement of inertia, to distinguish it from movement caused by newer or higher attraction; but the greater the bulk to move, the greater must be the force to accelerate or deflect it.

This seemed simple as running water; but simplicity is the most deceitful mistress that ever betrayed man. For years the student and the professor had gone on complaining that minds were unequally inert. The inequalities amounted to contrasts. One class of minds responded only to habit; another only to novelty. Race classified thought. Class-lists classified mind. No two men thought alike, and no woman thought like a man.

Race-inertia seemed to be fairly constant, and made the chief trouble in the Russian future. History looked doubtful when asked whether race-inertia had ever been overcome without destroying the race in order to reconstruct it; but surely sex-inertia had never been overcome at all. Of all movements of inertia, maternity and reproduction are the most typical, and women's property of moving in a constant line forever is ultimate, uniting history in its only unbroken and unbreakable sequence. Whatever else stops, the woman must go on reproducing, as she did in the Siluria of *Pteraspis;* sex is a vital condition, and race only a local one. If the laws of inertia are to be sought anywhere with certainty, it is in the feminine mind. The American always ostentatiously ignored sex, and American history mentioned hardly the name of a woman, while English history handled them as timidly as though they were a new and undescribed species; but if the problem of inertia summed up the difficulties of the race question, it involved that of sex far more deeply, and to Americans vitally. The task of accelerating or deflecting the movement of the American woman had interest infinitely greater than that of any race whatever, Russian or Chinese, Asiatic or African.

On this subject, as on the Senate and the banks, Adams was conscious of having been born an eighteenth-century remainder. As he grew older, he found that Early Institutions lost their interest, but that Early Women became a passion. Without understanding movement of sex, history seemed to him mere pedantry. So insistent had he become on this side of his subject that with women he talked of little else, and — because women's thought is mostly subconscious and particularly sensitive to suggestion — he tried tricks and devices to disclose it. The woman seldom knows her own thought; she is as curious to understand herself as the man to understand her, and responds far more quickly than the man to a sudden idea. Sometimes, at dinner, one might wait till talk flagged, and then, as mildly as possible, ask one's liveliest neighbor whether she could explain why the American woman was a failure. Without an instant's hesitation, she was sure to answer: "Because the American man is a failure!" She meant it.

Adams owed more to the American woman than to all the American men he ever heard of, and felt not the smallest call to defend his sex who seemed able to take care of themselves; but from the point of view of sex he felt much curiosity to know how far the woman was right, and, in pursuing this inquiry, he caught the trick of affirming that the woman was the superior. Apart from truth, he owed her at least that compliment. The habit led sometimes to perilous personalities in the sudden give-and-take of table-talk. This spring, just before sailing for Europe in May, 1903, he had a message from his sister-in-law, Mrs. Brooks Adams, to say that she and her sister, Mrs. Lodge, and the Senator were coming to dinner by way of farewell; Bay Lodge and his lovely young wife sent word to the same effect; Mrs. Roosevelt joined the party; and Michael Herbert shyly slipped down to escape the solitude of his wife's absence. The party were too intimate for reserve, and they soon fell on Adams's hobby with derision which stung him to pungent rejoinder: "The American man is a failure! You are all failures!" he said. "Has not my sister here more sense than my brother Brooks? Is not Bessie worth two of Bay? Wouldn't we all elect Mrs. Lodge Senator against Cabot? Would the President have a ghost of a chance if Mrs. Roosevelt ran against him? Do you want to stop at the Embassy, on your way home, and ask which would run it best — Herbert or his wife?" The men laughed a little — not much! Each probably made allowance for his own wife as an unusually superior woman. Some one afterwards remarked that these half-dozen women were not a fair average. Adams replied that the half-dozen men were above all possible average; he could not lay his hands on another half-dozen their equals.

Gay or serious, the question never failed to stir feeling. The cleverer the woman, the less she denied the failure. She was bitter at heart about it. She had failed even to hold the family together, and her children ran away like chickens with their first feathers; the family was extinct like chivalry. She had failed not only to create a new society that satisfied her, but even to hold her own in the old society of Church or State; and was left, for the most part, with no place but the theatre or streets to decorate. She might glitter with historical diamonds and sparkle with wit as brilliant as the gems, in rooms as splendid as any in Rome at its best; but she saw no one except her own sex who knew enough to be worth dazzling, or was competent to pay her intelligent homage. She might have her own way, without restraint or limit, but she knew not what to do with herself when free. Never had the world known a more capable or devoted mother, but at forty her task was over, and she was left with no stage except that of her old duties, or of Washington society where she had enjoyed for a hundred years every advantage, but had created only a medley where nine men out of ten refused her request to be civilized, and the tenth bored her.

On most subjects, one's opinions must defer to science, but on this, the opinion of a Senator or a Professor, a chairman of a State Central Committee or a Railway President, is worth less than that of any woman on Fifth Avenue. The inferiority of man on this, the most important of all social subjects, is manifest. Adams had here no occasion to deprecate scientific opinion, since no woman in the world would have paid the smallest respect to the opinions of all professors since the serpent. His own object had little to do with theirs. He was studying the laws of motion, and had struck two large questions of vital importance to America — inertia of race and inertia of sex. He had seen Mr. de Witte and Prince Khilkoff turn artificial energy to the value of three thousand million dollars, more or less, upon Russian inertia, in the last twenty years, and he needed to get some idea of the effects. He had seen artificial energy to the amount of twenty or five-and-twenty million steam horse-power created in America since 1840, and as much more economized, which had been socially turned over to the American woman, she being the chief object of social expenditure, and the household the only considerable object of American extravagance. According to scientific notions of inertia and force, what ought to be the result?

In Russia, because of race and bulk, no result had yet

shown itself, but in America the results were evident and undisputed. The woman had been set free — volatilized like Clerk Maxwell's perfect gas; almost brought to the point of explosion, like steam. One had but to pass a week in Florida, or on any of a hundred huge ocean steamers, or walk through the Place Vendôme, or join a party of Cook's tourists to Jerusalem, to see that the woman had been set free; but these swarms were ephemeral like clouds of butterflies in season, blown away and lost, while the reproductive sources lay hidden. At Washington, one saw other swarms as grave gatherings of Dames or Daughters, taking themselves seriously, or brides fluttering fresh pinions; but all these shifting visions, unknown before 1840, touched the true problem slightly and superficially. Behind them, in every city, town, and farmhouse, were myriads of new types — or type-writers — telephone and telegraph-girls, shop-clerks, factory-hands, running into millions of millions, and, as classes, unknown to themselves as to historians. Even the schoolmistresses were inarticulate. All these new women had been created since 1840; all were to show their meaning before 1940.

Whatever they were, they were not content, as the ephemera proved; and they were hungry for illusions as ever in the fourth century of the Church; but this was probably survival, and gave no hint of the future. The problem remained — to find out whether movement of inertia, inherent in function, could take direction except in lines of inertia. This problem needed to be solved in one generation of American women, and was the most vital of all problems of force.

The American woman at her best — like most other women — exerted great charm on the man, but not the charm of a primitive type. She appeared as the result of a long series of discards, and her chief interest lay in what she had discarded. When closely watched, she seemed making a violent effort to follow the man, who had turned his mind and hand to mechanics. The typical American man had his hand on a lever and his eye on a curve in his road; his living depended on keeping up an average speed of forty miles an hour, tending always to become sixty, eighty, or a hundred, and he could not admit emotions or anxieties or subconscious distractions, more than he could admit whiskey or drugs, without breaking his neck. He could not run his machine and a woman too; he must leave her, even though his wife, to find her own way, and all the world saw her trying to find her way by imitating him.

The result was often tragic, but that was no new thing in feminine history. Tragedy had been woman's lot since Eve. Her problem had been always one of physical strength and it was as physical perfection of force that her Venus had governed nature. The woman's force had counted as inertia of rotation, and her axis of rotation had been the cradle and the family. The idea that she was weak revolted all history; it was a palæontological falsehood that even an Eocene female monkey would have laughed at; but it was surely true that, if her force were to be diverted from its axis, it must find a new field, and the family must pay for it. So far as she succeeded, she must become sexless like the bees, and must leave the old energy of inertia to carry on the race.

The story was not new. For thousands of years women had rebelled. They had made a fortress of religion — had buried themselves in the cloister, in self-sacrifice, in good works — or even in bad. One's studies in the twelfth century, like one's studies in the fourth, as in Homeric and archaic time, showed her always busy in the illusions of heaven or of hell — ambition, intrigue, jealousy, magic — but the American woman had no illusions or ambitions or new resources, and nothing to rebel against, except her own maternity; yet the rebels increased by millions from year to year till they blocked the path of rebellion. Even her field of good works was narrower than in the twelfth century. Socialism, communism, collectivism, philosophical anarchism, which promised paradise on earth for every male, cut off the few avenues of escape which capitalism had opened to the woman, and she saw before her only the future reserved for machine-made, collectivist females.

From the male, she could look for no help; his instinct of power was blind. The Church had known more about women than science will ever know, and the historian who studied the sources of Christianity felt sometimes convinced that the Church had been made by the woman chiefly as her protest against man. At times, the historian would have been almost willing to maintain that the man had overthrown the Church chiefly because it was feminine. After the overthrow of the Church, the woman had no refuge except such as the man created for himself. She was free; she had no illusions; she was sexless; she had discarded all that the male disliked; and although she secretly regretted the discard, she knew that she could not go backward. She must, like the man, marry machinery. Already the American man sometimes felt surprise at finding himself regarded as sexless; the American woman was oftener surprised at finding herself regarded as sexual.

No honest historian can take part with — or against — the forces he has to study. To him even the extinction of the human race should be merely a fact to be grouped with other vital statistics. No doubt every one in society discussed the subject, impelled by President Roosevelt if by nothing else, and the surface current of social opinion seemed set as strongly in one direction as the silent undercurrent of social action ran in the other; but the truth lay somewhere unconscious in the woman's breast. An elderly man, trying only to learn the law of social inertia and the limits of social divergence could not compel the Superintendent of the Census to ask every young woman whether she wanted children, and how many; he could not even require of an octogenarian Senate the passage of a law obliging every woman, married or not, to bear one baby — at the expense of the Treasury — before she was thirty years old, under penalty of solitary confinement for life; yet these were vital statistics in more senses than all that bore the name, and tended more directly to the foundation of a serious society in the future. He could draw no conclusions whatever except from the birth-rate. He could not frankly discuss the matter with the young women themselves, although they would have gladly discussed it, because Faust was helpless in the tragedy of woman. He could suggest nothing. The Marguerite of the future could alone decide whether she were better off than the Marguerite of the past; whether she would rather be victim to a man, a church, or a machine.

Between these various forms of inevitable inertia — sex and race — the student of multiplicity felt inclined to admit that — ignorance against ignorance — the Russian problem seemed to him somewhat easier of treatment than the American. Inertia of race and bulk would require an immense force to overcome it, but in time it might perhaps be partially overcome. Inertia of sex could not be overcome without extinguishing the race, yet an immense force, doubling every few years, was working irresistibly to overcome it. One gazed mute before this ocean of darkest ignorance that had already engulfed society. Few centres of great energy lived in illusion more complete or archaic than Washington with its simple-minded standards of the field and farm, its Southern and Western habits of life and manners, its assumptions of ethics and history; but even in Washington, society was uneasy enough to need no further fretting. One was almost glad to act the part of horseshoe crab in Quincy Bay, and admit that all was uniform — that nothing ever changed — and that the woman would swim about the ocean of future time, as she had swum in the past, with the gar-fish and the shark, unable to change.

31

The
Grammar
of Science

(1903)

Of all the travels made by man since the voyages of Dante, this new exploration along the shores of Multiplicity and Complexity promised to be the longest, though as yet it had barely touched two familiar regions — race and sex. Even within these narrow seas the navigator lost his bearings and followed the winds as they blew. By chance it happened that Raphael Pumpelly helped the winds; for, being in Washington on his way to Central Asia he fell to talking with Adams about these matters, and said that Willard Gibbs thought he got most help from a book called the "Grammar of Science," by Karl Pearson. To Adams's vision, Willard Gibbs stood on the same plane with the three or four greatest minds of his century, and the idea that a man so incomparably superior should find help anywhere filled him with wonder. He sent for the volume and read it. From the time he sailed for Europe and reached his den on the Avenue du Bois until he took his return steamer at Cherbourg on December 26, he did little but try to find out what Karl Pearson could have taught Willard Gibbs.

Here came in, more than ever, the fatal handicap of ignorance in mathematics. Not so much the actual tool was needed, as the right to judge the product of the tool. Ignorant as one was of the finer values of French or German, and often deceived by the intricacies of thought hidden in the muddiness of the medium, one could sometimes catch a tendency to intelligible meaning even in Kant or Hegel; but one had not the right to a suspicion of error where the tool of thought was algebra. Adams could see in such parts of the "Grammar" as he could understand, little more than an enlargement of Stallo's book already twenty years old. He never found out what it could have taught a master like Willard Gibbs. Yet the book had a historical value out of all proportion to its science. No such stride had any Englishman before taken in the lines of English thought. The progress of science was measured by the success of the "Grammar," when, for twenty years past, Stallo had been deliberately ignored under the usual conspiracy of silence inevitable to all thought which demands new thought-machinery. Science needs time to reconstruct its instruments, to follow a revolution in space; a certain lag is inevitable; the most active mind cannot instantly swerve from its path; but such revolutions are portentous, and the fall or rise of half-a-dozen empires interested a student of history less than the rise of the "Grammar of Science," the more pressingly because, under the silent influence of Langley, he was prepared to expect it.

For a number of years Langley had published in his Smithsonian Reports the revolutionary papers that foretold the overflow of nineteenth-century dogma, and among the first was the famous address of Sir William Crookes on psychical research, followed by a series of

papers on Roentgen and Curie, which had steadily driven
the scientific lawgivers of Unity into the open; but Karl
Pearson was the first to pen them up for slaughter in the
schools. The phrase is not stronger than that with which
the "Grammar of Science" challenged the fight: "Anything more hopelessly illogical than the statements with
regard to Force and Matter current in elementary textbooks of science, it is difficult to imagine," opened Mr.
Pearson, and the responsible author of the "elementary
textbook," as he went on to explain, was Lord Kelvin
himself. Pearson shut out of science everything which the
nineteenth century had brought into it. He told his scholars that they must put up with a fraction of the universe,
and a very small fraction at that — the circle reached by
the senses, where sequence could be taken for granted —
much as the deep-sea fish takes for granted the circle of
light which he generates. "Order and reason, beauty and
benevolence, are characteristics and conceptions which
we find solely associated with the mind of man." The
assertion, as a broad truth, left one's mind in some doubt
of its bearing, for order and beauty seemed to be associated also in the mind of a crystal, if one's senses were
to be admitted as judge; but the historian had no interest
in the universal truth of Pearson's or Kelvin's or Newton's
laws; he sought only their relative drift or direction, and
Pearson went on to say that these conceptions must stop:
"Into the chaos beyond sense-impressions we cannot
scientifically project them." We cannot even infer them:
"In the chaos behind sensations, in the 'beyond' of sense-
impressions, we cannot infer necessity, order or routine,
for these are concepts formed by the mind of man on this
side of sense-impressions"; but we must infer chaos:
"Briefly chaos is all that science can logically assert of
the supersensuous." The kinetic theory of gas is an asser-

tion of ultimate chaos. In plain words, Chaos was the law of nature; Order was the dream of man.

No one means all he says, and yet very few say all they mean, for words are slippery and thought is viscous; but since Bacon and Newton, English thought had gone on impatiently protesting that no one must try to know the unknowable at the same time that every one went on thinking about it. The result was as chaotic as kinetic gas; but with the thought a historian had nothing to do. He sought only its direction. For himself he knew, that, in spite of all the Englishmen that ever lived, he would be forced to enter supersensual chaos if he meant to find out what became of British science — or indeed of any other science. From Pythagoras to Herbert Spencer, every one had done it, although commonly science had explored an ocean which it preferred to regard as Unity or a Universe, and called Order. Even Hegel, who taught that every notion included its own negation, used the negation only to reach a "larger synthesis," till he reached the universal which thinks itself, contradiction and all. The Church alone had constantly protested that anarchy was not order, that Satan was not God, that pantheism was worse than atheism, and that Unity could not be proved as a contradiction. Karl Pearson seemed to agree with the Church, but every one else, including Newton, Darwin and Clerk Maxwell, had sailed gaily into the supersensual, calling it: —

> "One God, one Law, one Element,
> And one far-off, divine event,
> To which the whole creation moves."

Suddenly, in 1900, science raised its head and denied. Yet, perhaps, after all, the change had not been so sudden as it seemed. Real and actual, it certainly was, and every newspaper betrayed it, but sequence could scarcely be denied by one who had watched its steady approach, thinking the change far more interesting to history than the thought. When he reflected about it, he recalled that the flow of tide had shown itself at least twenty years before; that it had become marked as early as 1893; and that the man of science must have been sleepy indeed who did not jump from his chair like a scared dog when, in 1898, Mme. Curie threw on his desk the metaphysical bomb she called radium. There remained no hole to hide in. Even metaphysics swept back over science with the green water of the deep-sea ocean and no one could longer hope to bar out the unknowable, for the unknowable was known.

The fact was admitted that the uniformitarians of one's youth had wound about their universe a tangle of contradictions meant only for temporary support to be merged in "larger synthesis," and had waited for the larger synthesis in silence and in vain. They had refused to hear Stallo. They had betrayed little interest in Crookes. At last their universe had been wrecked by rays, and Karl Pearson undertook to cut the wreck loose with an axe, leaving science adrift on a sensual raft in the midst of a supersensual chaos. The confusion seemed, to a mere passenger, worse than that of 1600 when the astronomers upset the world; it resembled rather the convulsion of 310 when the *Civitas Dei* cut itself loose from the *Civitas Romae*, and the Cross took the place of the legions; but the historian accepted it all alike; he knew that his opinion was worthless; only, in this case, he found himself on the raft, personally and economically concerned in its drift.

English thought had always been chaos and multiplicity itself, in which the new step of Karl Pearson marked only a consistent progress; but German thought had affected system, unity, and abstract truth, to a point that fretted the most patient foreigner, and to Germany the voyager in strange seas of thought alone might resort with confident hope of renewing his youth. Turning his back on Karl Pearson and England, he plunged into Germany, and had scarcely crossed the Rhine when he fell into libraries of new works bearing the names of Ostwald, Ernst Mach, Ernst Haeckel, and others less familiar, among whom Haeckel was easiest to approach, not only because of being the oldest and clearest and steadiest spokesman of nineteenth-century mechanical convictions, but also because in 1902 he had published a vehement renewal of his faith. The volume contained only one paragraph that concerned a historian; it was that in which Haeckel sank his voice almost to a religious whisper in avowing with evident effort, that the "proper essence of substance appeared to him more and more marvellous and enigmatic as he penetrated further into the knowledge of its attributes — matter and energy — and as he learned to know their innumerable phenomena and their evolution." Since Haeckel seemed to have begun the voyage into multiplicity that Pearson had forbidden to Englishmen, he should have been a safe pilot to the point, at least, of a "proper essence of substance" in its attributes of matter and energy; but Ernst Mach seemed to go yet one step further, for he rejected matter altogether, and admitted but two processes in nature — change of place and interconversion of forms. Matter was Motion — Motion was Matter — the thing moved.

A student of history had no need to understand these scientific ideas of very great men; he sought only the relation with the ideas of their grandfathers, and their common direction towards the ideas of their grandsons. He had long ago reached, with Hegel, the limits of contradiction; and Ernst Mach scarcely added a shade of variety to the identity of opposites; but both of them seemed to be in agreement with Karl Pearson on the facts of the supersensual universe which could be known only as unknowable.

With a deep sigh of relief, the traveller turned back to France. There he felt safe. No Frenchman except Rabelais and Montaigne had ever taught anarchy other than as path to order. Chaos would be unity in Paris even if child of the guillotine. To make this assurance mathematically sure, the highest scientific authority in France was a great mathematician, M. Poincaré of the Institut, who published in 1902 a small volume called "La Science et l'Hypothèse," which purported to be relatively readable. Trusting to its external appearance, the traveller timidly bought it, and greedily devoured it, without understanding a single consecutive page, but catching here and there a period that startled him to the depths of his ignorance, for they seemed to show that M. Poincaré was troubled by the same historical landmarks which guided or deluded Adams himself: "[In science] we are led," said M. Poincaré, "to act as though a simple law, when other things were equal, must be more probable than a complicated law. Half a century ago one frankly confessed it, and proclaimed that nature loves simplicity. She has since given us too often the lie. To-day this tendency is no longer avowed, and only as much of it is preserved as is indispensable so that science shall not become impossible."

Here at last was a fixed point beyond the chance of confusion with self-suggestion. History and mathematics agreed. Had M. Poincaré shown anarchistic tastes, his evidence would have weighed less heavily; but he seemed to be the only authority in science who felt what a historian felt so strongly — the need of unity in a universe. "Considering everything we have made some approach towards unity. We have not gone as fast as we hoped fifty years ago; we have not always taken the intended road;

but definitely we have gained much ground." This was the most clear and convincing evidence of progress yet offered to the navigator of ignorance; but suddenly he fell on another view which seemed to him quite irreconcilable with the first: "Doubtless if our means of investigation should become more and more penetrating, we should discover the simple under the complex; then the complex under the simple; then anew the simple under the complex; and so on without ever being able to foresee the last term."

A mathematical paradise of endless displacement promised eternal bliss to the mathematician, but turned the historian green with horror. Made miserable by the thought that he knew no mathematics, he burned to ask whether M. Poincaré knew any history, since he began by begging the historical question altogether, and assuming that the past showed alternating phases of simple and complex — the precise point that Adams, after fifty years of effort, found himself forced to surrender; and then going on to assume alternating phases for the future which, for the weary Titan of Unity, differed in nothing essential from the kinetic theory of a perfect gas.

Since monkeys first began to chatter in trees, neither man nor beast had ever denied or doubted Multiplicity, Diversity, Complexity, Anarchy, Chaos. Always and everywhere the Complex had been true and the Contradiction had been certain. Thought started by it. Mathematics itself began by counting one — two — three; then imagining their continuity, which M. Poincaré was still exhausting his wits to explain or defend; and this was his explanation: "In short, the mind has the faculty of creating symbols, and it is thus that it has constructed mathematical continuity which is only a particular system of symbols." With the same light touch, more destructive in its artistic measure than the heaviest-handed brutality of Englishmen or Germans, he went on to upset relative truth itself: "How should I answer the question whether Euclidian Geometry is true? It has no sense! . . . Euclidian Geometry is, and will remain, the most convenient."

Chaos was a primary fact even in Paris — especially in Paris — as it was in the Book of Genesis; but every thinking being in Paris or out of it had exhausted thought in the effort to prove Unity, Continuity, Purpose, Order, Law, Truth, the Universe, God, after having begun by taking it for granted, and discovering, to their profound dismay, that some minds denied it. The direction of mind, as a single force of nature, had been constant since history began. Its own unity had created a universe the essence of which was abstract Truth; the Absolute; God! To Thomas Aquinas, the universe was still a person; to Spinoza, a substance; to Kant, Truth was the essence of the "I"; an innate conviction; a categorical imperative; to Poincaré, it was a convenience; and to Karl Pearson, a medium of exchange.

The historian never stopped repeating to himself that he knew nothing about it; that he was a mere instrument of measure, a barometer, pedometer, radiometer; and that his whole share in the matter was restricted to the measurement of thought-motion as marked by the accepted thinkers. He took their facts for granted. He knew no more than a firefly about rays — or about race — or sex — or ennui — or a bar of music — or a pang of love — or a grain of musk — or of phosphorus — or conscience — or duty — or the force of Euclidian geometry — or non-Euclidian — or heat — or light — or osmosis — or electrolysis — or the magnet — or ether — or *vis inertiae* — or gravitation — or cohesion — or elasticity — or surface tension — or capillary attraction — or Brownian motion — or of some scores, or thousands, or millions of chemical attractions, repulsions or indifferences which were busy within and without him; or, in brief, of Force itself, which, he was credibly informed, bore some dozen definitions in the textbooks, mostly contradictory, and all, as he was assured, beyond his intelligence; but summed up in the dictum of the last and highest science, that Motion seems to be Matter and Matter seems to be Motion, yet "we are probably incapable of discovering" what either is. History had no need to ask what either might be; all it needed to know was the admission of ignorance; the mere fact of multiplicity baffling science. Even as to the fact, science disputed, but radium happened to radiate something that seemed to explode the scientific magazine, bringing thought, for the time, to a standstill; though, in the line of thought-movement in history, radium was merely the next position, familiar and inexplicable since Zeno and his arrow: continuous from the beginning of time, and discontinuous at each successive point. History set it down on the record — pricked its position on the chart — and waited to be led, or misled, once more.

The historian must not try to know what is truth, if he values his honesty; for, if he cares for his truths, he is certain to falsify his facts. The laws of history only repeat the lines of force or thought. Yet though his will be iron, he cannot help now and then resuming his humanity or simianity in face of a fear. The motion of thought had the same value as the motion of a cannonball seen approaching the observer on a direct line through the air. One could watch its curve for five thousand years. Its first violent acceleration in historical times had ended in the catastrophe of 310. The next swerve of direction occurred towards 1500. Galileo and Bacon gave a still newer curve to it, which altered its values; but all these changes had never altered the continuity. Only in 1900, the continuity snapped.

Vaguely conscious of the cataclysm, the world sometimes dated it from 1893, by the Roentgen rays, or from 1898, by the Curies' radium; but in 1904, Arthur Balfour announced on the part of British science that the human race without exception had lived and died in a world of illusion until the last year of the century. The date was convenient, and convenience was truth.

The child born in 1900 would, then, be born into a new world which would not be a unity but a multiple. Adams tried to imagine it, and an education that would fit it. He found himself in a land where no one had ever penetrated before; where order was an accidental relation obnoxious to nature; artificial compulsion imposed on motion; against which every free energy of the universe revolted; and which, being merely occasional, resolved itself back into anarchy at last. He could not deny that the law of the new multiverse explained much that had been most obscure, especially the persistently fiendish treatment of man by man; the perpetual effort of society to establish law, and the perpetual revolt of society against the law it had established; the perpetual building up of authority by force, and the perpetual appeal to force to overthrow it; the perpetual symbolism of a higher law, and the perpetual relapse to a lower one; the perpetual victory of the principles of freedom, and their perpetual conversion into principles of power; but the staggering problem was the outlook ahead into the despotism of artificial order which nature abhorred. The physicists had a phrase for it, unintelligible to the vulgar: "All that we win is a battle — lost in advance — with the irreversible phenomena in the background of nature."

All that a historian won was a vehement wish to escape. He saw his education complete, and was sorry he ever began it. As a matter of taste, he greatly preferred his eighteenth-century education when God was a father and nature a mother, and all was for the best in a scientific universe. He repudiated all share in the world as it was to be, and yet he could not detect the point where his responsibility began or ended.

As history unveiled itself in the new order, man's mind had behaved like a young pearl oyster, secreting its universe to suit its conditions until it had built up a shell of *nacre* that embodied all its notions of the perfect. Man knew it was true because he made it, and he loved it for the same reason. He sacrificed millions of lives to acquire his unity, but he achieved it, and justly thought it a work of art. The woman especially did great things, creating her deities on a higher level than the male, and, in the end, compelling the man to accept the Virgin as guardian of the man's God. The man's part in his Universe was secondary, but the woman was at home there, and sacrificed herself without limit to make it habitable, when man permitted it, as sometimes happened for brief intervals of war and famine; but she could not provide protection against forces of nature. She did not think of her universe as a raft to which the limpets stuck for life in the surge of a supersensual chaos; she conceived herself and her family as the centre and flower of an ordered universe which she knew to be unity because she had made it after the image of her own fecundity; and this creation of hers was surrounded by beauties and perfections which she knew to be real because she herself had imagined them.

Even the masculine philosopher admired and loved and celebrated her triumph, and the greatest of them sang it in the noblest of his verses: —

"Alma Venus, coeli subter labentia signa
  Quae mare navigerum, quae terras frugiferenteis

Concelebras.......
Quae quoniam rerum naturam sola gubernas,
Nec sine te quidquam dias in luminis oras
Exoritur, neque fit laetum neque amabile quidquam;
Te sociam studeo!"

Neither man nor woman ever wanted to quit this Eden of their own invention, and could no more have done it of their own accord than the pearl oyster could quit its shell; but although the oyster might perhaps assimilate or embalm a grain of sand forced into its aperture, it could only perish in face of the cyclonic hurricane or the volcanic upheaval of its bed. Her supersensual chaos killed her.

Such seemed the theory of history to be imposed by science on the generation born after 1900. For this theory, Adams felt himself in no way responsible. Even as historian he had made it his duty always to speak with respect of everything that had ever been thought respectable — except an occasional statesman; but he had submitted to force all his life, and he meant to accept it for the future as for the past. All his efforts had been turned only to the search for its channel. He never invented his facts; they were furnished him by the only authorities he could find. As for himself, according to Helmholz, Ernst Mach, and Arthur Balfour, he was henceforth to be a conscious ball of vibrating motions, traversed in every direction by infinite lines of rotation or vibration, rolling at the feet of the Virgin at Chartres or of M. Poincaré in an attic at Paris, a centre of supersensual chaos. The discovery did not distress him. A solitary man of sixty-five years or more, alone in a Gothic cathedral or a Paris apartment, need fret himself little about a few illusions more or less. He should have learned his lesson fifty years earlier; the times had long passed when a student could stop before chaos or order; he had no choice but to march with his world.

Nevertheless, he could not pretend that his mind felt flattered by this scientific outlook. Every fabulist has told how the human mind has always struggled like a frightened bird to escape the chaos which caged it; how — appearing suddenly and inexplicably out of some unknown and unimaginable void; passing half its known life in the mental chaos of sleep; victim even when awake, to its own ill-adjustment, to disease, to age, to external suggestion, to nature's compulsion; doubting its sensations, and, in the last resort, trusting only to instruments and averages — after sixty or seventy years of growing astonishment, the mind wakes to find itself looking blankly into the void of death. That it should profess itself pleased by this performance was all that the highest rules of good breeding could ask; but that it should actually be satisfied would prove that it existed only as idiocy.

Satisfied, the future generation could scarcely think itself, for even when the mind existed in a universe of its own creation, it had never been quite at ease. As far as one ventured to interpret actual science, the mind had thus far adjusted itself by an infinite series of infinitely delicate adjustments forced on it by the infinite motion of an infinite chaos of motion; dragged at one moment into the unknowable and unthinkable, then trying to scramble back within its senses and to bar the chaos out, but always assimilating bits of it, until at last, in 1900, a new avalanche of unknown forces had fallen on it, which required new mental powers to control. If this view was correct, the mind could gain nothing by flight or by fight; it must merge in its supersensual multiverse, or succumb to it.

32

Vis Nova

(1903–1904)

Paris after midsummer is a place where only the industrious poor remain, unless they can get away; but Adams knew no spot where history would be better off, and the calm of the Champs Élysées was so deep that when Mr. de Witte was promoted to a powerless dignity, no one whispered that the promotion was disgrace, while one might have supposed, from the silence, that the Viceroy Alexeieff had reoccupied Manchuria as a fulfilment of treaty-obligation. For once, the conspiracy of silence became crime. Never had so modern and so vital a riddle been put before Western society, but society shut its eyes. Manchuria knew every step into war; Japan had completed every preparation; Alexeieff had collected his army and fleet at Port Arthur, mounting his siege guns and laying in enormous stores, ready for the expected attack; from Yokohama to Irkutsk, the whole East was under war conditions; but Europe knew nothing. The banks would allow no disturbance; the press said not a word, and even the embassies were silent. Every anarchist in Europe buzzed excitement and began to collect in groups, but the

Hotel Ritz was calm, and the Grand Dukes who swarmed there professed to know directly from the Winter Palace that there would be no war.

As usual, Adams felt as ignorant as the best-informed statesman, and though the sense was familiar, for once he could see that the ignorance was assumed. After nearly fifty years of experience, he could not understand how the comedy could be so well acted. Even as late as November, diplomats were gravely asking every passer-by for his opinion, and avowed none of their own except what was directly authorized at St. Petersburg. He could make nothing of it. He found himself in face of his new problem — the workings of Russian inertia — and he could conceive no way of forming an opinion how much was real and how much was comedy had he been in the Winter Palace himself. At times he doubted whether the Grand Dukes or the Czar knew, but old diplomatic training forbade him to admit such innocence.

This was the situation at Christmas when he left Paris. On January 6, 1904, he reached Washington, where the contrast of atmosphere astonished him, for he had never before seen his country think as a world-power. No doubt, Japanese diplomacy had much to do with this alertness, but the immense superiority of Japanese diplomacy should have been more evident in Europe than in America, and in any case, could not account for the total disappearance of Russian diplomacy. A government by inertia greatly disconcerted study. One was led to suspect that Cassini never heard from his Government, and that Lamsdorf knew nothing of his own department; yet no such suspicion could be admitted. Cassini resorted to transparent *blague:* "Japan seemed infatuated even to the point of war! But what can the Japanese do? As usual, sit on their heels and pray to Buddha!" One of the oldest and most accomplished diplomatists in the service could never show his hand so empty as this if he held a card to play; but he never betrayed stronger resource behind. "If any Japanese succeed in entering Manchuria, they will never get out of it alive." The inertia of Cassini, who was naturally the most energetic of diplomatists, deeply interested a student of race-inertia, whose mind had lost itself in the attempt to invent scales of force.

The air of official Russia seemed most dramatic in the air of the White House, by contrast with the outspoken candor of the President. Reticence had no place there. Every one in America saw that, whether Russia or Japan were victim, one of the decisive struggles in American history was pending, and any pretence of secrecy or indifference was absurd. Interest was acute, and curiosity intense, for no one knew what the Russian Government meant or wanted, while war had become a question of days. To an impartial student who gravely doubted whether the Czar himself acted as a conscious force or an inert weight, the straightforward avowals of Roosevelt had singular value as a standard of measure. By chance it happened that Adams was obliged to take the place of his brother Brooks at the Diplomatic Reception immediately after his return home, and the part of proxy included his supping at the President's table, with Secretary Root on one side, the President opposite, and Miss Chamberlain between them. Naturally the President talked and the guests listened; which seemed, to one who had just escaped from the European conspiracy of silence, like drawing a free breath after stifling. Roosevelt, as every one knew, was always an amusing talker, and had the reputation of being indiscreet beyond any other man of great importance in the world, except the Kaiser Wilhelm and Mr. Joseph Chamberlain, the father of his guest at table; and this evening he spared none. With the usual abuse of the *quos ego,* common to vigorous statesmen, he said all that he thought about Russians and Japanese, as well as about Boers and British, without restraint, in full hearing of twenty people, to the entire satisfaction of his listener; and concluded by declaring that war was imminent; that it ought to be stopped; that it could be stopped: "I could do it myself; I could stop it to-morrow!" and he went on to explain his reasons for restraint.

That he was right, and that, within another generation, his successor would do what he would have liked to do, made no shadow of doubt in the mind of his hearer, though it would have been folly when he last supped at the White House in the dynasty of President Hayes; but the listener cared less for the assertion of power, than for the vigor of view. The truth was evident enough, ordinary, even commonplace if one liked, but it was not a truth of inertia, nor was the method to be mistaken for inert.

Nor could the force of Japan be mistaken for a moment as a force of inertia, although its aggressive was taken as methodically — as mathematically — as a demonstration of Euclid, and Adams thought that as against any but Russians it would have lost its opening. Each day counted as a measure of relative energy on the historical scale, and the whole story made a Grammar of new Science quite as instructive as that of Pearson.

The forces thus launched were bound to reach some new equilibrium which would prove the problem in one sense or another, and the war had no personal value for Adams except that it gave Hay his last great triumph. He had carried on his long contest with Cassini so skillfully that no one knew enough to understand the diplomatic perfection of his work, which contained no error; but such success is complete only when it is invisible, and his victory at last was victory of judgment, not of act. He could do nothing, and the whole country would have sprung on him had he tried. Japan and England saved his "open door" and fought his battle. All that remained for him was to make the peace, and Adams set his heart on getting the peace quickly in hand, for Hay's sake as well as for that of Russia. He thought then that it could be done in one campaign, for he knew that, in a military sense, the fall of Port Arthur must lead to negotiation, and every one felt that Hay would inevitably direct it; but the race was close, and while the war grew every day in proportions, Hay's strength every day declined.

St. Gaudens came on to model his head, and Sargent painted his portrait, two steps essential to immortality which he bore with a certain degree of resignation, but he grumbled when the President made him go to St. Louis to address some gathering at the Exposition; and Mrs. Hay bade Adams go with them, for whatever use he could suppose himself to serve. He professed the religion of World's Fairs, without which he held education to be a blind impossibility; and obeyed Mrs. Hay's bidding the more readily because it united his two educations in one; but theory and practice were put to equally severe test at St. Louis. Ten years had passed since he last crossed the Mississippi, and he found everything new. In this great region from Pittsburgh through Ohio and Indiana, agriculture had made way for steam; tall chimneys reeked smoke on every horizon, and dirty suburbs filled with scrap-iron, scrap-paper and cinders, formed the setting of every town. Evidently, cleanliness was not to be the birthmark of the new American, but this matter of discards concerned the measure of force little, while the chimneys and cinders concerned it so much that Adams thought the Secretary of State should have rushed to the platform at every station to ask who were the people; for the American of the prime seemed to be extinct with the Shawnee and the buffalo.

The subject grew quickly delicate. History told little about these millions of Germans and Slavs, or whatever their race-names, who had overflowed these regions as though the Rhine and the Danube had turned their floods into the Ohio. John Hay was as strange to the Mississippi River as though he had not been bred on its shores, and the city of St. Louis had turned its back on the noblest work of nature, leaving it bankrupt between its own banks. The new American showed his parentage proudly; he was the child of steam and the brother of the dynamo, and already, within less than thirty years, this mass of mixed humanities, brought together by steam, was squeezed and welded into approach to shape; a product of so much mechanical power, and bearing no distinctive marks but that of its pressure. The new American, like the new European, was the servant of the power-house, as the European of the twelfth century was the servant of the Church, and the features would follow the parentage.

The St. Louis Exposition was its first creation in the twentieth century, and, for that reason, acutely interesting. One saw here a third-rate town of half-a-million people without history, education, unity, or art, and with little capital — without even an element of natural interest except the river which it studiously ignored — but doing what London, Paris, or New York would have shrunk from attempting. This new social conglomerate, with no tie but its steam-power and not much of that, threw away thirty or forty million dollars on a pageant as ephemeral as a stage flat. The world had never witnessed so marvellous a phantasm; by night Arabia's crimson sands had never returned a glow half so astonishing, as one wandered among long lines of white palaces, exquisitely lighted by thousands on thousands of electric candles, soft, rich, shadowy, palpable in their sensuous depths; all in deep silence, profound solitude, listening for a voice or a foot-fall or the plash of an oar, as though the Emir Mirza were displaying the beauties of this City of Brass, which could show nothing half so beautiful as this illumination, with its vast, white, monumental solitude, bathed in the pure light of setting suns. One enjoyed it with iniquitous rapture, not because of exhibits but rather because of their want. Here was a paradox like the stellar universe that fitted one's mental faults. Had there been no exhibits at all, and no visitors, one would have enjoyed it only the more.

Here education found new forage. That the power was wasted, the art indifferent, the economic failure complete, added just so much to the interest. The chaos of education approached a dream. One asked one's self whether this extravagance reflected the past or imaged the future; whether it was a creation of the old American or a promise of the new one. No prophet could be believed, but a pilgrim of power, without constituency to flatter, might allow himself to hope. The prospect from the Exposition was pleasant; one seemed to see almost an adequate motive for power; almost a scheme for progress. In another half-century, the people of the central valleys should have hundreds of millions to throw away more easily than in 1900 they could throw away tens; and by that time they might know what they wanted. Possibly they might even have learned how to reach it.

This was an optimist's hope, shared by few except pilgrims of World's Fairs, and frankly dropped by the multitude, for, east of the Mississippi, the St. Louis Exposition met a deliberate conspiracy of silence, discouraging, beyond measure, to an optimistic dream of future strength in American expression. The party got back to Washington on May 24, and before sailing for Europe, Adams went over, one warm evening, to bid good-bye on the garden-porch of the White House. He found himself the first person who urged Mrs. Roosevelt to visit the Exposition for its beauty, and, as far as he ever knew, the last.

He left St. Louis May 22, 1904, and on Sunday, June 5, found himself again in the town of Coutances, where the people of Normandy had built, towards the year 1250, an Exposition which architects still admired and tourists visited, for it was thought singularly expressive of force as well as of grace in the Virgin. On this Sunday, the Norman world was celebrating a pretty church-feast — the Fête Dieu — and the streets were filled with altars to the Virgin, covered with flowers and foliage; the pavements strewn with paths of leaves and the spring handiwork of nature; the cathedral densely thronged at mass. The scene was graceful. The Virgin did not shut her costly Exposition on Sunday, or any other day, even to American Senators who had shut the St. Louis Exposition to her — or for her; and a historical tramp would gladly have offered a candle, or even a candle-stick in her honor, if she would have taught him her relation with the deity of the Senators. The power of the Virgin had been plainly One, embracing all human activity; while the power of the Senate, or its deity, seemed — might one say — to be more or less ashamed of man and his work. The matter had no great interest as far as it concerned the somewhat obscure mental processes of Senators who could probably have given no clearer idea than priests of the deity they supposed themselves to honor — if that was indeed their purpose; but it interested a student of force, curious to measure its manifestations. Apparently the Virgin — or her Son — had no longer the force to build expositions that one cared to visit, but had the force to close them. The force was still real, serious, and, at St. Louis, had been anxiously measured in actual money-value.

That it was actual and serious in France as in the Senate Chamber at Washington, proved itself at once by forcing Adams to buy an automobile, which was a supreme demonstration because this was the form of force which Adams most abominated. He had set aside the summer for study of the Virgin, not as a sentiment but as a motive power, which had left monuments widely scattered and not easily reached. The automobile alone could unite them in any reasonable sequence, and although the force of the automobile, for the purposes of a commercial traveller, seemed to have no relation whatever to the force that inspired a Gothic cathedral, the Virgin in the twelfth century would have guided and controlled both bag-man and architect, as she controlled the seeker of history. In his mind the problem offered itself as to Newton; it was a matter of mutual attraction, and he knew it, in his own case, to be a formula as precise as $s = \dfrac{gt^2}{2}$, if he could but experimentally prove it. Of the attraction he needed no proof on his own account; the costs of his automobile were more than sufficient: but as teacher he needed to speak for others than himself. For him, the Virgin was an adorable mistress, who led the automobile and its owner where she would, to her wonderful palaces and châteaux, from Chartres to Rouen, and thence to Amiens and Laon, and a score of others, kindly receiving, amusing, charming and dazzling her lover, as though she were Aphrodite herself, worth all else that man ever dreamed. He never doubted her force, since he felt it to the last fibre of his being, and could not more dispute its mastery than he could dispute the force of gravitation of which he knew nothing but the formula. He was only too glad to yield himself entirely, not to her charm or to any sentimentality of religion, but to her mental and physical energy of creation which had built up these World's Fairs of thirteenth-century force that turned Chicago and St. Louis pale.

"Both were faiths and both are gone," said Matthew Arnold of the Greek and Norse divinities; but the business of a student was to ask where they had gone. The Virgin had not even altogether gone; her fading away had been excessively slow. Her adorer had pursued her too long, too far, and into too many manifestations of her power, to admit that she had any equivalent either of quantity or kind, in the actual world, but he could still less admit her annihilation as energy.

So he went on wooing, happy in the thought that at last he had found a mistress who could see no difference in the age of her lovers. Her own age had no time-measure. For years past, incited by John La Farge, Adams had devoted his summer schooling to the study of her glass at Chartres and elsewhere, and if the automobile had one *vitesse* more useful than another, it was that of a century a minute; that of passing from one century to another without break. The centuries dropped like autumn leaves in one's road, and one was not fined for running over them too fast. When the thirteenth lost breath, the fourteenth caught on, and the sixteenth ran close ahead. The hunt for the Virgin's glass opened rich preserves. Especially the sixteenth century ran riot in sensuous worship. Then the ocean of religion, which had flooded France, broke into Shelley's light dissolved in star-showers thrown, which had left every remote village strewn with fragments that flashed like jewels, and were tossed into hidden clefts of peace and forgetfulness. One dared not pass a parish church in Champagne or Touraine without stopping to look for its window of fragments, where one's glass discovered the Christ-child in his manger, nursed

by the head of a fragmentary donkey, with a Cupid playing into its long ears from the balustrade of a Venetian
palace, guarded by a legless Flemish *leibwache*, standing
on his head with a broken halbert; all invoked in prayer
by remnants of the donors and their children that might
have been drawn by Fouquet or Pinturicchio, in colors
as fresh and living as the day they were burned in, and
with feeling that still consoled the faithful for the paradise
they had paid for and lost. France abounds in sixteenth-
century glass. Paris alone contains acres of it, and the
neighborhood within fifty miles contains scores of
churches where the student may still imagine himself three
hundred years old, kneeling before the Virgin's window
in the silent solitude of an empty faith, crying his culp,
beating his breast, confessing his historical sins, weighed
down by the rubbish of sixty-six years' education, and
still desperately hoping to understand.

He understood a little, though not much. The sixteenth
century had a value of its own, as though the ONE had
become several, and Unity had counted more than Three,
though the Multiple still showed modest numbers. The
glass had gone back to the Roman Empire and forward
to the American continent; it betrayed sympathy with
Montaigne and Shakespeare; but the Virgin was still supreme. At Beauvais in the Church of St. Stephen was a
superb tree of Jesse, famous as the work of Engrand le
Prince, about 1570 or 1580, in whose branches, among the
fourteen ancestors of the Virgin, three-fourths bore features of the Kings of France, among them Francis I and
Henry II, who were hardly more edifying than Kings of
Israel, and at least unusual as sources of divine purity.
Compared with the still more famous Tree of Jesse at
Chartres, dating from 1150 or thereabouts, must one declare that Engrand le Prince proved progress? and in what
direction? Complexity, Multiplicity, even a step towards

Anarchy, it might suggest, but what step towards perfection?

One late afternoon, at midsummer, the Virgin's pilgrim was wandering through the streets of Troyes in close and intimate conversation with Thibaut of Champagne and his highly intelligent seneschal, the Sieur de Joinville, when he noticed one or two men looking at a bit of paper stuck in a window. Approaching, he read that M. de Plehve had been assassinated at St. Petersburg. The mad mixture of Russia and the Crusades, of the Hippodrome and the Renaissance, drove him for refuge into the fascinating Church of St. Pantaleon near by. Martyrs, murderers, Cæsars, saints and assassins — half in glass and half in telegram; chaos of time, place, morals, forces and motive — gave him vertigo. Had one sat all one's life on the steps of Ara Cœli for this? Was assassination forever to be the last word of Progress? No one in the street had shown a sign of protest; he himself felt none; the charming Church with its delightful windows, in its exquisite absence of other tourists, took a keener expression of celestial peace than could have been given it by any contrast short of explosive murder; the conservative Christian anarchist had come to his own, but which was he — the murderer or the murdered?

The Virgin herself never looked so winning — so One — as in this scandalous failure of her Grace. To what purpose had she existed, if, after nineteen hundred years, the world was bloodier than when she was born? The stupendous failure of Christianity tortured history. The effort for Unity could not be a partial success; even alternating Unity resolved itself into meaningless motion at last. To the tired student, the idea that he must give it up seemed sheer senility. As long as he could whisper, he would go on as he had begun, bluntly refusing to meet his creator with the admission that the creation had taught him nothing except that the square of the hypothenuse of a right-angled triangle might for convenience be taken as equal to something else. Every man with self-respect enough to become effective, if only as a machine, has had to account to himself for himself somehow, and to invent a formula of his own for his universe, if the standard formulas failed. There, whether finished or not, education stopped. The formula, once made, could be but verified.

The effort must begin at once, for time pressed. The old formulas had failed, and a new one had to be made, but, after all, the object was not extravagant or eccentric. One sought no absolute truth. One sought only a spool on which to wind the thread of history without breaking it. Among indefinite possible orbits, one sought the orbit which would best satisfy the observed movement of the runaway star Groombridge, 1838, commonly called Henry Adams. As term of a nineteenth-century education, one sought a common factor for certain definite historical fractions. Any schoolboy could work out the problem if he were given the right to state it in his own terms.

Therefore, when the fogs and frosts stopped his slaughter of the centuries, and shut him up again in his garret, he sat down as though he were again a boy at school to shape after his own needs the values of a Dynamic Theory of History.

33

A Dynamic Theory of History

(1904)

A dynamic theory, like most theories, begins by begging the question: it defines Progress as the development and economy of Forces. Further, it defines force as anything that does, or helps to do work. Man is a force; so is the sun; so is a mathematical point, though without dimensions or known existence.

Man commonly begs the question again by taking for granted that he captures the forces. A dynamic theory, assigning attractive force to opposing bodies in proportion to the law of mass, takes for granted that the forces of nature capture man. The sum of force attracts; the feeble atom or molecule called man is attracted; he suffers education or growth; he is the sum of the forces that attract him; his body and his thought are alike their product; the movement of the forces controls the progress of his mind, since he can know nothing but the motions which impinge on his senses, whose sum makes education.

For convenience as an image, the theory may liken man to a spider in its web, watching for chance prey. Forces of nature dance like flies before the net, and the spider pounces on them when it can; but it makes many fatal mistakes, though its theory of force is sound. The spider-mind acquires a faculty of memory, and, with it, a singular skill of analysis and synthesis, taking apart and putting together in different relations the meshes of its trap. Man had in the beginning no power of analysis or synthesis approaching that of the spider, or even of the honey-bee; but he had acute sensibility to the higher forces. Fire taught him secrets that no other animal could learn; running water probably taught him even more, especially in his first lessons of mechanics; the animals helped to educate him, trusting themselves into his hands merely for the sake of their food, and carrying his burdens or supplying his clothing; the grasses and grains were academies of study. With little or no effort on his part, all these forces formed his thought, induced his action, and even shaped his figure.

Long before history began, his education was complete, for the record could not have been started until he had been taught to record. The universe that had formed him took shape in his mind as a reflection of his own unity, containing all forces except himself. Either separately, or in groups, or as a whole, these forces never ceased to act on him, enlarging his mind as they enlarged the surface foliage of a vegetable, and the mind needed only to respond, as the forests did, to these attractions. Susceptibility to the highest forces is the highest genius; selection between them is the highest science; their mass is the highest educator. Man always made, and still makes, grotesque blunders in selecting and measuring forces, taken at random from the heap, but he never made a mistake in the value he set on the whole, which he symbolized as unity and worshipped as God. To this day, his attitude towards it has never changed, though science can no longer give to force a name.

Man's function as a force of nature was to assimilate other forces as he assimilated food. He called it the love of power. He felt his own feebleness, and he sought for an ass or a camel, a bow or a sling, to widen his range of power, as he sought a fetish or a planet in the world beyond. He cared little to know its immediate use, he could afford to throw nothing away which he could conceive to have possible value in this or any other existence. He waited for the object to teach him its use, or want of use, and the process was slow. He may have gone on for hundreds of thousands of years, waiting for Nature to tell him her secrets; and, to his rivals among the monkeys, Nature has taught no more than at their start; but certain lines of force were capable of acting on individual apes, and mechanically selecting types of race or sources of variation. The individual that responded or reacted to lines of new force then was possibly the same individual that reacts on it now, and his conception of the unity seems never to have changed in spite of the increasing diversity of forces; but the theory of variation is an affair of other science than history, and matters nothing to dynamics. The individual or the race would be educated on the same lines of illusion, which, according to Arthur Balfour, had not essentially varied down to the year 1900.

To the highest attractive energy, man gave the name of divine, and for its control he invented the science called Religion, a word which meant, and still means, cultivation of occult force whether in detail or mass. Unable to define Force as a unity, man symbolized it and pursued it, both in himself, and in the infinite, as philosophy and theology; the mind is itself the subtlest of all known forces, and its self-introspection necessarily created a science which had the singular value of lifting his education, at the start, to the finest, subtlest, and broadest training both in analysis and synthesis, so that, if language is a test, he must have reached his highest powers early in his history; while the mere motive remained as simple an appetite for power as the tribal greed which led him to trap an elephant. Hunger, whether for food or for the infinite, sets in motion multiplicity and infinity of thought, and the sure hope of gaining a share of infinite power in eternal life would lift most minds to effort.

He had reached this completeness five thousand years ago, and added nothing to his stock of known forces for a very long time. The mass of nature exercised on him so feeble an attraction that one can scarcely account for his apparent motion. Only a historian of very exceptional knowledge would venture to say at what date between 3000 B.C. and 1000 A.D., the momentum of Europe was greatest; but such progress as the world made consisted in economies of energy rather than its development; it was proved in mathematics, measured by names like Archimedes, Aristarchus, Ptolemy, and Euclid; or in Civil Law, measured by a number of names which Adams had begun life by failing to learn; or in coinage, which was most beautiful near its beginning, and most barbarous at its close; or it was shown in roads, or the size of ships, or harbors; or by the use of metals, instruments, and writing; all of them economies of force, sometimes more forceful than the forces they helped; but the roads were still travelled by the horse, the ass, the camel, or the slave; the ships were still propelled by sails or oars; the lever, the spring, and the screw bounded the region of applied mechanics. Even the metals were old.

Much the same thing could be said of religious or supernatural forces. Down to the year 300 of the Christian era they were little changed, and in spite of Plato and the sceptics were more apparently chaotic than ever. The experience of three thousand years had educated society to feel the vastness of Nature, and the infinity of her resources of power, but even this increase of attraction had not yet caused economies in its methods of pursuit.

There the Western world stood till the year A.D. 305, when the Emperor Diocletian abdicated; and there it was that Adams broke down on the steps of Ara Cœli, his path blocked by the scandalous failure of civilization at the moment it had achieved complete success. In the year 305 the empire had solved the problems of Europe more completely than they have ever been solved since. The Pax Romana, the Civil Law, and Free Trade should, in four hundred years, have put Europe far in advance of the point reached by modern society in the four hundred years since 1500, when conditions were less simple.

The efforts to explain, or explain away, this scandal had been incessant, but none suited Adams unless it were the economic theory of adverse exchanges and exhaustion of minerals; but nations are not ruined beyond a certain point by adverse exchanges, and Rome had by no means exhausted her resources. On the contrary, the empire developed resources and energies quite astounding. No other four hundred years of history before A.D. 1800 knew anything like it; and although some of these developments, like the Civil Law, the roads, aqueducts, and harbors, were rather economies than force, yet in northwestern Europe alone the empire had developed three energies — France, England, and Germany — competent to master the world. The trouble seemed rather to be that the empire developed too much energy, and too fast.

A dynamic law requires that two masses — nature and man — must go on, reacting upon each other, without stop, as the sun and a comet react on each other, and that any appearance of stoppage is illusive. The theory seems to exact excess, rather than deficiency, of action and reaction to account for the dissolution of the Roman Empire, which should, as a problem of mechanics, have been torn to pieces by acceleration. If the student means to try the experiment of framing a dynamic law, he must assign values to the forces of attraction that caused the trouble; and in this case he has them in plain evidence. With the relentless logic that stamped Roman thought, the empire, which had established unity on earth, could not help establishing unity in heaven. It was induced by its dynamic necessities to economize the gods.

The Church has never ceased to protest against the charge that Christianity ruined the empire, and, with its usual force, has pointed out that its reforms alone saved the State. Any dynamic theory gladly admits it. All it asks is to find and follow the force that attracts. The Church points out this force in the Cross, and history needs only to follow it. The empire loudly asserted its motive. Good taste forbids saying that Constantine the Great speculated as audaciously as a modern stock-broker on values of which he knew at the utmost only the volume; or that he merged all uncertain forces into a single trust, which he enormously over-capitalized, and forced on the market; but this is the substance of what Constantine himself said in his Edict of Milan in the year 313, which admitted Christianity into the Trust of State Religions. Regarded as an Act of Congress, it runs: "We have resolved to grant to Christians as well as all others the liberty to practise the religion they prefer, in order that whatever exists of divinity or celestial power may help and favor us and all who are under our government." The empire pursued power — not merely spiritual but physical — in the sense in which Constantine issued his army order the year before, at the battle of the Milvian Bridge: *In hoc signo vinces!* using the Cross as a train of artillery, which, to his mind, it was. Society accepted it in the same character. Eighty years afterwards, Theodosius marched against his rival Eugene with the Cross for physical champion; and Eugene raised the image of Hercules to fight for the pagans; while society on both sides looked on, as though it were a boxing-match, to decide a final test of force between the divine powers. The Church was powerless to raise the ideal. What is now known as religion affected the mind of old society but little. The laity, the people, the million, almost to a man, bet on the gods as they bet on a horse.

No doubt the Church did all it could to purify the process, but society was almost wholly pagan in its point of view, and was drawn to the Cross because, in its system of physics, the Cross had absorbed all the old occult for fetish-power. The symbol represented the sum of nature — the Energy of modern science — and society believed it to be as real as X-rays; perhaps it was! The emperors used it like gunpowder in politics; the physicians used it like rays in medicine; the dying clung to it as the quintessence of force, to protect them from the forces of evil on their road to the next life.

Throughout these four centuries the empire knew that religion disturbed economy, for even the cost of heathen incense affected the exchanges; but no one could afford to buy or construct a costly and complicated machine when he could hire an occult force at trifling expense. Fetish-power was cheap and satisfactory, down to a certain point. Turgot and Auguste Comte long ago fixed this stage of economy as a necessary phase of social education, and historians seem now to accept it as the only gain yet made towards scientific history. Great numbers of educated people — perhaps a majority — cling to the method still, and practise it more or less strictly; but, until quite recently, no other was known. The only occult power at man's disposal was fetish. Against it, no mechanical force could compete except within narrow limits.

Outside of occult or fetish-power, the Roman world was incredibly poor. It knew but one productive energy resembling a modern machine — the slave. No artificial force of serious value was applied to production or transportation, and when society developed itself so rapidly in political and social lines, it had no other means of keeping its economy on the same level than to extend its slave-system and its fetish-system to the utmost.

The result might have been stated in a mathematical formula as early as the time of Archimedes, six hundred years before Rome fell. The economic needs of a violently centralizing society forced the empire to enlarge its slave-system until the slave-system consumed itself and the empire too, leaving society no resource but further enlargement of its religious system in order to compensate for the losses and horrors of the failure. For a vicious circle, its mathematical completeness approached perfection. The dynamic law of attraction and reaction needed only a Newton to fix it in algebraic form.

At last, in 410, Alaric sacked Rome, and the slave-ridden, agricultural, uncommercial Western Empire — the poorer and less Christianized half — went to pieces. Society, though terribly shocked by the horrors of Alaric's storm, felt still more deeply the disappointment in its new power, the Cross, which had failed to protect its Church. The outcry against the Cross became so loud among Christians that its literary champion, Bishop Augustine of Hippo — a town between Algiers and Tunis — was led to write a famous treatise in defence of the Cross, familiar still to every scholar, in which he defended feebly the mechanical value of the symbol — arguing only that pagan symbols equally failed — but insisted on its spiritual value in the *Civitas Dei* which had taken the place of the *Civitas Romae* in human interest. "Granted that we have lost all we had! Have we lost faith? Have we lost piety? Have we lost the wealth of the inner man who is rich before God? These are the wealth of Christians!" The *Civitas Dei*, in its turn, became the sum of attraction for the Western world, though it also showed the same weakness in mechanics that had wrecked the *Civitas Romae*. St. Augustine and his people perished at Hippo towards 430, leaving society in appearance dull to new attraction.

Yet the attraction remained constant. The delight of experimenting on occult force of every kind is such as to absorb all the free thought of the human race. The gods did their work; history has no quarrel with them; they led, educated, enlarged the mind; taught knowledge; betrayed ignorance, stimulated effort. So little is known about the mind — whether social, racial, sexual or heritable; whether material or spiritual; whether animal, vegetable or mineral — that history is inclined to avoid it altogether; but nothing forbids one to admit, for convenience, that it may assimilate food like the body, storing new force and growing, like a forest, with the storage. The brain has not yet revealed its mysterious mechanism of gray matter. Never has Nature offered it so violent a stimulant as when she opened to it the possibility of sharing infinite power in eternal life, and it might well need a thousand years of prolonged and intense experiment to prove the value of the motive. During these so-called Middle Ages, the Western mind reacted in many forms, on many sides, expressing its motives in modes, such as Romanesque and Gothic architecture, glass windows and mosaic walls, sculpture and poetry, war and love, which still affect some people as the noblest work of man, so that, even to-day, great masses of idle and ignorant tourists travel from far countries to look at Ravenna and San Marco, Palermo and Pisa, Assisi, Cordova, Chartres, with vague notions about the force that created them, but with a certain surprise that a social mind of such singular energy and unity should still lurk in their shadows.

The tourist more rarely visits Constantinople or studies the architecture of Sancta Sofia, but when he does, he is distinctly conscious of forces not quite the same. Justinian has not the simplicity of Charlemagne. The Eastern Empire showed an activity and variety of forces that classical Europe had never possessed. The navy of Nicephoras Phocas in the tenth century would have annihilated in half an hour any navy that Carthage or Athens or Rome ever set afloat. The dynamic scheme began by asserting rather recklessly that between the Pyramids (B.C. 3000), and the Cross (A.D. 300), no new force affected Western progress, and antiquarians may easily dispute the fact; but in any case the motive influence, old or new, which raised both Pyramids and Cross was the same attraction of power in a future life that raised the dome of Sancta Sofia and the Cathedral at Amiens, however much it was altered, enlarged, or removed to distance in space. Therefore, no single event has more puzzled historians than the sudden, unexplained appearance of at least two new natural forces of the highest educational value in mechanics, for the first time within record of history. Literally, these two forces seemed to drop from the sky at the precise moment when the Cross on one side and the Crescent on the other, proclaimed the complete triumph of the *Civitas Dei*. Had the Manichean doctrine of Good and Evil as rival deities been orthodox, it would alone have accounted for this simultaneous victory of hostile powers.

Of the compass, as a step towards demonstration of the dynamic law, one may confidently say that it proved, better than any other force, the widening scope of the mind, since it widened immensely the range of contact between nature and thought. The compass educated. This must prove itself as needing no proof.

Of Greek fire and gunpowder, the same thing cannot certainly be said, for they have the air of accidents due to the attraction of religious motives. They belong to the spiritual world; or to the doubtful ground of Magic which lay between Good and Evil. They were chemical forces, mostly explosive, which acted and still act as the most violent educators ever known to man, but they were justly feared as diabolic, and whatever insolence man may have risked towards the milder teachers of his infancy, he was an abject pupil towards explosives. The Sieur de Join-ville left a record of the energy with which the relatively harmless Greek fire educated and enlarged the French mind in a single night in the year 1249, when the crusaders were trying to advance on Cairo. The good king St. Louis and all his staff dropped on their knees at every fiery flame that flew by, praying — "God have pity on us!" and never had man more reason to call on his gods than they, for the battle of religion between Christian and Saracen was trifling compared with that of education between gun-powder and the Cross.

The fiction that society educated itself, or aimed at a conscious purpose, was upset by the compass and gun-powder which dragged and drove Europe at will through frightful bogs of learning. At first, the apparent lag for want of volume in the new energies lasted one or two centuries, which closed the great epochs of emotion by the Gothic cathedrals and scholastic theology. The moment had Greek beauty and more than Greek unity, but it was brief; and for another century or two, Western society seemed to float in space without apparent motion. Yet the attractive mass of nature's energy continued to attract, and education became more rapid than ever before. Society began to resist, but the individual showed greater and greater insistence, without realizing what he was doing. When the Crescent drove the Cross in ignominy from Constantinople in 1453, Gutenberg and Fust were printing their first Bible at Mainz under the impression that they were helping the Cross. When Columbus discovered the West Indies in 1492, the Church looked on it as a victory of the Cross. When Luther and Calvin upset Europe half a century later, they were trying, like St. Augustine, to substitute the *Civitas Dei* for the *Civitas Romae*. When the Puritans set out for New England in 1620, they too were looking to found a *Civitas Dei* in State Street; and when Bunyan made his Pilgrimage in 1678, he repeated St. Jerome. Even when, after centuries of license, the Church reformed its discipline, and, to prove it, burned Giordano Bruno in 1600, besides condemning Galileo in 1630 — as science goes on repeating to us every day — it condemned anarchists, not atheists. None of the astronomers were irreligious men; all of them made a point of magnifying God through his works; a form of science which did their religion no credit. Neither Galileo nor Kepler, neither Spinoza nor Descartes, neither Leibnitz nor Newton, any more than Constantine the Great — if so much — doubted Unity. The utmost range of their heresies reached only its personality.

This persistence of thought-inertia is the leading idea of modern history. Except as reflected in himself, man has no reason for assuming unity in the universe, or an ultimate substance, or a prime-motor. The *a priori* insistence on this unity ended by fatiguing the more active — or reactive — minds; and Lord Bacon tried to stop it. He urged society to lay aside the idea of evolving the universe from a thought, and to try evolving thought from the universe. The mind should observe and register forces — take them apart and put them together — without assuming unity at all. "Nature, to be commanded, must be obeyed." "The imagination must be given not wings but weights." As Galileo reversed the action of earth and sun, Bacon reversed the relation of thought to force. The mind was thenceforth to follow the movement of matter, and unity must be left to shift for itself.

The revolution in attitude seemed voluntary, but in fact was as mechanical as the fall of a feather. Man created nothing. After 1500, the speed of progress so rapidly surpassed man's gait as to alarm every one, as though it were the acceleration of a falling body which the dynamic theory takes it to be. Lord Bacon was as much astonished by it as the Church was, and with reason. Suddenly society felt itself dragged into situations altogether new and anarchic — situations which it could not affect, but which painfully affected it. Instinct taught it that the universe in its thought must be in danger when its reflection lost itself in space. The danger was all the greater because men of science covered it with "larger synthesis," and poets called the undevout astronomer mad. Society knew better. Yet the telescope held it rigidly standing on its head; the microscope revealed a universe that defied the senses; gunpowder killed whole races that lagged behind; the compass coerced the most imbruted mariner to act on the impossible idea that the earth was round; the press drenched Europe with anarchism. Europe saw itself, violently resisting, wrenched into false positions, drawn along new lines as a fish that is caught on a hook; but unable to understand by what force it was controlled. The resistance was often bloody, sometimes humorous, always constant. Its contortions in the eighteenth century are best studied in the wit of Voltaire, but all history and all philosophy from Montaigne and Pascal to Schopenhauer and Nietzsche deal with nothing else; and still, throughout it all, the Baconian law held good; thought did not evolve nature, but nature evolved thought. Not one considerable man of science dared face the stream of thought; and the whole number of those who acted, like Franklin, as electric conductors of the new forces from nature to man, down to the year 1800, did not exceed a few score, confined to a few towns in Western Europe. Asia refused to be touched by the stream, and America, except for Franklin, stood outside.

Very slowly the accretion of these new forces, chemical and mechanical, grew in volume until they acquired sufficient mass to take the place of the old religious science, substituting their attraction for the attractions of the *Civitas Dei*, but the process remained the same. Nature, not mind, did the work that the sun does on the planets. Man depended more and more absolutely on forces other than his own, and on instruments which superseded his senses. Bacon foretold it: "Neither the naked hand nor the understanding, left to itself, can effect much. It is by instruments and helps that the work is done." Once done, the mind resumed its illusion, and society forgot its impotence; but no one better than Bacon knew its tricks, and for his true followers science always meant self-restraint, obedience, sensitiveness to impulse from without. "Non fingendum aut excogitandum sed inveniendum quid Natura faciat aut ferat."

The success of this method staggers belief, and even to-day can be treated by history only as a miracle of growth, like the sports of nature. Evidently a new variety of mind had appeared. Certain men merely held out their hands — like Newton, watched an apple; like Franklin, flew a kite; like Watt, played with a tea-kettle — and great forces of nature stuck to them as though she were playing ball. Governments did almost nothing but resist. Even gunpowder and ordnance, the great weapon of government, showed little development between 1400 and 1800. Society was hostile or indifferent, as Priestly and Jenner, and even Fulton, with reason complained in the most advanced societies in the world, while its resistance became acute wherever the Church held control; until all mankind seemed to draw itself out in a long series of groups, dragged on by an attractive power in advance, which even the leaders obeyed without understanding, as the planets obeyed gravity, or the trees obeyed heat and light.

The influx of new force was nearly spontaneous. The reaction of mind on the mass of nature seemed not greater than that of a comet on the sun; and had the spontaneous influx of force stopped in Europe, society must have stood still, or gone backward, as in Asia or Africa. Then only economies of process would have counted as new force, and society would have been better pleased; for the idea that new force must be in itself a good is only an animal or vegetable instinct. As Nature developed her hidden energies, they tended to become destructive. Thought itself became tortured, suffering reluctantly, impatiently, painfully, the coercion of new method. Easy thought had always been movement of inertia, and mostly mere sentiment; but even the processes of mathematics measured feebly the needs of force.

The stupendous acceleration after 1800 ended in 1900 with the appearance of the new class of supersensual forces, before which the man of science stood at first as bewildered and helpless, as in the fourth century, a priest of Isis before the Cross of Christ.

This, then, or something like this, would be a dynamic formula of history. Any schoolboy knows enough to object at once that it is the oldest and most universal of all theories. Church and State, theology and philosophy, have always preached it, differing only in the allotment of energy between nature and man. Whether the attractive energy has been called God or Nature, the mechanism has been always the same, and history is not obliged to decide whether the Ultimate tends to a purpose or not, or whether ultimate energy is one or many. Every one admits that the will is a free force, habitually decided by motives. No one denies that motives exist adequate to decide the will; even though it may not always be conscious of them. Science has proved that forces, sensible and occult, physical and metaphysical, simple and complex, surround, traverse, vibrate, rotate, repel, attract, without stop; that man's senses are conscious of few, and only in a partial degree; but that, from the beginning of organic existence his consciousness has been induced, expanded, trained in the lines of his sensitiveness; and that the rise of his faculties from a lower power to a higher, or from a narrower to a wider field, may be due to the function of assimilating and storing outside force or forces. There is nothing unscientific in the idea that, beyond the lines of force felt by the senses, the universe may be — as it has always been — either a supersensuous chaos or a divine unity, which irresistibly attracts, and is either life or death to penetrate. Thus far, religion, philosophy, and science seem to go hand in hand. The schools begin their vital battle only there. In the earlier stages of progress, the forces to be assimilated were simple and easy to absorb, but, as the mind of man enlarged its range, it enlarged the field of complexity, and must continue to do so, even into chaos, until the reservoirs of sensuous or supersensuous energies are exhausted, or cease to affect him, or until he succumbs to their excess.

For past history, this way of grouping its sequences may answer for a chart of relations, although any serious student would need to invent another, to compare or correct its errors; but past history is only a value of relation to the future, and this value is wholly one of convenience, which can be tested only by experiment. Any law of movement must include, to make it a convenience, some mechanical formula of acceleration.

34

A
Law of
Acceleration

(1904)

Images are not arguments, rarely even lead to proof, but the mind craves them, and, of late more than ever, the keenest experimenters find twenty images better than one, especially if contradictory; since the human mind has already learned to deal in contradictions.

The image needed here is that of a new centre, or preponderating mass, artificially introduced on earth in the midst of a system of attractive forces that previously made their own equilibrium, and constantly induced to accelerate its motion till it shall establish a new equilibrium. A dynamic theory would begin by assuming that all history, terrestrial or cosmic, mechanical or intellectual, would be reducible to this formula if we knew the facts.

For convenience, the most familiar image should come first; and this is probably that of the comet, or meteoric streams, like the Leonids and Perseids; a complex of minute mechanical agencies, reacting within and without, and guided by the sum of forces attracting or deflecting it. Nothing forbids one to assume that the man-meteorite might grow, as an acorn does, absorbing light, heat, electricity — or thought; for, in recent times, such transference of energy has become a familiar idea; but the simplest figure, at first, is that of a perfect comet — say that of 1843 — which drops from space, in a straight line, at the regular acceleration of speed, directly into the sun, and after wheeling sharply about it, in heat that ought to dissipate any known substance, turns back unharmed, in defiance of law, by the path on which it came. The mind, by analogy, may figure as such a comet, the better because it also defies law.

Motion is the ultimate object of science, and measures of motion are many; but with thought as with matter, the true measure is mass in its astronomic sense — the sum or difference of attractive forces. Science has quite enough trouble in measuring its material motions without volunteering help to the historian, but the historian needs not much help to measure some kinds of social movement; and especially in the nineteenth century, society by common accord agreed in measuring its progress by the coal-output. The ratio of increase in the volume of coal-power may serve as dynamometer.

The coal-output of the world, speaking roughly, doubled every ten years between 1840 and 1900, in the form of utilized power, for the ton of coal yielded three or four times as much power in 1900 as in 1840. Rapid as this rate of acceleration in volume seems, it may be tested in a thousand ways without greatly reducing it. Perhaps the ocean steamer is nearest unity and easiest to measure, for any one might hire, in 1905, for a small sum of money, the use of 30,000 steam-horse-power to cross the ocean, and by halving this figure every ten years, he got back to 234 horse-power for 1835, which was accuracy enough for his purposes. In truth, his chief trouble came not from the ratio in volume of heat, but from the intensity, since he could get no basis for a ratio there. All ages of history have known high intensities, like the iron-furnace, the burning-glass, the blow-pipe; but no society has ever used high intensities on any large scale till now, nor can a mere bystander decide what range of temperature is now in common use. Loosely guessing that science controls habitually the whole range from absolute zero to 3000° Centigrade, one might assume, for convenience, that the ten-year ratio for volume could be used temporarily for intensity; and still there remained a ratio to be guessed for other forces than heat. Since 1800 scores of new forces had been discovered; old forces had been raised to higher powers, as could be measured in the navy-gun; great regions of chemistry had been opened up, and connected with other regions of physics. Within ten years a new universe of force had been revealed in radiation. Complexity had extended itself on immense horizons, and arithmetical ratios were useless for any attempt at accuracy. The force evolved seemed more like explosion than gravitation, and followed closely the curve of steam; but, at all events, the ten-year ratio seemed carefully conservative. Unless the calculator was prepared to be instantly overwhelmed by physical force and mental complexity, he must stop there.

Thus, taking the year 1900 as the starting point for carrying back the series, nothing was easier than to assume a ten-year period of retardation as far back as 1820, but beyond that point the statistician failed, and only the mathematician could help. Laplace would have found it child's-play to fix a ratio of progression in mathematical science between Descartes, Leibnitz, Newton, and himself. Watt could have given in pounds the increase of power between Newcomen's engines and his own. Volta and Benjamin Franklin would have stated their progress as absolute creation of power. Dalton could have measured minutely his advance on Boerhaave. Napoleon I must have had a distant notion of his own numerical relation to Louis XIV. No one in 1789 doubted the progress of force, least of all those who were to lose their heads by it.

Pending agreement between these authorities, theory may assume what it likes — say a fifty, or even a five-and-twenty-year period of reduplication for the eighteenth century, for the period matters little until the acceleration itself is admitted. The subject is even more amusing in the seventeenth than in the eighteenth century, because Galileo and Kepler, Descartes, Huygens, and Isaac Newton took vast pains to fix the laws of acceleration for moving bodies, while Lord Bacon and William Harvey were content with showing experimentally the fact of acceleration in knowledge; but from their combined results a historian might be tempted to maintain a similar rate of movement back to 1600, subject to correction from the historians of mathematics.

The mathematicians might carry their calculations back as far as the fourteenth century when algebra seems to have become for the first time the standard measure of mechanical progress in western Europe; for not only Copernicus and Tycho Brahe, but even artists like Leonardo, Michael Angelo, and Albert Dürer worked by mathematical processes, and their testimony would probably give results more exact than that of Montaigne or Shakespeare; but, to save trouble, one might tentatively carry back the same ratio of acceleration, or retardation, to the year 1400, with the help of Columbus and Gutenberg, so taking a uniform rate during the whole four centuries (1400–1800), and leaving to statisticians the task of correcting it.

Or better, one might, for convenience, use the formula of squares to serve for a law of mind. Any other formula would do as well, either of chemical explosion, or electrolysis, or vegetable growth, or of expansion or contraction in innumerable forms; but this happens to be simple and convenient. Its force increases in the direct ratio of its squares. As the human meteoroid approached the sun or centre of attractive force, the attraction of one century squared itself to give the measure of attraction in the next.

Behind the year 1400, the process certainly went on, but the progress became so slight as to be hardly measurable. What was gained in the east or elsewhere, cannot be known; but forces, called loosely Greek fire and gunpowder, came into use in the west in the thirteenth century, as well as instruments like the compass, the blow-pipe, clocks and spectacles, and materials like paper; Arabic notation and algebra were introduced, while metaphysics and theology acted as violent stimulants to mind. An architect might detect a sequence between the Church of St. Peter's at Rome, the Amiens Cathedral, the Duomo at Pisa, San Marco at Venice, Sancta Sofia at Constantinople and the churches at Ravenna. All the historian dares affirm is that a sequence is manifestly there, and he has a right to carry back his ratio, to represent the fact, without assuming its numerical correctness. On the human mind as a moving body, the break in acceleration in the Middle Ages is only apparent; the attraction worked through shifting forms of force, as the sun works by light or heat, electricity, gravitation, or what not, on different organs with different sensibilities, but with invariable law.

The science of prehistoric man has no value except to prove that the law went back into indefinite antiquity. A stone arrowhead is as convincing as a steam-engine. The values were as clear a hundred thousand years ago as now, and extended equally over the whole world. The motion at last became infinitely slight, but cannot be proved to have stopped. The motion of Newton's comet at aphelion may be equally slight. To evolutionists may be left the processes of evolution; to historians the single interest is the law of reaction between force and force — between mind and nature — the law of progress.

The great division of history into phases by Turgot and Comte first affirmed this law in its outlines by asserting the unity of progress, for a mere phase interrupts no growth, and nature shows innumerable such phases. The development of coal-power in the nineteenth century furnished the first means of assigning closer values to the elements; and the appearance of supersensual forces towards 1900 made this calculation a pressing necessity; since the next step became infinitely serious.

A law of acceleration, definite and constant as any law of mechanics, cannot be supposed to relax its energy to suit the convenience of man. No one is likely to suggest a theory that man's convenience had been consulted by Nature at any time, or that Nature has consulted the convenience of any of her creations, except perhaps the *Terebratula*. In every age man has bitterly and justly complained that Nature hurried and hustled him, for inertia almost invariably has ended in tragedy. Resistance is its law, and resistance to superior mass is futile and fatal.

Fifty years ago, science took for granted that the rate of acceleration could not last. The world forgets quickly, but even to-day the habit remains of founding statistics on the faith that consumption will continue nearly stationary. Two generations, with John Stuart Mill, talked of this stationary period, which was to follow the explosion of new power. All the men who were elderly in the forties died in this faith, and other men grew old nursing the same conviction, and happy in it; while science, for fifty years, permitted, or encouraged, society to think that force would prove to be limited in supply. This mental inertia of science lasted through the eighties before showing signs of breaking up; and nothing short of radium fairly wakened men to the fact, long since evident, that force was inexhaustible. Even then the scientific authorities vehemently resisted.

Nothing so revolutionary had happened since the year 300. Thought had more than once been upset, but never caught and whirled about in the vortex of infinite forces. Power leaped from every atom, and enough of it to supply the stellar universe showed itself running to waste at every pore of matter. Man could no longer hold it off. Forces grasped his wrists and flung him about as though he had hold of a live wire or a runaway automobile; which was very nearly the exact truth for the purposes of an elderly and timid single gentleman in Paris, who never drove down the Champs Élysées without expecting an accident, and commonly witnessing one; or found himself in the neighborhood of an official without calculating the chances of a bomb. So long as the rates of progress held good, these bombs would double in force and number every ten years.

Impossibilities no longer stood in the way. One's life had fattened on impossibilities. Before the boy was six years old, he had seen four impossibilities made actual — the ocean-steamer, the railway, the electric telegraph, and the Daguerreotype; nor could he ever learn which of the four had most hurried others to come. He had seen the coal-output of the United States grow from nothing to three hundred million tons or more. What was far more serious, he had seen the number of minds, engaged in pursuing force — the truest measure of its attraction — increase from a few scores or hundreds, in 1838, to many thousands in 1905, trained to sharpness never before reached, and armed with instruments amounting to new senses of indefinite power and accuracy, while they chased force into hiding-places where Nature herself had never known it to be, making analyses that contradicted being, and syntheses that endangered the elements. No one could say that the social mind now failed to respond to new force, even when the new force annoyed it horribly. Every day Nature violently revolted, causing so-called accidents with enormous destruction of property and life, while plainly laughing at man, who helplessly groaned and shrieked and shuddered, but never for a single instant could stop. The railways alone approached the carnage of war; automobiles and fire-arms ravaged society, until an earthquake became almost a nervous relaxation. An immense volume of force had detached itself from the unknown universe of energy, while still vaster reservoirs, supposed to be infinite, steadily revealed themselves, attracting mankind with more compulsive course than all the Pontic Seas or Gods or Gold that ever existed, and feeling still less of retiring ebb.

In 1850, science would have smiled at such a romance as this, but, in 1900, as far as history could learn, few men of science thought it a laughing matter. If a perplexed but laborious follower could venture to guess their drift, it seemed in their minds a toss-up between anarchy and order. Unless they should be more honest with themselves in the future than ever they were in the past, they would be more astonished than their followers when they reached the end. If Karl Pearson's notions of the universe were sound, men like Galileo, Descartes, Leibnitz, and Newton should have stopped the progress of science before 1700, supposing them to have been honest in the religious convictions they expressed. In 1900 they were plainly forced back on faith in a unity unproved and an order they had themselves disproved. They had reduced their universe to a series of relations to themselves. They had reduced themselves to motion in a universe of motions, with an acceleration, in their own case, of vertiginous violence. With the correctness of their science, history had no right to meddle, since their science now lay in a plane where scarcely one or two hundred minds in the world could follow its mathematical processes; but bombs educate vigorously, and even wireless telegraphy or airships might require the reconstruction of society. If any analogy whatever existed between the human mind, on one side, and the laws of motion, on the other, the mind had already entered a field of attraction so violent that it must immediately pass beyond, into new equilibrium, like the Comet of Newton, to suffer dissipation altogether, like meteoroids in the earth's atmosphere. If it behaved like an explosive, it must rapidly recover equilibrium; if it behaved like a vegetable, it must reach its limits of growth; and even if it acted like the earlier creations of energy — the saurians and sharks — it must have nearly reached the limits of its expansion. If science were to go on doubling or quadrupling its complexities every ten years, even mathematics would soon succumb. An average mind had succumbed already in 1850; it could no longer understand the problem in 1900.

Fortunately, a student of history had no responsibility for the problem; he took it as science gave it, and waited only to be taught. With science or with society, he had no quarrel and claimed no share of authority. He had never been able to acquire knowledge, still less to impart it; and if he had, at times, felt serious differences with the American of the nineteenth century, he felt none with the American of the twentieth. For this new creation, born since 1900, a historian asked no longer to be teacher or even friend; he asked only to be a pupil, and promised to be docile, for once, even though trodden under foot; for he could see that the new American — the child of incalculable coal-power, chemical power, electric power, and radiating energy, as well as of new forces yet undetermined — must be a sort of God compared with any former creation of nature. At the rate of progress since 1800, every American who lived into the year 2000 would know how to control unlimited power. He would think in complexities unimaginable to an earlier mind. He would deal with problems altogether beyond the range of earlier society. To him the nineteenth century would stand on the same plane with the fourth — equally childlike — and he would only wonder how both of them, knowing so little, and so weak in force, should have done so much. Perhaps even he might go back, in 1964, to sit with Gibbon on the steps of Ara Cœli.

Meanwhile he was getting education. With that, a teacher who had failed to educate even the generation of 1870, dared not interfere. The new forces would educate. History saw few lessons in the past that would be useful in the future; but one, at least, it did see. The attempt of the American of 1800 to educate the American of 1900 had not often been surpassed for folly; and since 1800 the forces and their complications had increased a thousand times or more. The attempt of the American of 1900 to educate the American of 2000, must be even blinder than that of the Congressman of 1800, except so far as he had learned his ignorance. During a million or two of years, every generation in turn had toiled with endless agony to attain and apply power, all the while betraying the deepest alarm and horror at the power they created. The teacher of 1900, if foolhardy, might stimulate; if foolish,

might resist; if intelligent, might balance, as wise and foolish have often tried to do from the beginning; but the
forces would continue to educate, and the mind would
continue to react. All the teacher could hope was to
teach it reaction.

Even there his difficulty was extreme. The most elementary books of science betrayed the inadequacy of old
implements of thought. Chapter after chapter closed with
phrases such as one never met in older literature: "The
cause of this phenomenon is not understood"; "science no
longer ventures to explain causes"; "the first step towards
a causal explanation still remains to be taken"; "opinions
are very much divided"; "in spite of the contradictions
involved"; "science gets on only by adopting different
theories, sometimes contradictory." Evidently the new
American would need to think in contradictions, and instead of Kant's famous four antinomies, the new universe
would know no law that could not be proved by its
anti-law.

To educate — one's self to begin with — had been the
effort of one's life for sixty years; and the difficulties of
education had gone on doubling with the coal-output,
until the prospect of waiting another ten years, in order
to face a seventh doubling of complexities, allured one's
imagination but slightly. The law of acceleration was
definite, and did not require ten years more study except
to show whether it held good. No scheme could be suggested to the new American, and no fault needed to be
found, or complaint made; but the next great influx of new
forces seemed near at hand, and its style of education
promised to be violently coercive. The movement from
unity into multiplicity, between 1200 and 1900, was unbroken in sequence, and rapid in acceleration. Prolonged
one generation longer, it would require a new social mind.

As though thought were common salt in indefinite solution it must enter a new phase subject to new laws. Thus far, since five or ten thousand years, the mind had successfully reacted, and nothing yet proved that it would fail to react — but it would need to jump.

35

Nunc Age

(1905)

Nearly forty years had passed since the ex-private secretary landed at New York with the ex-Ministers Adams and Motley, when they saw American society as a long caravan stretching out towards the plains. As he came up the bay again, November 5, 1904, an older man than either his father or Motley in 1868, he found the approach more striking than ever — wonderful — unlike anything man had ever seen — and like nothing he had ever much cared to see. The outline of the city became frantic in its effort to explain something that defied meaning. Power seemed to have outgrown its servitude and to have asserted its freedom. The cylinder had exploded, and thrown great masses of stone and steam against the sky. The city had the air and movement of hysteria, and the citizens were crying, in every accent of anger and alarm, that the new forces must at any cost be brought under control. Prosperity never before imagined, power never yet wielded by man, speed never reached by anything but a meteor, had made the world irritable, nervous, querulous, unreasonable and afraid. All New York was demanding new men, and all the new forces, condensed into corporations, were demanding a new type of man — a man with ten times the endurance, energy, will and mind of the old type — for whom they were ready to pay millions at sight. As one jolted over the pavements or read the last week's newspapers, the new man seemed close at hand, for the old one had plainly reached the end of his strength, and his failure had become catastrophic. Every one saw it, and every municipal election shrieked chaos. A traveller in the highways of history looked out of the club window on the turmoil of Fifth Avenue, and felt himself in Rome, under Diocletian, witnessing the anarchy, conscious of the compulsion, eager for the solution, but unable to conceive whence the next impulse was to come or how it was to act. The two-thousand-years failure of Christianity roared upward from Broadway, and no Constantine the Great was in sight.

Having nothing else to do, the traveller went on to Washington to wait the end. There Roosevelt was training Constantines and battling Trusts. With the Battle of Trusts, a student of mechanics felt entire sympathy, not merely as a matter of politics or society, but also as a measure of motion. The Trusts and Corporations stood for the larger part of the new power that had been created since 1840, and were obnoxious because of their vigorous and unscrupulous energy. They were revolutionary, troubling all the old conventions and values, as the screws of ocean steamers must trouble a school of herring. They tore society to pieces and trampled it under foot. As one of their earliest victims, a citizen of Quincy, born in 1838, had learned submission and silence, for he knew that, under the laws of mechanics, any change, within the range of the forces, must make his situation only worse; but he was beyond measure curious to see whether the conflict of forces would produce the new man, since no other energies seemed left on earth to breed. The new man could be only a child born of contact between the new and the old energies.

Both had been familiar since childhood, as the story has shown, and neither had warped the umpire's judgment by its favors. If ever judge had reason to be impartial, it was he. The sole object of his interest and sympathy was the new man, and the longer one watched, the less could be seen of him. Of the forces behind the Trusts, one could see something; they owned a complete organization, with schools, training, wealth and purpose; but of the forces behind Roosevelt one knew little; their cohesion was slight; their training irregular; their objects vague. The public had no idea what practical system it could aim at, or what sort of men could manage it. The single problem before it was not so much to control the Trusts as to create the society that could manage the Trusts. The new American must be either the child of the new forces or a chance sport of nature. The attraction of mechanical power had already wrenched the American mind into a crab-like process which Roosevelt was making heroic efforts to restore to even action, and he had every right to active support and sympathy from all the world, especially from the Trusts themselves so far as they were human; but the doubt persisted whether the force that educated was really man or nature — mind or motion. The mechanical theory, mostly accepted by science, seemed to require that the law of mass should rule. In that case, progress would continue as before.

In that, or any other case, a nineteenth-century education was as useless or misleading as an eighteenth-century education had been to the child of 1838; but Adams had a better reason for holding his tongue. For his dynamic theory of history he cared no more than for the kinetic theory of gas; but, if it were an approach to measurement of motion, it would verify or disprove itself within thirty years. At the calculated acceleration, the head of the meteor-stream must very soon pass perihelion. Therefore, dispute was idle, discussion was futile, and silence, next to good-temper, was the mark of sense. If the acceleration, measured by the development and economy of forces, were to continue at its rate since 1800, the mathematician of 1950 should be able to plot the past and future orbit of the human race as accurately as that of the November meteoroids.

Naturally such an attitude annoyed the players in the game, as the attitude of the umpire is apt to infuriate the spectators. Above all, it was profoundly unmoral, and tended to discourage effort. On the other hand, it tended to encourage foresight and to economize waste of mind. If it was not itself education, it pointed out the economies necessary for the education of the new American. There, the duty stopped.

There, too, life stopped. Nature has educated herself to a singular sympathy for death. On the antarctic glacier, nearly five thousand feet above sea-level, Captain Scott found carcasses of seals, where the animals had laboriously flopped up, to die in peace. "Unless we had actually found these remains, it would have been past believing that a dying seal could have transported itself over fifty miles of rough, steep, glacier-surface," but "the seal seems often to crawl to the shore or the ice to die, probably from its instinctive dread of its marine enemies." In India, Purun Dass, at the end of statesmanship, sought solitude, and died in sanctity among the deer and monkeys, rather than remain with man. Even in America, the Indian Summer of life should be a little sunny and a little sad, like the season, and infinite in wealth and depth of tone — but never hustled. For that reason, one's own passive obscurity seemed sometimes nearer nature than John Hay's exposure. To the normal animal the instinct of sport is innate, and historians themselves were not exempt from the passion of baiting their bears; but in its turn even the seal dislikes to be worried to death in age by creatures that have not the strength or the teeth to kill him outright.

On reaching Washington, November 14, 1904, Adams saw at a glance that Hay must have rest. Already Mrs. Hay had bade him prepare to help in taking her husband to Europe as soon as the Session should be over, and although Hay protested that the idea could not even be discussed, his strength failed so rapidly that he could not effectually discuss it, and ended by yielding without struggle. He would equally have resigned office and retired, like Purun Dass, had not the President and the press protested; but he often debated the subject, and his friends could throw no light on it. Adams himself, who had set his heart on seeing Hay close his career by making peace in the East, could only urge that vanity for vanity, the crown of peacemaker was worth the cross of martyrdom; but the cross was full in sight, while the crown was still uncertain. Adams found his formula for Russian inertia exasperatingly correct. He thought that Russia should have negotiated instantly on the fall of Port Arthur, January 1, 1905; he found that she had not the energy, but meant to wait till her navy should be destroyed. The delay measured precisely the time that Hay had to spare.

The close of the Session on March 4 left him barely the strength to crawl on board ship, March 18, and before his steamer had reached half her course, he had revived, almost as gay as when he first lighted on the Markoe house in I Street forty-four years earlier. The clouds that gather round the setting sun do not always take a sober coloring from eyes that have kept watch on mortality; or, at least, the sobriety is sometimes scarcely sad. One walks with one's friends squarely up to the portal of life, and bids good-bye with a smile. One has done it so often! Hay could scarcely pace the deck; he nourished no illusions; he was convinced that he should never return to his work, and he talked lightly of the death-sentence that he might any day expect, but he threw off the coloring of office and mortality together, and the malaria of power left its only trace in the sense of tasks incomplete.

One could honestly help him there. Laughing frankly at his dozen treaties hung up in the Senate Committee-room like lambs in a butcher's shop, one could still remind him of what was solidly completed. In his eight years of office he had solved nearly every old problem of American statesmanship, and had left little or nothing to annoy his successor. He had brought the great Atlantic powers into a working system, and even Russia seemed about to be dragged into a combine of intelligent equilibrium based on an intelligent allotment of activities. For the first time in fifteen hundred years a true Roman *pax* was in sight, and would, if it succeeded, owe its virtues to him. Except for making peace in Manchuria, he could do no more; and if the worst should happen, setting continent against continent in arms — the only apparent alternative to his scheme — he need not repine at missing the catastrophe.

This rosy view served to soothe disgusts which every parting statesman feels, and commonly with reason. One had no need to get out one's notebook in order to jot down the exact figures on either side. Why add up the elements of resistance and anarchy? The Kaiser supplied him with these figures, just as the Cretic approached Morocco. Every one was doing it, and seemed in a panic about it. The chaos waited only for his landing.

Arrived at Genoa, the party hid itself for a fortnight

at Nervi, and he gained strength rapidly as long as he made no effort and heard no call for action. Then they all went on to Nauheim without relapse. There, after a few days, Adams left him for the regular treatment, and came up to Paris. The medical reports promised well, and Hay's letters were as humorous and light-handed as ever. To the last he wrote cheerfully of his progress, and amusingly with his usual light scepticism, of his various doctors; but when the treatment ended, three weeks later, and he came on to Paris, he showed, at the first glance, that he had lost strength, and the return to affairs and interviews wore him rapidly out. He was conscious of it, and in his last talk before starting for London and Liverpool he took the end of his activity for granted. "You must hold out for the peace negotiations," was the remonstrance. "I've not time!" he replied. "You'll need little time!" was the rejoinder. Each was correct.

There it ended! Shakespeare himself could use no more than the commonplace to express what is incapable of expression. "The rest is silence!" The few familiar words, among the simplest in the language, conveying an idea trite beyond rivalry, served Shakespeare, and, as yet, no one has said more. A few weeks afterwards, one warm evening in early July, as Adams was strolling down to dine under the trees at Armenonville, he learned that Hay was dead. He expected it; on Hay's account, he was even satisfied to have his friend die, as we would all die if we could, in full fame, at home and abroad, universally regretted, and wielding his power to the last. One had seen scores of emperors and heroes fade into cheap obscurity even when alive; and now, at least, one had not that to fear for one's friend. It was not even the suddenness of the shock, or the sense of void, that threw Adams into the depths of Hamlet's Shakespearean silence in the full flare of Paris frivolity in its favorite haunt where worldly vanity reached its most futile climax in human history; it was only the quiet summons to follow — the assent to dismissal. It was time to go. The three friends had begun life together; and the last of the three had no motive — no attraction — to carry it on after the others had gone. Education had ended for all three, and only beyond some remoter horizon could its values be fixed or renewed. Perhaps some day — say 1938, their centenary — they might be allowed to return together for a holiday, to see the mistakes of their own lives made clear in the light of the mistakes of their successors; and perhaps then, for the first time since man began his education among the carnivores, they would find a world that sensitive and timid natures could regard without a shudder.

THE END

Index

A Note about
the Production
of This Book

The text of this special edition of *The Education of Henry Adams* is set in Linotype Janson, which is based on a 17th Century typeface designed by the Leipzig type cutter Anton Janson.

I

The paper, TIME Reading Text, is from The Mead Corporation, Dayton, Ohio. The cover stock is from The Plastic Coating Corporation, Holyoke, Massachusetts.

"A brilliantly written book that should be on every dog lover's bed stand. Charleson's use of language is so rich I'm not sure if I want to read her book or eat it."
— Patricia B. McConnell, author of *The Other End of the Leash*

"In a dog book, I look for great information, a wonderful story about the relationship between humans and dogs, and anecdotes that are funny, insightful, and memorable. Rarely do all three components come together, but Susannah Charleson's memoir has the whole package. Beautifully written, informative, charming in every detail that chronicles the life and work of Susannah and her dog Puzzle, and laugh-'til-you-snort funny, it's a magnificent work." — *Bark*

"Heartwarming, heart-achingly poignant, and riveting from page one. Puzzle had me from her first joyous wroo!"
— Hallie Ephron, author of *Never Tell a Lie*

"This book is a fantastic discovery! Dog and human decipher each other's language and behavior to solve the mystery of the missing, and find their bonds of love, trust, and friendship grow. I loved this book." — Lynne Cox, author of *Swimming to Antarctica* and *Grayson*

"Riveting . . . I found myself spellbound by their ability to read and unravel clues in their SAR work, as well as moved by the deep bond the two form to make an inseparable team." — *Modern Dog*

"The transformation of Puzzle the cuddly pup into Puzzle the professional search-and-rescue dog would be story enough, but Susannah Charleson gives us far more. With lean, lovely prose she takes us on a clear-eyed, compassionate journey into a mysterious world in which every story begins as a ghost story."
— Michael Perry, author of *Population: 485*

"*Scent of the Missing* contains wonderful writing about dogs and plenty of powerful, compassionate writing about the community of mankind. In its telling, it is respectful of life and celebrates the living."
— Rick Bass

Scent *of the* Missing

Scent *of* *the* Missing

LOVE AND PARTNERSHIP WITH A
SEARCH-AND-RESCUE DOG

Susannah Charleson

Mariner Books
Houghton Mifflin Harcourt   BOSTON   NEW YORK

First Mariner Books edition 2011

Copyright © 2010 by Susannah Charleson

www.hmhbooks.com

Library of Congress Cataloging-in-Publication Data
Charleson, Susannah.
  Scent of the missing : love and partnership with a
search-and-rescue dog / Susannah Charleson.
    p. cm.
  ISBN 978-0-547-15244-8
  ISBN 978-0-547-42257-2 (pbk.)
  1. Rescue dogs — Texas—Dallas — Anecdotes. 2. Search
dogs — Texas — Dallas — Anecdotes. 3. Search-and-rescue
operations — Texas — Dallas — Anecdotes. 4. Golden retriever
— Texas — Dallas — Anecdotes. I. Title.
  SF428.55.C43 2010
  636.7'0886 — dc22   2009033783

Book design by Melissa Lotfy

Printed in the United States of America

DOC 10 9 8 7 6 5 4 3 2 1

PHOTO CREDITS: All photographs by Susannah Charleson except as fol-
lows: *Skip Fernandez and Aspen: Dallas Morning News*/Louis DeLuca.
Fleta and Saber: Mark-9 Search and Rescue. *Max and Hunter:* Mark-9
Search and Rescue. *Jerry and Shadow:* Mark-9 Search and Rescue. *Max
and Mercy:* Kurt Seevers/Mark-9 Search and Rescue. *Fo'c'sle Jack:* Devon
Thomas Treadwell. *Confidence on a rappel line:* Sara Maryfield/Mark-9
Search and Rescue. *Certified Puzzle:* Daniel Daugherty.

For Ellen Sànchez, who always believed, and brought a thousand cups of tea to prove it.

For Puzzle. Good dog. Find more.

CONTENTS

AUTHOR'S NOTE

Scent of the Missing is a memoir of my experiences as a field assistant and young search-and-rescue canine handler. Unless otherwise attributed, the perspectives and opinions expressed here are my own and do not necessarily reflect those of teammates and colleagues in the field.

Though this book is a nonfiction account of working search-and-rescue, compassion for the affected families and respect for their privacy have directed me to change names, locations, and identifying circumstances surrounding the searches related here. Who, where, and when are frankly altered; what, why, and how are as straightforward as one person's perspective can make them.

The dogs are all real. You can hold up a biscuit and call them by name.

Scent *of the* Missing

1

GONE

I N THE LONG LIGHT of early morning, Hunter circles
what remains of a burned house, his nose low and brow
furrowed. The night's thick air has begun to lift, and the
German Shepherd's movement catches the emerging sun. He is a
shining thing against the black of scorched brick, burned timber,
and a nearby tree charred leafless. Hunter inspects the tree: half-
fallen, tilting south away from where the fire was, its birds long
gone. Quiet here. I can hear his footpads in the wizened grass, the
occasional scrape of his nails across debris. The dog moves along
the rubble in his characteristic half-crouch, intense and communicative, while his handler, Max, watches.

Hunter rounds the house twice, crosses cautiously through a
clear space in the burned pile, and returns to Max with a huff of
finality. *Nothing,* he seems to say. Hunter is not young. There are
little flecks of gray about his dark eyes and muzzle, and his body
has begun to fail his willing heart, but he knows his job, and he is a
proud boy doing it. He leans into his handler and huffs again. Max
rubs his ears and turns away.

"She's not in the house," I murmur into the radio, where a colleague and a sheriff's deputy wait for word from us.

"Let's go," says Max to Hunter.

We move on, our tracks dark across the ash, Hunter leading us forward into a field that lies behind the house. Here we have to work a little harder across the uneven terrain. Max, a career firefighter used to unstable spaces, manages the unseen critter holes and slick grass better than I do. Hunter cleaves an easy path. Our passage disturbs the field mice, which move in such a body the ground itself appears to shiver.

Wide sweeps across the field, back and forth across the wind, Hunter and Max and I (the assistant in trail) continuing to search for some sign of the missing girl. Hunter is an experienced search dog with years of disaster work and many single-victim searches behind him. He moves confidently but not heedlessly, and at the base of a low ridge crowned by a stand of trees, he pauses, head up a long moment, mouth open. His panting stops.

Max stops, watches. I stand where I last stepped.

And then Hunter is off, scrambling up the ridge with us behind him, crashing through the trees. We hear a surprised shout, and scuffling, and when we get to where he is, we see two men stumble away from the dog. One is yelping a little, has barked his shin on a battered dinette chair he's tripped over. The other hauls him forward by the elbow, and they disappear into the surrounding brush.

A third man has more difficulty. He is elderly and not as fast. He has been lying on a bare set of box springs set flat beneath the canopy of trees, and when he rises the worn cloth of his trousers catches on the coils. We hear rending fabric as he jerks free. He runs in a different direction from the other two — *not their companion,* I think — and a few yards away he stops and turns to peek through the scrub at us, as though aware the dog is not fierce and we aren't in pursuit.

Our search has disturbed a small tent city, and as we work our way through the reclaimed box springs and three-legged coffee tables and mouse-eaten recliners that have become a sort of home for its inhabitants, the third man watches our progress from the edge of the brush. This is a well-lived space, but there is nothing of the missing girl here. Charged on this search to find any human scent in the area, living or dead, Hunter has done what he is supposed to do. But he watches our response. From where I stand, it is clear Hunter knows what we've found is not what we seek, and that what we seek isn't here. He gazes at Max, reading him, his eyebrows working, stands poised for the "Find more" command.

"Sector clear," I say into the radio after a signal from Max. I mention the tent city and its inhabitants and learn it is not a surprise.

"Good boy," says Max. Hunter's stance relaxes.

As we move away, the third man gains confidence. He steps a little forward, watching Hunter go. He is barefoot and shirtless. "Dog, dog, dog," he says voicelessly, as though he shapes the word but cannot make the sound of it. "Dog," he rasps again, and smiles wide, and claps his hands.

Saturday night in a strange town five hundred miles from home. I am sitting in a bar clearly tacked on to our motel as an afterthought. The clientele here are jammed against one another in the gloom, all elbows and ball caps bent down to their drinks — more tired than social. At the nearby pool table, a man makes his shot, trash talks his opponent, and turns to order another beer without having to take more than four steps to get it. This looks like standard procedure. The empty bottles stack up on a nearby shelf that droops from screws half pulled out of the wall. Two men dominate the table while others watch. The shots get a little wild, the trash talk sloppier.

A half-hour ago, when I walked in with a handful of teammates, every head in the bar briefly turned to regard us, then turned away in perfect synchronization, their eyes meeting and their heads bobbing a nod. We are strangers and out of uniform, but they know who we are and why we are here, and besides, they've seen a lot of strangers lately. Now, at the end of the second week of search for a missing local girl, they leave us alone. We find a table, plop down without discussion, and a waitress comes out to take our orders.

She calls several of us "honey" and presses a hand to the shoulder of one of us as she turns away.

Either the town hasn't passed a smoking ordinance, or here at the city limits this place has conveniently ignored the law. We sit beneath a stratus layer of cigarette smoke that curls above us like an atmosphere of drowsy snakes, tinged blue and red and green by the neon signs over the bar. Beside the door, I see a flyer for the missing girl. Her face hovers beneath the smoke. She appears uneasy even in this photograph taken years ago, her smile tentative and her blond, feathered bangs sprayed close as a helmet, her dark eyes tight at the edges, like this picture was something to be survived.

I have looked at her face all day. On telephone poles, in the hands of local volunteers, over the shoulder of a big-city newscaster at noon, six, and ten o'clock. She is the ongoing local headline. She's the girl no one really knew before her disappearance, and now she's the girl eager eyewitnesses claim to have known all their lives. It's hard to tell what's real and what isn't, but for the most part that's not our job. We go where law enforcement directs us. We run behind search dogs who will tell us their own truths in any given area: *never here, was here, hers, not hers, blood, hair, bone, here, here, here.*

We humans aren't talking about the search, our first day at work in this town. Inappropriate discussion in a public place, and we are exhausted with it anyway. Though today's bystanders seemed to think we could take our dogs to Main Street and race them outward across all points of the compass — first dog to the victim wins — canine search-and-rescue doesn't work that way. Assigned to locations chosen by law enforcement, we work methodically, dividing a region into sectors to be searched by individual dog-and-handler teams. It's a meticulous process, but trained dogs can quickly clear a large area it would take humans days to definitively search.

Even so, we could be here for weeks. We already feel the trackless absence of this girl. Her hometown is small, but its outlying population is widespread, and there are places to hide a living woman or the remains of a dead one that cross lines into other states. Today we were sent to clear more "hot spots" — places where bodies have been dumped before. Shrouded, ugly areas they were too, scarred from previous events, but not this girl, this time. All day the dogs have been telling us: *Not here. Not here. Not here.*

I look at her photograph again. A big guy shifting on his stool blocks the ambient light from the bar, causing the girl's face to purple beneath the neon and the whites of her eyes to swallow the irises. Her gaze no longer connects. It's a condition that was true of her in life, some say. She has a history of scuttling head down, of sitting at the back of the class, never speaking unless spoken to, and even then as briefly as possible. She sounds uncertain on her voicemail greeting, enunciating her name with a rising inflection that suggests she isn't quite sure of it.

We hear fragments. The cumulative description adds up to a girl who began inching away from this town six years earlier, who saved her allowance and bought a junky car simply to have her first job at a truck stop in another town fifteen miles up the road, who saved her paychecks to buy a used laptop, and who had begun re-creating herself in variations all across the Web. *No judgment,* says a neighbor. *An accident waiting to happen,* says one interviewee. Authorities suggest she might be a runaway if it weren't for the methodical, calculated nature of her young choices. She might be a runaway if it weren't for her purse, cell phone, keys, car, and laptop left behind at her grandmother's house, the last place she was seen alive.

We're told she has a tattoo, inked by a trucker where she worked: a butterfly with the letter *K* on her left wrist. The tattoo is in honor of an online friend, Katie, who had slashed her own wrists in a successful suicide — or so it was rumored, until Katie returned to a chat room a month later with a new location, new name, new boy-friend, holding up her woundless wrists for photographs, laughing at the duped online friends who thought they knew her, who had responded to her loss with depression, Paxil, and new tattoos in her honor. April Fools, all.

Did our girl admire her, forgive her? I wonder. *Is this a copycat drama?*

I turn away from her photograph. She's not my daughter, but I feel a mother's impulse to push the bangs from her eyes, the rescuer's urge to put two fingertips to her carotid to check for a pulse.

We're a quiet group, tight and preoccupied. Still wired from the day's search, we lean forward over our food, weight on the balls of our feet with our heels lifted, as though we'll push up at any moment to go back to work. Unlikely. We're stood down for the night and have an early call in the morning. It always takes a while to let go enough to sleep, especially as a search presses forward over days and investigators' verbs begin to change from *she is* to *she was.* That little shift in tense is enough to keep us awake all night, revisiting the day's barns, ravines, burned houses, tent cities, and trailer parks, triple-checking ourselves against the signals from the dogs. To say this girl haunts us is to overdramatize. But we all mull choices made in the field long after we should be sleeping. I stab at my coleslaw and wonder when one of us will finally relax into the back of a chair.

In time, Terry, a canine handler, leans over to say to me, "Hey. I hear you're going to work a dog."

The others look up.

"Yes," I say. The word feels huge as a wedding vow.

I've been on the search-and-rescue (SAR) team for a while now, running beside certified dogs and their handlers, working as a field assistant responsible for navigation, radio communication, medical assessment, and other pragmatics of a working canine search team. After three years, I'm senior enough to have earned the next open slot to train and run beside a search dog. I am excited about this, but a little nervous too. Having run with more than a dozen breeds and their handlers, having searched night into day for the living, and having knelt over the dead, I'm aware how serious a proposition bringing a new dog to the team is. Working search is not a hobby or a Sunday pastime.

"What breed you thinking of running?" he asks. He handles a

MISSING TEEN and UNIDENTIFIED REMAINS UNCOVERED IN STATE PARK ten years from now seems narrow.

Time and numbers make me urgent. I cannot train my new dog too soon.

Next morning's light is hard as a slap. The community has rallied beneath a red, white, and blue striped tent donated by a used car dealership half the state away. The structure is shabby; its attached bunting is worn. The top line sags. A good wind could be a problem here, but the morning is windless.

At this early hour, the sun shines in at a slant, but it is already too warm inside the tent. Two hundred or so volunteers jockey for position behind the darker canvas of the wide blue stripes. We suck down donated orange juice or strong coffee or both — an unwise choice. The port-a-potties have not yet arrived, and today's search has staged in the middle of nowhere, from a plain so flat that any thought of a quick whip around a bush to pee should assume an audience, both local and televised. A caravan of mobile units from TV stations miles away has also arrived. Their antennae and cranes have already begun to extend.

We hear more cars exit the road and crunch across the gravel and brush. Doors slam, and a voice from near the tent flap says that the sheriff's here with the parents, and we should be starting soon. I don't think so. I read a similar doubt on the faces of my teammates. *Hurry up and wait* is the case more often than not on large searches, and this one, with its ambiguous geography and its swelling ranks of volunteers, has become a large search. We were told to be on-scene at 7:00 A.M., and we've been here ninety minutes. I think if we deploy by 9:30, we'll be lucky.

"I'm going to check on the dogs," says Terry, four bottles of water in the crook of his elbow. The dogs are crated behind the shade of our cars with Ellen, a field assistant, in attendance. I can see them through the tent flap. They look a whole lot more comfortable than we do.

Aware they are on-scene to work, the dogs are alert. Collie Saber, German Shepherd Hunter, Border Collie Hoss, and Buster, a Lab. They scrutinize all newcomers, nostrils knitting and ears perked forward, their expressions speculative. I wonder how they sort passersby: *old guy with a kidney problem . . . nice lady who ate bacon for breakfast, come* here, *nice lady . . . this guy's got two dogs — one of them, oh, one of them's in heat! . . . hey, that kid dropped McMuffin on his pants.* Terry's approach makes them turn and grin. Their wagging tails *bang-bang-bang* against the bars of their crates.

Here in the tent, a community group has made T-shirts for its members, purple T-shirts bearing several photos of the missing girl. WE'LL FIND YOU promise the shirts on the front. WE LOVE YOU they say on the back. Several participants have their video cameras out to record today's events. The sheriff walks in with two deputies and the missing girl's parents, and the group falls silent. A man whips his Tilley hat off. His friend with a digital camera continues to shoot: sheriff, mom and dad, TV reporter, crowd. A deputy's leaden gaze stops her. I hear the little *scree* of it winding down. She puts the camera in her purse.

The sheriff's briefing tells us little that gossip hasn't already introduced. Yesterday's search found nothing relevant to the missing girl. But, we are reminded, every area cleared contributes something to a final answer. The sheriff's baritone is edged with weariness, ragged on its ending syllables, yet he speaks well. His words are clear and urgent. The community group will be divided into four units who will work, geographically, across today's new areas. We should expect hardship, he says. These places are ugly and brushy and filled with debris from illegal dumping. High boots are recommended. There will be broken glass. There could be snakes. A woman in front of me, wearing shorts, sandals, and a baby in a papoose on her back, looks at her husband. He looks pointedly at her feet, and she sets her jaw and turns away.

The sheriff pulls the girl's parents forward. Though the woman appears shattered with fatigue while her husband's face is tight and reserved, it is his voice that gives way as he thanks the crowd. "Find our girl," says his wife in his wordlessness. She guides him away from the television camera, but he turns and gives the lens a long look in passing.

"All right," says the sheriff. "We've got no better reason to be here." The crowd stirs beneath the tent, convicted again. As two deputies step forward to divide the ground-search volunteers, I feel a tug on my arm. "We're going," mouths Johnny. He jerks his head in the direction of another officer discreetly leading us out of the tent and away from the crowd.

As we gather around the deputy and the dogs press their noses to the crate bars to smell him, he opens a map on the hood of a truck and shows us where we're headed. "The word is this may be it," he says. "We think she's here." He points to a spot and then makes a wide circle with a forefinger.

"Why here?" asks Terry. The retired detective in him is never far away.

The deputy shrugs. "Anonymous tip." He stares at the map a long moment. "That's all we've got."

The dogs quiver and circle and pee as we release them from their crates. A few bark excitedly as we load them into the trucks, engines and air conditioners on. Safe now in transport crates, they are ready to go. I can hear them winding themselves up behind the glass, scuffling and muttering, that signature dog sound that's more grumble than growl.

Three dogs work separate sections of the area we've deployed to, fifty acres of patchy terrain, dried creek bed, and dumped appliances. A variable wind has risen, strong enough to make a little thunder in our ears, but born of ground radiation, it offers no relief from heat. The dogs will use the wind, though. Turning east, north, then west, through binoculars I watch them sweep their individual sectors, heads up and tails visible above the bending grass, handlers following yards behind.

Collie Saber moves across the scrub at a steady trot, despite his heavy coat and the day's temperature. I hardly need binoculars. He is easy to see from a distance, a tricolored boy flashing against the dun terrain. Fleta follows, watching him thoughtfully, with Ellen in trail behind them both, taking notes. The scruffy field is flat. Saber's wide sweeps are clean and unbroken. At the end of the sector, they pause. The Collie looks back to Fleta and turns with a movement very like a shrug of his great ruff — an *all clear* that's readable even from where I stand. I see Fleta turn and shake her head to Ellen. A moment later, Ellen's voice crackles across the radio that they're coming in.

Max and Hunter are winding their way through a clutch of small trees that cling to the edge of a rainwater runoff gully. I watch the German Shepherd's great dark ears working independently as he penetrates the sector, as though there is much to hear skittering in the grass. A nervous prairie bird flushes yards away from where they walk, and both Hunter's ears come forward so rapidly that the light spots within them seem to blink like eyes. He doesn't turn for the bird, however, continuing on his course, nose thrust forward. He leads Max through the trees and they disappear behind them, visible only as an occasional twitch and flash of Max's red shirt as they work the rest of the sector.

Trained to alert differently on the living and the dead, the dogs' demeanor across the area is consistent. No pause, no head pop, no sudden, energized movement, no bark. Their passage stirs rabbits and shivers a few snakes from the brush, but the dogs communicate their disinterest. They all seem to agree that nothing's here.

The deputy watches quietly. "I hunt with a Lab," he says, looking out to Johnny and Buster. "Great dogs. Can't stop them."

Fleta has already returned with Saber. Max comes in with Hunter, shaking his head. Hunter takes a drink of water as fast as Max pours it and flops down with a sigh. A few minutes later Johnny returns with Buster. "Nothing," he says. "Except a bunch of baby rabbits in a washing machine out there."

"Aw," says Ellen. "Bunnies. How many?"

"Dunno," Johnny replies. "Enough to be breakfast, lunch, and dinner for the snakes."

"God." Ellen folds her arms across her chest and shakes her head. Ellen's worked ranches, but she's ready for any kind of good word here.

The deputy says, "Thing is . . ."

We look at him. His cell phone buzzes, and he walks away, muttering into it, one hand pressed to the opposite ear to block the wind.

A new search area, and we are moving fast. Ground searchers have found a location where the scent of death is strong, and third-hand word to the deputy by cell phone suggests the presence of possible evidence too. Now a potential crime scene, the area has been cleared, and the sheriff waits for the dogs. We'll use a different approach: one way in, one way out — a cautious trail rather than a wide sweep — to confirm or deny what's been found.

We park at the base of a shallow rise crisscrossed with bike trails and more dumped appliances, a whole host of abandoned cars. Our deputy gives a little jerk of his head as we look upward, waiting for clearance to deploy.

"Kids park here," he says.

I think of sex in this tangled, airless scrub and feel old. "Really?" I ask, doubtfully.

"The stars are nice," he replies. A little twist of his mouth suggests he knows this from experience, and I wonder if he's busted kids here or was once one of them himself.

His cell phone buzzes again. After a few moments he turns to us. "Thing is," he says, "there's a smell in a locked car, and an object not far away that may have been a weapon, and fresh clothes in the mud. Because this might be a crime scene — if not this one, then another one — we don't want you to track the whole area, but we'd like you to bring the dogs and see what they think about the car."

Fleta and Saber, Max and Hunter, Ellen and I follow the deputy up the thin trail to the top of the rise. A distance away, perhaps two football fields long, I can see a group of volunteer searchers watching us, their purple shirts dark as a bruise against the buff-colored ground. I hear the huddle of voices when the breeze shifts and I am downwind. At the top of the rise, the sheriff and two deputies are still and expectant. They turn to lead us carefully to the car in question, a battered blue '72 Impala. Just beyond it, a stainless butcher knife lies in the dirt. The knife is clean and bright. Next to the Impala, a pair of crumpled blue jeans rest in such a way that it appears someone dropped his pants right there and stepped out of them. The jeans remain in that position, the legs stacked, the fly open, the waist upward and wide. A thread of dust marks a few denim folds that I can see, but it doesn't appear to me that the jeans have been here long.

Ellen and I are taking notes as first Saber, then Hunter slowly circle the car. Both are experienced cadaver dogs, and though they sniff every crevice, neither gives a flicker of interest. Fleta shakes her head, and minutes later, Max does too.

"No," says Max. "The dogs say no."

The sheriff gestures us all closer forward, and the fug of decomposition is palpable. "Have any of you ever smelled a dead body?" he asks. Fleta, Max, and I nod and step nearer, and without thinking about it, we simultaneously put our noses just above the trunk. The air is thick and foul.

"This doesn't smell right," I murmur just as Fleta also shakes her head. I always have difficulty explaining it, but to me dead human smells different from squirrel, rat, or possum on the side of the road. Not just more scent — human death seems specific and particular. I don't know the why behind the chemistry. All that shampoo, maybe, or trans fat or antiperspirant, or maybe we're all pickled in Coca-Cola, like the urban legend says.

"Something's dead in here," says Fleta, "but I don't think it's human."

Max guides Hunter forward again, watching. "Where's the dead thing, Hunter?" he says. Off-command to find human scent, Hunter circles the car in the way of any curious dog, stopping warily and putting his nose to the back left wheel well. Max kneels into the area, then drops his head. "Got it," he says, his voice sad. "It's a dog."

We all bend down, and there, caught above the back axle, we can see a dog's paws and its limp head dangling. A medium-size mixed breed, brown fur ticked with black. The flesh of its mouth is pulled back from the teeth; the eyes are muddy and glazed. The pads are intact but slightly shriveled, and I can see a small white stone between two of them. This dog was either hit by the car or crawled up there to die. An uncomforted end. I hear the lazy drone of flies.

"Dead for a while," says Max.

"Well, okay," says the sheriff. He gets up stiffly. Though he is sunburned, the flesh beneath his eyes is gray.

"Got anywhere else for the dogs to search?" asks the deputy.

The sheriff shakes his head. "Don't have anywhere else for anybody." Then he adds, "This search is going to be a long one. Guess you folks can go home. We'll call you back if we get something for the dogs."

We stand a moment. He gazes along the rise to the motionless group of volunteers. Below us, another vehicle has pulled up and parked. The car doors slam, *thunk,* and — slower — *thunk.* The sheriff turns.

"Right," he says. "I'll go tell the parents."

He walks down the path, and they walk up toward him. As they near, I watch the sheriff stand a little straighter. The father, too, lifts his head and squares his shoulders and pulls his wife to his hip as they climb. And in that moment before they connect, on day thirteen of a search for a missing local girl, I wonder how they can bear the unknowing, what these parents most wish for — words that leave the door open or words that press the door closed.

Our cars are loaded for the long drive home, and the dogs are having a last romp in a small park along a stream. Two of the local volunteers on today's search stand with us beneath the shade of a pecan tree. One is about to drive back to her college for summer classes. The other has had a quick shower and will head another direction to her restaurant shift miles away.

One asks what we think the dogs know about this search. Do they feel what we feel? Does the search continue to trouble them, as we humans are troubled?

Fleta shakes her head, pointing out that from the dogs' perspectives, this search was successful. They were asked to do a job: *find the missing girl or indicate definitively she's not here*, and they did. Apart from three vagrants in a tent city, no one living or dead was there to be found. And after the day's sectors were done, volunteers hid so the dogs could find them, a quick and upbeat conclusion to a hard workday, a game that fools no one but keeps motivation high. These dogs are all praise-hounds. They played along, finding and grinning and capering.

No, Fleta suggests. There are exceptions, but usually the dogs let go of a day's search better than we do. We trust them to do their jobs, and they trust us to tell them they have done it well. And when we tell them, they believe us.

I watch them play. Common goals aside, these dogs are complete individuals in the field. I have searched beside Hunter's intensity, Saber's calm authority, and Buster's bounding accuracy. Even this evening's pleasure they pursue in different ways. The German Shepherd noses for critters in the brush, while the Lab snaps at minnows in shallow water, trying to catch them. We tease him, and Buster raises his head with muzzle dripping, looking fusty and bemused, but he grins at the sound of his name and tries for fish again. The beautiful Collie, Saber — much-admired and he knows it — rolls ungracefully in the grass, groaning *unnh-unnnh-unnhhhhh-mmmmmmm*. His white ruff is streaked with green when he gets up, and his coat splays every which way. He is thoroughly happy to be such a mess. "Brickhead," says Fleta, hugging him as he nuzzles her ear. "Doofus."

The Border Collie brings every one of us his ball. Hoss is a dog of great charm and is completely tone-deaf to rejection. It's time to leave, but he is persuasive. We throw and throw and throw again. "Fetch therapy" we call it, and it works. The local volunteers leave laughing, Hoss still petitioning them with his ball in his mouth all the way to their cars.

As we head out, I wonder what my own dog will bring to the work, to the team, and to me. I like the thought of a long drive home with a Golden snoring belly-up in the back of the car: a good dog who has worked well. A partner. A friend. After a search like this one, that companionship must take away a little of the ache.

2

DOG FOR THE JOB

I T'S 102 DEGREES when I step out of the airport in Midland, Texas, but my hands are cold. I've got a dog carrier, a collar and leash, and a canine SAR training vest. I'm wearing my team ID and a stunned expression I can describe only now as *deer in the headlights*.

After almost a year of research, breeder queries, and preemptive puppy-proofing at the house, I am a half-hour away from the Golden Retriever that will be my partner. Today there's little evidence of all the meticulous preparation: I look down and realize I'm wearing different-colored socks and that in my blind scramble to get from home to the airport at dawn, I also brought a new dog toy, size-appropriate for a Great Dane, a stuffed red lobster with "Cape Cod" embroidered on the claw. I don't remember picking it up at the house. I don't remember pushing it through security. I think the lobster is probably bigger than the puppy is.

"Where's the pet?" asks a cabdriver who sees me standing alone, cradling the empty carrier and the toy.

"I'm going to be having some puppy!" I babble, waving the lobster as if to clarify. The driver shakes his head and backs away from me, clearly figuring I'm not all there.

• • •

For so visible a presence in the public consciousness, the Golden Retriever is not an ancient breed. Though its early history is sometimes debated and there are folk stories of Russian dogs being the sire and dam of the first pups that would be Goldens, the Golden Retriever Club of America credits the Golden's origins to Sir Dudley Majoribanks, Lord Tweedmouth, who acquired the single yellow pup in a litter of black wavy-coated retrievers in Brighton, England, in the early 1870s. Lord Tweedmouth named the yellow dog "Nous" and added him to his pack of sporting retrievers at Guisachan House in the Highlands of Scotland, later breeding him with a liver-colored female Tweed Water Spaniel named "Belle." That mating yielded several yellow pups that would become foundation dogs for the Golden Retriever breed. "Crocus," a Nous and Belle pup, appears in photographs to bear a striking resemblance to the contemporary Golden. Golden Retrievers began appearing in British dog shows in the Retriever-Wavy or Flat-Coated category in the early 1900s, but the American Kennel Club did not recognize the breed until 1932. Goldens were a rare breed at the time.

Like their forebears, modern Goldens are intelligent dogs that are eager to partner humans in a variety of ways. Though bred to retrieve, they can also be talented, disciplined athletes in the agility ring and obedience trials. Many excel in tracking and at other scent-associated tasks. The AKC literature confirms they are loyal, loving companions. The breed's natural inclinations are all potential positives in the search field. I'd heard the general buzz for years, but during months of research prior to locating my puppy, it was good to see a solid reputation surface.

Now the Golden Retriever consistently places in the top ten most popular dogs in America — in part due to the word-of-mouth PR, perhaps in great part due to all the media exposure — a popularity that may contribute to the breed's serious problems. And there are some. In the open market, where supply meets demand, some smell the money to be made in Goldens, and commercial breeding can be haphazard. In the long months prior to finding my partner, I researched genealogies and read up on the breed's vulnerabilities, among them possible hip issues, heart issues, eye problems — and cancer, a common killer of Goldens, young and old. Hemangiosarcoma and lymphosarcoma: twin specters that shadow thousands of heartbroken posts on the Internet, lowering the Golden's average lifespan to ten and a half years. Deaths at age four or five are not uncommon. As a member of several online Golden Retriever forums, I read hard news from online friends and went to sleep some nights saddened by vicarious loss.

There were other caveats. For all their cuddly, genial good looks, Goldens are extremely social dogs who want to work beside their humans. The cute puppies that become grown dogs are ill-suited to haphazard training, intermittent contact, and banishment to the backyard. Hundreds of high-energy, anxious Goldens end up in rescues and city pounds every year, the result of poor choice-making on the part of owners who want a good dog at their leisure but don't want a Golden that jumps on them in the backyard, the ten-minute-a-day family pet now desperate for affection after long hours of abandonment. The collective research unanimously asserts that Goldens cannot be treated as accessories. This is true of all dogs, of course, but with a big dog like a Golden, the behavioral result of social neglect can be catastrophic for family and dog.

I was a newcomer to Goldens, but at least, I thought, I could promise attention, companionship, love. And work. The breed's drives and my own seemed right in sync.

I inquired with several Golden rescue organizations that promised to keep their eyes open for just the right young Golden that might work, but no solid leads emerged there. From pages of notes, I made ten breeder queries, nationwide. Four breeders indicated they had no new litters proposed for the year. Two had pups, but they were already sold. One seemed unwilling to believe I'd travel to get the right dog, no matter how much hypertext I used in my e-mails: *Plane! Car trip! Off for the summer!* Three others never responded. Nine months of close calls and almost-dogs that never came to pass — a whole series of Goldens that nearly came home to me. I had begun to wonder if a wiser universe was telling me something.

"No," said a neighbor, when I whined my frustration. "You said yourself this is more than a dog to be had and a thing to be done. You're being *prepared*." Gerand is a feng shui practitioner whom I've known to find a reasonable meaning in food poisoning and the bad chicken salad behind it, so I listened — and chafed — and waited.

In a moment of serendipity, a breeder who'd been recommended to me by five separate sources responded to tell me that she had a female named Spirit whose pregnancy was established, whose background was what I'd been looking for, and who might be very likely to bear a puppy with an aptitude for SAR. She sent me a link to information and images of her Spirit and the litter's sire, Ozzie, from another breeder on the East Coast. There was obedience, agility, and hunt in the merged background — good health and longevity too.

I already had notes on this breeder's line, but I took a day or so more to review them, imposing some kind of rationality while inside my heart leaped. Everything seemed right about this litter. I sent my application and puppy deposit and began a second wait for a Golden that wasn't yet born, charged with the idea that somewhere out there in the miracle of cell division and good dog DNA, my partner was becoming real.

"Look at that head," said Terry, weeks later. He was looking at a picture of Ozzie, my puppy's sire, a big boy with a genial, teddy-bear expression. "You've gotta smile at a face like that." I agreed. Another in the long list of reasons I wanted a Golden was the attraction factor. We search for children and Alzheimer's patients with some frequency, and I didn't want these victims more scared when they were found than when they were lost. I knew I wanted a light-faced dog with an open, kindly expression.

Terry looked at pictures of pretty mama Spirit, posed calmly in a "watch me" command, and he looked at my first pictures of her puppies, sent two days after the litter was born. Ten pups: nine girls and a boy. They looked like fuzzy tater tots, all butts and tiny ear flaps, their faces obscured as they huddled together. Each wore a little "collar" of colored rickrack for identification.

"I'm taking guesses," I said, pointing to the little tabs of rickrack. "Tell me which one you think will be my puppy, and if you guess correctly, I'll donate one hundred dollars to the Golden rescue of your choice." Terry pointed and picked. I'd played this game for a few days. Everyone had a reason for picking the puppy they did. "This one looks like she's protecting the others," one said. "This one has a big nose," said another. I made my choice last, picking a little blond pup curled on her side like a comma. In the picture, she was independent and apart from the others, wearing a yellow rickrack collar — and she was fat as a piglet, which suggested she could find something when she wanted it, and she didn't mind crawling over nine other puppies to get it.

As it happened, I guessed correctly, more fluke than intuition. "Yellow" and all the other pups were pretested for evidence of drive, confidence, and willingness to work for a human at six and again at ten weeks, and their breeder conferred with our SAR team head trainer. It was a close call indeed between this female and the little male. Breeder and trainer talked at length long-distance, and they made a decision for me — like an arranged marriage with four paws and a tail. I found out the day before I flew to Midland. "It's a girl," I was told. And she wore yellow rickrack.

Now it was just a matter of meeting her and bringing her home to join my family of three elderly cats and six adult dogs. I'd been raising dogs for years. I thought: *How hard could it be?*

Most of the animals in my house are rescues themselves. Coming from a family that always rescued cats from the pound, some part of me still draws energy from a rowdy, highly interactive little pack of animals, and I have one — a household of distinct personalities, none of them shy about expressing his point of view. A few dogs are fosters, living here on a temporary basis until they stabilize enough to be adoptable — plucked from animal shelters a day before their scheduled euthanasia. Excepting Pomeranians Fo'c'sle Jack and Mr. Sprits'l, the population here swells or decreases as this dog comes in to foster or that dog adopts a new family.

In the weeks preceding the new puppy, they were all aware of my changed motions, but only Sprits'l appeared deeply suspicious as I puppy-proofed the house, mutter-grumbling his way behind me, giving occasional "augh" barks of disapproval. He is a bright, fox-faced little guy, the color of a cigarette filter stubbed out into ash, which sounds ugly — but he is a good-looking dog. Sprits has small, dark eyebrows, and for a couple of weeks they were raised speculatively at the excessive housecleaning, the throwing away of once-loved-but-now-much-ignored small dog toys. The other dogs appeared curious but unconcerned.

Fo'c'sle Jack, the first Pomeranian in the pack, is much attached to me and has always been an easy dog. Jack came into the world mellow. Even though he was attacked by two large off-leash dogs as a pup, a violent event that shook both of us up for months, Jack recovered his equable nature. He doesn't rattle easily; he rarely barks. A soft and genial orange sable Pomeranian, his chief concern is food: *when's it coming, how much is coming, and by the way, you could give a guy a treat now and then.* With confident graciousness, Jack's seen foster dogs come and go. He was the least likely to be affected by this change, I thought, especially if I brought in a puppy of a breed known for its dog-friendliness.

By contrast, rescued Miss Whisky is all nerves, stretched tight as a violin string about to snap. When Whisky's previous owner, an elderly woman with advancing Alzheimer's, put a kitchen towel over a gas burner a few years ago, her whole house went up. The woman was pulled from the bedroom alive, and on his way out another firefighter found Whisky crouched in the kitchen between the refrigerator and a cabinet, semiconscious, the long fur of her tail already burning. He pulled the dog free, but in the aftermath of the fire, the woman's son placed his mother in a care facility and turned Whisky over to the pound. A poorly bred, cowering, traumatized black Pom with few social skills, she was given little time. A rescue organization got her out of the shelter, and I took her a few days later, the fur of her tail still crimped and scorched from heat. She is calmer now, but reactive: new neighbors throw her, the scrape and clunk of the mailman throws her. In truth, a strong breeze can still throw Whisky some days. She's in a state of almost permanent exclamation. Though she wags and smiles, her eyes are wary, and she barks about everything like an old record on the skip, shrieking a high note: *Wow! Wow! Wow! Wow! Wow!*

Whisky's staccato bark makes Salty Sophie blink, as though she winks away kickboxing butterflies. Sophie is the smallest of the Poms and perhaps the pluckiest. Another rescue, Sophie had been found duct-taped in a cardboard box and tossed in a Dumpster in Florida. A passerby heard her whimper, extracted the little dog, and then took her for veterinary care — despite the fact she could not keep Sophie herself. She came to us shaved free of mats and ticks, but with serious medical conditions: a collapsing trachea and congestive heart failure, both of which impair her breathing, particularly on hot, humid days. Despite her rough history and medical problems, Sophie is a cheerful, upbeat little dog, a round and waddling creature eager to keep up with household events. Dinnertime inspires Sophie to dance a doggy mambo, and occasionally she gets too excited about her coming food and falls over, dazed and blue about the mouth. But after a moment's pause, she is up again, does a little box step, and makes a honking sound through her nose, the closest she gets to a bark. Sophie is unruffled by the fosters who pass through on a layover to their new homes, and I think she'll get along with a new dog — even a larger dog — just fine, as long as the puppy has a little sense and equilibrium, thereby not sitting on small Sophie or spinning her silly on a race through the house.

The senior statesman of the household is Scuppy, aged twenty-one, another rescue who has already taught me much about how a smart dog works the wind.

A friend first e-mailed me about Scuppy after seeing a Petfinder ad pleading his case. A very senior dog who had been the pet of an elderly couple, he was abandoned when the couple died. Neighbors later said that the couple's adult children simply opened the front door and let the old Pomeranian out. Blind and deaf, he had wandered along the street, crossing traffic and colliding into unfamiliar fences for days until someone took him to the pound. There, the shelter's attending vet recognized Scuppy as one of his own former patients. A phone call confirmed the old dog's abandonment. No, the family denied, their mother's dog had died years ago. They knew nothing about a dog, about this dog, about any dog. Nothing, even when the vet's digital photograph exactly matched the stray Pomeranian sitting in a cage at the pound.

The shelter staff had made something of a pet of him as long as possible, but his age and disabilities made him unattractive for adoption. When I called eighteen hours before his scheduled euthanasia, the attendant on the phone wept. The Petfinder ad had been removed, she said. Scuppy couldn't be adopted because he was unneutered, and the law prohibited the adoption of an unaltered pet. But the shelter vet believed he would not survive surgical anesthesia due to his great age, and thus neutering was out of the question. One way or another, it looked like Scuppy would be put to sleep.

I asked about his health apart from the listed disabilities, and she said his condition was good for a dog both elderly and lately neglected. He was an active, mobile dog interested in exploring; he was gentle and responsive to touch. He was just very, very old. The shelter staff had been looking for someone to give him a soft place to live out his last months. But the decision had finalized today — he couldn't be adopted. The woman's voice was weary with the finality of it.

"What about foster?" I suggested. "Could I . . . sort of permanently . . . foster this dog?"

She put me on hold.

"What time can you get here?" she asked when she returned to the phone.

"What time do you close?"

"Five-thirty," she said.

"I can be there by five-thirty."

There was a pause. "Come at six," she said, and hung up the phone.

We met behind the shelter later that evening in the dark, where I signed paperwork I couldn't read. The young woman advised that the normal pet insurance that came with adoption was not available for fosters. Another attendant in the shadows, with bright-red hair lit only by the occasional flare of his cigarette on inhale, said I wouldn't be needing insurance, anyway: an old dog like Scuppy didn't have a whole lot of time. There was a little bundling movement, backlit in fluorescent from the shelter's half-cracked door. The two hustled something into my pet carrier, then scuttled back into the shelter. The whole thing was as quick and dark as an exchange of state secrets, and I would not have been able to recognize either one of them on the street in daylight. It would have been creepy if I'd not sensed how much these two wanted to avoid putting down yet another dog. Especially this one.

In the car, I unzipped the top of the carrier and saw him for the first time, a "clear orange" Pomeranian, his face sunken and white with age. His ears did not flick the way a hearing dog's would, and when I gently lifted his chin, I saw his clouded eyes. He was the oldest dog I'd ever seen. Toothless too. Accepting change with equanimity, he yawned, showing a wedge of bare, pink gums. I kept one hand down beside the old boy as I drove, feeling the soft, exploratory huff of his breath against my palm.

Once home, Scuppy accepted the other dogs calmly, submitting to their sniffs and prodding and circling without fuss or complaint. He clearly bewildered them, but something in his demeanor kept them respectful. At suppertime, he stood beside them in the kitchen, barked when he smelled dog food, and put his nose to his bowl as though he'd had this houseful of siblings his entire life. When he finished, he bobbed his nose and scented incoming air as I opened the back door for the other dogs, and he too headed outside, feeling his way along the porch to the ramp leading to the yard. There he revealed unexpected abilities. As he walked the backyard to become familiar with it, Scuppy marked the fence perimeter every few feet, demonstrating a bottomless bladder and a genius ability to meter his pee. He marked an entire fence line in that first single outing. The other dogs stood together and watched him, not one of the little males attempting to best the old boy by peeing over his mark.

He would mark further across the following days: trees, shrubs, the birdbath, a coil of garden hose, a clutch of flowerpots at a fork in the flagstone path leading to the garage. The outside water bowl too, which deeply offended the other Poms until I washed and raised it a little, allowing Scuppy's mark to land on the bricks beneath.

Scuppy clearly loved to be outdoors, and once he'd marked his territory, he never collided with objects again. He would walk the backyard for hours, then sit in the soft grass and lift his nose at the passage of squirrels on the fence or a fluster of pigeons beneath the feeder. When he was ready to come in, he would give a polite, solitary bark from where he sat — a little upward inflection like a query — *errrrr, now?* There he'd wait to be picked up, cuddled, and brought into the house. I learned that I could stand upwind of him many feet away and, waving my hands at knee level, would see him give the signature head pop of recognition I'd learned from the on-scent search dogs. When Scuppy caught the scent of me, he would rise, turn, and follow it to the source, his small tail wagging. And so it was that I learned how to call blind, deaf Scuppy and realized he could come when called just by the scent of me — even across the entire yard.

Having hidden electrical cords, replaced loose mattress batting, and installed some puppy gates, I took up all the cat toys and the small-breed toys, and I told the Pomeranians they'd just have to understand we couldn't have a puppy chew-and-choke hazard around for a while. The Poms tilted their heads when I spoke to them and looked even more speculative. *Something's changing,* their expressions said, *and it don't smell like bacon.* All this commotion began four weeks before Spirit's litter was due on the other side of Texas and fourteen weeks before I could bring the puppy home. I knew it was early, but I lay on the floor and tried to imagine this world through a Golden puppy's eyes. I wondered, in turn, what she would teach me and when.

When she sees me for the first time, Puzzle's expression is skeptical. I am another in a series of strangers bending over the x-pen. She considers and quickly rejects me, immediately gives me up for better things. A tug toy is more interesting. The open-bottomed bucket on its side, more interesting still. Our meeting is not a Hallmark moment between us. Mama Spirit welcomes me with soft generosity, but her blond, dark-eyed daughter with the fuzzy bottom turns away.

I sneak glances at her as Kim and I go through her puppy book and discuss her diet, vaccinations, and pending training. Puzzle isn't the biggest pup of the litter, nor the smallest. She moves through the x-pen with a bit of swagger, boxing toys, taunting her siblings until they wrestle. I see her swipe a stuffed duck from her sister and shoot a glance my direction. Puzzle drops the toy her sister wants and sits on it.

Somewhere in all of that, I think, *is my partner.*

Kim lifts her from the x-pen and puts her on the floor. "She knows 'Sit,' 'Stand,' and 'Come,'" Kim says. "And she should be pretty much housebroken."

"Sit," I say to Puzzle, who waits a molasses half-beat and then sits. And yawns.

"Good girl," I praise her.

Yada yada, her expression suggests.

I have never seen so intractable a puppy. My previous pups had cuddled at first meeting, but this one looks like she could spit at me like a llama. And might.

You have other dogs, I reassure myself. *This isn't all that new.* I want this ten-week-old Golden to be impressed with me, some-how — because I find her beautiful and full of possibility, and my heart is tight with months of waiting for her.

"Come," I say to Puzzle. She glances at Kim, then stands with elaborate slowness and saunters over. When she reaches me and I pick her up to praise and cuddle her, Puzzle doesn't yield. She leans back with stiff paws against my chest and gives me a long, level gaze.

I love her immediately. She hasn't learned to love me. But in her willingness to come I sense an ethic, and in her scrutiny I see intelligence. I think of the hard places we will go that need both: the disaster sites and gang-riddled neighborhoods, the lakes, the crime scenes and small town with a single missing girl whose case is on-going, whose fate remains unknown.

I return the puppy's gaze. What began as a late-night conversation in a bar has emerged as a Golden Retriever braced in the bend of my arms. She feels solid and capable. She feels right.

"Hi, sweetheart," I say to Puzzle. "Are you ready to go to work?"

3

INTO THE WIND

I CAME TO GROUND search-and-rescue from the air. The route was not direct. While I was working as a flight instructor in the early 1990s, an experienced student once asked me to fly with him to an area where he'd had a problem on a runway a few days before. A police officer and a talented pilot working on an advanced rating, he had been carrying other law enforcement personnel on a clear autumn day in his single-engine aircraft when, on landing, his plane shot off the end of the short, lakeside runway and down a small embankment before coming to a stop.

No one was hurt, the plane wasn't damaged, but he was an experienced pilot and the event concerned him. He wanted to discuss that landing with me and revisit the runway for touch-and-go practice. From his description of the plane's performance on final approach and the long, long streaks from his tires still visible on the asphalt when we got there, I suspected wind shear was responsible, and that his headwind had shifted to a tailwind at an unfortunate point in the landing sequence.

We had different conditions the day we revisited that airstrip, but we worked his touch-and-goes anyway. After a handful of successful, unassisted landings proved to him that the runway itself and his technique for landing on it were not an ongoing problem, he asked if I'd mind a flight around the lake before coming back to the runway to shoot more landings. The request surprised me a little — flight time is expensive — but I agreed.

A cold front had passed the day before. This afternoon was beautifully crisp and clear; low pressure had swept the air clean. From a plane flying low in this kind of weather, you can see the herringbone of wind on water, the definition of individual leaves, the colors on a bobber at the end of a fisherman's line. We made a circle of the lake's long shoreline, my student flying at the regulation altitude. I noticed, however, that his scan of instruments, sky, and ground included a lot of glances straight down, and having flown with him so long, I knew also it wasn't part of his standard procedure.

"What are we looking for, David?" I finally asked.

He didn't answer for a moment. Then he said, "We don't know what he did with her."

Without further comment, we circled the lake into evening, alternating who flew the airplane and who looked for the body of a woman along the lake's ragged shore.

That's how I began working search. In later months, through some grapevine I never completely understood, I gained a clientele who hired me to fly the press or personnel from other law enforcement agencies over variously troubled locations. For some clients, it was a matter of budget. My fixed-wing aircraft was less expensive than a helicopter. For others, it was an attempt to be nondescript: small planes in high-traffic areas attract less attention than rotorcraft. A few said they'd heard I was confident with the airplane; when asked to fly low and slow and stable, within regulations I could do it.

We flew over crime scenes and followed off-road trails suspected as body dumps. We traced the trajectory of downed aircraft in deep wood. As altitude restrictions expired, I flew with photographers over what remained of the Murrah Federal Building in Oklahoma City and the Koresh Compound in Waco, Texas. We plotted the paths of tornadoes. We circled livestock stranded on high ground by flood. From the vantage of a high-winged Cessna, my passengers — often press or insurance photographers — documented public and personal catastrophe. They unscrewed the window bracket for an unobstructed view and leaned outward as the slipstream held the window up. "Again," they'd gesture with a little twirl of the index finger, and around we'd go another time.

Not every client was clear about our objectives. Once, a man I took to be an insurance photographer (he came with multiple bags on shoulder straps), turned out to be the son of a rancher who had died. We unscrewed the window bracket so he could photograph the homestead in a long-shadowed sunset, and he did so, but when that was done he opened what I thought was a second camera case, drew out a large velvet bag, and prepared to drop his father's ashes over the family ranch. This kind of flight request is common, but problems are common too. It's a hire that recommends a good briefing. I saw what he was doing, was just about to give him — *hey!* — a quick word on ashes and slipstream when he, ahead of me, began to pour. Wind carried the ashes back through the window into the airplane, where they whistled around the tiny cabin and ended up all over us.

"Sorry," he said after an appalled moment. I tried to smile and felt the sheen of grit across my teeth, like I'd been testing pearls.

Not long afterward, another client had a similar request, but she was more straightforward on the hire and asked to sprinkle her father's ashes outside the small town along the interstate where he'd grown up. We had a good briefing on procedure, and I knew she understood, but when we got to the location she opened the window, took the soft case in her hands to hold it ready, then to extend it and pour — and dropped it entirely. The bag landed like a flour bomb in the middle of a Taco Bell parking lot just off the highway. We could see the astro-shaped burst of ash across the pavement.

We circled a little while in silence. I was thinking about the incident report I might need to file with the FAA. I don't know what she was thinking.

"Dad loved their Enchiritos," said my client at last, and she shut the window.

My own recent transitions were just as clunky. The flight career was still a fledgling; my twelve-year marriage, shot through with its own disasters, failed. And then I was alone. The family worried about my faltering income in "a man's profession," about their daughter newly divorced so young.

They worried about me in airplanes, but flight was perversely my good fortune. Then, as now, it was a mental and physical discipline, a blessed remove. I flew as often for hire as regulations allowed, grateful for the money of course, but I would have flown for free. During the period of divorce, I moved to a seedy, affordable apartment so near a runway that in the middle of the night I could identify individual planes by the grind of their starters, see the alternating flash of the airport beacon — green-white-green-white-green-white — like the *lub-dup* of a heart across the graceless walls of my bedroom.

It was a different time for general aviation before 9/11, when civilian pilots were not so readily framed as a threat. I would unlock the flight school on sleepless nights and check out a Cessna 152, file a flight plan, and go up to admire city skylines or make cross-country jaunts in the dark — flights I recall now for the occasional camaraderie over the radio with air traffic controllers and the night-flying freight dogs, but remember most for their exquisite aloneness. Moon and silver ground and the comfort of the Lycoming engine's cat-purr drone. I would set one radio receiver to the navigation facility closest to my home airport and the other receiver to the facility closest to the point of arrival, and I flew with the counterpoint of their Morse code identifiers beeping out of sync in my headset — literally the sound of where I was going and where I had been.

Though I think my family worried I might be suicidal (which I was not), and I know they would have been frightened to learn I flew in the middle of the night, flight gave me perspective. I think of those flights as private, invisible stitches across Texas in the dark, binding me to a world outside my own grief. Martha Graham once commented that she never thought of a dancer as alone on stage, that he or she was "always partnered by the surrounding space." It was a concept worth borrowing. And what space. On a clear night in still air, the stars were so close they shook up other senses, tempting me to open the window and put out my tongue to the spangle. I would have bet they had a taste, like pop rocks, maybe, or wasabi.

Other nights a blanket of stratiform cloud stretched wide above the little Cessna, and I flew small and secret, like a child with a flashlight under the blanket, flying beneath an eiderdown beautifully up-lit at its edges by the lights of cities on the horizon. The ground went dark for long passages over rural areas, defined by the deeper black of an occasional lake or edged by an interstate highway stippled with traffic. Small towns lay tidy as a tic-tac-toe grid beneath a handful of streetlights. But the peace and order were flecked occasionally with buildings afire, with the *uh-oh-uh-oh-uh-oh* twist of lights from emergency vehicles speeding down an unlit road. I could see them thirty miles away.

It wasn't in me to imagine my own catastrophe. Though there was one late night on an approach to the home airport's north runway that I felt a distinct unease at three hundred feet above the ground in the landing sequence, a sensation I couldn't validate with a crosscheck of the instruments, the sound of the plane, the feel of the air across the wings, or the sight of the windsock on the field. The unease was as profound as a waking shake on the shoulder, an imperative "go around." I followed instinct and aborted the landing, pressing the throttle forward, stabilizing the airplane, and retracting the flaps as airspeed allowed. The second approach was virtually identical to the first, the landing and roll-out uneventful. I taxied to the ramp and shut down the airplane, then walked to the edge of the tarmac and gazed out at the runway in the dark, wondering about my little mystery, looking for anything that might have been a problem on the first landing.

Nothing. South end of the field was quiet. I could hear wind tunneling through the windsock across the runway — a keening little song like a pissed-off fairy in a bottle. The beacon's double flash pulsed across the hangars, the planes, the tarmac, and me. Nothing. Nothing. Then movement: a stray dog winding west through the shadows at the end of runway 34. He paused and turned to look my way, caught by the scent or the sound of me. Was the dog what I had sensed earlier? Where had he been the first time I was approaching to land? A gangly, spotted mixed-breed, he blazed red in the glow of the runway end lights, his head lifted in a carrying posture of intelligence. We looked at each other a long moment, in our separate ways making sense of threat and possibility. The dog seemed to make his mind up first. When he turned and loped into the black field beyond, I felt an unreasonable urge to drop my flight case and follow.

Restless. I'd been feeling restless. The encounter with Runway Dog both provoked an urge for change and informed the relationship with my own dogs at home. In the months after that late-night experience at the airport, I paid even closer attention to dog ways of negotiating the environment. Eyes, ears, tongue, nose, pads — and that magical word *vibrissae*, the whiskers of the muzzle and eyebrows that can even perceive changes of airflow — I watched my little housedogs and saw them respond intuitively to a concert of sensory perceptions. Many of their skills were similar to stick and rudder skills I'd learned to use as a pilot — moving air is a whole kaleidoscope of changing textures, palpable to the pilot's hands, feet, and seat of her pants — but even the most sheltered dogs of my crew were better at making whole-body sense of their surroundings than I was.

When a leaf fell into a burning citronella candle and ignited on the back porch, three of the littlest dogs in the house raised their noses simultaneously, nostrils working, before they brought eyes and ears to bear and turned their heads to look in the direction of the fire, separated by a screen door and six yards away. Scent first indicated change; sight and sound were used to make better sense of it. Though all three dogs grew excited, Mr. Sprits'l alone ran to find me one room away, quivering and barking furiously, every hair electric, leading me back to the trouble. (When Sprits'l is excited, he tends to spin rather than travel in a straight line; this made our trip back to the porch rather like following a dreidel.)

Not a little fire. I extinguished the bucket of flame that had been a candle, thinking all the while about the clarity of Sprits'l's message: *Not normal. Not right. Back here. No, back here. Fix this.* He had not simply barked at the flame; he'd not run to another dog to telegraph the news. He'd come to me without hesitation, and when I went out the door to take care of it, Sprits did not attempt to follow. I realized that to this dog there were certain givens in our relationship, and that I was not only a bringer of food and a scratcher of chest, but I was also a trusted protector. I knew that, but I didn't know *he* knew that.

What else would dogs tell me? What else did dogs know?

Curiosity led me to consider volunteer opportunities with working dogs — dogs whose job descriptions included making sense of a changing environment and communicating that change to a human. I wanted to try for that kind of connection. And our large urban area presented plenty of opportunities. Depending on level of interest and commitment, I learned I could be a puppy-raiser for guide dogs, a once-a-week socializer of assist dogs, and — most interesting to me — an assistant in the field on a canine search-and-rescue team. They were all time-intensive opportunities, especially SAR. Three to seven training hours a week, plus expected home study, plus emergency calls.

One friend asked, "Does it pay well?"

A relative sighed, "You are never going to marry again."

My oldest friend understood. "Of course," Marina said. "You've got a history of getting out there. It makes sense you'd want to learn to fly a dog."

. . .

I visited the K9 team I would eventually join after finding a 1995 photograph from the *Dallas Morning News* that I'd cut out during the aftermath of Oklahoma City's Murrah Federal Building bombing. Skip Fernandez, a canine handler with the Miami-Dade County Fire Rescue team, sits on the ground with his head bowed and eyes closed against the back of his Golden Retriever, Aspen. The caption states that they have worked all night, and they look it. They are dirty. The dog sits rolled over onto one hip, propped up by her front legs. She looks tired. Her expression is subdued.

I don't know why I originally clipped the photo, but when I found it six years later, I felt convinced. While some disasters needed air support, almost all of them needed dogs on the ground to locate the living and the dead — and partners beside them to translate. Though the process itself was a mystery to me, I was eager to understand dogs better on their own terms. And perhaps I had something to contribute: As a pilot I had begun to learn the workings of the wind. I could talk on the radio. I wasn't squeamish or afraid of the dark. Surely that was enough to make a start at this. Nothing about the work looked easy, but canine search-and-rescue looked like work I wanted to do.

4

PUZZLE HAS LANDED

THE BAGGAGE HANDLER at ticketing doesn't speak much English. He makes a gesture when I bring Puzzle up to the counter—a funny little shoving motion that I can't quite make out, until he does the push gesture and a twist of his fingers, and I realize he's telling me that Puzzle should be in a hard-sided carrier to go in the belly of the airplane.

"No," I say. "This is a search dog in training, and she's coming home in the cabin with me." I show him the soft-sided, under-the-seat carrier. Puzzle will fit inside it, but I've been told earlier by the airline that because she's a search dog, she will be able to ride in the cabin in my lap or at my feet, as long as she has the appropriate credentials. Our trip home together involves elaborate explanation with some backstory; uncertain, the baggage handler shakes his head and leaves to find the ticket agent, who comes out wiping her hands, a daub of mustard on her nose.

"So what is this puppy supposed to do for me?" she asks a little skeptically, but she grins because Puzzle has suddenly turned on the charm, wagging and smiling and pawing at the agent's extended fingers.

"Well," I say. "She's not going to do anything but love you at the moment and maybe mooch a French fry, but she's passed her first aptitude tests, and she's heading home to train to be a search dog." I show her my team ID and Puzzle's green in-training vest, the smallest size of which is still three times too big for her. She looks like a puppy in a barrel.

The woman glances at the ID and the vest. "Wow. You are my first search-and-rescue dog," says the agent. She rubs Puzzle's ears, causing a sensation so pleasurable that the puppy's eyes almost cross.

"She knows 'Sit,' 'Stand,' and 'Come,'" I respond proudly — thinking, *boy, I hope she still does* — and resting Puzzle on the counter.

"Sit," says the agent, and Puzzle plops down on the counter with such gusto that she knocks my driver's license to the floor, grinning with her tongue out sideways. She clearly adores the woman, who leans closer. Puzzle licks the mustard from her nose.

"I couldn't do it," says the agent.

"Do what?"

"Train a puppy and then give it up to someone else."

I lean forward to help her untangle Puzzle's forepaws from her hair. "The good news," I say, "is that I won't have to make that choice. I'll be her working partner. She'll be a search dog, *my* search dog, but she'll also live with me."

"Ohhhhh — so she's going home, then," says the agent, handing me a boarding pass.

"Yes," I answer, reaching for the pass awkwardly, realizing Puzzle has somehow flipped in my arms and is butt-upward, her tail waving gently beneath my chin. "She's going home."

In the airline terminal, Puzzle is extremely social with two passing pilots, a child pushing her own stroller, and the three TSA agents who pass her among them after her collar, harness, and vest set off the security sensors. She tilts her head so winningly at a cowboy-booted man on a cell phone that he hangs up and crosses the gate area to pet her.

"Now this looks like a dog that could get away with anything," says the gentleman.

I tip her up to look into her face. "This sure looks like a dog who will try."

"She's got a good head, good big black nose. Gun dog?" he asks.

I shake my head. "Search-and-rescue."

"Bless you, Ma'am," he says, then, "You'd better give this one something to do *fast.*"

He pets Puzzle, engulfing her head in his large hand. Then he walks away with a chuckle, with a better-you-than-me shake of his head.

By contrast, our flight attendant, who later catches sight of Puzzle out of the corner of her eye during a trip down the aisle during the flight, gives a nervous little shriek. I feel sure the young woman saw the puppy come aboard, but now Puzzle sleeps upside down in my arms, her round belly upward, feet akimbo, head limp and lolling backward toward the aisle. Gravity has pulled down the puppy's ears and lips and bared her fangs. Her eyes are open but unseeing, rolled up in her head with the whites exposed. It's not a good look. It's not even canine — more Hell-Spawn Bunny of the Undead.

"It's a *puppy,*" says my seatmate, helpfully pointing to the paws, the nose, and the tail.

"I'm sorry," stammers the attendant. "F-for a second, I thought I was seeing some kind of a . . . a . . . mutant."

"She's going to be a search dog," I add. I exhibit the little green vest.

"Oh. I'm sure she'll be very good," says the flight attendant. But her expression is shifty. She hurries away.

The exchange has roused Puzzle a little. A couple of *huh? what?* snorts, and she stretches all four paws upward, trembling with the extension. She is briefly stiff as roadkill, then relaxes. In less than a minute she begins to snore: a treble *skkkiiiiinnnnnnnnk* from just behind her nostrils, then a deeper *skkunnnnnnnnnnnk* farther back in her muzzle. Her eyes roll slowly upward again, the whites staring dully across the aisle toward two other passengers.

One grins. The other flinches and turns back to his in-flight magazine.

I look down at Puzzle and consider that I've never seen a Golden puppy photographed from this unflattering angle. There are probably reasons for that.

"She doesn't have to be pretty," says the grinning man across the aisle, his voice kind. "She just has to be smart."

The Poms look like they've been to a horror show.

Puzzle's nap aboard the airplane has refreshed her, and she has entered the house all bounding energy and curiosity. It takes her only moments to put her nose to the butt of every Pom that rushes forward to inspect her, to flush a cat from the laundry basket, and to knock over a row of plastic bottles I have set aside for recycling. Now she has suddenly discovered the stuffed lobster that's made the trip with us, and she takes the over-large toy in her mouth, rushing up to little Sophie with it, shaking it meaningfully: *booga-booga-booga, lobster-booga!* Sophie honks and skitters, her dark eyes wide.

Undeterred, Puzzle drops the toy and prances up to Maddy, one of my oldest cats. Maddy has seen dogs come and has seen dogs go, and, totally fearless, has found a *laissez chien* attitude serves her well. She flops down on the floor as Puzzle approaches, squinching her eyes shut as though the puppy is something to be temporarily endured, like an enema. Puzzle moves very slowly, giving Maddy a thoughtful nose-over. The introduction seems to be going well until the puppy gets to Maddy's bottom. Some curiosity there gives Puzzle pause, and she huffs a snort straight up Maddy's backside, which causes the cat to loft with an insulted squawk and leap for the back of the couch. Maddy misses, overshoots, lands hard behind the couch, scrambling two other cats hiding back there — and they jointly riot, heading for the closest high thing any of them can find: a large potted ficus in a ceramic pot by the window. It is a big tree, in a big pot, but they are three senior cats with weight issues and motivation. As they struggle to climb frail branches, their weight overcomes the ficus, and it tips over before I can dodge the couch and get across the room.

Four things happen almost simultaneously. The tree falls, the pot shatters, the cats shoot apart like pieces of exploded TIE Fighter, and Puzzle leaps into the debris with the first bark I have heard from her: a bright, happy *hark!* of satisfaction. When I pull her from what's left of the tree, she has already snuffled into its root ball, emerging with a triumphant expression and a dirty nose flecked with Perlite. I get the sense that if a puppy could waggle her eyebrows at the lot of us, she would.

Wow! Wow! Wow! Whisky shrieks about the new dog in her house.

Augh! replies Sprits'l, apropos of it all.

5

ALL THE WRONG THINGS

PISSED AT HIS GIRLFRIEND, says the brother of the boy who is missing, or at least that's the version we get from the officer who interviewed family members an hour ago. *Pissed at his girlfriend and hitching a ride with a friend to Austin for the weekend.* He left the house before supper and slammed the door and headed right, said the brother, who watched him walk down the hill and out of sight. He was still wearing the khaki pants he'd worn earlier while waiting tables, stained with grease and ketchup. He was so mad he didn't stop to change. Just threw his things down and pulled on another shirt as he walked out the door, before their parents got home.

Two search dogs, however, disagree. Charged by their handlers to determine direction of travel, both dogs show little interest in the route suggested by the missing boy's brother. The dogs have been sent out to trail the boy separately, the second handler unaware of the conclusions drawn by the first team. Neither dog confirmed the brother's gestured route. Two officers clearly believe the dogs, while one is torn. The brother's story is brief and consistent. I've heard it twice myself, and it's not difficult to imagine the boy slamming out the door and hooking a right toward his friend's house, hitching a ride to Austin, and leaving the girl behind.

The friend in Austin, however, says by cell phone that he last saw the boy in question earlier that day at school. If he'd gone to Austin, says the friend, he didn't get there with him. And he adds, "Like his parents would even *let* him go."

The missing boy is a good-looking kid, two school pictures tell us. Last year's photo has a little baby fat that's missing from this year's shot. His hair is longer too. He appears confident and capable — he looks into the camera easily — and he was either cavalier about his sophomore picture or ill-prepared for it. He's wearing a faded, wrinkled T-shirt in this most recent photo, and his hair is mussed. There's a little tuft of it sticking upward from the back of his head, like a cowlick that aspires to a miniature peacock fan. His grin is crooked, and there's a pink scar from the corner of his mouth that points to his jaw. He appears uncertain in the freshman photo, but in the sophomore shot there's a little "dare me" expression in his eyes.

We get a lot of school photos in the pre-brief of searches for missing children, but sometimes a family will bring out their own candid shots too. It would be good to see a picture of this whole boy in the context of his house, his neighborhood. The way he dresses. The things he carries, values. But not this time. His parents, who made the 911 call after searching awhile themselves, offer a school picture and little else.

They stand silent on the porch of their house. His two younger brothers straddle bicycles a few feet away in the driveway. The bicycles are sized for smaller riders. Both boys have their feet on the ground and their knees rocked outward, their forearms resting on the handlebars. Though they stand apart, the family resemblance is apparent between parents and sons. Even at midnight in the shadows, I can see their faces settle into the same lines, pale and remote in the thin light of a waning moon and the streetlight one house over. They do not talk to one another or touch. They stand together but not together, the tension between them palpable.

The parents do not come forward to speak to us or to meet the dogs that will search for their son. It can go either way on a search; some families want that connection. Others do not. Neither has the community rallied to this search, which is also unusual. Though we see the occasional flick of light when a curtain is drawn back, no neighbors come out to support the family or speak with the police.

But before we arrived, the boy's mother located the jacket her son had tossed over the chair in his bedroom. A meticulous woman: she paid attention to the concept of a "scent article," bringing the jacket out caught between salad tongs so as not to touch and contaminate the fabric with her own scent. The officer that briefed us leads Jerry and Shadow again to the jacket now lying on the sidewalk of the house. Jerry directs Shadow to smell it, and she takes a brief, thoughtful scent. She knows the scent, has smelled it before an hour ago when sent out to confirm or deny the brother's statement. When Jerry commands her to "Find *that*," she ignores the eastward path the boy's brother says was the last way he went, choosing instead to wind her way north in the darkness. I am assigned to field assist the pair in this sector, and I follow a few steps behind, taking notes and watching Shadow. She avoids the street and the sidewalk of her chosen direction, sidestepping instead to an alley bounded by a mangled, uneasy fence that separates the neighborhood from open field beyond.

The wood and wire fence sags with the remembered weight of all the people who have climbed it. The field beyond is dark, broad, and scruffy — and for sale, weathered twin signs at either end seem to suggest — land waiting for development, only minimally kept neat. A line of trees bounds the far eastern edge of it. From this distance, the trees seem to hunch forward toward the field, like a line of vultures waiting for something to fall. The police say this field is a common thoroughfare for the dog-walkers and teenagers of the area. The dog-walkers let their dogs "run loose and shit free," as one officer puts it, while the teenagers use the field as a shortcut to a pizza joint and a convenience store. Sometimes the kids simply walk into the trees, for drugs or sex or both. The field and that stand of trees is a concern, a likely venue for poor choices or drug deals gone bad. Two busy streets intersect at the far edge of the wood, creating an area that is both quickly accessible and relatively obscured. There have been other kids in trouble there; other crimes across the four years the land has been for sale. Earlier this evening, police already searched into the tree line. They've found nothing.

Shadow walks along the alley, slipping through the infrequent light. Her liquid movement before us is beautiful: now a silver dog, now black, now silver, now black as she crosses in and out of the dark. About seven houses from where we began our sector, she slows, pauses, and mutters to Jerry. She puts her nose to a fence, then moves around the side of it, pawing at a warped gate buckling outside its frame, a gate that no longer aligns with its catch. Shadow is interested here. Very interested. She sticks fast with her nose to the gate.

Jerry moves to the front of the house to see its address, then calls the location to the officers in charge. They confirm this house is the home of another friend of the missing boy. But the officers have already visited it. Having spoken to the friend and his parents, they determined the boy is not there — though he'd visited there frequently, always coming in from the back gate through the kitchen. They say Shadow must be interested in old scent. The scenario is logical enough, and Jerry directs Shadow to move on. She does so with reluctance and some grumbling, a low, musical singularly Husky note. Her lope away seems unwilling.

Jerry wonders if anyone has checked with the boy's girlfriend. I call the question in by radio as we move northward down the alley to a dark area where a street lamp has gone out. We move with flashlights only now, Shadow glowing in the distance ahead of us. She pads steadily forward, but without the excitement of a dog on the scent she's been asked to find. Occasionally she pauses and turns her head to look back at us. Her pale blue eyes snap as they pass through the flashlights' beams. She turns away and lopes on.

The radio crackles; we have turned the volume down to prevent disturbing the neighborhood asleep. I murmur against the mike and hold the radio to my ear. Incident Command confirms that the girlfriend has been reached. She had no information about her missing boyfriend and (this said in low parenthesis) seemed surprised by any question that the two of them had fought. Jerry shakes his head and we walk on, coming to the end of the alley and turning eastward toward another street and a reverse sweep to the south.

Shadow grows less interested the farther we move east. She sparks again only once as we are southbound the next street over, crossing purposefully between two dark houses with us tiptoe-ing behind, then across the street. She mutters a little, working quickly, and as we watch the direction of her interest, Jerry recog-nizes we've returned to the front of the same house that she had originally engaged before. We call in second interest and head back to finish the sweep we'd briefly abandoned.

I can hear handlers calling Incident Command from their sec-tors southwest, southeast, and northwest of us. Routine calls not-ing time and location, none of the dogs showing any interest at all in their assigned areas.

Tonight we use an additional resource. One member of our team is a professional man tracker out of a police department in California. He and another FAS team member have begun "cutting sign," looking for footprints or other indicators that might confirm or deny the brother's story, anything that might suggest the boy's direction of travel. They know his shoe size and his height, have a fair approximation of his stride. By flashlight they will look for evidence of transfer: crushed grass in the road, alley dust in the grass, fresh mud on the depressed wire where someone has newly climbed over the fence. Man tracking is a painstaking process that requires good vision and an ability to note the signs of disturbance left by any creature that crosses ground. Terry's long experience makes him fast and efficient. Webb, his assistant, has caught on to the job quickly.

Jerry, Shadow, and I are at the farthest bound of our sector when Terry calls to Incident Command. He and Webb have found what appears to be likely prints in the grit of the alley we had first walked along. Not our boot prints; these belong to someone else. No sign that someone had gone over the wire and into the field today, but three prints in dust and tamped grass a few steps away suggest track — they lead to the area where Shadow had put her nose to the worn gate and held fast.

Jerry and I look at each other a moment. Shadow has worked ahead about a house-length, loping quietly southward now on the fourth street of our sector, but her demeanor suggests we are nowhere near the scent she has been told to seek. The other dogs are coming in. *Nothing*, their behavior tells their handlers. We conclude a final sweep and head back to the command area ourselves. As we walk, I can see flickers of light in my periphery from all quadrants: the other teams returning. Their flashlights punctuate every step, occasionally silvering the eyes of the dogs now trotting quietly beside them.

At Incident Command, two officers have agreed that fresh track and a dog's intense interest is enough to justify a second inquiry at the house seven doors to the north. They will return to that house and wake the family. Team by team, we head back to command and begin drafting our sector reports, chewing our pens and sketching sector maps, writing the narrative that explains who searched the sector, how it was searched, any problems in the sector, any area where the dogs might have shown significant response. We write, but we are all turned a little toward the command post radio. Our own radio is silent. I can occasionally hear the murmur of the police communication from the line of parked police vehicles near us, somehow sounding matter-of-fact and urgent at the same time, but nothing across ours.

Almost simultaneously, the dogs look north: noses up, ears wheeled forward. Their postures mark the boy's return before we see or hear it. He walks slowly back to his house with a police officer on either side. His head is down, and he walks with his arms folded across his chest. His right hand, beneath the fold of his left, is clenched into a fist. His parents meet him at the center of the yard, and the three stand rigid there, the boy and mother silent, the father speaking in short, emphatic tones with the officers who brought him back. The two younger boys retreat into the house. We never see them again.

After an exchange we cannot hear, one officer invites the dogs to meet the boy they have searched for. Perhaps the officer has seen them straining and wagging where their handlers stood. At the invitation, the handlers gesture and the dogs come together, and it's like a little ballet as they converge on the spot where the boy stands. Collie, German Shepherd, Husky, two Labs. From dropped shoulders and long arms, the boy turns his palms backward to allow the dogs to sniff, but he does not connect with them. He does not look up. Not at us. Not at the police. Not at his father who, after we begin to pack up for the night, lifts his hand as if to strike his son, then gives him an angry push into the house.

"Sometimes," says an officer, "it's tough to know if you've done a good thing or not."

6

FIRST LESSONS

THERE'S A STORY told about an experienced handler working a training scenario with a young dog who'd just begun to learn to search. The three-story warehouse where they sought a single volunteer victim was an ideal training environment: full of stacked crates, landscaping tools, out-of-season holiday decorations, window-cleaning equipment, discarded office furniture, and the occasional makeshift bed for a homeless person who'd snuck in. The lighting was poor. There were dark stairwells and disused elevator shafts, strange air currents and dead corners where scent hung motionless. The building challenged even experienced teams. But this dog was keen, and this handler wanted to give the building a try.

Working from the almost-empty ground floor up, the two swept the entire warehouse, and the Australian Cattle Dog pup hesitated in only one spot — a patch of cement strewn with the moldy remains of Halloween hay. He worried at the hay a little before the handler directed him away and upward to the second floor. From there they worked slowly through the still air, threading their way between the corridors of outcast computer desks and finding nothing. Up to the third floor, even more congested and dusty, peppered with pigeon feathers and owl droppings. They worked the room edges, the corners, and made back-and-forth sweeps across the middle of it through debris. The dog showed no interest at all. Knowing they had one planted victim, the handler reversed the search and again swept the third floor. Nothing. Second floor. Nothing still. Losing faith in the dog due to its youth and relative inexperience, the handler began opening crates and tilting boxes over, hoping to either find the victim himself or stir the air enough to shake loose significant scent. The dog did not respond. In frustration, the handler took the dog back to the first floor and moved through it again, quickly. The pup moved back to the flat scatter of hay, and the handler called him away from it twice, directing the dog to the edges of the elevator door.

The story goes that the dog had now had enough, ignored the handler and marched past him, oblivious to further commands, trotting out of the building straight to the head trainer and plopping down in her lap. The trainer says that when the handler came out, his face flushed with anger, the dog turned away. She says the dog too looked disgusted, like "ain't *he* a piece of work?"

After a few moments' debrief, the trainer asked if the dog had shown any interest in anything in the building at all. The handler dismissively mentioned the hay. The trainer stood up and led the pair back into the building, where she ran her foot across the hay and revealed a grate in the floor, and beneath the grate, a ten-year-old child sat patiently in the space of an air duct, looking upward at the three of them.

I've never heard how the story concluded — if the handler made nice to his dog at that moment, if the dog shrugged off the incident in the way of good-natured canines, how the pair of them fared on later searches. But the tale in all its versions is always cautionary, its warning perpetual: trust the dog.

It's not as easy as it sounds, because the handler developing trust is also raising a puppy still prone to scatterbrained antics. Many SAR dogs begin training as soon as their inoculations for rabies, distemper, and parvo allow it, between ten and twelve weeks old. Energetic, playful, sometimes highly distractible, they are introduced to search through "runaways," a game where a friendly assistant holds the new puppy and the handler runs a short distance away to hide. The assistant cries "Find!" and releases the dog, which ideally runs immediately for the handler and is praised and rewarded for the glorious find. Handler runaways are repeated enough times so consistent behavior is seen from the puppy, and then roles are reversed: the handler holds the dog and the assistant runs to hide. If the pup seeks the assistant as readily as she had sought the handler in previous exercises, learning has taken place — both for dog and handler. The dog has learned that "Find!" has an objective and a reward, and the handler has taken a first step toward trust. It's an encouraging moment when a handler sees his new dog willingly look for another person just as readily as he'd naturally run for the handler whom he has begun to love. When we see the dog successfully find a wide variety of people hiding in different places during "runaways," the dog demonstrates consistency and the handler's confidence rises.

From there, simple searches continue — one victim in a "sector" — but the victim's within a close, limited range of location. Now the handler cannot see the volunteer victim in hiding. And small as it may be, the sector is a mystery to the team. This is the moment when a basic understanding of wind direction and air currents makes all the difference to dog-and-handler strategy. It's also the moment where distractions for a young dog may tell — a blowing leaf kicks off a puppy's prey drive and off she goes to chase it; passersby fifty yards away tempt a friendly dog to break off the search and trot over to petition for petting. Another dog crosses into the puppy's field of vision, and the opportunity for play is irresistible.

It's a tough time for a handler, who can make several wrong choices at this crucial moment for a young SAR dog. Overdiscipline, and the dog can associate working search with punishment and become less willing. Overindulge, and the puppy learns that search is a casual, when-you-get-around-to-it affair. Perhaps the worst temptation is to deny that the young dog lacks focus at this point in training, to use your own eyes to find the victim and credit the dog with the find. Most training teams have an experienced handler or trainer supervising the search, but the opportunity to overcompensate for the dog's young nature still exists. More than false pride is implicated. Crediting a pup with more success than he has earned may push him into harder training scenarios that he is ill-equipped for; a frustrated dog (who may also intuit the handler's frustration) can quickly lose the sense of adventure and fun that fosters a consistent will to work. And the handler's confidence has taken a serious blow. Hide the puppy's immaturity at your peril. Eventually there will be search scenarios where your eyes can't do it and the dog, moved ahead in her training too fast, isn't willing to.

At eleven weeks old, Puzzle is all paws, fat belly, and big head. Her nose is large and very black, and she seems willing to use it to achieve a goal. There is a lot to smell in this house: food on the stove and leather shoes in closets, the other dogs and cats, and because the house is pier-and-beam, every mouse and squirrel running under the house too. She is not yet ready to begin search training. While we wait for her final Parvo vaccinations and the vet's all-clear to put her paws on new ground, we begin scent games in the house, designed to teach her to find things on command and to associate successful finds with praise. One game involves passing a treat from hand to hand behind my back, then extending both closed fists to the puppy, asking her to identify the hand with the treat and to bump that hand with her nose. Puzzle catches on quickly, and after a few attempts she recognizes the difference between faint scent (was there) and stronger scent (is there now), and she happily bumps my hand with her nose, sometimes chattering at me with yaps and moans to underscore her choice.

The Poms, too, enjoy the game. Blind Scuppy is invariably accurate. Fo'c'sle Jack, who loves food above all things, learns that the quickest path to a reward is to get the correct hand and be quick about it. Mr. Sprits'l is wary of the game. Inclined to sniff both hands critically, he tilts his head and considers in the way a gourmand might judge a mouthful of foie gras: *I smell the treat, but is it up to my personal standard?* When he chooses the correct hand and gets both treat and praise, Sprits takes the treat with great care, trotting off to private spaces, where he will work it with his paws and deliberate.

We play the "Which Hand?" game for a few days, then progress to a hidden treat beneath one of three clean, upended flowerpots. This advanced game requires that Puzzle not only identify the correct pot but also begin to maneuver to get to what she seeks. I watch these early efforts at problem-solving with some amusement. Puzzle lacks small motor skills and any sense of physics. She's inclined to identify the correct pot and then scoot it across the porch by bumping it with her head, the treat dragging along with it as she goes. After one such effort, she flops down on her bottom and barks angrily at the pot, then turns and barks indignantly at me. The message seems clear: *This won't cooperate, and it's All Your Fault.* Metatext aside, she has made a good choice. When she barks for my attention, I pick up the flowerpot and she gets her treat.

I am happy to see her accuracy and her perseverance. In the days that follow, I notice she pushes less and instead stands over the chosen flowerpot, barking for my attention much more quickly. I hope that this is the beginning of what will be direct, communicative alerts on Puzzle's search finds — a sort of *I've done my job, now you do yours.*

The games get more difficult, and I begin to hide the treats in the house and yard: under objects, on top of fence posts, wedged in the V-shaped branches of young trees. Puzzle is eager to play, and for a distractible puppy likely to abandon a butterfly she's chasing to flush a bird instead, falling over her own feet as she goes, Puzzle is all focus when the treats come out and I put on her little "search" collar that signals the work is about to begin.

The Poms watch us. Though they too get to play scent games

at least once in our daily training, I recognize they are aware that Puzzle gets more training and more treats. Feeling the pressure of hard gazes, I look up once in the backyard and see a row of three little fox faces staring out a bedroom window at us. Mr. Sprits'l gives a mutter, then an outraged *Augh!* of protest when the puppy scores her third treat in a row. I realize then that as soon as Puz can safely work outside the yard, we need to begin our training elsewhere. I am ill-versed in dog dynamics, but it seems to me that at least some of the Poms recognize the puppy's unfair share of my attention. Later that afternoon, we play again in the house, each dog taking turns at this scent game or that one. Sprits'l successfully finds a treat beneath my right foot, and when I raise my shoe he takes it after a long, guarded sniff. "Good boy!" I praise him as he stomps off — the treat in his mouth, his ears cocked back and his posture stiff with scorn.

Puzzle, in turn, watches the Poms. She is especially fascinated by Scuppy. The old dog navigates our yard quite easily, missing objects he has previously marked, sidestepping other dogs in his path as he orients to their scent and movement. Every once in a while I see a hint of what must have been his younger sense of mischief. He will pad slowly and quietly toward a huddle of pigeons, then make a little burst of speed and a bark like a toy trumpet with a mute. With only his nose to go by, Scuppy clearly demonstrates how scent moves, where it sticks, and how it pools. Watching him, I am aware of subtleties that he translates easily, though I cannot smell them at all.

Puzzle treats the old dog with kindly deference. She's inclined to rush and tumble the younger Poms, but she carefully sidesteps Scuppy and does not interfere with his flushed pigeons or his path through the yard. Sometimes she follows him as a sort of wingman. Other times she simply observes.

I leave the back door open and watch them lie together in the yard and ferret the scent of bird versus squirrel versus man-with-a-baby-jogger and girl-with-a-dog. Sometimes their noses bob to-

gether. Other times it's in a little sequence, like they're doing the
Wave. One night I slip out the back door and stand half the backyard away, upwind of them and silent. It's a warm, humid, windless evening. I lean over and wave my hands, wondering how long
it will take both dogs to catch scent enough to notice. It takes only
moments. Their noses bob with recognition, and Scuppy stiffly
rises, wagging, ready to come to me. Puzzle turns her head in the
easy pivot of a young dog and smiles from where she lies across the
slate. When she sees Scuppy heading my way, she too gets up and
follows at a careful distance. Scuppy finds me without a misstep,
puts his nose into my hands, and groans as I rub his soft ears, and
Puzzle, sometimes competitive and pushy for attention, does not
push him away.

Though I am eager for the day when Puzzle's safe to train with
the team, I recognize how much she's learned from all the dogs
here at home, quite apart from human instruction. She's a whole-
sense dog who will perk her ears at a baby's cry two doors down or
pause at the sight of a squirrel through a window, spinning with excitement as Sprits'l yaps through the glass, but it's Scuppy's unwit-
ting instruction that engages her most. A friend asks, "Are you sure
it's safe to leave the old guy alone with her?" — a question I have
never asked myself. Puzzle's twice his weight now and probably
ten times his strength, but in the backyard beside him she moves
gently, as though crossing a stream stone by stone. She models his
thoughtful inspection of the yard, corner to corner, scent by scent.
She mimics his position when they jointly lie across the cool slate
sidewalk in the evening. Best of all, she learns from Scuppy that
human scent has value.

Imagine you are walking through a small-town neighborhood at
midnight, the houses dark, televisions gone silent, the cars and
lawn mowers stilled. Though the cumulative daytime noise level is
down a few notches, you move, nonetheless, in a world of sound.
This is a time when you can hear small, specific noises and per-

haps identify them — the drone of separate air conditioners from three houses in a row or the jingle of collar tags hitting cement when a sleeping cat on a patio rolls onto its side. The ting of one pipe of a wind chime stirred by a moment's air. The strike of a match as someone sits smoking alone in the dark. The chirp of two crickets in conversation. They think better of it and stop their love song as you pass. Eighteen-wheelers on a highway half a mile away. Your own footsteps, of course, and the quality of them, down to the squidgy press of rubber soles on asphalt or the crunch and squeak of gravel you disturb.

Then imagine that it's your job to locate a single radio playing softly in the alley behind an unknown house in a five-square-block area. You could just run around randomly — hopeful of catching the sound by chance — or organize the process, sweeping back and forth down streets and alleys, attempting to quickly locate anything that sounds like it might be a radio. And though the old AM transistor you search for has a tinny, signature sound, when you move too quickly, that sound can be overcome or disguised by other noises. So you methodically work the area, and at some point in the process you believe you hear it. You move left or right, forward or back, turning in an attempt to narrow down the location, getting warmer or colder, as we say in children's games.

Warmer now and closer still, and the sound is undeniable, refining and separating itself from all others — you're hearing Sinatra or 50 Cent and then a PSA on sleep disorders. That definition makes things easier, and in a matter of moments you locate the house, the fence behind the house, the transistor radio sitting on a lawn chair just inside the fence.

Though you've engaged a different sense, in this scenario you've worked something like a search dog, moving through an area in a systematic fashion, acquiring, then filtering out environmental norms to hone in on a specific element. When we watch a SAR dog work, the process seems magical, but when we translate it to human sensory capabilities, we better understand what we ask the search dog to do with her nose: let every other smell go and find only *this*.

SAR dogs can demonstrate any number of nose-driven skills.

Air-scent dogs are frequently used in relatively unpopulated areas to find living victims. Trained to locate and follow the cloud of human scent made by the microscopic skin rafts we shed and odors we create just in the process of living and moving — think of Pig Pen, from the Peanuts cartoon, and you've got a fair visual on the evidence we leave — the air-scent dog is invaluable on disaster sites and in the wilderness lost-person scenario. Working quickly, a good air-scent dog can determine if a search area has no living person in it or, alternatively, hone to the scents of an injured family or a single person within a large search sector. Children, young people, or athletes with their higher metabolisms shed more rafts and create a greater cloud of scent. Those who are relatively motionless, like babies, or have a slowed metabolism, like the elderly, release fewer rafts. Even so, air-scent dogs are often successful at locating Alzheimer's patients who have wandered away and ended up stuck in brush or debris, unable to extricate themselves. An air-scent dog works very fast and largely nose up until near the source of the scent.

Trailing and tracking are terms often (incorrectly) used interchangeably. There are many approaches to both activities. The purist may note substantial differences in the two techniques: trailing uses a scent article; tracking may not, for example, or tracking is more likely performed "head down" on a harness, while the dog's head position moves up and down for trailing, and the lead is longer. There are those who might argue both claims.

Generally stated, trailing dogs may follow both scent in the air and scent that has fallen onto foliage, objects, cement, or dirt in trail. Using a scent article from a specific person, the handler exposes the dog to the scent and then instructs him to find more of it and follow. These dogs may work head up or head down and, once on the scent, trace the movements of the person they seek as closely as possible. Trailing dogs move quickly and randomly, their path transcribing the wide swath of scent left by a specific moving person. As noted in Jen Bidner's book, *Dog Heroes,* mid-twentieth-century experiments with suspension devices demonstrated that trailing dogs are able to follow a person who has never touched the ground.

Tracking dogs, on the other hand, may follow a combination of elements: disturbed vegetation and scent left by footsteps on the ground. An excellent tracking dog — sometimes called a "cold-scent dog" — can follow a path that is days or weeks old, even if the track has been blurred by the passage of numerous other people. This technique is often attributed to the Bloodhounds we associate tracking runaway criminals in novels and film noir, their nose-down posture as famous as their throaty bays. Bloodhounds are, however, excellent trailers on a cold scent too. The Bloodhound is famous for its number of scent receptors: 230 million as compared to other scent-working dogs, whose estimates range between 200 to 220 million. And both, of course, outstrip our human gift of scent. With forty times fewer scent receptors, we are significantly unversed about the spectrum and prevalence of human rafts.

Human Remains Detection (HRD) and cadaver dogs are trained to alert on the remnants of human death. The two terms are not necessarily synonymous. Cadaver dogs specifically recover deceased humans and locate skin, hair, bones, blood, and the indeterminate mix of scents made of semen, urine, sweat, and the process of decomposition, which has an evolving scent of its own. HRD dogs are also often able to discriminate between human and animal ash. These dogs may alert over graves from a century before. One of the most remarkable possibilities with the HRD dog occurs when human remains are buried near the root structures of trees. HRD dogs may put up their paws and stretch to alert on the relevant tree, which exudes human scent as part of its photosynthesis and related processes.

Search dogs can also effectively work from boats on water to recover the drowned. Though theories vary as to what, exactly, the dogs catch scent of from the water — some say the creation of gases an intact body creates, others suggest the more straightforward scent of natural oils, skin remnants, and decomposition — the SAR dog can be extremely useful to recovery dive teams and drag crews who need to narrow the range of an underwater search.

Skeptics abound. A SAR team's quickest allies come from the public who run hunt dogs, or those who work seizure-alert or cancer-detection dogs, from law enforcement officers with search, bomb-, or drug-sniffing canines of their own, and from those who are willing to suspend disbelief for the moment to learn. And the dogs don't necessarily make it easy to believe. To the uninitiated, a dog in a sector that doesn't have a workable scent can look suspiciously like a dog having a good time in the bushes. And a dog actually on a scent that's wavering in conflicted air can look downright confused — checking empty corners, turning circles on a sidewalk, or snaking sideways for a moment to pick it up again. It took me six months of running with experienced handlers before I could begin decoding the subtler signals of a searching dog in progress. And the dogs too finesse their skills with experience. Every time we train, I learn some new pause or movement from dogs I've worked with for years.

Where skepticism becomes a problem is at the point of deployment. A team can be called to a search because someone in charge has brought in all available resources, only to arrive and find that search management isn't sure how to assign the dog teams and is pretty much convinced that dogs are useless anyway. Persuasion and explanation on-site take time, time that some situations can't afford. And so the condition perpetuates itself: Bloodhounds are sent out to run a city park days after an abducted child has been taken to another area, or air-scent dogs are asked to track a single scent only after two hundred volunteers have grid-walked through the field the day before. Dogs are not "the magic bullet," as one trainer I know often says. Search dogs are a resource like any other, and their work must be understood if they are to search effectively.

"We hate to see the dogs come in," one detective said to me a few years ago. "It's a sign of defeat — means we've turned a corner and that the victim is probably dead."

I said, "Hey, we have dogs that do live finds too. With our dogs, it's such a priority that they certify in live finds first."

Perhaps he sensed I was about to go into an unwanted rafts and metabolism lecture or worse, into some fanciful realm he usually reserved for neighborhood psychics on a crime scene. "We only use dogs for human remains," he said definitively, shaking his head. "Live people just don't smell bad enough."

Head trainer Fleta holds Puzzle in the soft grass of a local fire training facility. Ahead of us is a railway tanker, to the left a double row of demolished cars, to the distant right a simulated disaster site, the "debris pile," where Puzzle will eventually learn to find victims buried in rubble. Today's training includes Puzzle's first "runaway" searches with the team. The objective is simple: find the woman who is now unseen and get the treat she took with her.

Puzzle may not yet have shown any deep affinity for me at home, but on command from Fleta she scrambles across the grass to find me where I've hidden behind a car. She gallops ungracefully, rounding the corner of a smashed vehicle too quickly. The physics of puppy fat and wayward legs aren't with her, and she falls over with a little skid, righting herself with a shake and continuing on to where I crouch. She wags wildly as we praise her. We do a second find-your-handler runaway, and the second time she measures her pace a little better. We see her briefly hitch at the place where she'd found me previously, but when I'm not there this time, she lifts her nose, snags a thread of scent, and pivots at that nose point, changing direction, heading for me in the new spot. This is a moment of revelation for both of us. Puzzle learns that sight has its own limitations and that in this game, scent prevails. I have the opportunity to watch her blink-quick decision to trust her nose.

We repeat the game with a reverse of position. I hold Puzzle while Fleta shows her a treat, then cover her eyes as Fleta runs and hides thirty yards away. At the command "Find!" Puzzle trots forward a few steps, then dashes wildly in the direction Fleta traveled. Following behind, I notice with some amusement that the puppy is wagging so hard her tail's propeller action almost seems to make her fat bottom loft. "Good girl!" I hear from Fleta. "Good girl!" I also praise. Puzzle takes her treats and trots back to what she must think is the starting point. She flops down in the green grass, snitzes once, and tosses her head with a grin so wide it eclipses the rest of her face. She looks like a little blond Halloween pumpkin laughing there, full of merry confidence and more than a bit of mischief.

The squirrels at home are less enthusiastic. Puzzle's nose has become a problem for them, and I see three lined up on the roof of the garage, leaning forward on their paws and cussing the puppy in long-winded bursts of angry chittering. I watch one deliberately push a broken stick until it falls and hits her over the head. It's a small stick that she ignores, because at the moment Puzzle is head down in her fourth newly dug hole. Quick and intent, she paws at the soft earth rapidly, her bottom high and little plumes of rich black dirt shooting out from between her legs. The more she digs, the more the squirrels scold, and as I watch I soon realize why: Puzzle is digging up their buried pecans. She doesn't eat them, preferring instead to drop them on the slate sidewalk, mission accomplished, then turn to nose across the ground to a new spot with a likely nut beneath.

It's eight in the morning, and as I look around the yard four holes are in plain sight. There could be more around the corners at the edges of the yard. In the half-hour since her breakfast, Puzzle has undone a single squirrel's long workday, unearthing a week of winter food. There is no doubt the squirrels are watching and disapproving. I guess that these three are probably residents and that it's their hard labor she's made short work of.

She turns her attention to a flowerpot whose plants have long since died dramatically. The coleus lies in a limp Sarah Bernhardt pose over one edge of the pot, but Puzzle is far more interested in the other side of it. The squirrels and I watch as she raises up on hind legs and balances her forefeet in the dirt, then begins scratching a hole in that uneasy position. It's slower work, involving balance and great care. I watch her occasionally pause to consider the hole, and at one point she puts her nose down into it and huffs. I hear the echo of her snort against the sides of the terra cotta, and I see a little blizzard of dirt fly immediately upward into her eyes. She lifts up, blinking a little, her nose black with dirt to her forehead, the tips of her paws also black to the wrists. She hops down from the pot, sauntering toward me in a posture of quiet triumph. The squirrels riot across the shingles as she drops a sheathed, very black pecan at my feet.

But before Puzzle and I can interact about the digging and the pecans, she stiffens, lifts her nose, and then trots to the edge of the backyard. She stands there a long moment, nostrils working, though there's nothing I can see through the thin spaces of the privacy fence. She huffs and moves forward, her tail slowly beginning to wag. I still see nothing.

"What have you got, Puz?" I ask her, just as I hear the rapid *tip-tip-tip* of paws and the harder, ungainly slap of feet as Gerand and his new dog, Token, approach the house. I can hear Gerand gasping, *Slow . . . down . . . dog . . . slow . . . down . . . dog,* but Puzzle wuffs happily and races Token on the other side of the fence, and neutered though he may be, it's the female dog Token pays attention to. He sparks to her unseen energy, showing off, perhaps, connects through the fence, then makes a little revving sound and pulls Gerand harder northward. Puzzle presses her nose to the place where he was, savoring the delicious last scent of them as they leave us. She heaves a little sigh, sits down with a plop.

"Good girl to let me know they were coming, Puz," I say, though I know she doesn't understand.

I haven't talked to Gerand in weeks. And it sure doesn't seem like I will today. I climb onto an overturned flowerpot and watch the pair of them go. Token, nose high, is on his own agenda, but when they turn the corner, Gerand has his own face lifted. He's moving well. He looks bright and engaged. And he looks happier than I've ever seen him. *The universe prepares you,* he once said to me. I look down at my own dog. Oh, doesn't it just.

7

TRUST FALL

WHEN YOU STAND at the edge of a building with your heels hanging free over the side, kinetics create a delicious little tension that travels right up the nervous system to your brain and to your heart — a hot, silvery sensation like breathing mercury or swallowing sparks. Standing there now, at the top of the "high-rise," a tall building used at the fire academy, I feel wind strum my rappel line, and I consider mortality. Or simply humiliation: a misstep that sends me flailing over the side to smack against a wall on the way down and my own late correction on the line that forces a teammate at the bottom, working safety, to pull taut and suspend me there like a spider caught in her own long thread.

There are a dozen ways to get stupid on a rappel line and just a few ways to be cool. I don't fear heights, which is in my favor. I'm still working on cool. I've already kissed brick a few times today, blowing out the left knee of my fatigues. Both my elbows are bloody and bruised.

Today marks Puzzle's third weekend to train with the team, and it's also the day that human teammates are scheduled to rappel and work on high-angle rescue. We are at a fire department training facility, and rookie firefighters are half a football field away from us, working a large engine, fighting a simulated tanker blaze. We have watched them climb a long ladder and sway there, and now they release water from that high angle of attack. This is the maneuver, backlit by flame, which we see so often in movies.

Autumn plays tricks with us. It's warm this morning, and a light wind carries mist as far as Puzzle's crate, which I have placed in the shade of the ladder tower a distance from where we work. Some dogs are prone to separation anxiety, a concern we don't want Puzzle or any young search dog to share, and so she is crated at a distance with her stuffed lobster and a treat and something to watch — in this case about twenty young firefighters working the tanker. She lies comfortably there, lifting her nose and squinching her eyes shut, happy about water in any form and particularly happy about this mist on a warm day in the shade.

When I walked away a half-hour ago, she didn't whimper. *A good sign,* said a colleague to me, but I remind myself that Puzzle hasn't yet seemed concerned when I've left her in any venue. I can see her from where I stand seven stories up, a blond bit of pocket fluff against the dark floor of her crate.

Earlier we rappelled from the ladder tower, much closer to where Puzzle lies, a three-story structure open on all sides planted in the middle of a parking lot. It's no great height, but the backward launch from the top of it can still be scary. I envied the double-handful of us that launched confidently backward with an arc of a jump and a landing soft as an astronaut on the moon. Three little swings and two little touches to the building and they were down on both feet, looking up and grinning to the rest of us. My own descents lacked that easy grace, characterized by an awkward spurt of trajectory that resembled a hippopotamus giving birth on the run. I had some trouble rappelling from the ladder tower, which has no walls but does have an open metal framework along the sides. The experts among us managed to *gaboing-boing-boing* down with their feet precisely contacting the framework. Not me. I either missed the framework entirely, swinging completely through and then banging it hurtfully on the way out again, or contacted the metal braces in a sort of straddle, a right smart rap on the backside, on the *ischiopubic ramus,* said one of our paramedics, which somehow made it hurt more.

Now, at the top of the high-rise, the wind is blowing warm and fitful from the south. We are rappelling down the protected side of the building out of the wind, but up here on the roof in queue for our turn to drop, the wind puts hair in my eyes and whips the sleeves of my T-shirt, making me feel a little shaky, a little scattered. I'm about tenth in line, with plenty of time to watch and learn. Or not. I peer over the side to Deryl, holding the line on the ground. He is an imposing man, but from the roof he seems small. When I go over the side, it'll be Deryl providing safety if I forget how to rappel. From here, it's not the size of the guy that makes me feel safer, it's the intensity of his focus. A good man. He would be quick on the line to stop my falling self two beats before I might know I'd lost it.

I move away from the edge of the tower. I look at the teammates ahead in line and realize that ten years ago, probably none of us would have forecast we'd be on the roof of a building together, preparing to step off the edge of it. Backward.

"You couldn't pay me to do that," said a visitor to a booth the team had hosted during a neighborhood safety fair. She was speaking collectively, gesturing to the brochures and photographs we had at the booth depicting the working life of a canine SAR team. They are candid shots without airbrush, and in them we are rappelling with dogs on line with us, pushing through mesquite thorns in the wilderness, sweating in 105-degree heat on the debris pile while we traverse it behind our dogs, watching for signs of human scent. When I told her that we are an all-volunteer group, she gave me a little laugh and a doubtful twist of her head, and said, "You do this for *fun?*"

It's a common question, and one I'm often at some loss to answer. *We do it for service* would be the summary response, and accurate too, but sounds a bit lofty, and canine SAR folk are not generally a lofty group. We trudge through Dumpsters too often, carry our dogs' warm poop bags too frequently to claim much glory. Though certainly some of the training is fun, the work itself is challenging in every respect.

Behind every experienced handler with a dog or assistant in the field is an implied rigor: years of training scenarios and practice searches — three to seven hours weekly in all types of weather, campouts involving ten to fifteen hours of wilderness training, classes in everything from scent theory to medical assessment to meteorology to report writing to building construction and situation size-up and, following that, required exams. And for many, daily training on some aspect of SAR, whether decoding dot-dashes from a Morse code CD or tying figure-eight knots on a bight with a sample bit of rope. And work with the canines at home too — a reliable dog on a disaster site may have hundreds of hours of "Heel" and "Down" and "Stay" from his handler, training that proves he can control himself amid chaos and respond appropriately on command. Early in my experience with the team, a colleague said, "To work volunteer SAR, your idea of what makes a good weekend has to be flexible."

A news reporter once mentioned off-camera that our volunteer status surprised her. She had figured "canine SAR teams were made up of elite, paid professionals." I'm not sure how she typified elite, but paid wouldn't apply to most canine SAR teams I know. The reverse is true: most of us pay to be able to do this. Canine SAR units are often not-for-profit organizations, but contributions rarely equal the yearly expense of running even one dog. Unpaid we may be, but *professional* we strive for. Canine SAR is part of America's long, worthy tradition of volunteer emergency response, going back to the earliest days of colonial firefighting.

Among our team members are a few common denominators. About half of us are former military. A good few are former or current first-responders — police, paramedics, firefighters. We have professional dog trainers among us. A handful of pilots. A few scuba divers and a couple of rock climbers. But we are also students, entrepreneurs, bookkeepers, schoolteachers, engineers, tech support personnel, and one of us aspires to be a pastry chef. Though our working backgrounds are disparate, we're generally outdoorsy and unafraid of getting dirty. And we all love dogs. It's also safe to say we share a deep sense of responsibility toward our fellow human beings, driven by an impulse to serve that training intensifies and the search field completes.

Canine search-and-rescue attracts a lot of interest — an interest that increases in periods following catastrophe or after a particularly riveting news story illustrates the poignant connection between a dog and the human he has found. Many teams have no lack of short-term volunteers, some who are simply interested in the work as a hobby, others who believe it's a simple matter of putting a family pet in a vest and walking around until he finds something, still others who are attracted to the media attention and vicarious glory. And some, of course, who have both an urge to contribute and a willingness to give up, in our case, weekend mornings and some weeknights to training. Work with our team also means risk: even in training we may crawl over unstable rubble, hike through wilderness and emerge from it bloody, or lie in crushed vehicles on a hot summer day while waiting to be found by a young search dog that is still learning.

Our team requires that new members train first to assist dog units in the field. These field assistants learn and are tested on map, compass, and GPS navigation, first aid, situation size-up, crime scene preservation, interviewing, interagency response protocols, and radio navigation before ever taking to the field to assist on a first search. Advanced training follows, with written and practical tests administered by NASAR (the National Association of Search and Rescue), FEMA, and the U.S. Fire Administration. Field assistants, or the FAS team, perform invaluable services during searches, freeing the handlers to concentrate on their dogs as they jointly work a sector.

Training and testing thoroughly is a long process, and many volunteers are surprised by all that the commitment involves.

Pushing through thorns in the sleet isn't fun. Wading through a floodwater debris field poxed with illegal dumping is nasty. If the poison ivy doesn't get you, the blisters will. And then there are the insidious, sulphur-resistant, omnipresent chiggers. A month or so into training, newcomer attrition is high.

It would be easy to think about quitting now. A colleague just ahead of me balks at the edge of the building. She did well rappelling off the ladder tower, but the distance down from this greater height seems a long, mortal drop onto brick and cement. Some loose-lipped sadist ahead of us in line talked about a recent rookie SWAT cop who'd come to grief by being careless during a shorter rappel (two broken ankles and four front teeth gone!), and the story has made a few of us pensive, a few of us a little manic — *ha,ha,ha* — as we cover our shaking knees.

My teammate feels the pressure of her indecision. No one rushes her, but we all want her to make the rappel. *I* want her to make the rappel, perhaps a little selfishly. Every success encourages the rest of us, gets us a little further from the image of the limping, gap-toothed former cop who can now hoover peas off a spoon. When I point out to her that she's a flight instructor who routinely teaches students how to recover spins and that this, by comparison, is no big deal, she seems encouraged, and in a swift, decisive moment calls out to Deryl on safety, checks her equipment, and steps over the edge. Her descent is quick and smooth, and we cheer when she lands squarely on both feet. *She made that look easy,* I think, as I hook onto the line, call down to Deryl, and stand poised at the edge of the roof.

Patience is as much a part of working search as commitment. When you consider the volunteer SAR team made up of adults from widely differing backgrounds, there's strong likelihood that they won't all be good at the same things. A great dog handler may struggle with compass navigation; a hard-charging brush buster who can search in the wilderness for days may get a little claustrophobic training in tight spaces; the compassionate field assistant who can imagine how a lost child might think may struggle with theory involving building construction and collapse. At our best, we are a collaborative team of teachers and simultaneously a team of learners. At our best, we remember what it was like not to know something.

I was fortunate as a field assistant — many of the required duties were similar to those needed to fly an airplane. Navigation, radio communication, and emergency protocols were already a part of my thinking. Translating those procedures to ground SAR wasn't difficult. The dog work was new, however, and I struggled for some time behind handlers in the field, all of whom seemed to want something different — *stay right beside me, stay fifty feet back, clear the area ahead for hazards before we get there, let the dog go in first* — an inconsistency that frustrated me until the training day when I ran after four dogs in the same sector, one after another in quick succession, and I saw, at last, that each one of them worked a given sector differently, taking to the terrain according to their individual gifts. The quick-scented and somewhat heedless dog needed more help avoiding hazards than the slower, more cautious dog who worked an area with efficient, deliberate care. Some dogs enjoyed moving quickly and, pack-oriented, wanted the presence of their human counterparts just behind them. Other dogs preferred to blaze ahead and communicate back across a half-acre of brush. I must have tried many a handler's nerve with my early one-size-fits-all approach to assisting them in the training field, but not one of them yelled at me for it, a compassion I admire, a patience I have an uneasy feeling I'm going to have to learn.

The young woman who rigged today's rappel system comes forward to me. She is patient, silent for a moment while I stand there, intuiting perhaps that I'm reviewing procedure and making sense of the physics behind the rappel. Or she may think I'm nerving myself up. All of which is true.

"I would like," I say, "not to slam into the wall this time. I understand what's got to happen from the point I step off the edge to the moment I connect against the wall, but somehow I'm just not moving quickly enough to do it."

She says, "If you can get past the idea of the fall, you'll step off and get your feet right. Right now, I think you're stepping off and going into a kind of fetal position, so it's your knees that hit the wall."

Fetal position. Though I don't think I feel scared, I'm amused that when I step over the edge, some part of me still curls up and cries Mommy. I'm not sure what I feel beyond a desire to get down neatly and with no new wounds.

She adds, "Try to think of it the way you would if you were stepping from one building to another over a gap that's seven stories down. Don't fixate on the hole. You want to visualize stepping off with one foot and connecting to the building across the gap. The fall is not the big deal. It's not the empty space that matters. It's the arrival."

That's a philosophy I'll have to remember to pass along to Gerand. "I'm sorry I'm taking so long," I say to the young woman.

She gives a little okay-by-me shrug, then says, "If you feel anxious about the force of the fall on the line — even though we've shown it's safe — you know you can *crawl* off the side of the building. That might help. Just lie down along the edge, pivot your legs off, bend at the waist, and find the wall with your feet, then establish tension on the line and start rappelling down."

Crawling off the building sounds almost as bad as fetal position. Her suggestion sounds easy and bloodless, but definitely uncool. *I can't be too bad off,* I think, *if my ego's still capable of wincing.* No, I have to trust this young woman, and I have to step over the side. I remember the scores of fourth-lesson flight students who took a deep breath and gave me a thumbs-up before I demonstrated their first stalls, their faith in me overcoming every instinct for self-preservation that screamed, "You're going to make the airplane *stop flying*?" Their actions shame me now. I look at the young woman and say, "I trust you." I give her a thumbs-up.

"On belay," I shout down to Deryl, who confirms the belay, and then I step backward. This time, there's a funny little *whoosh* of wind across the flat of my ears, a double buffet, as though the winds at the top edge of the building decided to smack me on each side of the head.

Three seconds of freefall aren't much in the grand sum of life's uncomfortable experiences, but they are memorable. It's a little like touching a fork to a filling while stunt-doubling a crash-test dummy just before the bang. My descent from the high-rise is safe enough — a little jump, an arc of a swing, and then several controlled collisions down and down and down to the ground. I walk away from the rappel with all my teeth intact and no new holes in the knees of my fatigues, but the knuckles of my left hand are scraped, as though I took a swing at the wall somewhere along the way.

The teammates above and below me cheer. Later I may be in for much teasing (was I upside down at one point? I have an uneasy recollection of the ground rushing up), but right now they're all about my success.

I've got to get better at this, I think. After I learn to make my own descents with confidence, there will be a point where I'll be put online with Puzzle, and we'll be raised and lowered together. Dog-and-handler rappelling works differently; it lacks the graceful *gaboing-boing* of the solo descent, but Puz will do better if the handler holding her on the way up or down is assured.

Puzzle squeaks happily when I open her crate, emerging from it wiggly and more overjoyed to see me than ever before. She squirms and mutters as I hold her in my lap, kissing my face and then sniffing carefully every bruised and bloody spot on my arms and knees. Teammate Michele says, "See! She's glad to see you." Birgit adds, "Looks like she knows she's your puppy now." I hope so. What's changed in the past ninety minutes? Perhaps she scents the slightly shaken cocktail of me, post-rappel: the adrenaline, sweat, torn skin, and blood. Perhaps her joy is a matter of timing.

She wants out of the crate, and I'm the one to free her. This sudden sure-do-love-you change is another of her dog mysteries.

I take her to socialize with the rest of the team. Some cuddle her, others bend down to rub her belly when she rolls over to expose it. Petting her is not an easy process. Our teammates are dog lovers, but they also know this socialization lays a strong foundation for the puppy who must learn not only to be a partner, but also a member of the larger pack that is our team. These are her instructors, her mentors, and the people who will hide for her hundreds of times, in all conditions and all weathers, as she trains toward certification. But for now the lessons are simpler: this is a fun place to be; trust and affection are the standard; humans are here to be partners and here to be found.

My colleagues try to hold conversations while Puzzle ping-pongs between them. She moves quickly among dogs and humans alike, and while I'm prepared for her puppy bounding and freakish attention span (*Is that a treat? What is a cigarette? Did you see that bird? Hey, this dog's got balls!*), my height, my center of gravity — and my steady stream of apologies — slow me down. Puzzle trips a teammate, runs completely under the belly of one dog, and steals the last part of a chew treat from another. I arrive just in time to see Collie Misty shoot yellow Lab Buster a thoughtful look. It's a brief communication — *discipline this youngster or let her slide?* Both dogs turn their heads away from Puzzle, allowing her the thievery. For now.

"That puppy license won't last long," says Fleta with a laugh.

"I'm surprised she's so dominant," I hear over my shoulder. "I expected a Golden to be softer."

She's not soft when it's her turn to search. At the command "Find!" Puzzle catapults from my arms, trips over her own feet while trying to lift her nose and run at the same time, spins angrily at her tail, and then ricochets across the rubble to locate the volunteer victim shrouded by debris and tall grass. We hear a little *oof!* as Puzzle lands on the young woman's chest. It's a successful find, but not a graceful one. The praise afterward goes straight to her head, and as we leave the search area, she saunters up to one of the senior dogs and starts to shadowbox. I see the wrinkle of his dark muzzle, just a little rickrack showing of bared white teeth. A warning. The four adult dogs standing there simultaneously lift their heads and turn away from her, a doggy snub executed like synchronized swimming. I'm not sure how much of it registers with Puzzle, who bounces off a couple of their backsides before she pogos across the grass to get the toy in her crate.

I look at my dog, now tugging at the embroidered left eye of Lobster. She has him gripped in fat paws, and she's working him over with a will. I hear little *pup-pup-pup* sounds of black thread pulling free. Every once in a while, she lifts her head to make eye contact with the nearby dogs or humans, her expression a little like a challenge, a little like a brag — a *wouldja get a load of me.*

A colleague puts his arm around my shoulder. "Good rappel there at the end," he says. "You landed on your feet. And you don't look like you lost too much blood." He grins toward Puzzle. "Fourteen weeks," he says in the same way one would say "tax audit," as though he remembers his own dog, as though Puzzle's age is a statement of condition.

"She's a natural disaster," I say and smile at her.

"A force to be reckoned with," my teammate amends. "But count all the plusses. You're doing good," he adds.

We both look at Puzzle, who has now beheaded her toy and makes *ack-ack-ptui* sounds, spitting out soggy bits of red plush. She smiles up at us with a wreath of Lobster's former innards around her muzzle. She appears to be having a very good day.

But I must look dazed. I can't imagine ever being able to step over a ledge and descend placidly with this dog. At this point, I can't imagine taking her off lead and expecting to ever see her again. After a moment, my teammate shakes his head and pats my arm. "Don't worry," he says. "It all works out. Remember she's got you. And you've got us."

8

SIX DAYS DOWN

A STEADY RAIN is falling when the pager goes off this morning, a rain that continues as we make our way out of town twenty minutes later, a rain that silvers the highway in the light of traffic inbound for the city. It is early and still very dark, and the rainfall—slow and insistent—is the kind guaranteed to make us sleepy, even though we've got coffee in a Thermos, oldies rock on the radio, and a cryptic note on the pager that indicates we will be looking for a drowned man likely six days down.

Which is unnatural, this failure to surface—a big man, we've learned, believed drowned in a small body of water in warm weather. According to our refloat tables, his body should have appeared days ago. A teammate and I discuss this as we drive. The situation suggests many things the team has seen before, among them the possibility that he's tangled in something beneath the surface, that heavy clothing has affected his buoyancy, or that his body did refloat days ago unseen and is now caught in shoreline debris, that local wildlife may have claimed and dragged him, and—apart from all of this—the chance that he may not be there at all.

The calling law enforcement agency believes he is.

I consider the effect of water on a victim submerged six days. If we do find the body of this man, the distortion will considerable. Horrific. I feel little internal latches begin to flip as the analytic part of my thinking steps forward and my other, more vulnerable responses head for cover. I have never seen a tidy death, and this one is unlikely to be the first.

A body under water still produces scent available to a dog.

"What are they smelling?" a reporter once asked me. "Perfume? Garlic? Laundry detergent?"

Yes, perhaps, but more so the distinctly human tissue byproducts that rise naturally to the surface and are released into air passing over water. Blood may be part of the scent artifact too. Unless in motion due to current or caught and suspended by something underwater, drowning victims always lie face down in the water, heads hanging, which causes blood pooling and any post-death injuries to seep. Some theorists suggest that the friction of water against skin and the friction of human body against underwater objects actually cause more scent production from a water victim than would naturally be produced by a victim on land.

The scent of underwater victims is also subject, like a sailing ship, to multiple forces. The scent of a victim in rivers or moving floodwaters is carried by current before it is released into the air, where it moves according to wind direction and terrain friction. The scent of a lake victim may be fragmented and distorted by the chop of passing boat and ski traffic. Additional factors like water temperature and composition, depth of water, and depth of victim sometime complicate the relationship between the victim and the rising point of the victim's scent.

Dogs working water are rarely able to hover directly over the location of a body in the water. Rather, from boats or shoreline they indicate the location where scent is first available to them above the surface. Our team uses multiple dogs for this effort, ruling out certain areas as "null" — or no indicated scent — and defining areas by GPS where more than one dog has indicated scent source, dogs

and handlers ideally refining that information to determine areas of faint, stronger, and strongest scent. The teams work "blind,"
meaning that they do not know the nature or location of information passed on from the previous canine unit, the better to ensure
that similar indications are not influenced for one handler by the
handler who has gone before.

Not yet a handler with a certified dog, for this search I will be
working along the shore or on the water with another dog unit.
Buster, Belle, Shadow, Hunter, or Saber: all are experienced water
and shoreline recovery dogs, partnered by handlers long with the
team.

While my colleague drives, I inspect my worn gaiters by flashlight. Warm weather has encouraged the snake population, and
though I have a live-and-let-live philosophy about them, I know
our blundering press through the brush along a shoreline can provoke a snake to strike in self-defense, if not aggression. On scene,
an officer confirms this. "Lotta snakes out there," he says, with a
gesture of disgust across the lake.

The rain has stopped, but the air is heavy and close. The area we
will search is small by our standards — a wattle-shaped inlet off a
thick neck of the lake, a good fishing spot that doesn't take much
effort to get to, bordered by a sheltered boat dock. The shoreline
is ugly and unkempt, a tumble of yellowish brush and trees fighting dumped garbage for space. The winning trees extend awkward
branches over brown water. Thick bramble competes below. The
shoreline appears impassable from where I stand.

During a momentary wind shift, I can smell rotting debris and
the stench of something dead from the opposite bank. The dogs
lift their noses but do not react. One of the officers tells us this is
a prime crappie fishing spot; locals have been dumping old furniture and Christmas trees, dead cars and small boats here for years
to give the fish a place to shelter and breed. Plenty of folks dump
along the shore too, not to improve the fishing, but just because

they can. "One-stop dumping," he calls it: do a little fishing, drop a lot of trash.

We look at one another. The boat work on this search should be relatively straightforward. The shoreline work will probably be more difficult. There's no scramble among us for the easier search, and I'm proud of that. Most of us stand with gaiters in one hand and a PFD in the other, ready to go whichever way the Incident Commander directs.

Meanwhile, the dogs are schooling among us. Two yellow Labs, a Husky, a Collie, and a German Shepherd. Their heads bob slightly as they ferret the thousands of scents drifting around us from the water, the shore, and the Dumpster behind the convenience store nearby. I watch their noses work and their ears prick to passing sounds, and I wish, as I always do, that I could experience the sensory world they interpret with calm curiosity.

We do not have a picture of our missing man, but his half-brother in another state has sent a photo. Apparently the two men are so similar they were mistaken for each other as children, and they are still much alike. We look at the image of this virtual twin. It is a birthday shot over a small cake ablaze with black candles. The twin's eyes squint shut with laughter. His moving hand is fuzzy where he tries to shield himself from the camera. From him we get an idea of size, muscle mass, and hair color. The first two are relevant to the victim's refloat projections; the third may be significant when we begin to work along the shore, where birds and other creatures sometimes furnish their nests with hair.

We're told the man we're looking for had come out here several days earlier to fish off the side of his boat. He was last seen arguing with a stranger outside a local fast-food restaurant, where he clutched a fresh six-pack to his chest, pointing first to himself and then toward the lake in an exchange no eyewitness can clarify. This account provokes ongoing speculation, raising the question of possible foul play — if not on his boat, then on another one, or somewhere else in the immediate area.

A couple of conflicting stories suggest the missing man may have been seen later on his boat, still docked, a little while before a late-evening thunderstorm hit. One version describes a man in the shadows sitting on the side of a boat that may have been his. Whoever he was, he ignored a friendly warning about the approaching storm; without reply, he stared across the inlet to a midpoint on the water where nothing moved.

Though officers shrug over the latter account, saying everyone wants to get in on the story and small towns make new ghosts fast, one of the search dogs shows interest around the victim's boat. Hunter paces restlessly along the dock, straining to cross onto the boat, but aboard it, he appears frustrated, as though the space has convoluted the scent. His handler remarks that this is interest, strong interest from his dog, but he is cautious. Hunter may be indicating human scent from what remained of the owner's personal belongings still aboard. His early interest is noted, and we all head to our separate sectors to confirm or deny the presence of the missing man there.

An hour later as Johnny, yellow Lab Buster, and I press forward through unforgiving brush, Buster works as quickly as the thick scrub and debris will allow. Thorny vines snag our clothing and our bootlaces. One particularly stubborn branch catches both my boots and penetrates my leather gloves, then flips the radio out of its holster when I cut myself free. Johnny says, "They'll all be on their second sectors by the time we get halfway through the first." I don't know whether to pity or envy naked Buster, who is scratched liberally but able to move much faster than we are.

And he is moving fast.

There is any amount of human scent here, but it is old, old scent that Buster wisely disregards. Decaying car seats, beer cans and Styrofoam cups, disposable diapers a decade old, shredded by a thousand field mice in nesting season. The promised snakes are here too. Most of them whip quickly away from our approach, but in the deepest part of the shoreline thatch, one young fellow, perhaps two feet long, slips over a low branch toward us, then pauses and coils with a neat little snap, his head flattish and his mouth gaping wide. Steady Buster gives him a peripheral glance and changes direction. Johnny and I do not stay long enough to differentiate the snake from his nonpoisonous imitators, though Johnny knows I am interested in snakes. Sidestepping, he grins and asks if I happened to notice whether there was a single or double row of scales on the underside of that tail. I did not, and I don't go back to look. It is enough that the snake was there, brilliantly patterned and smiling widely upward, the tip of his tail a shivering yellowish-green.

The dead thing I could smell across the water turns out to be the remains of a cow, in so strange and awkward a position that she appears to have been dumped there a while ago. The local wildlife has worked her over, and at this point she is mostly hair and hooves and curves of whitish bone already braided with vine. Buster acknowledges the cow but is not fooled by her scent. He continues forward through our sector, a strong and sensible dog who communicates clearly that while there are many interesting things where we are, not one of them is the reason we are here.

The dogs on the water have something else to say. I can see the last dog unit returning to the dock. In a series of blind searches where handlers did not know the response of previous dog units, three dogs have confirmed one another, indicating strong human scent from the water in a chain of points leading back to the docked boat. Two dogs have returned to the spot where Hunter strained to get at the water to chew it, his best method for discerning submerged human scent. One dog shows intense interest; one of them fully alerts a few feet over.

Two officers look down to the murky water surrounding the dock. A crappie hole encouraged by debris is not the safest place to send down divers, but that will be the next step in the search and recovery of the missing man, whose untouched six-pack still sits on the boat.

Having completed the search, Johnny, Buster, and I return. The team stands down. We write our sector reports — this is what we searched and how we searched it; this is how the dog responded. We notate wind, terrain, direction of travel, and percent of coverage. We debrief in the parking lot, reviewing the environment, the weather, the known, and the unknown about the victim. The dogs could not have been more unanimous in their signals to us. They are relaxed now, praised and satisfied, lying in confident postures. I make a map for my own notes, drawing Buster moving with long speed streaks behind him, with wheels instead of paws. I add little sketches for both the snake and the cow.

The divers say they'll let us know what they find after their own difficult searches, but they expect to find the missing man there, caught in debris or fishing line. Crime or misadventure? Those are the conclusions, long coming, that we rarely get. But I stroke Saber's cheek and think of a local family needing some kind of word, of the half-brother waving away his birthday photograph, and of the man caught beneath his boat waiting to be found. "Good dog," I say to Hunter, as Saber leans into my scratching hand and groans. We drive home beneath a sky that cannot commit to sun.

9

HOUSEBREAKING

OOGLE "GOLDEN RETRIEVER" and "temperament," and you'll likely come up with happy paragraphs describing the Golden's sweet nature, companionability, and eager desire to please. These are famous qualities, and it's no wonder that the Golden is one of the world's most popular dogs, the figural presence in TV commercials and greeting cards. Oh, those cute puppies, knocking over a houseplant, tumbling down a hallway with a roll of toilet paper! Theirs is a moment's mischief. Puzzle's shenanigans work overtime.

The Pomeranians are a little stunned at puppy behaviors from a dog that rapidly triples their weight. When she dances and boxes and bows in petition for play, they scatter for the first few weeks. Puzzle gets more action out of Maddy the cat, who after the first startled introduction seems to quite enjoy the puppy. In fact, the cat is the first four-footed member of the household who keeps Puzzle in line. Maddy stalks Puzzle when she is sleeping, creeping up behind her, circling, staring at her with a calculated, misleading benevolence, then popping her nose with a paw, causing the puppy to wake from her deep sleep dazed and scrambling for a cat that has long since skittered across the room and out the door.

Puzzle's not the only one who wakes stupid. Insomnia leaves me fuzzy-minded in the early morning, and I'm not yet used to the new dog rhythms. Puzzle, however, is housebroken. One early morning when she grumbles and I don't take the hint that she needs to go out, Puzzle pops me in the face with my house shoe. I open my eyes and watch her eyebrows knit and her expression change. She looks dubious and vaguely disappointed. Clearly she hopes I'm a little smarter after the slap.

Unfortunately, she has to do this the next day also. She wants to go out. I don't wake up. She wants to go out a little harder. I can be slow. And in time Puzzle figures out that if she slaps me, runs away with the house shoe, *and* drops it at the door, I've not only made the connection, but the one-shoe-on/one-shoe-off stumping to the door has thumped me awake enough to be able to unlock it.

Certainly there are softer ways to wake, but Puzzle's insistence interests me. Eventually she'll need to tell me other things, and there will be complicated, difficult moments when she has to figure out how to communicate what she knows. I imagine a few dog trainers would have something to say about this whole process with the shoe, about the metamessage of the slap to the head, about my slow responsiveness, about who's really in charge in these early days. But I can't argue with her success. I learn to wake at the first mutter of her grumble, and once I've demonstrated this for a week or so, she never slaps me with the house shoe again.

The other dogs have not reached a similar accord. Though I make allowances for the clumsiness of a developing puppy and her universal interest in provoking play, Puzzle's sideswipes of gentle eight-pound Jack seem to cross another line. She is testing her place in the pack and challenging any dog she considers a rival. She carefully steps around little Sophie, with her labored breathing and congestive heart failure, and treats five-pound Scuppy kindly, but for reasons I don't understand, Puzzle targets Jack with dedication.

It is an unfortunate choice. While on a leashed walk with me in 2002, puppy Jack was attacked by two large dogs running free, an attack that nearly killed him before I could kick the big dogs off and fall over him to block them. In the presence of Puzzle's swaggering dominance, her sideswipes and bared teeth, he — at four and a half years old — first stands his ground, then cries out and gives in to the five-month-old pup when she pins him down, his tail in her teeth. The line between play and bullying blurs here. I am inexperienced with it, and I'm never far from that 2002 attack. Apart from whatever it means in dog logic, Puzzle's new behavior worries me.

She is a dog who's got some lessons coming, I think. *She's a dog who needs to learn to respect me and to get some comeuppance from larger playmates, from a pack.* My little crew hasn't found their ground with her yet. But on neighborhood walks, we meet other dog owners with mature, puppy-friendly big dogs, and play-date interactions seem to ease some of the tension at home. *A tired puppy is a good puppy,* says the truism. In our case, a tired puppy seems less interested in collaring a Pomeranian just for the hell of it.

Weeks pass. At SAR, the team continues to let Puzzle mingle with the grown dogs. We watch carefully and hope they might check her pushiness. Only one of the males has so far given her a growl that means business.

"Can you hear them counting to ten?" one handler says to another about the dogs, as I rather desperately redirect Puzzle elsewhere, a wiggly and manic process, like juggling six baby sharks and a tuna.

The universal expectation was that she'd be pliable, friendly, and willing to work. The work part is true enough, but at home she retains a stubborn streak and the occasional tendency to bully. Puzzle on a playful scramble sends three Poms rolling like fuzzy croquet balls, yelping in surprise, but worse, she again corners Jack in the hallway minutes after they all have eaten, and when he backs against the wall and squeaks in fear, she jumps him, taking a mouthful of his ruff as though she were about to shake prey. She already outweighs Jack several times over, and in the tumble of them I cannot tell if this is extreme play or aggression. But it doesn't look good. I am between them and have the dogs apart in only seconds, Puzzle bemused and Jack trembling. This was unexpected and far too close a call, and I realize there are all kinds of problems with my inexperience here. I hire a dog trainer right away.

There is the old, old joke about the airline pilot so accustomed to a jet's roar that when its engines suddenly go silent, he screams, "What was *that*?"

I understand.

Silence in the household with a new dog can indicate a puppy sleeping or, more insidiously, a puppy occupied somewhere in the nether regions, ripping up carpet, chewing electrical cords, backing Pomeranians into corners and staring, staring, staring. Unless Puzzle's crated, unless I can see Puzzle sleeping, silence usually signals trouble. All those qualities that were a good sign on her aptitude tests — intelligent, curious, assured, resourceful, strategic — can translate differently at home. Intelligence directs her to prize open the latch to her crate, pad silently out, then wiggle through folding closet doors. Curiosity leads her to sample the cats' litter box (robust! salty! with just a hint of salmon back!) to taste-test my shoes (patent leather shares the same bouquet of dead cow but is more delightfully resilient than suede). At one point I walk down a hallway and find a Hansel and Gretel trail of buttons leading out of my bedroom. Resourceful, strategic: Puzzle had woken from a nap at my feet, tiptoed away on soft paws, jimmied into my closet, and de-buttoned five shirts back from the cleaners. Fortunately, she wasn't interested in eating them. The number of buttons dropped equals the number of buttons missing. She just likes the feel of them in her teeth, the little snap of release. Self-confident: when I catch her in misdeeds and scold her, she does not look ashamed.

I am, however. I thought I was prepared for the realignment of priorities any puppy brings, but either she is sly or my distraction level has made me oblivious, or a little bit of both.

The obedience trainer is frank. "You aren't being enough of a leader, here. She's a smart dog, and she's got time to think too much," Susan says. "Smart dogs are tougher than dumb dogs. For a while, you want her thinking what you need her to be thinking. You want her doing what you tell her to. It should be: sit for petting, sit for treats, sit for no reason at all other than I told you to. She should think her middle name is 'Sit.'" Susan's direction: watch her carefully, keep her directed, reward her for good behavior, set some standards, and make her stick by them. In fact, my leadership over all the crew is lacking. Make *all* the dogs stick to the rules.

I say "Sit" so much that even one of the cats drops his bottom at the sound of the word. I say "Sit" so much that when a salesperson hovers over my shoulder and interrupts me for the fourth time in a complicated transaction, I hold up my hand and reflexively say "Sit," as I lean over the contract. He blinks. I blink. "New dog," I say in apology. "Ah," he replies and points at the picture of his black Lab, all muscular intensity with a shining head. "How old?" I ask. "Ten months," he says. "Yours?" "Six months," I answer. We have a moment of empathy. He does not, however, interrupt me again.

Walks are also a challenge. The world is fresh and new to Puzzle, and my neighborhood is in a state of upheaval. Old houses are demolished for new-builds, and the sound of destruction and the smell of overturned earth is everywhere. Puzzle strains at her lead, occasionally porpoising to leap for some provoking scent. Downwind of a dog friend in a backyard two blocks away, Puzzle goes theatrical. *It's Roxie! Roxie! Roxie! and she's way up there and I'll DIE if I don't go VISIT.* She has a Roxie moan, a Jack-and-Lady grumble, an Annie mutter. The sounds are so separate and singular that at one point a friend on a walk with us recognizes the difference. "Oh," he says when Puzzle lifts her nose and mutters, "Annie must be out." She is.

I am not opposed to dog friends or playdates, but I'd like a better walk from Puzzle, a loose lead, a heel. "Keep her busy on her walks," says Susan. "Make her go on *your* walk. Be consistent with your words. Don't give her time to think about what she'd rather do."

In a few months, I get a casual, acceptable trot ahead from her, punctuated by only a few spasms of pull. The lead is frequently slack. I feel less like I'm walking a chain saw. But "Heel" Puzzle seems to find insulting. She veers away on her lead like a reluctant teenager in the company of a parent. We are irrevocably bound, but terribly uncool. She seems to be sure I'm unnecessary. She prefers to think I'm invisible too.

Even the sight of the lead is enough to set her spinning. Puzzle is young and winds up easily. Quick movement from me or a high, bright word, and she starts to ricochet across the house. I begin to approach walks as though I were headed for meditation, winding things down half an hour before we're likely to go out. I try speaking more quietly, moving more calmly and with greater purpose. I turn off the TV and the radio, and I avoid giving all the dogs high-energy treats. I am just one notch away from lighting incense and beating a few low-key brass gongs with cloth mallets before I suggest "walk" in a whisper.

Like the Poms, Puzzle is also keenly aware of body language, and though I try to disguise my intention to take her out for a walk until the moment I head for the leash, the puppy seems to anticipate me by minutes. I don't know what she senses in me; there is no noticeable routine of timing, clothing, or movement that I can see, but when I have a walk in mind, I notice her sudden omnipresence, and then her escalated breathing, and then a certain oingy-boingy quality that knocks over chairs and thumps pictures a-tilt on the walls. It is as though she can hear the bat's-squeak of the idea across the synapses of my brain. Sprits'l takes a cue from Puzzle and begins to bark, racing in circles in front of the door. Puzzle may be the one going out, but five-pound Sprits'l is just the man to scold her for what she's about to do, what she may do in the future, what she has certainly done in the past. To her credit, Puzzle accepts his noisy chiding with goodwill. She sidesteps Sprits'l and heads for the leash rack. She is all about the walk. I wonder if she can smell me mentally gearing up for the adventure with her that often feels like a cross between street fighting and deep-sea fishing.

Friends try to help. One night a teammate and I are both going to take Puzzle for her evening walk. Ellen has witnessed this spectacle in the past, and tonight we decide that we'll use the long SAR lead, which has a sense of weight and gravitas, and that we'll wear the puppy out with backyard games, wind down for an hour or so, and then take her out when she is mellow. Mellow. *As if,* Puzzle's expression seems to say when we bring her in from forty minutes of fetch and chase in the backyard.

"Maybe," Ellen says, "we should just up and go in the middle of a TV show. You know . . . sit and watch the show and then, all of a sudden, just get up and go." It is a good plan, meant to teach the puppy spontaneity and adaptability, but the truth is we hope to sneak the walk up on Puzzle and to teach her there's no need to make a fuss about something she does twice every day, anyway. No need to dismantle the dining room. The Poms do not have to be woofed, nor the cats flushed upstairs in happy anticipation.

Our plan fails on several levels. Puzzle is lying on the floor, tenderly beheading a stuffed octopus when I get up. She immediately drops the toy and rolls onto her chest to watch what I'll do next. I head for her long lead, and she's at my ankles, happy and wiggling as I snap it on. She's delighted with it. Gathering a knot of black webbing in her teeth, she trots toward the door with her head up and her fuzzy tail waving. As I move for my house keys and Ellen bends to re-tie her shoe, Maddy flashes through the room and right under Puzzle's nose, then skitters away. It is a direct provocation and one that Puzzle cannot resist. She scrambles after the cat, her long lead trailing, and before I can grab it, the end of the lead catches under the leg of the china cabinet. The cabinet shudders but does not fall. Before we can shriek "Puzzle, stop!" the lead snaps taut. Puzzle scrambles after Maddy, the uneasy cabinet makes a little hop, then pivots somehow on two feet that are free, turning ninety degrees clockwise on squat legs like a glass sumo wrestler, before its weight stops the puppy. Through some miracle of physics, the cabinet rests upright and perpendicular to the wall after the dance step, its curved glass intact. The china and crystal inside have shifted but have not shattered. Ellen and I gawp, wordless. I'm reminded of those magicians who can pull a tablecloth out from under a laden table and leave dinner, wine, and candles intact. Puzzle has felt the check on her lead and sits like a good dog, her expression a little wistful as Maddy rounds a corner out of sight.

Ellen finds her voice before I do. "Did you see that?" she shouts, waving her arms at the china cabinet. "Did you — DID YOU SEE THAT?" Her pitch rises to dog whistle altitudes and Puzzle gives a little woof. High octaves out of humans are very exciting. I extract the dog's lead and tell Puzzle to hold her sit, which she does, but I can feel the happy vibration of her down the long length of webbing. The puppy flashes me a loopy, tongue-sideways smile. A cat, a scramble, a spin, and a shriek: this is the way all walks ought to begin.

10

SOMEONE ELSE'S STORM

A SPONGY EVENING on the verge of spring, and I am driving up I-35 in a caravan of eight other cars. A teammate sits beside me. Frances has her knees propped on the glove box and her peanut butter sandwich on the dashboard. She's clearing waypoints from her GPS and humming along to Santana. I've got a Thermos of coffee wedged next to me in the seat. We've got a long drive ahead. The team has been preemptively deployed against bad weather in another state, and we're packed for several days of possible searches, heading out to serve as field assistants to the handlers with certified dogs.

We've driven north out of city lights and into the enveloping black of rural night sky, but we lose stars, too, by the minute as we head into the storm system moving toward central Oklahoma. On radar, the system's greatest violence and repeating hook echoes suggest that tornadoes are likely again in an area barely recovered from multiple disasters across the past decade. So we've been deployed to a staging area just outside the storm's projected path, the local police and fire departments now aware how long it can take specialty search-and-rescue teams to get to a disaster site after the fact. We'll move three hours closer to coming trouble, but not too close to become victims ourselves. With any luck there will be no trouble at all.

But the longer we drive, the more the angry sky defines itself. We watch the roil of cloud to cloud lightning and see, from one splendid chain reaction across the horizon, a dozen flashes and three separate cumulonimbus anvils backlit in perfect formation, firing on one another like ships of the line in the age of fighting sail.

To stay alert on the road, Frances and I trade storm stories. Frances grew up in New York and had never witnessed a tornado before she got here, but the first year she was in Texas as the young bride of an ex-military man, a storm out of nowhere hit when she was alone at the farm. The sky of that storm, she says, was unlike anything she'd ever seen: purple, silver, and green, pimpled with mammatus clouds — beautiful and surreal.

When the storm released, she heard all the windows of the house pop, as though the pressure in the house had suddenly changed. Hail the size of softballs killed some cattle, spooked horses in their stalls, and took out all the baby trees in the front yard. Hail fell so loud and so long, it was enough to make you crazy, she says. When her in-laws called afterward to make sure she was all right, Frances shouted into the receiver, unable to hear the caller and hardly able to hear herself.

This was her introduction to extreme Texas weather. It was enough to make her wish she'd married a guy from Rhode Island.

Frances says worse than the storm was her husband coming home to find out she'd forgotten to put his candy apple red '67 Mustang GT in the garage. She was too young to have gotten married, and things had gone south just afterward. They had been in all kinds of standoffs for months after the wedding. Thinking back, she says she might have forgotten the Mustang on purpose to shake things up, bring the storm inside a little, at least to know where she was with him, which it turned out was nowhere, but at least she knew.

Donny screamed at her for days after the storm, every time he caught sight of the GT's smashed windshield, the cratered hood peeling paint. When he threw a skillet and threatened to kill her dog, she packed while he was at work. She loaded his old army duffle full of clothes and that was it. Frances was eighteen at the time. She took her poodle and left, stepping over split baby trees, walking past the smoldering livestock that had died in the storm, piled into a mound to be written off as a loss, doused with gasoline, and torched.

"What about you?" Frances asks. "Do Texas kids just get used to this?"

I tell her that of all the things I could have been afraid of as a child, it was storms that scared me most. Which came first, storm phobia or *The Wizard of Oz*, already showing on television when I was small? While some of my playmates feared the flying monkeys or the talking trees, and others were spooked by the Wicked Witch of the West, for weeks after a rerun of *The Wizard of Oz*, I dreamed only of storms — nightmares I still remember — all lowering sky and wind rising, a whirl of flightless chickens, a tornado on the horizon, and the storm cellar bolted shut.

I had tangled reasons to be afraid, living with my parents near an air force base in an era of nuclear tension, housed on the leading edge of the Midwest's Tornado Alley. If The Bomb didn't get you there, said the sixth-graders (who knew it all), the tornadoes would. I was pretty much terrified of both. A few of the big boys talked about missiles in Cuba ("just a hundred miles away!"), little missiles with lasers and big ones with The Bomb, all of them most definitely aimed at us. But tornadoes were the stuff of better stories. Some of the sixth-graders had seen the Wichita Falls tornado of '64. Others pretended to have seen it. Those big kids fascinated and frightened us with their catalogue of bizarre outcomes: a toothpick stuck in the side of a car; a Cocker Spaniel found — still alive! — thirty miles from home *with its ears pulled right off its head;* a picture of a solemn, suit-wearing farmer holding a bald chicken, its exploded feathers plucked clean by the passing storm. Sometimes two boys would fight over whose uncle had the chicken and whose daddy had the earless dog. I had given up on Santa Claus by this time, but for some reason I believed every story from the sixth-graders about the tornado of '64.

Their tales were indirectly validated by our teachers. We were thoroughly prepared for disaster. On first-grade field trips, we memorized which buildings had the yellow and black FALLOUT SHELTER sign (post office, hospital, big school) and which did not (movie theater, grocery store, church). We learned which buildings were the safe places in storm or nuclear attack. The rules were simple: hear the siren, run for the sign.

We watched a lot of *Duck and Cover!* in those days. I still remember animated Bert the Turtle retracting into his shell at the first sign of trouble, the goofy kid in the jacket with the fur collar dropping his bicycle and flinging himself headfirst against a curb, the smiling teacher pointing out two types of nuclear attack on the chalkboard, the neat rows of schoolchildren hiding beneath their desks when something bright flashed white outside. When we ducked beneath our desks during drills, the rows were not so perfect, and our teacher didn't smile. Some kids giggled while the sirens wailed. A five-year-old first-grader, I always cried.

Tornado warnings caused sirens spring, summer, and autumn; civil defense drills brought sirens at least monthly year-round. The sound of that horn, just blocks from my house, the way it wound up and down its wail, went right through me. A latchkey kid after school while my parents searched in vain for childcare, on stormy afternoons I would hide in the closet beneath the stairs when the sky went black and the sirens went off, turtling like Burt, apart from my family like Dorothy Gale, ducking and covering and waiting for the house to fly.

I spent a lot of time in that closet. I can laugh a little about it now. "Duck!" I sing to Frances, ". . . and cover!"

She says, "You were one spooky kid."

· · ·

The southbound side of the highway is ablaze with headlights, people running from the storm; northbound traffic is sparse. "Looks like we're heading the right direction," says Frances. She has eaten her sandwich and pulled on her boots. We've finished the coffee.

The storm stretches wide, west to east in front of us. Lightning, now cloud to cloud, now cloud to ground, reveals five intact super-cells. One cell northwest of us surges powerfully upward, and its churning base has begun to droop toward the horizon.

We drive north in still air past all-night fast-food restaurants. It's business as usual for them, with lines of cars wrapped around the drive-through. (*Not a safe place*, I mutter.) Burger by burger, they seem impervious to storm. But we are twitchy with expecta-tion. We've turned off the music and turned up our team radios, the squelch crackling with storm discharge. I take off the cruise control so I can feel the car beneath my feet. I expect a blast of wind at any time.

A couple of years in Tornado Alley had its effects. When I was di-agnosed with an ulcer at six years old, my parents made arrange-ments for me to stay awhile with my grandmother. She was my fa-vorite relative, living in a small town with calmer weather — on the surface, this was a very good plan.

None of us remembered that my grandmother lived only a few blocks from the firehouse. One day just after our arrival, I was out-side playing barefoot in the grass when the fire siren went off — an all-purpose, small-town horn used to alert volunteer firefighters or warn of a coming storm. It was a higher-pitched, long-winded cousin of the civil defense sirens of Tornado Alley. When it wailed on that sunny afternoon, I didn't have a lot of logic going. *Hear the siren, run for the sign.* The closest one was the post office three blocks away. I ran across the yard for the house, to save my family, but ran straight into a patch of stickers, fell, ran again, fell again, and lay screaming with my arms over my head, curled into duck and cover.

The siren had to stop before my parents found me, doubled up, being sick in the grass. I remember my mother's stricken face and the single look she exchanged with my father. "There's not a storm," she said, bewildered. "There's not a storm." I wasn't able to tell her the sirens were terrifying enough. I feel compassion now for my parents, out of money and possibility, whose sick child had fears she couldn't explain. They had no other options. When they left a few days later, I knew why I stayed behind.

We watched them go, and my grandmother had her own ideas about storms and Susannah. She was in no mood for a summer of wailing. The next time the firehouse horn sounded, she held up a hand. "Ehh," she said, with a shushing motion. "Not every siren has to do with us. Not every storm is ours." She said what we needed was a little "equanimity." I had no idea what the word meant, but I used it every chance I could.

Now three state troopers and two trucks full of storm chasers pass us. Plastered with logos, their vehicles are whiskered with equipment, and they are driving fast.

"Would you do that?" Frances points to the storm chasers. "I'd do that."

I nod. *Me too.* Somewhere along the way, fear of storms had turned to fascination.

"DPS says stop at the Holiday Inn," crackles Johnny over the radio. We have come far enough.

We exit the highway in tandem, right blinkers flashing. They are a shocking red against the storm's white and black. We meet in the parking lot and climb out of our cars to move around while we can, stiff from sitting and sore from straining forward to see the weather ahead. The wind is strong, the air electric. Released from their crates, the search dogs pee and race and quibble with one another, stretch in the bending grass of a neighboring field.

"They feel it," says Deryl. We all do.

A state trooper pulls up. His car is muddy and already dinged with hail pocks. He has a rain cover on his hat. "You folks good to go?" he asks. He looks tired already, and this storm is young. "Probably won't be long now." In the radio calls of his colleagues, we hear a distant siren wail.

"We're ready," says Max.

One hour. Two. Three.

Hunter's head rests on his paws, but his eyes are open and his sensitive ears flick left and right as the pitch of the moving storm changes and one distant siren gives up as another begins to wail. Saber lies on his chest, his graceful head turned to the northeast. Though they lie almost immobile, I watch their nostrils twitch, and I imagine all that they must process between the local, familiar scent of teammates, the nearby restaurants, and the millions of shattered, disorganized town and country scents stirred by winds miles away.

Saber looks thoughtful, a paw extended to the side of his crate and resting upward against it, the pads touching the wire frame lightly. It's an attentive posture, the way an adult would hold up a hand and say *Hush!* to catch the second sound of something. The movement of Saber's nose is slight but precise. A change of scent: I see his head lift almost imperceptibly and turn an inch or so to the left, his nostrils working more rapidly. I look in the direction of his change. Moments later a restaurant employee appears from behind a brick wall surrounding a kitchen door. He carries a white paper bag in his hand. It looks like take-out: late supper, perhaps, early breakfast. In the dim light, I have an impression of short dark hair, dark pants, a white T-shirt, and running shoes. What does Saber know of him? A baseline scent of individual young man, plus soap and fry-cook grease, and the onions he ate on liver earlier in the day, a hint of vanilla and jasmine on his jacket, left by the embrace of a girlfriend, plus the white bag contents: the hamburger, the cold, greasy fries, and the wedge of pickle with a half-inch smear of mustard along its edge? One thing is certain: the dogs get more of him than I do in the shadows. When the young man gets in his car to drive away, Saber releases him of interest, turning his head slightly back in the direction of the storm.

We've parked close together; we talk car to car. Frances and I were not the only one trading storm stories, we learn as the team waits for word to deploy or stand down. Many among us have been caught out by violent Texas weather — survived flash floods, tornadoes, hurricanes. Several members of the team have worked Oklahoma tornadoes before, most notably the 1999 F5 tornado that began in Chickasha and tore through Bridge Creek and Moore before dissipating. We speak now of that past history and what these storms can produce: mass casualties and injuries, entire neighborhoods leveled, landmarks obliterated. In Moore, Fleta says, even firefighters born there could no longer always be certain where they were amid the rubble. She describes established neighborhoods where nothing left was more than waist high, the dogs threading their search through twists of raw metal, jagged wood, and shattered glass. A hard search on the humans, tough on the dogs — in some cases, human scent from survivors, the injured, and the deceased torn to fragments and strewn wide.

Moore had its oddities too. Max speaks of trees stripped of leaves and of bark, and of one tall tree blown completely bare, a desperate squirrel still alive and clinging to the slick of its topmost branches. The Toughest Squirrel in the World, Max calls that guy, a bright memory in Moore amid much darker ones. And just down the street from what might be the Toughest Dog too. On one neighborhood search, Max saw rubble shiver from a collapsed house across the street, and as he ran to assist whoever was moving beneath it, a battered Rottweiler emerged. Buried in rubble for two and a half days, injured and frightened, the dog had nonetheless dug his way out. Rescue responders led him to a local group that was there to provide veterinary care and help families recover their lost pets.

Sometimes, Fleta says, the loss gets even closer than you'd expect. In one sector, as she and Saber searched for victims down a

street of flattened houses, the firefighter working beside her gestured briefly to the rubble of the next house they approached.

"Empty," he said. "No need to search that one."

"How do you know?" Fleta asked.

He said, "Because it's mine."

I look at the dogs that have deployed with us on this search, lying quietly in their crates. Some of them are storm phobic at home
on their own time. But now in the environment of search, when
they can smell and feel as well as hear the storm, it's curious to me
how they seem to let their fear go. Several of these dogs are Oklahoma and Texas tornado veterans: they've spent plenty of long
days circling the rubble on command, expressions thoughtful as
they made their way to the center of this tumbled house or the
ragged edge of that one, finding dime-size fragments of the deceased in the remaining eggshell curve of a bathtub.

These are the searches that test the whole handler, the whole
dog — equanimity and stamina in good measure. After the search
for human casualties had been made in Moore, the same dog units
went out to assist dazed residents returning to what was left of
their homes. Some families needed help locating emergency
items — medication, insurance documentation, and the like. Others just needed hands to help remove mementoes left intact. Still
others wanted nothing more than the solace of the dogs. Many
residents turned to them, having lost their own. After disaster, the
Moore handlers say, a search team's job description expands. We
come to search, but we do *whatever*, Max says. You have to get a
little bigger, give up your fatigue and your ego and your own fears
to meet the need.

We sit all night.

"Damn lucky," says the officer who stands us down, eight hours
after we deployed. He's referring to the towns that lay along the
spent storm's path and were, apart from downed trees, hail damage, and lost power, spared disaster. The worst of the weather had
skipped across open fields, he says, and there were already storm

stories, reports of strange sights — a tractor overturned beside a truck left untouched, a windmill that had fallen and somehow trapped a cow in the mangle of it, the cow apparently uninjured *but really pissed off.*

No persons missing, no civilian casualties known. Damn lucky, he repeats. Damn close. The officer thanks us for being willing to sit the night on standby. He says, "Glad you were here, but really glad we didn't need you." We thank him, and we all exhale.

Here is equanimity. The dogs are always ready for whatever. They shrug off the night of standby and are running now, racing like puppies across the muddy field. We're also a little goofy with relief, and we play too, tugging toys, throwing balls. We set up practice searches. Dog by dog, they find those of us who've disappeared for them, leaving paw prints on the windows, the wet of their noses streaking the cars where we hide.

Piloting a Cessna 172
in 1995.

Dade County search-and-rescue handler Skip Fernandez and his partner,
Aspen, rest together after working all night in the rubble of the Murrah
Federal Building, Oklahoma City, April 1995.

Fleta and Saber search the rubble after the F5 tornado in Moore, Oklahoma.

Max and Hunter in a stream bed.

Jerry and Shadow rappelling, 2003.

Johnny and Buster in a wildlife preserve that requires on-lead searches.

Max and Mercy work in the chill air of an early morning.

Terry and Hoss search the wildlife preserve.

Fo'c'sle Jack is a certified therapy dog and enjoys interacting with children from the bow of his dread ship *Pork Chop* at charity events.

Ellen and Scuppy, age twenty-three, at a Christmas presentation for nursing home residents. Sociable and kindly, Scuppy became an unexpected role model for Puzzle.

Mr. Sprits'l on the couch he claimed — and Puzzle ate.

Puzzle, Fleta, and I observe Johnny and Buster finding a volunteer victim buried in debris. Moments later, Puzzle will duplicate the effort for her first formal search.

I found him! Puzzle and Matt, her first victim. She has swiped a piece of charred wood as a memento.

That's a lot of vest for a little dog. Puzzle relaxes off-lead at her second training session.

Left: Scent work in a fire academy "burn building"—Puzzle is twelve weeks old.

Below: Puzzle demonstrates "postural echo" in a gentle first greeting of Pomeranian Misty, subdued after the death of her owner just forty-eight hours before.

Search-dog training builds stamina and confidence. Puzzle works a fire escape in 2005.

Teaching the dogs confidence on a rappel line is a team effort.

Above: Vines, thorns, and the occasional snake: the Wilderness certification test in Texas.

Left: Puzzle posing after a morning on the debris pile—eleven months old.

Left: Mission ready: Team Puzzle after the challenging Urban/ Disaster cert test.

Below: The backyard "playhouse": *La Folie des Chiots.*

Happy at her work: a certified Puzzle finds a photographer in a ravine on a training search.

11

RUNNING WITH THE BIG DOGS

WHATEVER OUR TROUBLES at home, a different dog hits the ground in the early days of our search lessons. Puzzle has learned all the signals that suggest she's about to leave the house and head out to work. It does not take her long to assimilate the clunk of ice in the mini-cooler, the zip of my steel-toed boots, and the jingle and snap of her treat bag on my belt to know what they mean. She rushes out the back door and into the yard ahead of me, wearing the special harness that is another signal we're about to get down to business. Puzzle is all retriever. She has the lifted head and switchy prance of a dog born to carry things for their partners, and she swaggers around the yard with her own lead in her soft mouth. She is small but extremely prideful, dragging much of the webbing behind her as she trots beside me toward the car, crooning *wrrooo-ooo-wroooo-oo-oo*, universal Golden for *dig me*. This is just the kind of reaction we want from a search dog — self-confidence, awareness, and joy in the work to come.

But at the door of the garage she pauses, and there I see her first hesitance. Puzzle is quick to make connections, and just as she knows that certain clothes and objects mean search training, she has also associated car trips with nausea. At the door of the garage, I see her pause, drop her lead, and back up a little. She is torn. When I encourage her toward the Jeep (*Hey Puz! Oh boy! Let's go to work!*), she is all mixed signals. She wags and simultaneously scoots backward, plopping her bottom down and whimpering, miserable with the conflict of wanting to go but really, really, really not wanting to throw up all over the back seat again, a condition I understand and share.

Car sickness is fairly common in dogs. I had a Sheltie that invariably vomited in the first five minutes of motion and then loved every minute of any car trip, even those to the vet. He would wholeheartedly retch up whatever he had in him, then flash a hey!-beg-pardon-for-the-puke grin, and wiggle and wag the rest of the way. Puzzle has thrown up only once in the car, but she's drooled a little and hung her head several other times, and it didn't take much to sense that she felt awful. At three months old, she doesn't seem to be particularly afraid of the vehicle itself or its smell, or its shape, or the rumbling of the engine, but within a few minutes of any drive, she is trembling, and in a couple of minutes more, I can see her head droop and her nauseated salivation begin. She is a long way from grinning about it.

Remembering the puppy that flew home belly-up and snored through moderate turbulence, I believe the car sickness is a problem we can outwit. Unsure if she feels sick because she's afraid or if she's afraid because she once felt sick, I first try modeling fearless canine car travel. While she sits in the doorway, I bring Sprits'l out to the garage, where he bounds into the car and puts his paws up on the back window, grinning and yapping an ecstatic *neener-neener* through the glass at her. Puzzle is unimpressed with the effort and oddly seems to feel no urge to one-up the Pom behind the window. They take a short car trip together. Sprits is joyful; within a couple of blocks, Puzzle's head and ears are down. *Love the car,* Sprits'l Morse-taps across the window with his paws. Puzzle's sullen expression suggests: *Hate the car. Hate the drive. Think I hate you too.*

Other tactics are marginally successful. I begin feeding her at least an hour and a half before a car trip, giving her food a chance to settle. We try puppy ginger snaps. A little Rescue Remedy on her tongue or paws. I bring out all the tricks that flight instructors use to help nauseated student pilots: I raise the seats so that Puzzle can get her bearings and see out, redirect vents so that she stays cool, fresh air blowing over her as she travels. Airbags are dangerous for dogs, so I cannot put her in the front seat, but in the back seat I move her closer to the center of the vehicle, securing her to the seatbelt with a special canine harness for a sense of security, hoping also to eliminate any swing or yaw she might feel farther back.

We make a party out of it with friends and much praising, we vary short trips with longer ones, and sometimes we just go hang out in the back of the Jeep without going anywhere. Once she jumps into the back seat of her own accord — a huge jump for a small pup — and I am very proud, but this is no new standard. Puzzle does not quickly learn to love a car. She tolerates the drive and, I believe, understands it's the necessary evil that gets her to search training. Some days, she heads into the garage with only slight reluctance. Other days, she sits on the sidewalk and sighs into the darkness, following only when I take up the lead and walk her into the garage. Once in the Jeep, she gazes stoically out the window while we back out and begin to roll, gulping a little as nausea seems to threaten, rise, and abate.

Where car travel may be a misery, search training itself is a quick and early joy for Puzzle. By the time we pull into the parking lot, her nausea is forgotten, her paws are up to the glass and her nose to the crack of the window. I hear her breathing change as she *huff-huff*s the delicious scent of human teammates and the dogs schooling among them at knee-level. She wiggles as I unfasten her seatbelt harness and secure her lead, and she scrambles across the asphalt to greet all comers, wagging so hard that she pops herself in the face with her own tail, and no matter how many times she's done it, still looks surprised and affronted by the smack. She whips her head in a startled *who did that?* — but it's an insult that quickly evaporates in the presence of greater joys: dog friends! people friends! and *Oh! Oh!* the men of the team.

Puzzle is something of a hussy, as one teammate calls her, a man's dog, and though she's fond of the team's women and shows a particular affinity for Fleta, our lead canine instructor, it is the men of the team who make her go weak in the knees. Puzzle is all about the boys: petitioning them shamelessly for attention and petting. Most of these guys love her too. They are longtime dog owners, well-versed in the perfect scratch and ear rub. A few of them pick her up and strum her belly like a banjo. Others cradle her and rub her ears until she completely relaxes and her head dangles upside down. Sometimes she shoots me a look from this exalted position, and the message is pretty clear: *They're big, and they're strong, and they are so much cooler than you.*

Now one of them has gone missing. Puzzle would really like to find the former Marine voluntarily buried in the woodpile. We stand fifty yards away, watching as Johnny and Buster work the mound of charred debris. Our head trainer watches us, I watch my dog, and Puzzle watches Johnny and Buster. She is quiet and intent at the end of her lead. When Buster makes the find, she strains a little toward the scene, as though she wants to see the moment of connection. Buster likes to fetch a ball as reward for his searching, and off he scrambles after it while we watch. Puzzle's ears briefly perk at the sight of the ball, but she turns back to the debris pile with a fixed expression.

I have seen hundreds of training searches, but now I look down at Puzzle and try to imagine how she frames all of this. In intermediate dogs, we sometimes get the sense of wry exasperation: *Look, I found this guy twice today already, not two hundred feet from his own car. I'm telling you, he is freakin' hopeless.* Advanced dogs often seem to grin in conspiracy: *Okay, I know you're going to hide her in the trickiest place you possibly can, and I'm still gonna show you it ain't no thing.* But for Puzzle this is all still new. I wonder if Matt's predicament bemuses her — *hey buddy, whatcha doing in there?* — and if she can already clearly distinguish between the scent of normal human energy and genuine fear. Perhaps she saw Buster search the pile, make the find, and get to chase a ball afterward, and in all of that she sees the search as the greater game. There's no way to know.

We turn our backs and Matt, the Marine, is reburied in the woodpile, covered again where Buster had made short work of finding him. Maneuvering downwind of the pile, I give Puzzle the "Find!" command and off she races to the debris, circling it without question and giving a little happy hop of excitement when she picks up Matt's scent. She takes a moment to negotiate the loose debris, but when she gets to Matt and he weaves out a hand to touch her nose, she's all happy grins and wiggles. "Good girl!" we praise, and from beneath the debris we can hear the mutter of Matt laughing, praising her too. I offer her a bit of beef jerky with the *good girl*. She takes the treat daintily, and then drops it absently, unchewed, preferring to caper while we lay on the petting and praise.

As we carefully extract Matt, Puzzle steals a piece of burned wood from the debris pile. Matt carries her to the team to show off her success, and she has her head up, her trophy in her mouth. "Good girl!" they all praise. *Rooo-wooo-wrroooo*, Puzzle rumbles, wagging around the circle, showing off her burned stick. *Woooroo-woo*. I know the sound, but it's the first time the team has heard it from her. It's the sound of a dog who thinks she's hot stuff.

A harder lesson is learning to take her turn. Dogs that are not actively searching are waiting to search or are in "rehab," resting quietly with a bowl of water in the shade, recovering from a previous search and physically preparing for the next one. Puzzle will come off a search quietly, but her eyes follow the other dogs, and she springs to her feet when she hears the distant shout of handlers giving their dogs the "Find!" command. She watches and quivers, and occasionally when she can get the scent of a victim from where she waits, she whips her head around to look at me with great urgency and moans. *Put me in, Coach*, we call the yearning expressed by a line of search dogs, watching a distant dog and handler work a new scenario, waiting their turn. They all would be happiest if they had every search. Though their frustration is apparent, I believe that all that watching instructs the dogs too.

Puzzle enjoys her early days of search work. Our trainers say the dogs often catch on far more quickly than the handlers do, and Puzzle is quick to demonstrate that she knows what "Find!" means and that she doesn't care who she's finding. She likes the challenge; she likes the hunt and the strategy to get to the victim; she loves the praise. What I cannot tell in these early months is how best to reward her. The Labs and Collies and some of the German Shepherds of our team love to fetch a ball, and I try this with Puzzle, who cheerfully fetches in the backyard. After one training search, I take out a beloved tennis ball from home and throw it for Puzzle, who looks at me skeptically and ignores it. She watches the arc of the ball and the bounce and roll that follow, then looks at me as if to say, "You want it, *you* go get it." Search training does not seem to be the time or place for fetch in her view. Treats are possibly the better reward.

What Puzzle responds to most is the celebration that follows a successful find. Praise goes straight to her head, and she trots from a search expansive — chin up, high-stepping with her tail waving a happy flag. She croons her signature rumble until she's acknowledged by bystanders. In these early months, the work itself is Puzzle's best fun, and I get the sense that if I really wanted to reward her for a good search, I would give her another one.

Puzzle in the wilderness can move much faster than I can. Chalk it up to youth. Chalk it up to four paws on the ground and a lower center of gravity. Chalk it up to motivation too. Puzzle is from a line of dogs who love fieldwork, and she immediately shows me that crashing through brush and fording creeks to find a victim is most excellent fun. While I consider myself somewhat outdoorsy, wilderness search in Texas is never just a tidy hike through friendly wood. A wilderness search invariably means deep brush laced with mesquite thorns, poison ivy, and rugosa rose branches. Puzzle presses through such brush with equanimity, disregarding the pops and scratches and thorns in her paws. I have more trouble, bundling through the brush like a wounded bug, tripping over vines, thorns tangling the straps of my pack, snagging my clothing and sometimes shredding it as I pass.

An early morning cold front has passed on our first long day of wilderness training. We are all a little stunned by the shift from an 85-degree afternoon yesterday to a 36-degree morning today. The humans have swapped T-shirts for parkas, and we stand in a knot together, our shoulders hunched against the climate we're not yet acclimated to. The dogs, however, are bristly and alive with the cool, electric air, and as every one of them has some form of field impulse in their makeup, they look toward the wood with anticipation. *This*, their waving tails seem to say, *is gonna be great.*

Today's training will rotate between three sectors. Some feature wide plains of tall, stiff grass. Other sectors are mostly brush and huddled stands of trees, so thick that inside the huddle it is difficult to see open field beyond. The air is dense and heavy, but it's moving a little too. This morning's twelve-knot wind will shift scent in interesting ways, and when the ground warms after a few hours of sun, the same terrain will offer all-new scent patterns.

The dogs go into this with few preconceptions. It's the handlers who must be on their toes, and the risk for all of us, and particularly for me, the new handler, is that we'll search the dogs too rigidly according to our expectations, rather than trusting them to tell us where the scent actually is. Puzzle's urban work at the fire academy has shown me that when she's clearly got the victim, she is not a subtle dog. Her huge, happy alerts are visible sometimes to bystanders in the parking lot from a hundred yards away. But wilderness work demands that I be able to decipher when she has begun to pick up scent (interest), when she has narrowed it to a general location (indication), and when she has found the source itself (alert). And the heavy brush may prevent her from alerting the way she typically would. I watch the big dogs and their handlers head out into sectors, and I remind myself that when it comes to decoding my dog, I am a kindergartner at best. We have two objectives: Puzzle needs to find the victim, and I need to know when she's on her way to finding him.

I also need to learn how to watch my dog and stay upright. Our first wilderness sector, though not large, is uneven — full of gullies and sinkholes and unsteady stones, all of which are hidden beneath tall grass. The wind is from the north, and we begin sweeping east and west from the southern, most downwind point of our sector. The idea is that a dog may catch first scent at the farthest downwind point of a search area and, if so, will indicate and head for the victim quickly and efficiently. Puzzle quivers when I ask her if she's ready to work, and on command she barrels away from me. She moves quickly, but not as quickly as she will after losing that puppy weight. She's tough to follow, even so. Puzzle's nose and tail are up, and watching her, I fail to see a dip in the ground ahead of me. I fall flat for the first time, a right smack. I pick myself up, take two steps, and fall again, this time tangling my compass in the small branches of a young tree. Puzzle pauses briefly at the sound of my *oomph* and *oomph* again, but when it's time to move deeper into the sector and sweep the other way, she races ahead without concern.

On the second sweep, I see the sharp, characteristic pop of her head and a little push in her gait, as though an elf has kicked her in the backside. *She has something,* I think. We continue the sweep, but on the reverse pass, when she pops her head again parallel to the first, I'm sure she's got the scent. I let her have her head. Puzzle takes off northward at full speed, and I stump along behind her, tripping once but staying upright as I watch the flick of her tail through the brush, then falling flat again in a clump of brambles just as she bounds into a stand of trees. As I pull myself up a fourth time, the two field assistants running with me exchange looks.

"Are you all right?" asks one. I'm not sure if he's asking about possible injuries or just my curious inability to run without falling. They aren't having any trouble with it, clearly. But then, they aren't learning how to run after a dog, and I haven't learned how to watch mine and where I'm going at the same time.

In the stand of trees, I hear a yip, then a little grunt and a laugh, and I find Puzzle wiggling over Max, who's buried beneath a camouflage tarp. Max is an old hand at this and somehow manages to pet her, praise her, and extricate himself from his hiding place simultaneously. She is aware of her success and turns to each of us for the praise due. When the two field assistants compare GPS readings, she bumps them for second acknowledgment. I give her a treat and again, she accepts it politely but with no great desire, gives a halfhearted chew, and drops it. *Wroo,* she croons lovingly to Max and the two field assistants. *I need better treats,* I think, *or maybe I just need to understand what really motivates my dog.*

I ran behind many other dogs before Puzzle joined me, and even as we train together, I continue to work as a field assistant behind certified dogs on actual searches. Though it's easy for a new handler-in-training to dismiss this opportunity, running behind other teams is some of the best handler training there is. Because field assistants operate at some distance from the canine unit, we are often able to see parts of the nonverbal communication between dog and handler that even handlers cannot see from their closer position. Our handlers all use similar commands, but from the moment of encouragement and release, the partnership is unique. There is much to learn.

Jerry and Shadow have a relationship framed by easy camaraderie, absolute authority on Jerry's part, and their mutual understanding that she knows her job, he knows his, and Shadow doesn't need to be micromanaged. She isn't. She's a dog of great presence. Even strangers who meet her will mention the aloof carriage, the regal bearing. We call her "The Queen," not because someone came up with a nickname we all adopted, but by default. No other descriptor fits.

Shadow works off-lead entirely. After Jerry's low command and a bob of her head in acknowledgment, she enters a sector with immediate purpose. She is not a nervous or an effusive dog; her assessments are cool, but the humans behind her can clearly see the process of her choice making. Left, not right, scent, no scent. She enters an area and meticulously clears it with wide, confident sweeps, Jerry following quietly behind. There is no mad dashing and great noise with a Shadow/Jerry search, but it is highly efficient. When Shadow enters an area of interest, she moves immediately to it, hones scent to the victim quickly, and sticks there. She's a talky girl who often discusses the find — in long strings of multiple syllables — with Jerry when he comes to reward her. Shadow likes her beef jerky. She will take it with great care, eat it thoughtfully, and then talk about it as a human might give several points of critique. If Shadow believes more treats are in order, she's not above putting a paw to your knee and telling you so explicitly.

In contrast, Belle, a yellow Lab, is a dog of high energy and great dash, who quivers before her release and races into a sector at a speed even the most athletic of us could not match. I was a victim on one of her early wilderness training searches. Buried deep in brush up a small hillside, I remember hearing the distant "Find!" command and seeing Belle flash by below me within seconds, with her handler and a field assistant struggling through the brush in full gear behind. When Belle caught my scent and altered course, she leapt over brush and had to belly-crawl in to get to me. She remained there and had begun her happy bark of success well before handler and field assistant were able to clear the brush to get to us.

"Good dog!" Cindi cried, waving Belle's beloved ball, her reward.

"Oh . . . good . . . God," panted the field assistant, "the only way to follow Belle is stark naked and greased like a swimmer."

Cindi learned early that working Belle was not so much a matter of keeping up as recognizing Belle's communication from a distance. Belle's signals are broad — fast and muscular, a lot of motion, a snapping at the air as she narrows to the find, and a bark of excitement to say she deserves her ball.

Max and Fleta's first dogs, Hunter and Saber, were two of the team's foundation dogs. They are the senior dogs of the team with a large number of searches behind them, and both now approach retirement. I regret that I came to the team too late to witness their early careers and the dialogue with their partners as it evolved, but I have seen the end result. Hunter has long been a hard-charger in the field, known for pushing through debris and digging out victims, if he must, to show Max where they lie. His finds will not go unnoticed. Saber, by contrast, moves like the senior statesmen of search dogs. He is calm, methodical, and precise, and true to his breed's background protecting sheep, Saber is known for an intense, protective victim loyalty at the point of find. A confident boy with a stubborn streak, Saber early taught Fleta how a search would progress and how she would pay attention to his signals in the field. With Saber, there is no room for sloppiness or inattention.

Max began training his second partner, Mercy, a white German Shepherd, in 2001. Fleta's second partner, another Roughcoat Collie named Misty, arrived in 2003. On the surface, it might seem that choosing the same breed for second partner would make training the new dogs easier, but though the dogs shared a handful of common physical traits in the field, they were each unique — Misty as gregarious as Saber was cautious, Mercy's subtler signals demanding a watchfulness not required by Hunter's broad, masculine alerts. *Every dog is a new conversation,* says Fleta.

I am learning to speak Puzzle, and maybe she is learning to speak me. We have a little time — hundreds of training searches to become fluent in each other, months of work before we will challenge our certification tests as a canine team. It is a rigorous curriculum for both of us in wilderness, urban, and disaster environments. Canine teams emerge from this prepared for all live-find work, whether a missing child in a neighborhood, five Boy Scouts lost in a state park, or an unknown number of survivors trapped beneath a building collapse. When I look at Puzzle, the prospect seems years distant, but sometimes she runs into her practice sectors with an intensity that suggests I'd better learn the grammar of her soon.

Puzzle's eagerness is clear, but she has more energy than finesse. Her wayward motor skills are funny. On the "Find!" command, she gallops away with great joy, then slows to a thoughtful lope as she first enters an area that seems to have live scent. I watch her work across the wind and begin to refine how she uses her nose. From that easy trot, the first strong scent that snags her attention literally seems to hook her by the nostrils. I watch her pivot while the suddenly lifted muzzle appears to stay in one place. When she's got scent, Puzzle's nose directs all her actions; she turns where it goes, and simultaneously there's a little kick-in-the-pants movement and a quickening of gait. Her tail, once idly swaying, begins to wag.

The closer she gets to the scent source, the quicker she moves. These early searches are easy finds. Though fully hidden, the victims are within Puzzle's access, if not her immediate sight. She pushes aggressively through brush to a scent source in the wilderness, but in closed building scenarios, where scent may slide along walls or hang in corners like ghosts, she must work harder to move from faint scent to stronger and strongest. I hang back while she mutters in frustration, clearly catching the scent but not able to see the source. It's the same kind of sound one occasionally hears from a person who's lost her car key in her purse: *I know it's here somewhere, but I just can't find it.* This is her problem to solve, and with a few words of encouragement (*Work it out, Puz*), I wait for her to find her own way in to the victim she cannot see.

When she does, the transition from indication to alert is obvious. I see a bounce of excitement just before her bottom drops, her tail wagging hard enough that her whole back end sways. Occasionally she makes a little whine of pleasure, particularly if the volunteer victim is someone she knows well. Her early alerts are puppyish, and I wonder what she will keep of these markers as she matures, and what she will lose. At this point, her final alerts have begun to evolve. They are clear to me and unaggressive toward victims: she no longer jumps on their chests, scratches them with a forepaw, or presses her face to theirs to lick. I hope her paws-off alerts will continue. I praise her hugely for them. Victim-passive alerts will be more appropriate in the field, where someone could be hurt or afraid of dogs, or if the find is located in the middle of a crime scene that would be better left unmauled by a happy, successful search canine.

On a Saturday morning in late spring, I lie wedged beneath two slabs of cement tilted sideways over chunks of concrete and mangled rebar. I've been here about an hour, a buried volunteer victim in the debris pile, as a series of experienced and less-experienced search dogs work across the rubble to find me. I will be here a while, still. I've been well hidden below the crush of rock, and from where I lie, I can see little in the dim light — cement, a piece of what appears to be plywood, and, if I turn my head slightly, a few tufts of wild grass stretching up through rebar. The air that reaches me is warm and spongy with drizzle, but the cement itself is still cool from the night before. Over time, some of that cool has seeped into my bones. My left foot, wedged sideways in a ballerina's turnout, has gone numb. The rest of me feels plenty, though. Some of the cement beneath my back is jagged. There's a hard chunk of something pressed against two ribs. One piece of cement against my forehead is mercifully smooth, but if I turn my head to the left, a raw piece of metal snags my ear. This is not the most comfortable hiding any of us does for the search dogs, but it is some of the most realistic.

Between dogs, there is a debriefing for the previous handler and a briefing for the next one. Sometimes, if the wind is right, I can hear the handler's command and the occasional eager *woof* of the responding Lab or Border Collie or German Shepherd. Other times, I can hear nothing more than the whistle of draft side-winding through shattered cement. I have been here only a short time, but in the gaps between dogs it's not hard to think I've been forgotten even in this soft little while. I've started the day with a good breakfast and a quiet walk to the debris pile, and though I am in this place on a voluntary basis and I have no injuries, it's not difficult to imagine the fear and hopelessness of a victim caught, much worse than I am ever caught, for hours, even days, in the rubble following catastrophe.

Dog Number Five is ready to run, and from far away I hear the "Find!" command and a few distant thumps that may be running feet. The voice sounded like Deryl's, which means the dog searching will be Sadie, a German Shepherd. The wind has lessened, and within moments I can hear Sadie's progress around the pile and Deryl's footsteps after her. I hear the scrape of her claws as she scrambles upward, and then a moment of silence, as though she's poised to make a decision — this way or that way in the sticky air. It's an instructive moment, listening to the rhythm of the working dog in progress.

I hear Sadie's definite change of gait, beginning with a soft lope that quickens, a pause, and then the scrambling sound of the dog moving upward. It's a little difficult to be sure where she is as I hear her moving across the pile, until I hear her pad into a nearby vertical structure. Its floor is smooth, though littered with a scatter of heavy dust and bits of concrete. I am close, and I can hear the softer movement of Sadie circling inside it and then the quicker sound of her exit. She has rejected that space for a possible living victim. I hear the closer scrape of her climbing paws. Plywood lying nearby creaks, then makes a shuddering sound as it bears her weight. Above me, I hear a huff of breath, a mutter, and as I wind my hand up to touch her forepaw, a *woof* as she signals to Deryl she's made the find.

Though I have hidden in the debris pile countless times across the past five years, I still feel a surge of relief each time one of the dogs find me, here or any other place. Their successes increase my conviction and confidence in the work.

Two nights later, wedged into a closet between a wall and three stacked fire mattresses as we work on urban searching, I sit in the dark and listen to first Shadow and then Misty find me. Though I am two rooms away from the "Find!" command and do not hear it, Shadow's easy tread is so distinctive that she's unmistakable. I always think of Shadow searching with the precision of a surgeon: opening a space and making decisions as she moves, with great efficiency. As her pace quickens, she begins talking to Jerry long before she reaches the closet, where she puts her nose to the crack beneath the door, huffs, inhales, and huffs again. Then she talks — a long string of dog syllables that have an almost human cadence. She's got me. Jerry knows it. And when he opens the door, Shadow peers in at me and gives me a little *hmph* — like *is-this-the-best-hide-you've-got in you?* It is.

I take Shadow's apparent condescension as a challenge. For the next dog, I decide to lie between the fire mattresses in the same closet. They are heavier than I might have guessed, and little air gets through. It doesn't take long to break a sweat lying there, and I hope this isn't one of the brand-new dogs — then I realize: I have the brand-new dog, and she's out there and I'm in here. I hear the distant "Find!" and the sound of a dog on the move, and so I lie still, wondering how sweat adds to the overall composition of my scent. I can smell me, and I am not impressed, but I wonder if the coming dog notes only the chemical change: *Susannah freshly glazed with fresh water, salt, glucose, ammonia, and lactic acid. Oh, and she's lying on mattresses that have had fifty-six — no, fifty-seven — other humans on them. Two of them wore Old Spice.*

The coming dog is Misty, the Collie who moves through the large room like a thoroughbred on light feet. I can hear her steady gait quicken, then a pause as she picks her way through a series of ladders lying flat. At the door of the closet, I hear her breathing change from a pant to the rounder *huff, huff, huff* of a dog drawing scent into the cavern of her muzzle. She paws at the closet door, scratching and huffing with excited certainty. I hear a single little squeak. When her handler, Fleta, opens the door, Misty makes short work of finding me between the mattresses in the dark. I am a lovely, living human sandwich lying there. She is a tall, beautiful dog with a long nose, and she snakes between the mattresses to give me a joyful kiss on the mouth.

Months later, the sun is merciless on us one morning as the dog teams work scenarios involving debris, damaged cars, and the "burn building" — a concrete, one-story house routinely filled with wood and hay and set ablaze for training firefighters to put out. Today is more like summer than spring, and the burn building is stifling. A recent training burn has left it sooty and rich with the scent of charred wood, and with the iron windows latched closed, the structure has little air movement, making it harder to search. My eyes tear immediately when we enter. I imagine Puzzle's overwhelmed nose. Is an environment like this the olfactory equivalent of eighth-row center at a Metallica concert?

We need to work quickly too. We have volunteers sweltering in there, despite their gel-filled "cool down" neckerchiefs. The burn building is no place to be slow. Handlers and victims come out from that hot space bathed in sweat; the dogs make their finds and dash free of it as though their tails were afire. I have a bandanna tied around my forehead, but its cool is long gone. Perspiration has soaked through it and run into my eyes. On our last search in the burn building, I have to follow the vague, light swoosh of Puzzle's tail out of the darkness, the sweat having literally blinded me in the short time it took to clear six rooms and extricate a single victim.

We sit in rehab for twenty minutes, drinking water. I swab Puzzle's paws with cooling alcohol, then wipe my face and put on a new kerchief for the next round of searches. Puzzle lies in the shade of the fire hose rack and lifts her nose as the other dogs and handlers work across the various scenarios. Hard work today, but she twitches each time she hears the word "Find!" the command and its response now a reflex of muscle memory.

The heat from the debris pile radiates so powerfully that my face stings as we work it. I wonder about the dogs' paws as they scramble over its jagged, tumbled surfaces, but they give no sign of discomfort. Puzzle loves working debris, and she watches as the certified dogs circle the pile thoughtfully, choosing the tidiest way to a find, or dash across it with the precision of a tennis pro's return volley. A youngster still, she searches debris with a technique somewhere between the two — a mad gallop around the pile to what seems to be the best point of scent for her, then a happy scramble across its surfaces. She is still a little small and clumsy. Some leaps onto rubble require a second or third effort. Some finds must be achieved a different way. We work several debris searches, then stand down to rehab again, crossing the long stretch of green grass toward a shady area with more water and, for Puzzle, a couple of pieces of watermelon, a favorite post-search refreshment in the heat. The watermelon is no longer cold or even cool, but the deep pink chunks are sweet, and after a bite or two, we both feel energy begin to return.

Border Collie Hoss isn't feeling well today. He sits in the deep shadow of the ladder tower, watching the team work. He's alert, but his expression is tired and there is a sense about him of overall malaise. Hoss is a hard-working dog and compulsive about it too. He has worked a couple of searches at the training site, but Terry has noticed he's "off" and knowing that Hoss will rarely stand himself down, Terry has decided to let him rest for the remainder of the session in the shade in the back of the truck. His dog is obedient, but from his tucked posture and watchfulness across the training field, it's clear Hoss is at odds with himself. He feels sick but still wants to search. The truck is a good vantage for this boy who misses little. Over the course of the morning, he watches the FAS team rigging extrication systems and supervises the dog-and-handler teams working at a distance.

Hoss has always been kind to Puzzle. The few times she has been too obnoxious, hop-hopping at his side or pawing at his muzzle, Hoss has simply put a weighty paw over her shoulders and pressed her down to the ground in a decisive statement of authority. She's learned to accept this correction at the moment it is made, though

I sometimes wonder if the lesson will ever carry and if she will, in time, stop all the puppy stuff that requires dog-to-dog discipline in the first place.

Today she is a little bewildered that he's five feet above her. Trotting idly away from the rehab area, Puzzle stands beneath the truck and looks up to Hoss as he looks down at her. At the sight of him, she play bows in petition for a game, then stands looking at him bemusedly, apparently aware that he cannot come down from the truck to play, no matter how much both of them might like to. I watch the two dogs study each other.

Then Hoss disappears for a moment inside the truck, returning quickly with his ball in his mouth. He puts his head over the side, gazes at Puzzle briefly, and with a flip of his muzzle, drops the ball, where it bounces across the parking lot. Puz is off like a shot to fetch it, bringing it back to the truck and, on command, releasing the ball to me. I hand it to Hoss, who tosses the ball again for Puzzle to fetch. I can't quite believe what I'm seeing, and the three of us collaborate on the game for a few rounds before I call in a low voice to Terry, and say, "Don't move, but look at this." Terry stands still and watches his dog throw the ball for my pup, who brings it back for Hoss to throw again. "I'll . . . be . . . damned," Terry says, and signals to a couple of teammates to watch the game in progress.

Hoss and Puzzle are inexhaustible. Over and over, Hoss throws the ball from the bed of the truck, Puzzle brings it back and hands it to me. I give it to Hoss, who throws it again. Hoss has always been a ball dog, but he has always been the one on the receiving end of the throw. He has also always been a smart dog and, clearly analytic, he recognizes now that though he's in no position to fetch, he can still play ball just fine, thank you very much. Puzzle is glad to play with Hoss. If she didn't have so great a stretch to reach him, I get the sense that neither of them would need me there at all.

Perhaps every team has its smart dog stories. I've heard plenty of them and witnessed a few. These high-drive dogs, given a job very young, quickly learn they are valued for the ability to interpret a situation and make a decision about it. They use these skills in the field, but they are equally likely to use them off-duty. Underestimate a search dog at your peril.

Shadow has never been fond of leads. Her loyalty to Jerry and her confidence combine to suggest that she's going to stay near him wherever he needs her to be, but no way does she need to be tied to the man. In fact, she intensely resents it. She's a pack-oriented creature with her own agenda, who accepts being tied with limited patience. During the years of her training, when she was learning to work on a long, braided length of webbing, she systematically chewed through it a handful of times when left to her own devices. Jerry patiently spliced and knotted the lead each time, which gave it a beaded appearance from a distance.

One cool Saturday morning at the fire academy, the handlers all temporarily tied their dogs to the A-frame, a rooflike structure designed to teach firefighters how to chop and vent a house fire. The handlers left their dogs sitting happily in shady grass, heading inside the academy for a quick class before returning to scenario training again. About halfway through the class, a security guard knocked on the classroom door, asking the group "if they knew the dogs were outside and wanting to come in." He gestured over his shoulder, pointing to the building door. The handlers left what they were doing and saw five dogs with faces pressed to the glass. All of them dragged the remains of tattered webbing. The security guard reported that Shadow had been the first to chew through her lead, and then she moved from dog to dog apparently instructing or assisting them as they chewed through their own. When all were free, they moved as a pack to the door of the building, where they stood now. Some were grinning and wagging. Shadow's expression was conversely haughty: *we do not take kindly to being left outside, thank you.* When Jerry walked out the door, she gave him an earful in fully articulated Husky. An "equal-opportunity release artist," some of the team old-timers call Shadow. And they never leave her alone with a dog secured on a lead.

Hoss the Border Collie is another famous opportunist. One summer day during the debriefing after a search, Hoss, who had been beside his handler, suddenly disappeared. It was not like him to stray or to leave Terry for any extended length of time. When the group noticed he was missing, the dog had completely vanished: he was not with the search dogs, not with the other handlers, not with any of the law enforcement officers he might have schmoozed to throw a ball.

The search had generated a crowd of bystanders, and some grew concerned that perhaps Hoss had been dog-napped. There had been precedents; high-profile search dogs sometimes attract unwanted attention. And Hoss is a friendly, sociable boy, trained to walk on a lead beside strangers in emergency situations. He would not have snapped at someone who led him away. The search for him grew tense and hurried before someone noticed that one of the handlers, whose car was running in order to cool her own dog in the back of the vehicle, had left its front door slightly ajar. It had been ajar before too, when Hoss had prized the door open with a paw and leapt inside to stretch out across a seat, his belly positioned to the air conditioning vents. He pirated a candy bar and relaxed. When discovered, Hoss seemed oblivious to the worry he'd caused, a smart dog unto himself who saw an opportunity for comfort while his people rushed around in the 100-degree heat, waving their hands and yapping.

12

THE FAMILY STORY

EVEN JUST STANDING on the front lawn before we head out to sectors, it's difficult to find the missing woman at the center of this family argument. Her daughter Nora says Miss Celeste has always loved leaving. Nora's voice makes a hard little wobble when she raises it to talk over her father, who tells us all there's an open jar of peanut butter in the kitchen, and she struggles to be heard over two neighbors debating the year Miss Celeste moved into her daughter's house. Nora's so tired it appears the gray skin of her face hangs from the bones. She left work early, has been out looking for her mother all day, and now it is dusk going dark, and she is discouraged, frightened, and, she admits this, shot through with anger toward the living ghost of her mother that has no place to rest. Nora cannot blame her father, who is also frail and worried about the peanut butter and thought he'd locked the door. She cannot blame her thirteen-year-old son, who was already at school when his grandmother took it into her head to go. ("I didn't do it!" says the boy to anyone who will listen, "I didn't let her out.") Miss Celeste's daughter is afraid that in the heat of the afternoon, her disoriented mother dropped down dead in some space she couldn't get out of, lost in the tangle of old memory and new neighborhood and lacking all sense of time or orientation to save herself. Miss Celeste was diagnosed with Alzheimer's disease four years ago.

She is five foot two, 115 pounds, and only a little arthritic, a former dancer (a Rockette we hear from one bystander, a Vegas showgirl, says another). She still carries herself well: shoulders back, a slight turnout remaining in her walk. Salt-and-pepper hair she sets in rollers nightly — the same style she has worn for years. She knows her name, and though she could not recall meeting you an hour ago, she will recount the full detail of a trying day forty years before, when she had to leave a dress rehearsal because her first-grade daughter had forgotten her lunch and could not be consoled. Miss Celeste had boarded two buses wearing spangles and tights. It's the famous family story. Nora has heard it all her life. She repeats it to us, repeats that she's tired as a sort of apology. It's ironic, she says, that now she's the one leaving work to chase her mother down. Nora has produced photographs and a plastic bag with a nightgown folded inside it: a scent article for the dogs, the only thing of Celeste's not straight out of the wash.

A pair of house painters across the street told the police they saw Miss Celeste go, and they wondered a little about the elderly woman out alone on a hot day in her long coat — but they didn't wonder enough to approach her or call for help. Just a little after ten this morning, she went right down the sidewalk in her dress and coat and Mary Jane walking shoes, carrying a purse and brown paper bag in her hand. She went east around the curve of the sidewalk and from there, both witnesses say, passed right out of view.

Two dogs have already scented the nightgown and have gone out with their partners to confirm Celeste's direction of travel. Once we have word from them, search management will assign sectors for each dog team. We double-check our gear for extra water and first aid supplies relevant to Celeste's possible falls, dehydration, and hyperthermia.

Neighbors and family circulate among us, a crowd of twenty or more. One brings a stack of paper cups, a campsite Thermos of lemonade and coffee in a carafe. There are a lot of what-ifs and if-onlys said to one another and to us — *If only I had mowed the lawn today instead of yesterday, I would have seen her. If only she'd gone the other way, she would have passed right by me reading the paper on the porch. Normally I'm in the front room that time of the morning, but this time I was on the phone . . .* You hear sometimes about bystanders co-opting a family's emergency, wanting to share the drama, but there's a sense among these neighbors of failed responsibility. They replay the morning as though they could intervene and stop Miss Celeste before she disappeared.

The group on the lawn parts suddenly, like little fish scattering in advance of a big one. Daughter Nora steers her father aside by the elbow. Celeste's twin sister, Aunt Charm, has arrived to assist the family crisis. She looks like Celeste caught in the soft bend of a funhouse mirror. Her first words to me are about herself: she has Bell's palsy, contracted years ago when she put her face too long against the cold of an airplane window. Aunt Charm is a psychic with a husky tenor voice who graduated from a table in New Orleans's Jackson Square to more private consultations in a velvet- and sequin-draped room not far from Bourbon Street. And from there she had retired. *Retired well,* she tells me, there apparently being a good living in clairvoyance. She has charisma despite the comedy/tragedy conflict in the muscles of her face. Her glasses droop on the affected side, giving her a somewhat rakish expression, and her voice suggests both a smoking habit and a wise connection to unseen things. At the precise moment Celeste went missing, Aunt Charm says she felt her go — a little rift in the soul while she stood in the shower. As she bowed her head to rinse her hair, she felt Celeste too slipping quietly down a long, dark hole.

That doesn't sound so good to me, but Aunt Charm seems unworried by the image.

Celeste is always looking to escape, she says, present tense.

Even before she got sick, she was never really with us, explains Nora, as though she lost her mother long before this morning.

Aunt Charm adds an insight about her sister: Celeste will never speak in a voice above a whisper, if she speaks at all, and when she walks, she bends forward and rocks slightly on the balls of her feet as though to tiptoe. *Bullshit*, mutters Nora about the whispering, which Aunt Charm ignores. Aunt Charm describes their troubled childhood bound to a shattered father who never recovered from his experiences as a prisoner of war. He had refused to buy a television, had ripped the phone free of the wall. All their play had been some variation of the Quiet Game. She says it made his daughters good and sneaky.

Nora tells us that the elderly Celeste has wandered before, returned home by the mailman once, by the neighbors twice more. She came home each time flushed and unhappy, unable to describe her plans but clearly frustrated by the interference of others — and eyeing the door for next time.

I have heard Miss Celeste's description repeated so often that as we take additional information from the briefing, I seem to see her at the edge of every shadow. I've read of searches where the vague lost person stood among her rescuers unnoticed, and though Celeste isn't here, I see her standing in the yard nonetheless, considering, turning left as she headed from the house this morning. An estimated 80 percent of people who still retain directional skills will turn right when they are lost, but the Alzheimer's patient does not, necessarily. Celeste's condition has rapidly deteriorated. She has no more directional skills, no more right and left, even, no spatial orientation, no ability to recognize landmarks she has passed. She is all urge to go, but Celeste does not know she's lost.

Would she have taken help from someone she didn't know? Her daughter and Aunt Charm deliberate. Nora says yes. Celeste's sister closes her eyes and says no. Aunt Charm's voice has acquired a shortness, an edge, as though she senses old skepticism about her psychic gifts. The two of them spar a little at the edge of an argument. Forestalling an unspoken "prove it," Aunt Charm says Celeste gleams like a lost thing at the bottom of a drain. Nora pushes her lips forward and looks away.

The first two search dogs have confirmed Celeste's direction of travel. She's been gone more than nine hours, and while a strong woman her age could have walked one to two miles per hour and made some serious distance in that time, heat and Celeste's condition make it likely that if she had remained afoot, she'd be found closer to home. It's time for us to head out to the most immediate sectors. We wear gloves as we handle the plastic bag with her nightgown, and we do not touch it at all, but the dogs do, their curious noses snuffling over the cloth for a moment, memorizing her signature scent before they turn away.

"Find *that*," say four handlers to their dogs. Collie, German Shepherd, and two Labs spring forward in their separate directions, and the sector searching has begun. We hear a scatter of applause from the crowd on the lawn — the kindly, spirited presence of the dogs always injects a little hope. The windless air is thick with mosquitoes. As I jog away behind Johnny and Buster in the twilight, I can still hear Nora and Aunt Charm proving to each other which one knew the missing woman best.

We move quickly along the streets of our sector, dog, handler, field assistant, and a young police officer beside us who has never worked beside a search dog before. We are urgent with the sense of lost time and the extreme vulnerability of an Alzheimer's patient who may have gone all day without water. We look to Buster for some sign that he's caught any scent of Miss Celeste. We call her name hoping that she might call back to us. (*Yes she would*, says her daughter. *No*, says her sister, *but she might wave a little*.)

Miss Celeste seems to wander with intent, sometimes called "goal-directed" wandering, but she has also demonstrated the aimless path-following, or "critical wandering," that caused her to once get stuck in the tight space between a neighbor's garage and fence line. Today she could have begun with an agenda in mind and then lost it, following a travel aid — a sidewalk, road, or path through the grass worn flat by passing schoolchildren — until unable to go farther and unable to turn around and go back. In such cases, a search dog is an invaluable asset, charged only to find her scent without the constraints of human logic. And Alzheimer's wanderers often operate outside the margins. Any space a human searcher might reject is a possible find space to a search dog. If Miss Celeste lies huddled behind a row of garbage cans or is squeezed in the crawlspace beneath a playground slide or has stumbled from a park path into a ravine, the dogs will find her.

Intent. The coat, the purse, the brown paper bag all speak to me that Celeste had some kind of plan, at least for the first few steps down the sidewalk, but it's anyone's guess. I think of my own neighbor of twenty years ago, a neighbor who, at ninety-one, would sometimes walk out of her house in her good dress, pearls, and apron — dressed as though she were hosting a church social — and begin to rake the gravel in the alley behind us. She would rake with great determination deep along the alley, sometimes for blocks, until her son would drive down it and pick her up to bring her home, happy to have done so thorough a job all day.

We press on, moving fast, dripping muck sweat and attracting a lot of attention. Doors open and residents lean out to openly watch us. Others pretend not to watch us while they do something else. Some locals trot forward to ask if we're looking for the "lady they saw on the news." *We are,* we say at a jog while they move along the fence line in pace with us, *and have you seen her?* They have not. They promise to keep their eyes open.

At one point, I turn around and see an assortment of children following us half a block behind, their eyes locked on Buster, waiting for whatever magical thing it might be that a search dog will do. And Buster looks magical. It's dark now, and to the delight of the children we have clicked on our hazard lights: lights on us, lights on the dog. Some pulse red, others flash an alternating blue and white, some glow neon green. "Don't shoot me lights," I call them. They are meant to caution passing drivers, but I wonder how a frightened, lost woman might view us at night, glowing and blinking and descending upon her like aliens.

Miss Celeste's story has been well broadcast, and the farther we get from her home, the more neighborhood energy seems to shift from personal loss to a general excitement. *Celeste,* we call. *It's time to go home now.* Down the street the children's treble echo: *Celeste. Celeste. Celeste.*

We hear no answering call — and with every cry, Celeste seems a little more lost.

It's a busy night at the neighborhood park. There's a game going in the softball diamond, a pack of young men thumping and scudding across the basketball court, families in the brightly lit playground area, a party of some kind at the pavilion end of the green. The park is part of our sector, and Buster diligently sweeps across it in broad, generous strokes. He is uninterested in the hundreds of human scents available to him here, new scent, older, and oldest, his head up and down as he works the air for any trace of Miss Celeste. Buster works his way across the park, all concentration, and perhaps it's because of the crowd or perhaps it's because we are intent on his focus among all these people, but none of us quickly sees the charge of a large, off-leash dog who barrels through the crowd, teeth bared for Buster. He's a young, strong mixed-breed, and he clearly means business, but as he springs Johnny reflexively falls over his dog to protect him and grabs the attacking dog in midair, flipping him onto his back on the turf as though he were roping a calf. The dog makes a startled *huh?* sound and goes immediately passive where he lands, regressing to almost a puppyish wiggle beneath the flat of Johnny's hand on his belly. Muscular Buster, who in other contexts might have taken on the attacker, has stayed put where Johnny pushed him.

"*Shiiiit,*" says the officer, who finds his voice first.

I'm silent, still a little stunned — and feeling guilty because identifying hazards for the dog team is my job, and I didn't see this one in time.

A middle-aged man in running gear emerges from the shadows, his movement a little cramped, a little crablike, like he's not sure whether he wants to own up to this or not. There's a lot going on in his face. He doesn't have a leash, but it is his dog inverted in the grass, and there's a police officer with us who may or may not write a citation about the incident.

"Sorry," he murmurs, as he takes his now-simpering dog by the collar. The dog has his tail between his legs, his mouth also open in an apologetic grin.

"Better get control of your dog, sir," says the officer.

Man and dog slink off together.

"That was . . . that was . . . *something*, Johnny," I say, inadequate, in my mind years away from having that kind of confidence with a dog.

Johnny stands up, Buster rises and gives himself a little shake, and we are back to work.

By midnight, we have all gone out to multiple sectors. The closest have been cleared, farther ones have been searched, and the dogs have demonstrated interest in only two areas. Buster paused in the doorway of a local school building, and a few blocks away three of the dogs in blind verification all exhibited significant interest near a bus stop beside a busy road. Nothing across the street. Nothing at the nearby convenience store. The police ask us if this abrupt loss of scent indicates the woman got on a bus, and Fleta tells them that any number of factors could cause scent to disperse on a busy road. That she got on a bus is certainly possible. But there has also been foot traffic, car traffic, radiant heat, the day's earlier wind. It would be great to be able to say that when scent stops beside a road it's certain a missing person left by vehicle, but we cannot claim that absolute. The dogs jointly indicate that Miss Celeste was here. What we also know is that from this point, the dogs have nothing else.

Operating across several scenarios, the police will pursue the bus possibility further, while search management has developed sectors even farther from the neighborhood, including target areas where local buses might stop en route. We're about to go out again.

"How long will you search?" asks an officer.

"Until you tell us to stand down," says Fleta. "We're prepared to search as long as you need us."

The crowd too is steadfast. The gathering at the house has diminished only slightly. Neighbors sit in the grass or on the edge of raised flowerbeds. Nora stands alone beside her mailbox, head bowed, her arms folded across her stomach as though it hurts. I can hear the rasp of Aunt Charm in the huddle somewhere. Miss Celeste's husband is nowhere in sight. A few neighbors come forward toward the dogs, asking to pet them or to help them in some other way, wanting news. Bottles of water are poured into dog bowls, pressed into our hands. One nice fellow tells us he's hidden a pizza just for the dog team in his car.

"She's dead, isn't she?" I hear Nora say to a policeman. She has said it to several neighbors, to a couple of us, less a question as time passes and more like a truth she needs to acknowledge. The late hour and the dogs' return have discouraged her.

"Ma'am . . ." he says, shaking his head, then stops when another officer runs up to him, murmuring something. They walk away together, then come back with quick steps, not quite a run. "We've got her," he says quietly to Nora, who is now supported by friends who've rushed forward, but the words and his changed, relieved posture snap the news across the lawn. The crowd converges where they stand.

"Alive," I hear Nora say to the friends who are holding her.

"Of *course* she is," says Aunt Charm. She says it to those standing nearest, but loud enough to give Nora a little smack.

Alive, but in what condition? Even the authorities aren't sure, but they do know she's coming here.

It takes half an hour for a police car to arrive, and Miss Celeste has an audience when she is handed carefully from the vehicle into the headlight beam of a waiting ambulance. The dogs' heads instantly come up, and their tails wag. They do not have to be told. This is their person. Oh, definitely their person. She does not appear to see them, but they strain where they stand, wuffling pleasurably. Handlers exchange glances. Miss Celeste is too frail for a meeting, and the dogs remain where they are. Their partners bend quietly to them and praise. "Good *that*," they say, crackling open sleeves of beef jerky. "Good dog!"

Word travels fast: Miss Celeste had indeed caught a bus to a shopping center miles away. From there the driver had reported her disorientation and continued on. But before the bus dispatcher could communicate a description and location to police, she had vanished again. Further details are fuzzy. There had been at least one, possibly two car trips afterward. A Samaritan finally left her where he thought she wanted to go: an elementary school in an adjoining suburb. The police of that town found Miss Celeste lying on a stone bench in the doorway, wearing her coat, purse at her side, clutching a sack lunch — a peanut butter sandwich and apple juice. Now she appears pale and bewildered, but she is smiling a little as she stands in the light, nodding politely to the surround of loving strangers.

"Goddamnit, Mom," says Nora, like a tenderness. She throws her arms around her translucent mother and weeps, rocking her, one hand covering her eyes, the other clutching the brown paper bag.

13

THE SEARCH YOU'RE
CALLED OUT TO

D OG TEAMS ARE RARELY the first emergency response resource on the scene. For us, most pips of
the pager represent a chronology — someone has
been determined missing, caregivers, family, and friends may have
searched first, perhaps for hours, before calling 911. Police or firefighters (or both) arrive and make the search an official incident
and, having deployed according to their own procedures and having not located the victim, call additional resources if available:
air support, ground-walking search teams, and dog units. This
chronology may seem agonizingly slow to anxious families (and
to dog teams themselves — fresh scent is always better), but many
searches result in possible crime scenes that should be overseen by
law enforcement before additional resources could contaminate
the environment.

Many of our team's calls occur late in the evening — some for
immediate deployment, others (particularly when the victim is believed deceased) for early morning deployment the following day.
The pip and its text message are cryptic, with little information beyond the nature of the victim — missing toddler, Alzheimer's walk-

away, suspected drowning — and the search location. When the pager goes off, we respond immediately to the team manager if able to search.

Because these calls frequently come late at night, a first priority is to have a pager with a sound so distinctive it's likely to wake us. Salespersons are never quite sure what to make of me every time I buy a new cell phone (several of mine have come to grief in the water on searches). My priorities are odd. I need a phone large enough to hang on to, ideally with an available rubber cover — Day-Glo orange would be a plus — and I'll always trade sleek and pretty for solid and sturdy. But I also spend a lot of time reviewing each prospective new phone's standard ringtones, annoying other customers by repeatedly beta-testing an electronic version of *The 1812 Overture* at max volume next to my head as I lean over a counter, feigning sleep.

Would that wake me up? I wonder, and move on to the next phone, which lacks *The 1812 Overture* but may have the advantage of a particularly discordant *Beethoven's Fifth. Dit-dit-dit-BLAAAAT!*

My current phone is set to a pager ringtone that while melodious, goes on a long, long, long time, then follows with a nagging pip every few minutes if you fail to acknowledge the text. Though Puzzle is unmoved, something in this pager's electronic song rouses and infuriates the Poms, who bark as it plays. And plays. And plays. If the song doesn't wake me, the little dogs certainly will. Bonus!

The pager supercharges all activities that follow. When I was first qualified to go on searches, I made the mistake of preparing to deploy in tidy stages. It was an organized process, like an aircraft checklist, but too slow, and without a dog I still took twenty minutes or so to get out of the house, assuming I started off in pajamas and half-asleep. ("What's your best bare-ass to haul-ass time?" a colleague on another team once asked me. His own best time was astonishing, though his teammate did confide that the guy showed up to one search with his shirt on backward and Scooby-Doo boxers showing out of his unbuttoned trousers.)

In those early days, I was eager to better my time out of the house. Eventually I learned that I could call in my response to the team manager at the same time I put on my uniform, an exercise of balance and coherence. I would shimmy into the T-shirt with the phone in my left hand, then speed dial while I balanced on first one leg, then the other, pulling on my pants with the phone cradled beneath my chin. Lean against the bed, still cradling the phone with my jaw, pull on, lace, and strap down boots. By the time I had the boots on, the call had rung through and I'd have hands free to copy more specific instructions not available on the text message. This call-and-dress method has served me well in following years, as long as my foot doesn't somehow get caught in the pants. The unbalanced fall, the hot language, the dropped phone easily adds another two minutes to my departure.

Hair in a ball cap, glasses on, and I'm ready to load a little cooler with ice, water, and a couple of breakfast bars in case the search gets long. My gear is already in the car trunk — I never take it out except to repack or restock.

This all assumes a call-out in warm weather. Winter calls, with their necessary thick socks and long johns and turtlenecks and long-sleeved T's — and Thermos of hot cocoa for the rehab period — add time. But I keep my search clothes ready in one place. The cocoa and the Thermos are in the same cabinet, the electric kettle just three steps away. My best clock out of the house, sans dog, is eleven minutes — curiously, a winter search with the added clothing. Worst (a fall in tangled pants, failed speed dial, misplaced car keys) is about twenty-eight minutes, which may not seem too bad until you realize that most calls are to a location involving at least a half-hour drive at civilian speeds — we have no lights and sirens — and a slow departure plus drive-time means that you don't get in the search field for an hour or more. If the missing person is presumed alive and weather conditions or his own health is precarious, that hour comes at a price. Regretting the Keystone Kops quality of some of my late-night departures, I trade notes with teammates and try to learn from their strategies — particularly the dog handlers, who have to not only get themselves out the door, but also get their dog and the dog's fresh supplies out too.

Some of the dogs help at this, and some hinder. Max and Fleta's partners Mercy and Misty react immediately to the sound of the pager and the putting on of uniforms, blocking the door to prevent Fleta and Max from leaving without them. Jerry's Shadow gives him room to maneuver, but he notes that she pays attention to his changed movements. When she's on the way to training, she lies quietly in the back of the SUV, but while on her way to searches, Shadow senses Jerry's different energy; she hangs her head over the seat at his shoulder, as if scrutinizing the route, as if to ask, "Are we there yet?"

We are sure the dogs know the sound of the pager and anticipate what's coming next.

The Poms have learned that the pager's long chime means I'm going to be moving through the house very fast. Excitable Whisky likes to stand in the hallway and bark *Wow!* every time I pass through a doorway, which feels like my own private cheering section. The other dogs tend to stand off to the side silently, watching my back and forth like polite observers at a tennis match. Not yet certified to deploy, in the early days Puzzle also watched from the back of the couch, then would cheerfully move to her crate when I gave her the "House, house, house!" command, curling up in it and waiting for her peanut butter Kong. But she has since learned that the pager means search gear she recognizes, gear I frequently wear at training, and as she approaches certification, I see her expression change when I gear up and do not ask her if she's ready to go to work. She's made the connection. Sometimes, Puzzle gives me a baleful look as I gesture her into the crate, turning her nose up at the Kong. Sometimes, she gives me the look, adds a mutter, and then flops down in the crate with an elaborate sigh, turning her back my direction. *Go ahead,* her sullen posture suggests. *Search without me. And good luck with that.*

The road to a search has its own surprises. A fair percentage of the time we begin the drive out and the pager pips again, indicating the missing person has been found — a turnaround/stand-down page — which is universally good news but can do strange things to your biochemistry, the earlier flush of adrenaline now with no place to go but home. On one pair of back-to-back searches, I got to exactly the same place on the freeway when I heard the pip of the turnaround page. Two night calls. A turnaround page at exactly the same place on the freeway. What are the odds? I drove home calculating whether this might influence the likelihood of my getting struck by lightning or winning the lottery. So far, neither has happened.

I've never known a colleague to grumble about the interruption of a callout followed by a subsequent stand-down page, but we trade a few stories afterward. Without the hard activity of a search, blazing out the door only to return minutes later can take a bit to unwind. One colleague plays solitaire on the computer. Another watches *Fresh Prince* reruns in the small hours. I sometimes weed the rose garden at two in the morning beneath the light of a security lamp hanging off the garage. There's a strange Proustian moment of connection every time I prune back the mint growing among the roses. I now associate the dark, fresh scent of crushed chocolate mint with the good word that a toddler missing from a lakeside home — feared abducted, feared strayed, feared drowned — had been found asleep in her parents' laundry hamper before we got there. Two years have passed since that callout, but I think of that little girl every time I pinch mint for iced tea. She would be four now, or five, and I wonder if her nap in the basket has turned into the kind of family story that will be told on holidays, told to her fiancé and eventually to her children, just as she remains a figure on our side of the narrative — as a late-night call, a missing child in winter, an early find — *alive* — and a universal reprieve.

Some morning deployments tell a different story, particularly on weekday mornings, when a close search location can still take an hour or more to reach. One drowning call on a lake across the Metroplex was challenging enough to reach as depicted by map, the route served by a spider web of freeways that tapered off to county roads that fed to undeveloped residential streets that wound down to gravel paths and a boat ramp. Teammates were heading in from all directions (not one of us lived close to the search site), and on that particular winter morning every major freeway had a problem of one kind or another, from overturned eighteen-wheelers to burning cars to spilled green stuff from a produce truck made slick as it was overrun by traffic. Most of us left home before 7:00 A.M. for a 9:00 A.M. deployment. But by 8:45, we were all immobile and scattered wide across the two cities, unable to contact the officer leading the search, who was probably already on-site, and whose cell phone seemed to be out of range. Crazy-making conditions, but as I crept over the glaze of smashed tomatoes that had caused a few cars to spin out and into each other, I was grateful this was a recovery call for someone long deceased rather than a call for another strayed child or missing elderly patient, where every minute lost to traffic was potentially fatal.

Sometimes we have a little help getting there. Several years ago, a traffic jam on the major artery leading to the site of a search for a missing second-grader threatened to slow our arrival by an hour or more. Somehow local police got word and intervened, leading three cars of us out of the congestion via the shoulder of the freeway, one police car ahead of us and one behind as we drove in trail, passing a mile or more of motionless vehicles. So many frustrated drivers shot the bird at us as we passed that my memory of that drive bristles, as though the long row of cars had quills.

The dogs in general seem to handle the journey better than we do, perhaps because they're free of the deeper implications of each call. But no mistake, they are intensely aware of the job they are heading to. Some dogs take the travel a little harder than others, the adrenaline rushing straight to their digestive systems, resulting in nausea or diarrhea, or both, conditions they seem to shake off once on-site.

A handler acquaintance from another team once told me the story of his first dog, a chocolate-kiss-colored Lab, who would lie quietly in his crate on the way to training, but behaved differently on his way to searches, where he would stand in his crate and nuzzle the catch that latched the door shut — repetitively, rhythmically, *bang-bang-bang* — so much so that sometimes he emerged from his crate with the skin of his muzzle rubbed bare and bloody. By the time he retired, the old Lab, a veteran of many searches, had a callous on his nose. *How did he know?* the handler still wonders. *Why did he only bang the crate on callouts?* The gear was the same, the crate was the same, the car was the same. The only difference was the beep of the handler's cell phone and his own hasty motions to get them out the door. And of course, we both hazard, the changed scent from a human who just got a biochemical jumpstart in the middle of the night.

Some searches are short. We've had a handful of them in the history of our team. Jerry, first to arrive on a morning search for a missing adolescent believed suicidal, was briefed on the boy's description, the chronology of his previous actions and his current disappearance, and the cryptic messages the boy left across the sidewalk, words that could be variously interpreted as a suicide note or an homage to a popular rap song of the day.

"Did you . . ." Jerry asked the officers carefully, "check the girlfriend's house?"

Head shakes all around, and while the rest of us were en route, an officer found the boy at his girlfriend's house, where he'd been all night. The remaining dogs arrived just as the team was being stood down, a dogless search with a happy ending.

Another search for an Alzheimer's patient who'd been missing more than half a day had an ugly prospect. Fleta, Jerry, and

Shadow arrived at the facility where the elderly woman had gone missing. After the initial interview, they went upstairs to scent Shadow on the woman's bed and clothes, hoping to determine the woman's direction of travel. Jerry and Shadow went ahead, and Fleta remained behind to get a more portable scent article for the other coming dogs. While in the elevator returning to the ground floor, she heard Jerry say over the radio that they had the victim. Shadow had gone from the room, down the hall, out the front door and had found the woman less than thirty feet away from the facility entrance, lying wedged beneath a stiff row of bushes. Alive, just stuck. No broken twigs or disturbed leaves marked her presence, and the calling officer said he'd personally passed the hedge where she lay a number of times. Total time on the search from start to finish: less than ten minutes.

Some searches are just weird. An urgent out-of-state call to a remote location was the proposed scene of a homicide. The bones of what appeared to be a human foot had been found by hikers, and local authorities called in dog teams to find the disarticulated bones of the rest of the body. After a long journey to the location, the team arrived at a small area cordoned off with crime-scene tape. But on-site, none of the dogs indicated any interest in the foot, and none of the dogs seemed to find anything amiss in the deeper wood.

"Something wrong with your dogs?" drawled an officer testily, to which a handler responded, "I think something may be wrong with that foot." It was a potentially tense *oh-yeah-sez-who?* moment, but not long afterward, a forensic team arrived and quickly assessed the bones as bear, not human. A small bear, an adolescent bear, perhaps, with bones remarkably similar in construction to a human foot. *Understandable*, they assured the law enforcement agency that had called for search dogs. *These things happen all the time.*

A few officers graciously hid for the dogs, giving them a motivational find as a reward at the end of their long journey. Afterward, as the team loaded into cars for the long drive home, the calling agency deconstructed the cordoned area and opened it back up to hikers, a quiet aftermath save for the *pup-pup-pup* of the crime-scene tape as they tore it free.

People sometimes ask what kind of search we do most frequently. It's a question I've asked other teams myself — curious about the intersection of geography, calling authorities, population, and need. Some of their responses are what you'd expect. Teams located near the edges of national parks or major ski areas may do a lot of searches for lost hikers or strayed children in the woods, while those serving areas popular for water recreation — boating, fishing, swimming — may have a high percentage of drowning calls. Some responses were harder to predict. Two Californians from the San Francisco area once told me the majority of their recent winter calls had been for Alzheimer's walk-aways, while another handler from a picturesque town on the East Coast said he and his dog were most often called to suspected crime scenes in the thirty-mile stretch of woodland that separated his little town from the next.

Because our team is based in an urban area surrounded by wide stretches of ranchland and prairie and peppered with popular lakes, our calls come in for any number of reasons. Though there are exceptions, we typically work more drownings in late spring and summer, walk aways in the autumn and winter, despondent potential suicides after the turn of the New Year — and of course sit standby or deploy during tornado season and during the hurricane months summer through autumn. Weather causes many of our searches, and every changing season reminds us of the coming needs of the next one.

And still we get surprises.

Years ago, Max and Fleta deployed with Hunter and Saber to south Texas after a long period of hard rain and extensive flooding. Damage was widespread, and lives were known lost. Many residents were still missing. Served by the SAR dogs of a state task force, the search area seemed unending nonetheless. Max, Fleta, Hunter, and Saber worked for days across flattened, mud-bound farms and small towns.

One day's search required a helicopter transport. The waterline had risen far upland and roads were so completely impassable that the only way to get to the search site was by air. Handlers, dogs, and support personnel deployed to the top of a rise, their search sector an extensive area of flood debris field below.

As they prepared to begin their formal search, Fleta's Saber pulled away from the group and bounded uphill to a scruffy area of low mesquite trees. He pushed his way through the surrounding brush to a spot just beneath one young tree and began worrying at the dirt, pawing at it urgently. Though this was not the direction of the sector and she had never seen Saber behave this way on previous searches, Fleta knew from his intensity that something was up. She crawled awkwardly into the thicket after him, talking to the dog, looking for recognizable signals from him as he pawed the thick, heavy ground beneath the tree. The accompanying officer asked what was going on; Fleta could only answer that she wasn't sure, but that Saber was on to something he couldn't seem to get to. She gave Saber a few minutes working at the dirt, and when nothing quickly surfaced, she pulled him from the thicket and tied him to the base of a tree, where he sat and howled with frustration.

Max and Hunter went in for verification purposes. They approached the scene from a different angle, and like Saber, Hunter immediately pressed for the area beneath young mesquite. He too began to work the dirt in the spot where Saber had pawed his shallow hole. Seeing his dog's similar intensity, Max crawled into the area beside him as Hunter deepened the hole and Saber continued to protest yards away. Soon the shallow dip was deeper, and after a particularly furious spate of Hunter's digging, Max caught the first scent of cadaver: faint at first and then stronger as the dog worked.

A body in the brush, buried beneath a young tree that had partially grown over it, high above the flood's debris field. The disaster response crew with them offered to begin to dig, but Max shook his head. This, he said, was likely a crime scene. Better not touch. The group called the local sheriff's department, who asked if the handlers were sure the dogs hadn't caught the scent of dead animal.

They've been ignoring dead animals in the debris field for days, Max and Fleta responded. The scent was undoubtedly cadaver, and they believed the scent was undoubtedly human as well.

Overextended or skeptical, the sheriff's department didn't pursue the matter for a couple of days, long after the dogs and handlers had cleared the area and had been deployed to search another one. When law enforcement did dig beneath the tree, they found the decomposing remains of a man who'd been shot between the eyes. Dead and buried long enough for a young tree to grow over him, his death unrelated to the flood that brought the dogs there in the first place.

There's a saying in the SAR community: the search you're called out to may not be the one you end up on. Being prepared means being ready for anything.

14

HOME AND HEARTH

I'VE GOT TWO PUZZLES: the emerging search canine, confident and capable, and the adolescent family dog at home, beautifully housebroken, but in other behaviors unpredictable. I've read five training manuals, and the dogs have a trainer we all value, yet in the private hours, I'm clearly floundering — without guidebooks for steering a young dog along the fuzzy line that separates a well-behaved family pet and an independent leader in the search field. Puzzle must learn to be both. I need her obedient to me but not overly dependent, disinclined to jump on people who walk through the door, but stubborn enough to insist when I have made a wrong choice on a search and the scent we need is in another direction. She should be assured enough to search ahead of me, and I should have trust enough to let her work apart from my micromanagement.

And in all of this, I need to believe that dog peace will somehow return to the household.

Collaborative is the word I think of when I watch the other handlers with their dogs, the relationships long-defined and trust between them evident. I know things didn't start out that way. I've heard the puppy backstories and the way this handler or that one had to mediate between the new dog and the older ones in the family. I've heard about the wrecked landscaping at home and the dog-to-dog posturing and the squabbles over favorite toys. I know there are occasionally days when one of the senior search canines has an issue at home, then shows a little attitude at training — shooting the paw, we call it — and dog and handler have a stern exchange. I have even seen a mature search dog take it into his head to vanish in the middle of a training search — off on his own *yabba-yabba-woo-hoo!* — abandoning his handler for the first time in his dog life to go walkabout. I take a little comfort that I'm not the first handler to struggle with dog dynamics at work and at home, but right here, right now, the job sometimes seems a lot bigger than I am. And behind my frustration is the loom of coming failure, that somehow despite all the reading and note taking, despite wanting this as much as I do for both of us, I do not have it in me to effectively partner this dog.

At the house, we have forged a little order. The universal "Sit" command serves us well. Puzzle seems aware — and happier — that she's not the only one expected to behave. Sometimes the dogs are rewarded with treats for the obedience; sometimes they receive only praise. Though I watch Puzzle carefully for signs of resource guarding against the smaller Poms, when treats are doled out during a community sit, she politely waits her turn and concentrates on her praise, her treat alone. She is aware that I'm watching. Sometimes she looks back at me with a teenager's deadpan expression: *What?* she postures touchily. *What?*

Yay! Six dogs, six sits, six treats, no throwdown! But I can't take anything for granted. Puzzle is always ready to engage. Verbal Sprits'l's energy excites her, and Whisky's flash-paper hysteria escalates that excitement. If Whisky and Sprits'l squabble, Puzzle will launch into the thick of it. Worse, if Jack grumbles at Whisky for getting too close to his food bowl, Whisky's returned growl will provoke Puzzle to jump in and settle things, invariably landing on Jack, who squawks with terror, which escalates Puzzle's aggression — a situation I cannot allow.

Peace in our house during Puzzle Year One requires a constant presence of mind on my part. Like flying an airplane: this is where we are, this is what's coming next, and this is what we do ahead to prevent bad things from happening. The dogs all eat at a distance from one another, and Puzzle eats in an area where no presumptuous Pom can challenge her and where she, in turn, cannot stalk a dog with his head in the food bowl and begin the stare-down that precedes a fight over the dish. My job is to get the bowls up before Puzzle has access to the smaller dogs' eating area. After eating, each goes outside for a little constitutional, and Puzzle — a slow, dainty, dispassionate eater — is always the last. They go out separately, they come in on their own timing, and after dinner they all meet up in the kitchen, where a sit is expected on my part and an after-dinner dental treat is expected on theirs.

The routine is consistent, the system works very well, and denied the situations that lead to problems, Puzzle and Jack get along with quiet reasonableness. Jack is cautious and wary around her, but I'm pleased to wake one night to find him huddled against Puzzle for warmth and Puzzle lying belly-up next to him in sleepy companionship.

Puzzle's early aggressiveness toward Jack still concerns me. What was that? Why did it happen? Though I believe the original conflict was about power, I can't be sure if Jack's wariness and fear send off "weakling" signals that arouse the bully in her, or if she reads his sidelong gaze and stiff posture (or his thick, stand-on-end coat, according to one behaviorist) as a direct challenge that she is willing to address. After Puzzle has similar skirmishes with Whisky and with Sprits'l, also relatively young and relatively strong, over high-value items, I hypothesize that my smart but immature Golden is determined to rise in pack status and is willing to take on any dog that she believes stands in her way. Clearly, the senior, special-needs dogs don't stand in her way. Apart from the occasional play bow, Puzzle ignores wobbly Sophie. Scuppy she defers to, following him in the yard, examining what he too pauses over, lying near him when he settles.

· · ·

They do not cuddle together, but the oldest dog of the pack and the youngest one have forged a connection none of the rest of the dogs share. In January 2005, when twenty-three-year-old Scuppy begins having occasional seizures, Puzzle is the dog who first shows me he's in trouble. One cool evening when they have been lying together on the day-warm sidewalk, I hear her thump the back screen door and whine a single urgent note to get my attention. This is not usual behavior from Puzzle, and when I push through the door to her, she immediately jumps away to the center of the yard, looking at me as though waiting. It's the same wait I have seen from her in the search field when she has raced ahead to a space I must catch up to. As I move to her, she jumps away again, heading down the long fence to the base of a pecan tree where Scuppy lies on his side, one leg contorted and trembling. He is conscious but bewildered, the foreleg drawn up awkwardly. His mouth is open, and he is panting rapidly. I touch the leg, which seems intact, and in a few minutes this first focal seizure releases him and he sits up, dazed and withdrawn. I carry him to the house, but once inside he walks gingerly on his own. The paw is down, but he seems dissociated from it, as though he doesn't trust it or isn't sure it's there.

He is terribly thirsty. Scuppy drinks deeply from the water bowl and removes himself to one of the dog beds by the hearth, where he lies quietly the rest of the night. Puzzle lies next to him on the floor, and a few hours later, Sprits'l joins her there. Neither stretches out. They sleep in cautious poses, on their chests, chins on paws. When I walk in the room, their heads raise. Scuppy is deeply asleep on his side and does not stir.

The seizures continue. Infrequently at first — weeks apart — but they appear to be worsening, as our vet thought they would. Puzzle shows the greatest concern of any of the dogs when Scuppy has a seizure, sometimes waking me in the night when he has begun to go rigid but not yet to howl, a new byproduct of the seizing. We sit together by the old dog on his soft bed next to the fireplace, waiting for the episode to let go and for him to return to us. Each time, he comes out of it a little more slowly.

Across the next few months, Scuppy retains his voracious appetite and his impeccable sense of 7:00 A.M. breakfast and 5:00 dinnertime, but grows weaker. He takes shorter walks in the backyard, where self-involved Puzzle forgets herself and supervises from a distance. She has ceased to play anywhere near him, as though recognizing that he is fragile and will easily topple. In time, the old boy begins to wobble to the back door and mutter — a signal to me that he needs help out to the yard and back in again. He grows content to remain on his cushion beside the fire; Maddy the cat occasionally cuddles him and Puzzle lies not far away. Sprits'l tends to visit and briefly hover, then goes away to return again later. The other dogs watch from a cautious distance. They are uneasy with his frailty. But Scup continues to eat and wags his fuzzy, upturned tail at the first scent of peanut butter, his favorite treat.

Lab tests show no treatable condition for Scup, and our vet advises that the best we can do is keep him comfortable, spoiled, and happy to the end, which the vet believes may be coming soon. The seizures have become more frequent, and Scuppy is losing weight, but he still retains an interest in the household, a pleasure in the outdoors, and a passionate attachment to his dinner.

The old dog brings out a maturity in Puzzle that she has not previously demonstrated at home. She moves slowly and quietly around Scuppy. Beside him she is a different, softer, wiser dog. I do not understand it, but I'm grateful he has her warmth on cold evenings and her canine companionship in addition to human affection. As he grows more introspective and slips farther from us, sometimes Puzzle alone will perk his interest in the goings-on of the house.

In time, he moves beyond even her reach. One Monday afternoon in late March, Scuppy has a seizure that runs abnormally long, recovers, and within hours has two others. I gently bathe the urine from him, and he groans and nuzzles into my hand when I rub his ears, but by evening he has begun refusing food. As does Puzzle. As does Sprits'l. In the night, he has another seizure, and by morning is too weak to even raise his head. Though I had hoped

Scuppy might die peacefully in his sleep, he grows feebly nause-ated, retching up bile as his kidneys begin to fail.

I cannot allow him to suffer. I wipe his coat clean and comb him lightly, stroking and talking to him very gently before wrapping him in a towel for a last trip to the vet. Puzzle watches us from a slight distance, but when Scuppy makes a little mutter, she gets up to wash his face. She sniffs him thoroughly, curiously; her face is anxious, and I recognize that by the scent of him she may know far more about his condition than I do. I allow them this time to-gether, and then I bundle Scuppy close to my chest and make my way with him out the back of the house to the garage and to the car. In my arms, he feels light as spun glass, his bones hollow as a bird's. At first, Puzzle seems to think I'm just taking the old boy out for his toddle around the garden, but as I turn with him to pull the garage door closed, I see Puz at the door of the screen porch look-ing out at us. Her tail waves slowly as I look back at her, and then it stops.

Have a friend long enough, and in time he or she is going to have to break bad news to you. Ellen has been the bearer of bad news more than once. Some of it dog-specific. In 1989, when my hus-band and I were on a trip to Minneapolis for the Twin Cities Mar-athon, Ellen dog-sat our Bogie, a Shetland Sheepdog and my first dog. High-energy Bogie had taught me valuable lessons about the perils of puppyhood and boredom, lessons that my husband and I believed we had mastered by the time we went to Minneapolis. Bogie was about eighteen months old at the time.

On the first evening of our trip, I called Ellen to check on Bogie.

"How's it going? How's Bog-dog?" I asked.

She said "Fine," but the word had a tightrope quality to it. A little extra fricative on the *F*, and the long *I* sound slightly drawn out.

"Everything okay?"

"Yes." The second yes almost seemed convincing, but when

I hung up the phone, I turned to my husband and said, "Something's wrong at the house."

We gave it a few minutes, and then I called her back. Ellen came clean. She hadn't wanted to worry my husband the night before his big run, but the truth was . . . Bogie ate a chair.

"Ate a *chair*?"

I had heard correctly. Bogie had stripped a bentwood rocker completely free of its wicker seat and back, leaving only the curved wood behind. The chair looked, she said, like what cicadas leave behind when they slip out of old skin. Maybe it could be upholstered. The wood was pristine. He had not actually eaten the wicker, though it was gnawed into a pretty fringe — piled up in a soggy little stack in the hallway. And he had done the whole job with an assassin's silent efficiency. One minute, Ellen was watching TV and Bogie was asleep in the hallway. The next minute, the dog was asking her for a game of tug, and the chair guts lay where he had been sleeping.

This was the first piece of furniture Bogie ever ate, but in the course of his extended puppyhood, he also stripped a bathroom of carpet from the comfort of his crate and kindly disposed of a set of mauve hand towels we had received as a wedding present and had loathed for years. When Bogie got through with them, there wasn't enough left to successfully wipe a dipstick. Bogie was a voracious and indiscriminate destroyer of furnishings, whose tastes went everywhere. But he had a private standard. He never once touched a houseplant, a roll of toilet paper, or a shoe.

Fifteen years later, I thought I came to Puzzle wiser. But Ellen's voice on the other end of the phone suggests otherwise. She has been dog-sitting the crew on evenings when I teach a night course. When I call her to let her know I'm on my way home, I hear the guarded tone she'd used with Bogie all those years before.

"What?" I say.

"Your dog," she replies. And though I have six dogs, I know which one she's talking about straightaway.

"What?" I repeat.

"She ate the fainting couch." Then she clarifies. "Well, first she dug the stuffing out of it, and then she stripped off the rest of the upholstery, and then she ate . . ."

"What?" I imagine a Golden Retriever full of foam rubber and upholstery tacks.

". . . all the treats Sprits'l had been hiding between the arm and the seat cushion."

I sputter a little, trying to frame this, and then I remember all those "Sit" commands in the kitchen, and Sprits'l trotting off with his treat and his small, superior posture, and I think of the early search games I had done with Puzzle, hiding treats in the house — yes, God help me, even in pockets of the furniture — and I can't do anything but laugh.

When I get home, Ellen shows me what's left of the antique couch, and I peer down at what's left of the treats too. Puzzle has left a few crumbs that are fresh, but other untouched biscuits are discolored and hard as rocks. Sprits has claimed that couch since puppyhood. Sprits has been hiding his treats in the deep fold of that upholstery a long, *long* time.

I'd thought I kept a tidy home. I remember his other favorite spots, and before Puzzle can do a thorough shakedown of the entire house, I search under his preferred dog bed, the spot beneath my dresser where he likes to lie behind the curtains. I don't find biscuits, but I do find his collection of stolen leather things: a key fob with one of my old office keys, a cell phone cover, the luggage tag off my briefcase. Sprits'l has long been given to thieving and now, I realize, to hoarding.

The disemboweled couch has ended his career, and I go back to look at what remains of it. Unlike Bogie, who chewed wicker from a chair for the sheer pleasure of worrying it free, Puzzle has gutted the couch not for its own sake, but in order to find the treats she could smell deep within the folds of its upholstery, deeper than my vacuum cleaner ever reached. It's too late to punish her, and what would I punish her for? Initiative and success at a game I had originated?

Ellen comes in with all the dogs. Sprits'l knows immediately that something's up with his couch, and he is outraged at the violation. He huffs over the crumbs, circling and chattering. Puzzle watches me study her handiwork. She has no interest at all in the fainting couch now, but she leans against my knee, her tail faintly waving, as though to say *yes, it was quite the job, but I got through it.* I make a mental note to find an upholsterer tomorrow, and I consider the digging and tugging Puzzle must have gone through to get all the way down to the couch's wood frame. Making the best of a bad thing, I throw a coverlet over the couch, and I hope Puzzle will search for the source of human scent with the same conviction.

Goldens are soft dogs, I was told by more than one person in the days before Puzzle. *Goldens can be easily wounded. They're so eager to please that a sharp word can destroy them. It is so easy to break their hearts and spirits.* Some of this seems melodramatic to me, and counterintuitive, since plenty of Goldens are working dogs of all kinds. Puzzle has not yet shown me any great fragility — in fact, quite the contrary. I have let loose a few sharp words, and though she seems to recognize the knock-it-off meaning behind the tone, she has certainly never cowered. But I move forward with her thoughtfully. Behind the puppy willfulness and general blockheaded egocentrism could be a soft, sensitive dog in the making, I suppose, though you would still never know it at this point while on a walk with her.

As our walk saga continues, I have tried various collars, harnesses, and the Gentle Leader, a check device that wraps over the muzzle and, when the dog pulls ahead too hard, turns the dog's head due to the inappropriate tension on the lead. The idea is that most dogs will learn that pulling too hard results in a self-generated check. Puzzle strains against all collars; she disregards the changed locus of control with a harness. She responds well to the Gentle Leader for a few, optimistic steps, then suddenly porpoises in a spasm of dislike, landing on her side to paw at her muzzle or try to wipe the hated Gentle Leader off in the grass. The more elaborate the device, the less progress we make. For a number of reasons, I do not use a prong collar on Puzzle. Her puppy and adolescent testing suggested that her threshold for discomfort is very high, and there's the possibility that I could do her genuine harm with a prong collar before she ever truly perceived the check.

"Why does it matter how she walks?" asks a friend. "Won't she do most of her SAR work off-leash?"

I try to explain that a good walk is at the heart of obedience, and that obedience is at the heart of good search partnership. The controlled cross of a busy highway, an emergency stop when I shout that command from a distance, a responsive "Down" in the presence of structural instability — all these demands in the SAR field grow out of respect and accord begun on something as basic as a walk.

Trainer Susan weighs in on my two Puzzles. "At search," she says, "she seems more mature than she is because she loves the work. She likes the challenge. And you're following *her*. But on a walk, you're telling her to do what she doesn't necessarily want to do. To her, obedience is boring. Remember," she adds, "she may look like a big girl now, but she's still a puppy in the head."

Puzzle and I walk twice every day, an event I try not to dread. She is remarkably strong, fully capable of going from a nice trot to a doggy broad jump in moments. Walks have left me exhausted, bruised, and sore a few times, and though I pride myself on a long fuse before I get angry, walks have also occasionally left me purple with frustration. *The leash is a telegraph line,* I'm told by more than one trainer, and I know any tension I have at the outset of the walk communicates directly to her. At this point, she is rarely *on my walk,* as Susan would put it, and I wonder if Puzzle feels my tension down the leash in the same way she picks up on Jack's guard-up wariness in the kitchen. I wonder if she perceives this as a similar advantage to be pressed.

We walk on, regardless. I try all the tactics suggested by trainers, dog whisperers, competition obedience instructors, and sympathetic friends with senior dogs who ruefully remember their early days with leashes and "Heel" commands. One Golden owner, who repeated puppy class three times with her beautiful, reddish male, tells me it's just a matter of patience.

"Walks were hell for the longest time, and then at one point I looked up when Pico was two years old, and I had the perfect dog. People would stop me and say, 'I want a dog like yours,' and I would think, 'Like *mine*?' My commands for Pico weren't any different. They just finally sank in."

Two years old, I think, and gulp. Puzzle has just had her first birthday. Even though passersby often comment that she's remarkably mellow for a young Golden, I'm privy to all the shades of Puzzle on a walk, and *mellow* is not the word I would choose.

We head out one cool afternoon following a rainstorm, and Puzzle is charged with excitement after being housebound the majority of the day. She's an especially pretty, spirited dog on this walk, glowing in the muted light after the storm, splashing happily through the occasional puddle. People smile passing us. I smile back, huff-huffing. We wrestle for the first block until she settles into the walk by the second. *A settle by block two may be some improvement*, I think as she trots ahead of me on a "Wander" command, where she is free to explore ahead in an easy lope, stopping and sniffing and occasionally rolling in soft grass, as long as she doesn't pull on the lead and obeys when we pass a dead squirrel or dog poop and I say, "Leave it."

"Wander" is getting better, but "Heel" is still awful. In heel, she continues to veer away on a diagonal, as willful a disengagement as she can make while still attached to a lead. We work on "Heel," "Stop," "Sit," "Turn," "Wait," "Leave it," and "Stay" as we walk, with modest success. "Sit" is pretty strong; "Leave it" seems to be the only command with 100 percent obedience. Puz is happy to ignore anything I say no to — an excellent behavior for the search field. "Heel," "Stop," "Stay," and "Wait" need a lot more work. Today I'd be happy for improvement on even one of these.

This is a dog who will tell me she has found a person tucked in a pipeline beneath three feet of rubble. *But, Puzzle, why won't you just walk with me?*

I muse on strategy as we turn another corner and head for a busy intersection that borders a park where we often train. Puzzle pads ahead easily, but she must heel while crossing streets with me. I'm preparing for the inevitable struggle across the approaching four-lane when I step on a loose piece of sidewalk that comes up the moment I put weight on it. I come down, smacking my forehead against cement, my right wrist snapping hard beneath my weight. There's a roar in my head, like the rush of decompression out a hole in an airplane, and though my eyes are open, I realize that for the moment I can't see. I have dropped the leash and hit my head, and when I try to turn to look for my dog, I can't see her. I'm aware that I'm near to blacking out.

"Puzzle, *wait*," I say, and with a heart sink that I'm probably going to lose her, it's the last thing I remember for I don't know how long.

I wake to the huff of her breath in my ear, and I open my eyes to see Puzzle in full alert above me, her leather lead dragging free behind her. *How long have we been here?* I wonder. The daylight seems changed, but my vision is still not right. We are a few yards from the busy intersection, and my dog has not, apparently, left my side. I sit up. The right wrist is bad. My cell phone is shattered. I use my left hand to touch my head for blood and find a chestnut-size lump. Best to sit a moment. Puzzle sits beside me and attends, offers once to lick my face and then waits quietly minutes later when I try first to rock to my knees and then to stand.

Five blocks from home on a weekday afternoon. I'm not in great shape, but I have no idea who in this neighborhood would be home at the moment to help us and who would not. I take Puzzle's lead in my left hand, and on the "Wander" command she moves soberly forward without pulling. I'm still dazed, but Puzzle heads for home as though she recognizes the reverse course or intuits our walk is done. She moves gently, ignoring the challenge of two barking Dobermans in a backyard we pass. Here is the obedience we've been working on for almost a year, and I cannot know what provokes it — only that she obeyed a "Wait" command while I lay unconscious, either as a form of obedience or a concern that I had fallen, and now she walks ahead as if chastened by the experience.

"Good girl," I say to her when we get back in the house. She follows me to the refrigerator for ice and to the phone as I call a friend for a ride to the emergency room, and to her credit, she saves me from additional embarrassment when she puts her muzzle to my backside and I feel the cool wet of her nose against my skin. It's then I realize that not only have I blown out the seat of my jeans and my underwear, but I also walked all the way home mooning anyone who cared to note the tall, shattered woman walking behind a very good dog.

15

THIS BOY HERE

WE THUMP ALONG the shadowed lanes of a mobile home park, awkward behind the steady grace of a moving dog. Heavy in our boots, prickly with sweat, we've been out only a few minutes, and we're chafing already beneath the unforgiving rub of packs — packs in which we've crammed every possible thing we might need in the rescue of a six-year-old boy who's ten hours gone. He is asthmatic, diabetic, allergic to bees, frightened of punishment, inclined to run.

Braden has light brown hair and blue eyes. Earlier today, he wore blue shorts and a red T-shirt, green and yellow athletic shoes, and glasses. Two front teeth are missing. He was last seen with other children, older neighbors, squabbling over a Game Boy. Up to this year, he's been a city child, but now he lives in this mobile home park that is rural in three directions and suburban only if you look out the front gate and stretch your eyes toward a gated community across the freeway. Braden was not reported missing until he failed to show up for supper.

Near midnight, his young mother can barely get a word out, sitting on a picnic table beside her boyfriend, also silent, who has an arm around her shoulders. Her head is down. His is up, attentive, watching each addition to the search. Three, four, five police cars, two fire trucks, and now the dogs. A clutch of other family members stand in the strip of yard beside the missing boy's home. They pulse red-blue in the flash of police-car lights and stand disengaged, watching the search but apart from it. There is an open animosity among some of the group that carries out to where we are. Comments are made, derisive laughter even. Some nod while others shift slightly away.

"Oh, *hell* no," said one woman at the earlier arrival of the dogs. She shook her head, went inside, and slammed the door.

"Now this boy here," says an uncle who has come forward, "has a history of this." The uncle is a tall man standing in the cold pool of a street lamp with his hands in his pockets, head bare, his face flecked with leaf shadow from the hackberry tree that crowds the light. He is the designated family representative, and he has not moved from the place where he stands the entire time we've been here.

Place Last Seen, Direction of Travel, Containment, Attraction: these terms can direct a missing-person rescue, allowing responders to choose the place to begin and the first direction for search, to prevent a moving victim from traveling outside the immediate area, and to provide attractors that can lead a missing person to safety. In a perfect scenario, the PLS is consistent among eyewitnesses, the direction of travel known. The missing person doesn't fear responders and is excited to see the flashing lights or hear the quick, light chirps of a siren. He is physically and cognitively able to head for help.

We rarely get the perfect scenario — I cannot recall *ever* getting it — and on this search, our understanding of Braden wavers. Runaway, abduction — or something else? The PLS is in a constant state of revision. Witnesses disagree on his direction of travel. What seems to be a common theme is that Braden is deeply afraid of getting into trouble with adults, and there is a changeable story about this afternoon that describes a fight over a favorite toy — that may or may not have been dismembered by another child — a bro-

ken window at a friend's house, a pair of soiled pants, and then a
hard run away from feared punishment. One version of the story
leaves out the fight and concentrates on the toy that Braden may
have tried to walk to a supermarket to replace. Other stories detail
Braden's two previous runaway events. Once, because he was mad
about a broken promise to go swimming. A second time when he
was left behind with a new babysitter he didn't much like.

The uncle says, "Braden doesn't make trouble, but he brings
trouble on."

In the smoke of conflicting stories, anything may be possible
behind Braden's disappearance. His medical needs are a concern
among us. The time gone even more so. When a young child has
been missing for more than two hours, successful rescue probabil-
ities drop. We know today's high temperatures. We all sense the
time passed and quickly passing, and though we never think it's
possible to move any faster, somehow in the search for a child, we
do, pushing hard behind the dogs. They also seem to feel the extra
urgency, so much so that even the quiet ones bark before they gear
up to run.

The earliest dogs out could not confirm either of the directions
Braden was said to have traveled, but this isn't really surprising,
considering the relatively small area, the passage of hours, and a
great deal of foot traffic in every direction. Braden could have been
here, or here, or here, his scent now lost in the blanket of other
scents dropped more recently. The other possibility is that something else has happened to him, and he was never in any of these
directions at all. We search as though either condition is true.

I run behind a handler whose dark dog lopes easily down the
narrow streets, threading his way between trailer pads. Missing
Braden is public knowledge here. The police have already questioned local residents, and now we move house to house among
watching bystanders. Some homes are dark at this late hour, others flicker blue and yellow with the glare of television screens, and
others still are ablaze with light. Venetian blinds bend a little, ex-

posing people looking out at us as we look back at them, their movement catching our attention. A couple of teenagers come forward to ask if they can help, clutching a photocopied picture of Braden police had given them earlier. They are the only ones to do so. Other residents watch silently from porches, their expressions withdrawn, some with arms folded, flicking cigarette ash onto cement. One man calls from a porch that his baby is sleeping and that we'd better not set the alarm off on his car. When our passing search canine causes a housebound Chihuahua to bark, we hear the bang of a screen and another man shout that he's "gonna fucking kill me a goddamn dog" — sharp words flung our direction that make my stomach knot until our pace jars it free.

This community has not softened to Braden's trouble, and it strikes me that maybe it cannot. We have been on searches where local police offered us Kevlar vests, and though this isn't one of them, I feel our vulnerability here as well as his, a twitchy awareness as we jog behind the dog, calling for the child within a neighborhood that seems . . . something. Hostile? Wary? Frightened?

It seems a hard place for a little boy to get lost. I think of diabetic Braden, who is last known to have eaten a bologna sandwich at lunchtime. I have two energy bars, beef jerky, and a juice box in my backpack. With every step I hear the slosh of it, a little chug like *I-think-I-can*.

I am childless, which is not to say I never had a child. In the decade of my marriage, I almost had five of them — pregnancies reflecting the fitful stages of our good years together and twice, our duress. Because I never knew them, I think of these children now by the placeholder names we briefly gave them then: Baby 1, Baby 2. We called them this not for want of better names, but because we learned to hold our collective breath and carefully round the corner on each trimester. My sensible, hard-working husband with a wild streak was a closet conservative. He valued an even keel. When our first loss came six months into our marriage, an early surprise and a devastating blow, we would not be jinxed again. So we didn't get too hopeful, too excited about another pregnancy, ever. We didn't actively try, and we instinctively knew it was harder to lose a baby already named than one affectionately known by the order of conception.

After the first miscarriage, we conceived again a year later, then a third time after I graduated with my master's. Again two years later, in a moment of feeling flush enough to send a baby to college (Baby 4). And finally, after three years of job losses, financial struggle, and temptation in various forms, again. Baby 5 was the child I carried into a car accident and out of it, the pregnancy that held the longest, and the baby whose miscarriage began while I was piloting an airplane. Physically stunned by the sudden, catastrophic labor and the loss fully formed enough to see, to hold, we fell to earth — my husband and I — within the year, and that would be the end of us.

He took the cat, I took the dog. We separated nightstands and divided dishtowels. We argued over bills, taxes, apartment deposits. And then it was done. We moved to separate cities and licked our wounds in private.

Those babies return to me as yearning when I least expect it. Sometimes, all these years later, Baby becomes an individual, and I see the cut of my ex-husband in a boy at the supermarket. Or a girl on the street stops to ask directions, and the flash of her form in the glass of a moving door is something like me.

I've been asked if these losses are why I work search — some Freudian byproduct or act of reparation, of denial. I don't think so, of course, but friends say I might be denying that too. It's a well-worn concept and a repeated one. A few kind souls suggest a nobler motive: on searches involving children, perhaps I'm saving some other mother the grief I've known myself. That sounds very good, but I don't think about motive much. I work search the way I plodded through the muddy aftermath of miscarriage and divorce: one foot before another, hoping for good but prepared for grief, and following the dog ahead anyhow.

. . .

There are a hundred or more mobile homes here, but the community sits tight enough that occasionally I see the flicker of other canine units on their neighborhood sweeps. We call out to the little boy, telling him he's not in trouble, that it's time to go home. Our flashlights silver the underbellies of trailers, the interiors of cars. After a time, the bystanders retreat to their houses, and we're left with only the glittering eyes of crouched housecats, their gazes hard on the dog as we pass.

Near the farthest reaches of our sector, the dog we follow rushes suddenly forward to the door of one mobile home. He thumps so hard against it that the door pops open, revealing a half-dressed man bent down to the bins of his fridge, fishing for something in the crisper. The man yelps with surprise at the sight of the dark, powerful dog, almost falling as he rights himself. Lights come on in the neighboring home, shouts back and forth. The handler apologizes and pulls his dog from the doorway. We step cautiously back as the man slams his door onto its latch and then locks it.

"No radio," says the handler quietly, aware that anything we say broadcasts widely across team radios and could be audible to bystanders near other dog teams. "I think we'd better walk this one back in."

That strong indication in a doorway, two other dogs responding markedly on the trunk area of a car. This is what the dogs have given us. It can be a strange moment describing tangible responses to trace evidence that humans cannot smell — you always hope the authorities understand what the dogs are truly doing. This time, when handlers relay their separate information to police, investigators confer together and tell us the indications make sense. The doorway marks an area where the boy often visited, where in fact he may have played today. The car, owned by a friend of the family, was one Braden had ridden in a lot. That the dogs indicated strongly here, in a neighborhood where the child has also been in other houses, other cars, and on the playground swing set seems significant to us. Why so much fresh scent here? Perhaps it's significant to investigators too, though we are not included in their deliberations. We stand by at a distance as they bend over the hood of a police car, pooling the known information from interviews and the interest of the dogs.

A mutter in the distance, then loud and louder still: a police helicopter passes low over the mobile home park and outward to the fields beyond it, pilot and spotter flying an airborne version of the tight sweeps we have made on the ground. The intensity of the helicopter searchlight and the heavy *whup* of rotor blades have likely wakened every living creature in the area. And for the time it is with us, the helicopter now makes dog work virtually impossible, the downwash from the blades creating a scatter of scent worthy of a small tornado.

Now we stand with the dogs that lie flat in the cool grass along the street. They are less interested than we are. They have seen and heard helicopters before, and this rest with their water bowls is welcome to them. We humans watch trees whip and objects blaze in the bright circle of light that slips easily from the helicopter across the neighborhood, and though I have no reason to fear that scrutiny, something in the nearness and approach of it makes me want to run.

I wonder what sense Braden makes of all this, if he is alive and conscious, if he knows the helicopter's there for his sake. I say as much to a young officer standing nearby, who shakes his head. He says over the noise that the residents of this mobile home park are pretty familiar with that helicopter. There's a lot of crime here: bad drug deals, abuse cases, robberies that turn to assault and, occasionally, to murder. Many of the longtime residents are too poor to move away. The officer's voice is matter-of-fact, but he says with some compassion, "They never know anything about anything when we show up, because they've got to live here after we've gone."

We count twenty-two passes before the helicopter rises easily away, slides winking into the darkness. When it's gone, I feel my knees begin to shake. I'm tired and more than tired — heartsick with certainty that Braden isn't here. I don't say anything. None of us says anything. With a gesture, an officer stands the dog team down. He tells us that tomorrow we'll search more widely: the surrounding fields, the farther places where bodies have been found before.

Seven hours later, I'm rested and well-juiced with coffee, in the left seat of a Cessna 152 a thousand feet above the ground, while a spotter gazes down from the right seat. I'd expected to run with the dogs again today, but at check-in, the Incident Commander said, "We'd like to send you up, if you're willing. It would be good to have you overfly areas that might be tough for the dogs, so that we can sector and prep the teams appropriately before they go out." Twenty minutes later, I was at the airport renting the Cessna. Twenty minutes after that, we were aloft.

This morning's heat is already surly, and the little plane is battered by thermals as we circle potential points of interest and fly gridlines over empty fields. I'm grateful the spotter is a fellow pilot from the flight school, unlikely to get airsick from the heat, the maneuvers, or the turbulence. He is a calm young man with sharp eyes, and he calls what he sees to me: the arrival of additional resources for today's sectors: horseback riders, ATV drivers, and a large crowd in a supermarket parking lot that could well be intended to walk certain areas a few feet apart, scanning the ground for any physical evidence that might be tied to the missing boy. At least a hundred more volunteers will join the search today, and it won't be an easy one.

We see unmowed fields. Plenty of creek beds surrounded by heavy brush. Several construction sites and a junkyard. A ribbon of road that was once a main thoroughfare from country to town. As we fly, the spotter jots terrain details on our photocopied map. We take turns flying, alternating who spots, our eyes straining for some sign of Braden on the move below. Now at five hundred feet above the ground, we should be able to see the missing boy in open areas, but there is nothing of him in the tall grass or flat spaces. Nothing in grass verges beside the road. What we do see is terrain it could take days to thoroughly cover.

We land, call in the information, and take off again. By the time we are airborne, ground searchers are on the move. We overfly their sectors for the rest of the day, hoping the presence of searchers will provoke some kind of movement from the missing child. And if they can't see him, we might be able to.

It's the call we understand but never like to hear. Whether out of ideas or having information they have not shared with any of us, investigators stand down the search in the late afternoon. Every sector has been covered — some by separate resources — and no trace of the boy has been found. "Abduction" is the rumor floating among the assembled company, always a possibility, now widely believed if not confirmed. Many of the searchers offer to remain here on standby, despite the 105-degree heat and the injuries already among some of the volunteers: heat exhaustion for several, a sprained wrist, a horse that took a bad fall crossing a ravine. The authorities decline. They too are pulling out. The case isn't over, but the ground search is.

The exhausted dogs load quietly into their cars and their crates, drooping over their water bowls, some of them dozing before they take the time to lie down. We're a subdued group, leaving with a few pats on the shoulder between us and little to say.

On my way home, I drive through the mobile home park a last time. Not much adult movement there in the heat of the day, but on one of the empty trailer pads, four shirtless boys play Keep Away with a deflated basketball. They stop and point a little as I pass, a *who's-that?* gesture and a brief stare before they turn away. A few streets over, an elderly woman sits with a small child in a kiddie pool. She nods as I drive by; the little girl waves wildly. In the unapologetic light of this summer afternoon, in a mobile home park half a century old, last night's search for Braden seems unreal. There are no cars in front of the house where he lives. It is quiet, cloth awnings collapsed against the windows to better block the sun.

A few hours after the search stands down, a park resident walking her dog smells smoke, peers into a ditch not far from the community, and finds a roll of smoldering carpet wedged into a drainage pipe, carpet from which a child's foot protrudes. He is found just feet away from the verge where investigators had parked, in a pipe that had been searched several times, penetrated by flashlight the night before. Days pass before we learn what is thought to have happened. There's word of a playmate's accident with a gun, the collaboration of adults to hide the matter, a transport somewhere else — and the return of Braden's body only after the search had terminated. The dogs' indications were relevant. The recovery raises questions we will never know the answer to. What was the message behind his return — a desire for discovery? A belief he would not be found in a place already searched? Or a more pointed message to authorities?

When we debrief the search a week later, several of us acknowledge the nightmares and insomnia that have followed it. Some of us are angry, some so sad we can barely speak. Rescues that become recoveries are never easy. Recoveries involving children — whether we are there at the moment of find or not — may be the hardest of all. In time, we go on to other searches and other sectors behind the dogs. But I am never far away from Braden. For months, he remains a figure in the corner of my dreams, with a wound to the head and a wound to the palm, as though he saw what was coming and put up his hand in the moment of flash.

16

FEAR STAGES

I FEEL THE THUNDER before I hear it. Five-pound Pomeranian Sprits'l is on the bed, tap-dancing on my chest. He senses a line of storms approaching from the south. Early morning storms in Texas are often the worst, especially during shifts of season, and I never know if Sprits hears them, smells them, senses the drop in pressure, or hears the change of wind, but for the last two years he has become increasingly storm phobic. He isn't hysterical or destructive during storms, but deeply anxious, panting rapidly and kneading his paws on any available human who will hold him. Now he is squeaking and gibbering in my arms. Four A.M., and if I squinch my eyes shut and block the ticking of the alarm clock, I think I can hear thunder miles and miles away. He always knows long before I do.

Sprits is the only dog that's nervous. I have three others on the bed — I can make out Fo'c'sle Jack and Sophie at the foot, their heads pressed together as they sleep, and Puzzle, whose snores I hear and whose dead weight I feel against my back. She is sleeping hard. I lie in the dark and idly scratch Sprits'l's chest, which seems to help him a little. He stops the tap-dancing but stares out the window toward the southwest, rigid and expectant. He is not my first storm-phobic dog, and I wonder if he learned to fear storms from our late English Setter who was afraid of them in a big way—an eighty-five-pound dog circling, pacing, and wedging himself under chairs, digging frantically in the bathtub, his head down as though he were receiving blows. Sprits as a puppy was never nervous about bad weather, but I have to wonder if he watched old Chevy and learned what it is to be anxious, or whether he evolved to this on his own.

And I wonder too about Puzzle, who has never yet been disturbed by storms. Will she in time come to dread them? The condition is apparently common in Golden Retrievers—so common that acquaintances who find out about Puzzle often say *Oh-you-have-a-Golden-Retriever-and-is-she-scared-of-storms?* in one breath.

If Puzzle is going to have a problem with storms, it isn't this morning. The wind rises, and the cross-draft in my old house makes the glass in the windows rattle with each change of pressure and thunderclap. Jack and Sophie have raised their heads and grumbled a little before settling back down. Storms hassle their dream cycles. I roll to my side and let Sprits tuck himself in the *V* at the back of my knees. He settles there, and I lean toward Puzzle's warm, sleepy presence. I have always loved cuddling a dog during bad weather, and she's a good size now for a full-body hug. I press my cheek to her forehead and drape my arm across her middle. Every crash and bang of thunder makes Sprits squeak a little, but Puzzle refuses to rouse. *What a steady girl,* I think. She rolls belly-up and sighs, and the storm's bright crashes have resolved to the occasional flicker and boom.

A free-floating statistic you hear in canine SAR states that 80 percent of would-be search dogs wash out. They can't do the work or won't do the work or too many things stress them to overload and they shut down. Aptitude testing for puppies gives an initial idea of a puppy's overall assurance, but there are no guarantees which way the maturing dog will go. I heard the statistic long before I got Puzzle, and I went into our partnership knowing there was more than just *can-she-smell-it-and-tell-me* involved: a search dog's drive and confidence are as important as good gifts of scent and smarts.

I watched her go into and out of the first puppy "fear stage," when she suddenly was averse to wheeled things and to toddlers, a condition that faded with desensitization as weeks passed. Now Puzzle's due for another one. A second fear stage is common between six and fourteen months. So far she hasn't reacted strongly to anything, but knowing the speed of her changes, I try to calmly show her the whole range of bizarre stimuli that for a search dog is common ground. I hope this can be a bonding opportunity: a *here is this thing we respect but don't need to fear — trust me.*

This morning, young firefighters are learning how to drive the big trucks. Two fire engines round a corner and flash past us at the fire academy. Sitting with me in the grass five feet from the curb, Puzzle could be nervous. That's a lot of truck and very close. There's much for a dog to be afraid of as the engines tilt and blaze through their paces — turning corners, braking suddenly, navigating through tight lanes, backing up. But Puzzle doesn't seem to be afraid at all, regarding the fire engine maneuvers with calm, unmoving benevolence. When the trucks stop and the firefighters jump out, she occasionally wags her tail as she scents one who is an old friend.

Puzzle has grown up with big noise, living in a house that sits next to ongoing construction. If houses aren't being torn down to the left or the right of us, the city is tearing up the streets, repairing aged infrastructure. The daily noise and dust have made me cranky, but — credit where it's due — the cement mixers, dump trucks, and backhoes may have accustomed Puzzle to big vehicles and the noise they're capable of making. I have seen her belly-up sleeping in the backyard grass while jackhammers pound asphalt twenty feet away.

For all she accepts storms and fire trucks with equanimity, this is not to say Puzzle is fearless. She is of two minds about the firefighters themselves. From puppyhood, she has schmoozed the men and women of local fire departments for petting when they are in civilian clothes. (We joke that she simpers, "They're big and strong and lightly smoked!") But a recent experience with a firefighter in turnout gear has dampened her enthusiasm a little.

The firefighter is Max, a team colleague and a thirty-one-year firefighter, the subject of Puzzle's deep devotion. On a bright, windless training day, out of sight from the dogs of the team, he puts on full turnout gear and oxygen system. It's an important part of their training. The youngest dogs of the team have never seen (or heard) a firefighter in full gear up close, and today is the day we hope they will make the association that the lumbering yellow creature with the shiny visor, indecipherable expression, and raucous breathing is a human underneath. Many dogs dislike their first experiences. Puzzle has seen quite a few firefighters in full gear from a distance, and in the engine bay she has sniffed curiously at long rows of pants and boots dropped in a neat, vertical, waist-open stack for quick gear-on — but this will be her first up-close experience with a firefighter in full gear.

Max rounds a corner and approaches the group of young dogs, all of whom shy, most of whom bark. His own search dog, Mercy, backs and barks in alarm for a few seconds until she connects the changed form with the scent of her handler. Two others are pointedly wary until Max gets on one knee and speaks to them. Whether his scent or posture tell them this guy's okay, they come forward with hesitance, then greater confidence.

Puzzle, however, is having nothing of him. She went skittish the moment she saw Max, and as he stands near her, speaking to her in a voice distorted by the mask and rasp of the SCBA, calling her by name, she cowers and pulls away, trembling. When he extends a hand down to offer a treat to her, she huddles behind me and submissively pees — something I have never seen her do before or since. In time, she takes a tentative sniff of his gloved hand and offers a tentative wag, but there seems to be nothing about this experience that comforts her.

Max wisely moves away — no sense in making the first experience a permanent problem. Puzzle watches him go, calming as he turns his masked face away from her and heads back the direction that he came from. I cannot make out if she failed to recognize the scent or sound of Max in the gear, or if she knew it was him and was terrified by his great change. I don't have to wonder long. When Max returns in his civilian clothes, Puzzle shies from him for the first time in her life. She presses to me for protection and looks briefly up at him with a betrayed expression on her face. She clearly knows what's what: the funky, stomping guy with the shiny face and distorted voice was Max. Her Max! It is not difficult to see the friction of her cognitive dissonance: *Max is a friend. Why would he scare me like that?*

It is a grudge she holds for months. Though every interaction with Max warms slightly, we all notice her subsequent hesitance in approaching him, as though she thinks in a flash he might change into the monster that first offered a treat, then scared and shamed her into peeing herself.

"Puzzle," Max says six weeks later, "are you ever going to forgive me?"

One thing's certain, Puzzle needs more turnout gear experience. I take her through the engine bays every training session, allowing her to walk the room's periphery where all the gear hangs, and after a moment of wariness, she thoughtfully sniffs the trousers, boots, coats, and gloves as we pass. "Own this," I say to her. "And this . . . and this." "Own," in our language, means *check this out, get comfortable with it.*

We acquire an old turnout coat and pair of trousers, and I bring them home, first throwing them haphazardly on the porch for all the dogs to sniff. Sprits'l to the rescue: from the first, he stomps over the gear fearlessly, his small, curious nose working it over, punctuating the inspection with an occasional snitz. The other Pomeranians follow, and a friend remarks that this process looks a little like a science-fiction movie, where fuzzy, fox-faced space parasites somehow swallow a firefighter whole without making a mark on the gear left behind.

Days later, I move both coat and trousers to an outdoor chaise longue, draping them over the frame as though it were a human lying there. Again the outfit looks like the person inside has been sucked right out of it by tidy aliens. Nevertheless, I hide treats in the thick yellow folds. Puzzle is somewhat curious about the change of position, only mildly interested until Sprits'l jumps on the chair and bounces across the coat and pants to find the hidden treats; then suddenly competitive Puzzle wants in on the action.

For the next week, I putter around the yard wearing that turn-out gear and yellow ladybug galoshes. This firefighter rig once belonged to a large man — the pants are seven inches too long and the jacket could hold three of me — and I wonder what that long-retired fellow might make of me toddling around the rose garden in his bright yellow pants and coat while holding a pair of clippers and a watering can. The ensemble has a makeshift crazy-lady air. Once, when I carry a bag of clippings to the compost heap at the side of the house, two neighbors laugh aloud before shifting to the other side of the street to avoid me. The next time I cross their path, they stare. They seem disappointed I don't have my little outfit on.

In time, my gardening, lounging, and taking tea in the turn-out gear have the desired effect. Puzzle comes to accept it calmly during training exercises, particularly when firefighters go about their business uninterested in her. I watch her watch the rookies suit up. She tilts her head and brings her ears to bear now and again when a person she recognizes slides into the heavy coat and trousers, looking speculative when their heads disappear beneath a helmet with a shield and mask. When it's someone she's fond of, I see the characteristic Golden furrow of the brow, an almost maternal look of concern, like *Oh, I wish you wouldn't do that.* On several training sessions, we hide volunteers in a turnout coat and pants, face-down in a tumble of wood, and — good news — Puzzle shows no qualms about finding them in it.

But her memory of Max in the suit remains fresh. Long months after he approached her for the first time fully suited in firefighter gear, he hides for her one day in the engine bay, wedging himself in the space behind a rack of the heavy yellow coats and trousers, helmets, masks, and boots. Puzzle has happily found other victims similarly hidden, but this time she runs into the room, clearly orients the scent in one corner of the bay, and screeches to a stop about six feet away from where Max is hidden. From that comfortable distance, she alerts to me, she alerts to the head trainer, and just to make sure we get it, she alerts to us both again. I encourage her to move closer to Max, but there is no way this time she's going to breach the space between them. *Fool me once . . .*, she seems to say, staring hard at the spot where Max crouches behind a row of turnout coats. She is sure and she is stubborn. She knows it's Max hiding back there, and — nothing doing — she knows what he gets up to when he gets a little access to that gear.

I make a note to myself: hide Max in turnout clothes more often. And I add a second note: maybe invite him to suit up and come over to pull a few weeds.

Thunderstorms, fire engines, jackhammers — not a problem. Toddlers and turnout gear, getting there. Puzzle moves forward, but I too have issues that I need to get past. Puzzle's a year into her training and doing well. She has more than two hundred successful scenario searches behind her. Urban streets and buildings, wrecked cars and mangled aircraft, debris fields, dense wilderness. Now, because half or more of the team's searches take place at night, we train accordingly.

I'm not at all afraid of the dark, but some night spaces make me a little uneasy even by flashlight. This is particularly true of building searches. It's my own clumsiness at issue: I don't want to fall over things I can barely see. I've had a few missteps with and without my dog, falling once face-first onto an oxygen tank. Puzzle, however, is comfortable in dim light, padding through dim warehouse and furniture-tumbled apartment spaces, climbing stairs with easy confidence.

Wilderness night work is her particular favorite. The Golden grows more joyful as the light fades, as though the diminished view intensifies all the things available to her other senses. Not that her night vision is necessarily bad: though information on canine sight is sometimes contradictory, contemporary research suggests that dogs have much better night vision than we do — more rods than cones, an assist to night hunting, while our cone-rich eyes give us better color vision. Puzzle and the other dogs seem to bear this out, bounding forward at the "Find!" command with the same ease they demonstrate by day.

While the dogs take darkness in stride, volunteer victims are relieved when the search canines work quickly at night. It can be an interesting hour, hidden somewhere in deep brush without a flashlight, waiting for a series of dogs to suss you out in the brambles, even as the nocturnal wildlife comes forward to make sense of you in the stillness. Our volunteers have come back a few times with their eyes wide and neck hair prickling. They've brought back stories of creeping sounds and snapping sounds and unblinking eyes that flicked once or twice in the moonlight.

It isn't hard to feel lost out there, and it's not difficult to be joyful when the dogs make the find. I've hidden in the brush for every dog on the team except my own, peeking through vines to watch them sweep their sectors, imagining how a stranger would see them — the light dogs ghosting along in the moonlight, the dark dogs unreadable, their easy trot almost wolflike in the dimness. The volunteers know what's coming — from the dogs, anyway — but I think of those who are genuinely lost and realize again the importance of people-friendly dogs out doing this work. I'm glad of my light-coated girl with the whole body wag and the smiling puppy-soft face.

But she scares me sometimes, does Miss Puzzle Boldly-Go, who seems to trot from light into darkness without pause. What I've learned across this year with her is that I can face my own fears at this work, light or dark, and push through them, but I am much more anxious about Puzzle. It's the parent's conundrum that I have sidestepped in my childlessness: that conflict between love, protection, and a young one's developing independence. It lands on me in full force now.

In familiar territory, we work primarily off-lead, and though Puzzle is well past her flight impulse, and her willingness to check in with me doesn't vary from day to night, I find myself stiffening before I take off her lead and give her the "Find!" command. This is particularly true in wilderness or debris fields where I have little ability to be a second set of eyes for her, to see what might be a threat from yards away. Coyotes. Stray dogs. Vagrants with a grudge. Anything could be out there, and sometimes is. Puzzle wears a set of blinking lights on her collar that helps me plot her movements when I cannot hear them. That helps. But in the dark, I seem to quiver with protective antennae. It's hard not to hold her back.

A trainer I know says that some of those 80 percent dogs wash out because of their handlers, and now, in the latter stages of our training together, I'm first aware that I could be the weak link between us. This is not a job for the merely well-intentioned. I have the training, the head skills, and the physical and emotional stamina for this, but Puzzle provokes my vulnerabilities.

One night at the fire academy, our trainer hides a victim on a high A-frame built to simulate a roof for training firefighters. The victim clings by his hands to the roof's peak, his body dangling out of sight down the other side. Puzzle and I are working a sector that includes mangled cars and railway tankers, and on this clear, cool night, the victim's scent is sweet and strong for her. After a couple of sweeps through the area, my dog rejects the tankers and the cars and dashes for the A-frame, lifting her head once at the bottom of it and then racing up the incline to the top, wagging and alerting on the victim draped down the other side, licking his hands. "*Woop!*" she says, the joy of the find making a little pop like a consonant at the end of her croon.

At the base of the A-frame, I'm about to climb to meet her when she dashes down the incline to get me and lead me back. "Good girl," I praise, and she bolts up the roofline again, alerts again, then scrambles down the roof to meet trundle-bug me only halfway up. She's made a good find and a great alert, and though I'm pleased at her insistence, she's terribly excited, scrambling from the victim back to me several times as I climb. Every dash down the roof seems closer to the edge of it in the dark — a ten-foot drop at its greatest height, a drop onto cement and training equipment she seems oblivious to. Or perhaps she can see that edge clearly, has it all under control.

"Puzzle," I call to her at the top of the roofline. I hear my voice quavering. "Good girl. Good girl. But 'Stay.'"

She does — oh, beautiful stay — balancing there with the victim at the top of the peak, wiggling her great joy of the find, tongue lolling. In the darkness, she is all light coat and dark eyes and *ha-ha-ha* exhalation.

"Hi," I huff to the volunteer victim at the top.

"Hi," he says back.

"Ten bucks says she makes it down from the roof before we do."

"Not gonna take that bet," he replies. I see him grin. With one hand hanging on and the other free, he gives her a scritch on the cheek before we begin our careful slide down the incline to the ground. On the release word, Puzzle, with her lower center of gravity, skitters easily down the slope. She stands on the asphalt and smiles up at my slower progress, her tail waving idly.

As I make my way down, I decide to teach Puzzle a "Creep" command, a word for "go slow beside me" in cases like these. I can imagine other scenarios where such a command might be useful — crawling under barbed-wire fences, making our way through damaged houses — anywhere slow progress might be the safest course. *Woo*, she says to me cheerfully when I arrive, a little encouragement for the human from the dog.

Night work is good for both of us. I have lessons of confidence to learn in this uneasy space between Puzzle's puppy foolishness and adulthood. Across the coming months, we train on, and I begin to understand how she makes sense of her surroundings at night. She's not heedless. With her nose in motion, her paws outstretched, her gaze extended, and her ears brought forward to bear, Puzzle is capable of making good choices. But I watch her light form flash over debris in the darkness, and because I love her as well as respect her gifts, I hold my breath when she slips out of sight. It's a hard-won peace, this letting the dog do her job outside the scope of my protection.

17

SNAKE-PROOFING

I AM UPSTAIRS, tapping away at my journal with the stereo on, and Puzzle has been whining at the puppy gate for several minutes. She's come in from outside, and now she wants to come up.

"*Wait,* Puz," I call, using our words. Trainer Susan would be proud. "Let me finish this, and I'll come down and let you in."

She whines again. Nothing doing on the *wait.* I hear her somehow pop the latch and press through the puppy gate, bounding up the steps to find me. She pushes her way between the hassock and my chair to sit nearby. Without looking away from the computer, I reach my hand to her face and feel her snuffling there.

Okay, I shouldn't be pleased. She didn't wait. (Trainer Susan would *not* be proud.) But this is a cozy, friendly connection, and for the division of a minute, I am first bemused by a dog who has figured out how to open the puppy gate and grateful also for the adolescent Golden who has finally begun to seek me out for companionship. We've had a number of little breakthroughs recently. Partners at last.

Stroking her idly while I reread today's journal entry, I'm only half paying attention to my dog. It takes a moment to realize that her face feels misshapen, and I recognize that the snuffling I heard against my hand didn't stop when she pulled away from it. I look down to Puzzle, and a Puzzle in trouble looks up at me, the left side of her head swollen twice its size, her eyes terrified. She is struggling to breathe. Saliva she cannot seem to swallow runs from the sides of her mouth, soaking the fur of her chest.

I drop down beside her, turning her face in my hands. This looks like anaphylaxis, an allergic reaction to something she'd eaten, gotten into, or the result of a bite or a wound. Her head seems to be swelling more even as I touch it, and when I find two small puncture marks just below the edge of her mouth in the soft flesh that joins face to throat, I know this is an emergency issue. Somehow I lift her up, get her down the stairs, and into the car. A neighbor agrees to drive while I hold Puzzle upright. She is gasping now, the inside of her mouth tinged blue.

The emergency vet is just a few miles away, but this Friday night the direct route is choked with restaurant and club traffic. Puzzle is propped in my arms, trembling as I lift her chin with my fingertips and hold up her head, the only position that seems to relieve her labored breathing. My friend drives carefully. We try not to further distress the dog, so we speak in low voices about whether we tough out the traffic or try longer, alternate routes. I wonder if Puzzle feels my racing heart against her shoulder. It takes only minutes but seems forever to get to the vet.

The receptionist at the emergency clinic takes one look at her and triages us into an examining room quickly, where the on-duty vet examines Puzzle at once, noting the double puncture wound. Rodent, possibly, but snake far more likely by the look of the injury, and this is the season for them. I think of my house's proximity to water and of the undisturbed woodpile in the backyard, both attractive resources for a snake even in a residential area. Still, it's hard to believe. *We're out working in all kinds of wilderness, and she gets a snakebite at home?*

"These bites are very painful," the vet says. He disinfects the area, gives Puzzle a shot of Benadryl and another of antibiotic, and starts an IV. She doesn't growl or resist, tilting her chin up to rest on my shoulder as I lean down to her. And then I hold her and we all watch, waiting for the swelling to come down and her breathing to ease. Long minutes of no change at all. She struggles to get comfortable. The random scrabble of her feet against the table is so helpless a sound I fight tears.

After a time, she stops drooling, and a little while after that she swallows. When Puzzle opens her mouth to pant, I no longer hear a labored rasp, and I can see the flush of pink tongue. "Things are looking up," the vet says, and he leaves us to attend the other emergencies that have crashed through the door. Across the next hour, we hear the click of nails on the lobby tile, bright thank-yous in the corridor, and later, a young man weeping. I stand in the examining room with my head bowed to Puzzle. I too have lost loved animals at this clinic, even in this room. But not this time.

We drive home more slowly than we'd left it. Whether sedated from the Benadryl or relieved that she can breathe easily, Puzzle no longer trembles in my arms, but lies awake and occasionally gulping. I can feel her pulse beneath my fingers, the motion of her swallow against my arm.

She is strong enough to walk, but we carry her gently into the house and put her across my bed, where she lies without protest. The little dogs yap and chitter, and lifted to the bed, they give her the obligatory vet trip sniff-over. And then they settle, all of them, the way she had once settled near Scuppy. Jack, shy and wiggly, gives Puzzle's face an experimental lick. She seems unaware of all of them, her eyes following me as I draw the curtains and change into my pajamas. When I leave for a glass of water, she immediately tries to jump to the floor.

Puzzle is needy — a condition I have never seen in her. I prop us both up on pillows and curl beside her on the bed, feeling the press of her spine against my chest. In time, she sighs, a relaxed heave and an exhale that suggests all is better, if not well. She sleeps easily, but I do not, realizing how serious this could have been had she not come to me. And I wonder what went through her dog mind as she bumped free the puppy gate separating us and bounded up the stairs to put her face into my palm.

I can easily imagine Puzzle putting her nose to something rustling in the woodpile. Was the snake a resident or a transitional character? How long after she'd been bitten did she come to me? I think of the Poms, equally curious and one-fifth of Puzzle's body weight. Tonight's situation, already bad enough, could have been much worse.

The next day, wearing boots and leather gloves, friends and I disassemble the woodpile with much noise and crashing, and we move it behind a gated fence inaccessible to the dogs. And I make a plan to disturb that woodpile daily. Come winter, we will burn it all up.

Puzzle is eighteen months old and has not yet been "snake-proofed," in the traditional sense. Snake-proofing is a common procedure for field and search dogs, involving a shock collar and thoughtful, controlled access to a living snake, which is not harmed. From a considered distance, the dog is allowed to get the scent of the snake and see the nature of its motion, and at the point the dog exhibits any interest, a mild shock is applied via the collar — ideally teaching that the snake has a painful potential and is to be avoided at all costs. Some dogs get the point with little provocation from the collar. Even the tiniest shock elicits a start and a *yike*, and a second view of a snake causes a backpedaling motion worthy of Wile E. Coyote. One of our handlers laughs that his dog, generally calm and relatively fearless in the search environment, leaps straight up at the sight of a snake in the brush, landing in his arms with Scooby-Doo's "ruh-roh!" expression on her face. Other dogs require greater deterrence. Belle, a yellow Lab with a high pain threshold who has grown up around snakes, would not be put off no matter how high the setting on the collar, a shock she did not even seem to feel.

I wonder how Puzzle will respond at her own snake-proofing session. She's a dog of great curiosity, but also a dog of deep grudges against things that have frightened her. This could go either way.

Puzzle's regular vet examines her face the next day. He is an upbeat, confident man with an easy laugh that fills the room, and no matter how many times Puzzle goes to the vet for one injection or another, she adores him, tolerating any number of pokes and prods and sharp sticks to be with him. Now she stands quietly as he examines her, trembling a little with the intensity of our joint scrutiny. Dr. Yzaguirre confirms the snakebite — probably copperhead, probably juvenile. The swelling has diminished this morning, and the neat double-slash of the bite is clearly visible. He shakes his head a little, then gives Puzzle a stroke and a playful tug of her ear. A lot of venom in these young snakes; a little lower on the jaw, and this could have been very bad. I mention Puzzle's future snake-proofing session, and the vet laughs a little. He would be surprised, he says, if she needs it.

Puzzle seems to agree. Across the following weeks, she watches our regular disturbance of the woodpile, raising up on her hind legs to peer over the fence at what we are doing, and though she has always loved stealing kindling, she has little interest in joining us.

We go to formal snake-proofing as soon as possible. I'm not sure what to expect as Fleta fits the shock collar around Puzzle's neck in the parking lot of a wildlife rehabilitation facility near one of our local parks. A wildlife handler brings out a large, lidded plastic tub carrying a de-venomed diamondback rattlesnake. The lid has holes in the top of it, and we begin the training procedure by simply allowing Puzzle to approach the tub in the way of any curious dog. As she approaches and her nose begins to work the scent of it, Puzzle has already stiffened and become wary. Her path forward has altered to a cautious half-circle. I watch her nostrils work, and though she is receiving small, increasing shocks, she doesn't seem to notice them. At the most downwind point to the tub, Puzzle veers abruptly away.

Fleta and I deliberate. Initially, Puzzle was a little too curious about the tub, but the moment of strongest scent and strongest shock seemed quite clear to her. She had no interest in approaching the tub again. The snake handler suggests that we move to the next stage, allowing Puzzle to both see and scent the snake in order to gauge her true response. This takes little time. The handler places the snake on the ground, where it begins its graceful side-slither to the north, and Puzzle backs up to the fullest extent of her lead, circling wide away from it, every muscle stiff with alarm. Though she had received the associated shock, she did not react to it — not even a flinch — as though every part of her awareness was focused on the snake.

The snake pauses a moment in its own meander, splendidly poised, then slopes into motion again. Puzzle responds with another half-arc away from him.

Good choice, I think, and because I'm too often from the if-a-little-is-good-more-is-better school, I ask if we should double-check Puzzle's aversion with another exposure to the snake, another shock.

Fleta shakes her head, grinning a little, watching my dog counter-curve away from the snake on tiptoe, her fur on end and tail rigid. "No shock on that last one," she says. Puzzle's expression is so tense she appears walleyed. "But I think we can safely say this is one dog that's snake-proofed. And then some."

18

A HANDLER'S GUIDE TO
RISK MANAGEMENT

THE ELECTRIC FENCE isn't live, authorities tell us, just minutes before Buster brushes against it at the edge of our sector, catapults back, and yelps from the shock. Snow has been falling heavily for the past hour or more, and the fence has become almost impossible to see in the first place, especially where it threads through overgrowth and seems to disappear. The farm we search on this midwinter day is decrepit; the three houses sitting on the land haven't been lived in for a long while, but the property is in use. The fence is certainly live — perhaps to discourage predators or trespassers, or to keep the livestock out of what once would have been the farmhouse yard.

Buster shakes off his shock and, after a word of encouragement from Johnny, continues working his sector, stepping deliberately over a woundless dead rabbit, so newly dead that when I pull off my glove and hover my hand over its fur, I feel the rabbit's residual warmth. Snow has fallen thickly in past minutes, and now the dead rabbit appears to be made of lace, her dull eye frosted over. Soon she will disappear entirely, as the ground has quickly disappeared beneath our feet.

Our search here, two states away from home, is just as ambiguous. There could be the remains of one teenager on this land, or two, or none. The authorities are guessing, pursuing a lead from a lead from a lead that has led them in unexpected directions on a case almost a year old. The area is remote. Where once this farm might have been on the far side of the small town it adjoins, hard decades have caused the town to recede and the outlying farms to fall to ruin or give over to other forms of enterprise.

The three houses here reflect generations across a previous century. Unbound by city code or ordinance restrictions, they are placed in a haphazard clutch on the land, as though to take advantage of utilities connected to each house on the property before. The oldest of them — a modest structure with a wide front porch — was probably built in the early 1900s, the smallest of the three looks like a 1950s ranch with its red brick and wide windows, and the last of the group, closest to the road, appears to be the newest of the homes, built perhaps forty years ago at the height of a neo-Mediterranean era. It is a light brick house with arched windows and iron burglar bars, black scrollwork on the porch railing, and a rusty iron Don Quixote lying face-down in the dirt. This would be a quiet, uninterrupted place to hide someone — living or dead — which is the possibility now. I'm working a sector beside Johnny and Buster that involves the Mediterranean house and a long, narrow stretch of land behind it that includes pasture, outbuildings, a burn pit, and a row of stables leaning over to the point of collapse.

Though the snow gives the scene an air of gentle benediction, we are all tense here. We came to this search after a two-day briefing that warned about possible dangers in the area. The calling agency has been frank: in the places we are to search, there are likely hazards. There may be meat-baited, cyanide-laced coyote traps, the so-called M-44s that can look deceptively like pieces of old pipe or sprinkler heads. These could be an obvious danger to our dogs and even to us. Before we deployed, we studied pictures of the devices and a whole series of warning signs required to be posted on property where the traps are embedded — and then we were told that plenty of ranches have the traps but not the signs, worn away by weather or never posted in the first place. Several of our handlers shook their heads at the briefing, unwilling to risk this danger to their dogs. The calling agency answered with a promise to have the search areas swept first by grid walkers trained to identify and dismantle the devices.

The coyote traps are not the only possible problem. There are meth labs deeply hidden in some pockets of this terrain, protected by homemade explosives on tripwires. Some of the labs may be abandoned, but the explosives could remain. Day two of our briefing included pictures and samples of the devices and tripwires, often more difficult to see than the coyote traps. There seemed to be a thousand ways to blow up unwelcome strangers, and that would be us. Any search is better with a good prebrief, but despite the promise of trained ground sweepers clearing the way ahead of our work, we ended the briefing session pensive. We made the long trip to the search area subdued.

Today, the farm where we search has been swept and theoretically cleared of all dangers, including the electric fence, supposedly off, that shocked Buster. This does not inspire confidence. After apologies and assurances, we work forward, hoping the fence is the only surprise we'll get in the field. Johnny and Buster move carefully ahead while I sweep sideways back and forth beside them, looking beyond them both to anything that appears to be a threat. Lovely as it is, the snowfall doesn't help matters much as it obscures the ground before us. I see livestock moving easily a distance away — perhaps this suggests the area is safe.

There is a small herd of pygmy goats on this land, and a few donkeys. We've been warned that the donkeys are probably not dog-friendly. It's hard to know what to make of their stares as they approach the fence that cuts our sector in half. The fence is live, and they seem to know it. They are cautious not to touch the posts and strands, but they crane their heads carefully over the side. They gaze at us steadily with an air of expectation, their fuzzy faces sugared with snow, and one occasionally extends his jaw forward and brays. The hard, metallic screech of the animal echoes less now than it did an hour ago, softened by the snow's accumulation. When we approach the fence as part of our search sweep, two donkeys bring their ears forward and one lays his ears back. I don't know much about donkeys, but my money bets the one with the big brown spot on his forehead and the laid-back ears is the dog hater of the group. The others just seem social. One pretty chocolate-colored creature extends quivering lips toward the pocket of my jacket as I pass, which suggests someone else has been feeding her treats from pockets. Every time she does it, the tender expression in her eyes looks like she just wants to give me a little taste.

The goats are even more aggressive. Not one of them is taller than my knees, but what they lack in height, they make up for in confidence. They are not shy, rushing forward as though we are the bearers of food or god-sent relief from goat boredom. Two of the smallest, twin silver and black Agouti doelings, seem to have something of a crush on Buster. As we leave one part of our sector and enter the next where the goats wander, these two rush forward to sniff at his haunches. There's a funny, complicit little tremble between them that shudders snow off their coats. They begin to follow him as he works. Buster's a farm dog and used to barnyard animals, but he's not sure what to make of his growing entourage when the rest of the herd follows these two from a respectful distance. When he stops, they stop. When he turns, they pivot also, plodding his new direction, their small heads bobbing.

"Shoo — go on now," says Johnny, clapping his hands and waving. The herd skitters slightly sideways a few steps, but their focus is on the two females who are love-locked behind Buster and who have ignored Johnny entirely.

I know less about goat dynamics than I do about donkeys, but it's interesting to watch the rest of the goats defer to these two small females, who seem to be the power players here. Who are they to the herd? What about them makes them leaders? Charisma aside, they don't make this sector easy to search, and Johnny and I confer a moment. As Buster and Johnny move forward, I begin stomping and waving every few feet, singing off-key to distract the goats enough to give the dog some room to work. Some of the herd isn't sure what to make of me and scatter a little farther. Buster's two smoke and silver girls shoot me cynical looks from the slit pupils of their golden eyes, and then they ignore me too.

The herd follows us to the white brick house with the burglar bars, but they pause at the edge of what would formerly have been a yard. They come no farther. We step onto a bare cement porch that has a fragment of a woman's shirt lying a few feet away from the door. It was once part of a western shirt, red yoke and sleeves, white from the yoke to the waist. One pearl and metal snap remains. It looks too clean to have been here long. Buster is uninterested in it. I note the scrap of fabric but don't touch it, writing down its description, and we enter the house, which smells of moldy shag carpet and cat pee.

Someone lived here and someone left here with little thought to resale. There are empty, yellowed fast-food sacks on an abandoned dinette table, overturned cereal boxes speckled with rat excrement, and old, old food in the refrigerator. Dirty dishes in the sink, the remains of several meals dried and crusted over. The bathroom has so strong a smell that Johnny and I recoil, breathing through our mouths as we walk down the hallway. Though his nose is more sensitive than ours, the heavy air doesn't dissuade the dog. Buster lifts his nose thoughtfully in the fug — a whole host of rich, human smells — but he turns away, indicating nothing suggests a violent human crime here.

I stand at the edge of what would have been a living room and watch him work, relieved to think that the dog found no death and no evidence of recent life in this space, that perhaps this house didn't hold missing teenagers for the last days of their lives.

The dog pads out of the house and we mark it as cleared, making our reverse way back through the waiting goats, who caper a little with excitement as we separate the herd and cause them to regroup and hustle to follow us. Buster's two little goat friends join him, breaking into a trot as he moves out of the pasture as quickly as possible. We slip through the gate, frustrating their follow, and we leave the goats behind. They press against the fence line, their expressions wistful. The Lab shoots us a disgusted look and something of a dog shrug, then sets back to work.

We enter a long field, where a flock of peacocks joins us in the farthest part of the sector. They follow in a stately progression beside us, replacing the goats that have been left behind. The birds are unafraid of us, unworried about Buster. We search and they move quietly in trail, picking their way with great care, without fluster or gibber. The vivid males and speckled, elegant females are remotely beautiful against the falling snow, creating the surreal impression of a search sector embroidered in brightly colored thread.

"Is it just me," says Johnny, ever understated, "or does this search just get more weird?"

Buster seems relieved to be rid of the goats and unworried by the peacocks. He works quickly, crossing the area in four easy sweeps and rejecting it of any interest. We leave the birds to their field and the goats to their pasture and enter the leaning, shabby outbuilding that lacks a door. The first room is full of feed bags and smells of dust, grain, and bird droppings, but the second room is curiously empty apart from a cushioned rocking chair sitting in the center of the floor. Buster moves to the chair, circles it thoughtfully, and as he is sweeping the little room, suddenly yelps softly and backs away in haste, winking his eyes and snorting. We smell nothing, but Buster certainly does. Not a response to human scent, it's as though something burns.

Johnny looks to his dog that's now pawing at his nose, and we move away from the building as Buster's eyes begin to water and he begins to breathe heavily.

"What the hell?" says Johnny, bending down to examine Buster's face. He has never seen his dog react so. I circle the outbuilding and peer into the room that gave him the problem, and I can see nothing but the battered chair and dusty floor. Our tracks in. Buster's circling paw prints. Our tracks out.

I make a note of Buster's curious response, call it in on the radio, and rejoin Johnny. "How's he doing?" I ask.

"He's okay."

"Not a good day at the office for Buster."

"No," says Johnny, still bending down with a careful eye to his dog.

Buster recovers in moments, but he's eager to move away from that outbuilding, and he's quick to go back to work. The dog scrambles across the field, lifting his nose in the direction of a row of adults watching from an adjoining property, yards and yards away. Three are standing. Two sit in lawn chairs and gaze in our direction over the backs of several abandoned cars. They are swaddled in parkas and hats; some of them cradle a Thermos. I flick a nod of acknowledgment, but they do not respond.

We finish the sector and head back to Incident Command, where we are introduced to two men and a woman who are, we are told, anthropologists and archaeologists here to potentially protect any find of human remains that may be irrelevant to our search and have historic or tribal significance. One of the young men had seen Buster's contact with the fence and heard about his experience in the outbuilding over the radio, and he bends over the dog now, talking to him kindly and rubbing his ears. The three have come prepared to watch and to wait.

Several local officers walk across the snow in the field near the oldest house, probing it gently with a pike designed to penetrate dirt and allow buried scent to rise. There's a chance that this current search sweeps over old, old graves. The anthropologists watch, their eyes on the officers but their conversation directed to us. The dogs fascinate them, they say; they have never seen this kind of work before. While I write up the sector report and sketch a map to attach to it, Johnny and others talk with them about the use of dogs for the recovery of human remains from ancient sites. One of the anthropologists jokes that what they really need are "dig dogs," trained to keep archaeologists and anthropologists from picking at the dirt too hastily. A good dog alert could make all the difference. Sometimes, he says, a single strike of pick and mallet can bring up things you weren't quite ready to see.

There is nothing visibly amiss in the oldest of the houses, but a police canine and Saber have shown strong interest in a bedroom windowsill and upward along a wall beside it. They have also shown interest in a dark spot on the floor. On a blind search after the others had emerged from the house, Belle, working in the basement, went "straight up the wall," according to her handler, stretching toward the same floor area from below. *Human scent here*, the dogs separately suggest, though the house is remarkably neat and still bears the faint scent of cleanser. Blood spatter from an attack, semen, or old blood from a commonplace injury? Learning that two of our dogs confirmed the police canine, the officers overseeing the search stand together in the snow with their hands deep in the pockets of their black leather jackets and their shoulders hunched forward against the cold. Though the search has recovered no bodies here, the floor, wall, and windowsill of the oldest house merit forensic examination, and we are far from any place with those resources. Several officers continue to confer while one goes to release the anthropologists and another tells us they have nowhere left for the dogs to search.

Our work is done, and after the calling agency releases us, we begin to pack our equipment and prepare the dogs for travel. They are tired and withdrawn, ready to go off-duty and sleep in the protective warmth of their cars and their crates. We're ready too. This kind of work needs to be done, and the team exists to do it, but the possibility of poison and explosives on this search made the already difficult work even harder. None of us knows what to make of Buster's response in that outbuilding. Nothing about it looked good.

Thick snow still falls, and we push through it shin-deep, some of the dogs wading through drifts that brush against their bellies. Despite protective footwear and heavy socks, many of us can no longer feel our feet. The dogs' paws are icy between the pads. Icicle beads have formed like tribal necklaces around the ruffs of the ones with long coats.

"God," says Cindi, shaking off the search and its dangerous possibilities, "I'm glad that's over." I breathe deeply and rub my eyes, feeling a little winded afterward, suddenly aware of how often I'd held my breath through that sector, how hard I'd stared forward into the white of the snow.

As we load the vehicles and Buster, Belle, Saber, and Hunter are defrosted and made safe for transport, I look across the fields where we searched, now completely blanketed with snowfall. The human audience is packing up, retracting lawn chairs, their bright Thermoses tucked beneath their arms. The peacocks have taken to branches of low trees, to the dividing fence that separates them from the goats. They huddle beside one another silently, their graceful heads bowed and the trailing plumage of the males counterbalancing their forward weight. The little goats have carved a trail for themselves to the leaning shed. One of the females has jumped onto an overturned trough. She gazes toward the truck Buster leapt into, but the rest of the goats don't seem to notice our departure. They saunter idly along the trail to the shed and back again, the untouched snow that borders their route so deep that from where I stand the goats appear to be swimming, only their dark, bobbing heads visible above the white.

I am home very late from the search. It feels strange, light, and heedless to walk easily through my backyard without scanning for cyanide traps. The dogs have been long asleep when I come in, and they rouse a little fustily, the Poms briefly deliberating whether they should riot when the door opens and then, seeing that it's me, deciding not to. They rise, stretch, and wobble forward in greeting while Puzzle, who cocked an eye in my direction when I came in the door, remains belly-up on the back of the couch.

Too tired to sleep, I sit beside her, stroking the fine line from her throat along the jaw to her soft ear. She has always seemed a sturdy dog, but tonight I think of tripwires and coyote traps, and I'm aware of her fragility. Had this search been mine to choose as a handler, would I have made the choice to work her, despite the known risks and failed assurances? I don't know. But this is no reprieve. The decision could come up again, and soon. Puzzle is only weeks from her certification tests.

"Here's a handler's guide to risk management: don't live vicariously through your dog," an experienced handler from another team once said to me, "and for God's sake, don't get attached." The best handling, he said, is done from a distance. He had dogs at home that he loved, but his search dog was not one of them — a working dog in a different place with him. He had to keep her there. They were functional partners only as long as the handler held real affection for her at bay.

I wonder what he would have made of this search and its potential hazards. Would he have been hesitant at all? Would he have been cautious only due to the investment risk? Or were those long-ago comments to me made in a moment of posturing, and did his colleagues know him as a man who split his hamburger in the truck and let his search dog sleep on the bed? The fellow had been insistent. He had worked several dogs in his search career, and when he told me that "loving a search dog screws with your priorities," I understood his perspective. But I couldn't agree with it. I wondered then and I wonder now if I could ever be capable of that kind of remove.

19

SHOW AND TELL

A T THE END of a long corridor smudged dark with recent smoke, Puzzle stands with her nose to a door, her tail waving faintly. Six rooms, six closed doors, and behind one of those, a single volunteer victim buried in rubble. We are in the fire department burn building, and today Puzzle is telling me which closed door to open and which others to ignore. She was given the "Find!" command yards from the building, and in she ran, smiling, her tongue out sideways. I am steps behind her, running from bright into immediate gloom. The air here is thick with soot and the dust of spent hay, and in the flashlight's beam, I can see the swirls of Puzzle's slipstream wash up against the wall like an airplane's wingtip vortices. If she were to disappear down some dark passage, for a time at least I could track her path through dusty air. I sneeze, then sneeze again.

The airflow here is tricky. The burn building's outside windows are open to today's southerly breeze, while all its internal doors are closed. Here, the scent of a human hidden in a single room can easily slip out the bottom of one door and wash up against neighboring walls or onto the closed door opposite, sticking there in the dust and damp. "Scent traps," these are called, and scent can be deceptively strong there, misleading the dog trying to pinpoint the source. In this exercise, Puzzle's got to know better, and she's got to show me how much she knows better.

These closed-door drills are some of the hardest, most intuitive work a dog team can do. In a damaged office building full of locked doors, a dog that can indicate the right door to kick in for rescue is a tremendous help to the firefighters who have to break through them. In past training, we've not been entirely successful. Because I didn't yet know how to read my dog, when scent was faint, I was inclined to open every door. And Puzzle was glad to let me do so, smiling there and sometimes moving idly into the empty room and sometimes not, as if uncertain how much to humor me. With closed-door drills, I had to learn to hang back, to stop doing the work and stop opening doors just as a given. When I frustrated Puzzle with our slowness, she began to make her cues bigger: a little scent there, A LOT OF SCENT HERE.

Today she has her nose to one door and stands expectant. It's clear which one she wants. Last door on the left at the end of the corridor. As I approach it, her wagging tail wags faster: *oh-yeah-oh-yeah-this-one-oh-yeah*. I decide to test her loyalty to that door, and at the last minute I put my hand to the latch of the door opposite, a *wrong* choice. Puzzle's tail stops wagging, and when I grind the latch slightly, I hear a little *pffft* snort out of her that could be a sneeze but sounds like disgust. She does not turn away. She sticks to the door she prefers.

I stop and turn to the door where she stands. "Is *this* the one you want, Puz?" I ask her. There is the briefest brow-furrow, an expression of incredulity at my indecision (like a doggie *Duh!* — I'm not kidding), then a harder wag when I put my hand to the right door latch. She is all encouragement. When I pop open the door, Puzzle gives her two-boing hop as she bounds across the threshold toward the victim for the find. And then she turns and beams at me, giving me so thorough an *atta-girl* that I laugh out loud.

It is a perfect moment of joyful understanding between us. From the depths of her total dogness, Puzzle is pleased, and she knows that I am pleased, and after I help the victim from the rubble, she spins and capers down the corridor, smudging herself liberally with soot.

And what of snakes? In the months after Puzzle's snake-proofing, I realize her experience with the snake in the woodpile was profound. Clearly Puzzle saw the snake before the strike to her face, and its shape, coil, and movement made an impression she remembers.

After the bite, she immediately became wary of coiled rope and occasionally jittery on walks when we passed someone pulling a garden hose through tall grass. Once, when strong wind catches a length of black rubber tubing and blows it into the street in front of us, Puzzle freezes and barks furiously. I maneuver her downwind of the object, where she wuffles her cheeks for the scent of snake, relaxing only when the scent isn't there.

And she is willing to generalize. On one training day at the fire academy, Puzzle and I cross a parking lot to get to the training area and approach a fat, hay-stuffed silt filter placed over an open gutter. Puzzle catches sight of the silt filter in her periphery, starts, then presses her body against my legs, refusing to move forward and refusing to let me move forward, either. Her eyes are dark and wide. She barks furiously where she stands. The silt filter is about four feet long and perhaps ten inches in diameter, and to her dog eyes I suppose it looks like the tubby mother of all snakes. Puzzle looks up at me where she has frozen, her expression dumbfounded, as if to say "Look at *that* mama-jama!" We are upwind, so we circumnavigate the object, and she works her nose downwind of it. A couple of good inhales and Puzzle seems a little sheepish when she recognizes her mistake. She immediately saunters over to the silt filter as if to hide her earlier alarm. There are times when Puzzle's face-saving maneuvers remind me of a cat.

I look back at the silt-filter episode with interest. When Puzzle had been afraid of Max in turnout gear months ago, she had hidden behind me. When the silt filter first appeared like a snake to her, she instead froze in *front* of me, unwilling for either of us to go forward. I appreciate that double caution. Is my dog becoming protective of me as she matures?

Though her sight response suggests what may have happened that night in the woodpile, I don't want Puzzle afraid of every snake-shaped object that we pass. There are too many hoses and ropes in our future. At the fire academy, I lead her past every coil of rope and hanging line, every type of fire hose in motion with the rookie firefighters. The acclimatization works. Puzzle gives these things an eyeball in passing, and that nose works rapidly both on approach and departure, but she no longer spooks as she once did. The garden hose at home she ultimately forgives. She no longer scuttles away, but she knits her brow every time I move it, as though she sure wishes I would smell it first.

Puzzle has other opinions she's happy to share. On a warm evening, she has stopped in the middle of a training search and has deliberately taken her long lead in her mouth, growling and tugging as though to pull it from my hand. We are searching for a single victim in a mixed sector — partly urban, bordered by scruffy, unimproved "wilderness" acreage — and after I've had to stop and untangle her lead from mesquite thorns three times, my dog is clearly telling me I'm slowing her down.

"She wants to work off-lead," I say to Deryl, who runs with me.

"So take her off," he replies, swatting at a mosquito.

It's a simple solution, but I hesitate. Tonight she's on-lead because we're training in an area we've never been to before. If Puzzle were to take it into her head to run, to let go of this training search and flee on some whim of her own, it would be almost impossible to find her. It's an uneasy moment, and one that plenty of other handlers have experienced before me. The 100 Percent Recall: the dog who always comes back when called. When do we trust a dog's emerging commitment? With a search dog it's got to be solid. It should be solid for Puzzle now.

It's not hard for me to remember the puppy that ignored my "Come" commands in our own backyard, but Puzzle has become more than that dog. In environments we know well, she commonly works off-lead. And her long wait beside me after my recent neighborhood fall demonstrated loyalty or obedience or a mixture of both. I know I should trust her now. But I dither. *I don't know this area,* I think. *Anything could be out there. And it's getting dark.* I make plenty of excuses not to trust her, not to take the chance.

While Puzzle stares at me with challenge, Deryl waves away the mosquitoes that have surrounded us in so thick a cloud I can hear them singing against my ears. We're getting chewed to bits while I deliberate and, worse, whoever the poor soul is out there hiding for us in the mesquite and poison ivy has been chewed even longer.

"Has she ever run away from you before?" Deryl asks.

"Not since she was a puppy. And never from a search."

Deryl is a military man of quick decision, but he says gently, "You've gotta let her go."

I take off the lead, and Puzzle doesn't have to be prompted. She's off with purpose — moving quickly while we run behind her. I'm better now at watching my dog and not falling into holes, but this terrain, with its universally high brush covering uneven ground and dried creek beds, is still a challenge. We crash and huff and stumble, chest-high in the scrub that Puzzle presses through. She moves without pausing, and though I only occasionally see an ear or the flip of her tail as she winds her way between the trees, the sound of her suggests she's on to scent. This is not the intermittent, tentative snap and crackle of a dog casually nosing around. I have begun to learn the sound of my working dog as well as the sight of her.

We are losing light. The deepest part of the brush has already gone gray, and as I cut myself free of brush, I realize that I've lost sight of Puzzle altogether. We stop, and in the distance to our right, I can hear my dog's rapid scrambling through the thicket, maybe thirty or forty yards away.

"She's got him," I say to Deryl. "Or at least she's got *someone*," I mutter. The team has had a few surprises in the wilderness, finding people who'd sought out private spaces and, surprised (and naked), were not prepared for the launch of a joyful search dog in their midst. Now we are veering right and pushing hard to make our way to the dog, and now we're in the strange nether of light between dusk and dark when flashlights don't help much, but the ambient light is too faint to distinguish low branches and braided vines covered in thorns. *I'll start falling any minute now,* I think, just as a branch flips my glasses off my face and over my head, where they land like a horseshoe around the upturned limb of a young tree.

"Do you hear her?" I ask, blundering forward again.

Deryl shakes his head. In the distance, probably from the direction of a housing community on the other side of this land, I can hear two dogs barking frantically, and I have to wonder if Puzzle has thrown off the search out of boredom or disgust with my slowness, and if she's now a football field or more away, pressed to some fence and taunting those dogs.

I'm about to call her name when I fall hard, landing face first in a thick clutch of poison ivy thrust upward from the base of a tree, twisting my pack off one shoulder and losing my glasses again.

"You all right?" asks Deryl.

I am not all right in any sense, I think to myself, feeling impotent, swallowing frustration — and worse, weak and nauseated after the fall. I am gathering my glasses, shredded gloves, and twisted backpack when I hear the snapping of branches just ahead and Puzzle moaning her victory *wroo,* a sound which unfailingly means she has found the victim and is proud of it. And because I was not right behind her, this time she has come back to get me and take me to him — a "re-find," we call it. Re-finds can be a trained technique, but Puzzle, never one to let her achievements go unnoticed, does not have to be prompted to go back. She pushes her cold nose to me and quivers a little.

"Where is he, Puz?" I ask, as her movements into the brush quicken. She crawls through some low spots and bounds over vines in others, and a few minutes later I hear her *wroo* again, see the light flash of her tail as she alerts on our patient volunteer, lying supine in a tangle of thicket.

"Good find! Good girl!" I shout to her, fumbling mangled treats from my pocket as Deryl helps the volunteer out of the brush and Puzzle bounces and preens. It was a good find. Direct, purposeful, independent, and — loyal. Loyal to the victim, loyal to the work, loyal to me. It was not enough to find the fellow once. In the absence of her handler, tonight Puzzle understood the job wasn't finished until she came back and showed him to me.

"See?" said Deryl. "She told you. And know what else she's telling you?"

"What?"

"She's telling you she's ready. And you better be too."

We are days away from the first of three certification tests — Wilderness, Urban/Disaster, and Clear Building — and now is when our strengths and weaknesses will show. In the plus column is certainly Puzzle's great enthusiasm for this work, our joint tolerance for discomfort, our experience together across all kinds of scenarios (now more than 250 training searches with the team or apart from it), and the fact that neither of us gives up easily. In the minus column is certainly that this dog is much faster than I am. We're not a slow team, but I can't help imagining Puzzle with a younger, stronger handler — an even match for her speed. I have seen her pause just so that I could catch up.

Puzzle, just a few months shy of two, is in that marvelous place where puppy energy and adult strength and coordination intersect. This is a happy time for her, and it shows. After training with the team or after training sessions at home, she is talkative and cheeky, full of dog mutters for me and play bows for the Poms, tossing toys their direction for a game. Her engagement with the world is a pleasure, her energy a challenge.

One afternoon, she finds a swatch of my discarded red SAR shirt, torn by thorns in the day's earlier training, and she runs outside with it to taunt the Poms: *I have this and you don't.* Dog Keep

Away is a very real game. Sprits'l is easily incensed and begins to chase her; Whisky's provoked to chase them both; two new little foster Poms get in on the action; and then Jack has to follow, his signature bark like a rooster's crow. The backyard is in an uproar, and when I go out to investigate, I find all the Poms chasing the Golden. They're galloping and barking and chasing her in great circles around the yard. They are amused to be furious, and Puzzle canters before them, tossing her head, the bit of red shirt waving from her mouth like a flag.

No video camera on hand. I sit down on the stoop and think, *Watch this and remember.*

I look at the Golden and feel the challenge of her. I was forty-four when Puzzle came to me, and I'm forty-six now. I keep reading that forty is the new thirty, and I don't want to acknowledge that a body slows down, but I've already noticed a change in my own stamina just in the time Puzzle's been by my side. *I should be getting stronger with all that running after her,* I think. But even the neighborhood walk with the forty-pound SAR pack has become tough sometimes. Other days after training, I'm so tired I go to bed with the six o'clock news. What is up with that?

I'm a healthy eater, get plenty of exercise, am not overweight. I scrutinize my diet with the help of a nutritionist. I take more yoga, more dance lessons, walk farther with and without the pack. I've never been a fan of elevators, but now I try to jog rather than walk up every set of stairs. This dog is ready to run, and I want to run this dog.

"Getting old," says my father about both of us when I tell him I've been tired lately. He is maybe joking, maybe not.

She's ready, Deryl said. *And you better be ready too.*

There are plenty of dog handlers who are older than I am, running young dogs and making very good work of it. I'm determined not to give in to this — even if I have to eat daily bowls of Wheaties in Geritol, or whatever the modern equivalent is.

20

THE WILDERNESS TEST

I MAY BE the one who pulled up a satellite image and the local weather data, studying them over coffee I couldn't taste, but Puzzle is the one who, on a bright March morning in 2006, looks far more prepared to run a certification test than I do. She strains impatiently at the end of her long lead as she waits at the edge of a nature preserve. She can already scent people on the trails. In a few minutes, we will be given a wilderness sector with zero to three victims and an hour and fifteen minutes to find them. The weeks just before Puzzle's Wilderness cert test, some days I felt ready, and other days completely vulnerable, like those dreams about exams you haven't studied for that you somehow end up taking anyway, stark naked.

Today I feel thoroughly prebriefed, which should inspire confidence. I know the area, the terrain, the weather conditions, and I know how my dog works. But I also know the wicked, thriving brush that fills the off-trail areas of the lowest parts of this preserve, which is built on a set of rolling hills. No examiner is going to give us a sector as easy to walk as a city park. And I'm betting my sector will include the low spaces. This is brush with teeth that in some areas grows as high as my chest. Not just uncomfortable. Not just impassable in some places. Scent muddles and meanders through it, and Puzzle and I must get through it too. There is my chief concern.

Puzzle will push her way through anything if it's physically possible to do so. She never seems to feel the thorns and slows only when a web of vines is thick enough to trap her. I'm not as quick to follow, though, and if there's a graceful way to get through this kind of terrain on two legs — even with a knife or small machete — I haven't yet mastered it. The brambles here can check me at every pass — snagging my boots, gaiters, pants, shirt, pack, hair, and hat to the extent that I have to cut myself free. It's the snagging and the cutting I'm not too sure about. (Maybe I *should* take this test naked.) I am concerned that Puzzle might find scent and push to it beyond my ability to follow. I'm now confident she would wait with her victim, vocalize his presence, or come back to return me to that place; what I don't know is how my slowness might eat up our total test time. There's every chance I could be the one to fail us, and I know it.

I've been warned by the examiners who set up the test. All victims are camouflaged. And all victims have been instructed not to make a sound in reward to Puzzle until I make contact and acknowledge finding them.

Matt will run FAS team for us and has been similarly told to do nothing more than define the odd-shaped edges of the sector and radio call the finds. He is ready to go too. He stands a little apart, and Puzzle wanders over to nuzzle him, wagging as he strokes her head. Puzzle loves Matt. He was her first volunteer victim and is one of her favorite field assistants now. Matt's in his twenties. Puzzle is not yet two. They look capable standing together, very much up to the task. I close my eyes and hope to channel a little of that.

In the presence of modern technologies, there are those who suggest that the canine wilderness search will become a thing of the past. Some canine teams already seem to feel the change. At a conference in Baltimore, I spoke with a woman who had once been on a search team that had primarily worked wilderness, a team that eventually folded because they no longer got calls. "Everyone has a cell phone these days," she said. "And a lot of people have GPS units," added another. Some care organizations serving Alzheimer's or dementia populations have expanded their own protection initiatives for patients — shifting from identifying patches on clothing to GPS locators that make it possible for caregivers to track a lost patient via satellite, even in the woods.

Yet lost children on camping trips and hikers who fail to come home are still a part of the news, as are the disoriented elderly, many of whom are found not far away from the care facility or the home they left, but are found hidden in the undeveloped land that surrounds it, having fallen or strayed into terrain they can't escape. Cell phone batteries die, and it may be a while before every individual in a kayak or out for a hike has a GPS locator around his neck. We train forward. In an urban area like the Dallas–Ft. Worth Metroplex, our wilderness searches are not confined to Boy Scouts who got separated on a field excursion. The chain-link fence behind a housing development may be all that separates civilization from an expanse of owned but unimproved land, rapidly changing a so-called urban search into a wilderness search that can stretch on for miles.

A potential suicide case we worked years ago centered on the deep brush surrounding a steep ravine and the creek that wound through it — all sandwiched in the middle of a fully developed city. Working across that area, we sometimes couldn't see teammates standing eight feet away — the brush was that thick. Yet there was evidence of human traffic and in the most remote corners, for those who knew the way, wild and sometimes beautiful spaces. A winding stream, untouched bird nests, yellow wildflowers peering over the edge of the ravine, a little waterfall. But if you stood still and the wind was blowing from the right direction, you could hear the distant sounds of organized life: traffic, certainly, and a girl shouting to a friend, "Don't be that way!" Someone with an open window calling his child to come in for the night.

And so we continue to train wilderness, knowing an hour from now we could be called to work a state park or the scruffy back forty behind a multimillion-dollar housing development. Easily half our searches result in some sectors that require compass navigation, GPS orientation, and an ability to watch your dog and where you're going at the same time.

The first two I've got. The last one, not so much.

A word from the test coordinators and we are off, heading eastward along a road to the most downwind point of the sector. With any luck, on the way out Puzzle will get a little scent against the wind and either find a victim outright or forecast hot search spots when we come the other way. The breeze, warm at the front and cool at the trailing taper of each gust, invigorates her. She trots out along the cedar trees that border the sector with her head up. She's not pulling on the lead, but I can feel her excited tension on the line. I always think of the poet Robert Herrick's phrase — "that brave vibration each way free" — when Puzzle quickens before a search.

At the edge of the sector, I give her a brisk rubdown to stimulate her circulation and rev her charge even more. I ask if she's ready to go. She is. Puzzle flips her head around with a grin, and I feel her shiver pleasurably beneath my palms. "Find!" I shout, releasing her from the lead, and off she dashes, nosing immediately into the brush to begin our series of wide sweeps perpendicular to the wind. She is quick as I thought she'd be, and in these early minutes I'm having a better time of following her than I had forecast. The woods here consist more of young trees than brush, and as Puzzle winds her way across the area, I see her stiffen, her head pop up, and she makes an abrupt change of direction, nosing through the wood without a sidestep, working a scent cone. In just a few minutes, she has found the first victim, Don, huddled against a tree beneath a camouflage jacket.

Six minutes.

"Good girl!" I praise her. Don laughs. Tight nerves and a mild cedar allergy make my voice a little warbly, and from a distance I can see Matt also grinning. I sound like a squeaky eighth-grader. Puzzle takes her treat and gives Don a second kiss, and when I call "Find more!" in the most masterful voice I can conjure, she heads back to her sweeps.

We make several difficult presses through the woods again, but I see no sign of scent from her until the fourth sweep, when she leaves the woods entirely and crosses to the path in the middle of our sector. I watch her make a little arc with her muzzle and her eyes narrow with thoughtful appreciation. It's like watching dog radar. By all the signs I know from Puzzle, this dog is about to lock in and run.

I push out of the woods after her and raise up a few feet from the clearing. But I raise up prematurely, just in time to be caught by the low branch of a tree — a right sharp smack to the forehead. "Ohhh —" says Matt, in the way crowds go "Ohhh" after a hard hit on the football field. His face is red. I think he's trying not to laugh. My hat has gone, but before I can retrieve it, Puzzle gathers herself for a leap into the opposite brush. I see her head come up, and she is off and running uphill before I'm clear of the woods she had left.

I ignore the hat, which I can come back for after the test, and run after Puzzle, desperately trying to follow her course through the woods. Puzzle chooses a path that bends to the east before it curves back southwest, and behind me I hear Matt call that we may be crossing out of the sector. I can't be sure, moving as fast as we are, but my dog is certainly onto something human. She scrambles upward along uneven stones, and at the top of a rise, she pauses, as though the scent she'd been certain of had suddenly disappeared. For dog and handler, it's a peculiar "what the —" sensation when a dog runs out of a scent cone. Like being in the middle of a deflating hot-air balloon — a moment of great *hoosh* and then, *now what?*

It's a critical point for the handler too, but I've learned that in the wilderness, Puzzle never seems to fret over the *now what*. She's good about working her way back to the last point of scent. Today, all jumped up in the hard light of the cert test, I'm as likely to misdirect her as to do anything useful for the search. So I just shut up and watch. Difficult to do. Hard not to hurry her. But I've pressed Puzzle in previous training, tried to do the job for her, and have seen the exasperated confusion that followed. Sometimes to be faster, you have to be absolutely still.

Puzzle stands quietly, turning her head slightly to the left and the right. I see her mouth open slightly and her nostrils work. She reminds me of a boy I once played Hide-and-seek with as a child. He was fast and intuitive about all the good places his playmates would hide, and at the moment he ran out of good leads, he'd stand perfectly still and wait for someone to betray themselves by sound. It always worked, and stillness will work for Puzzle too, with her nose lifted to catch the thinnest strand of human scent on the wind. One wayward little gust or one movement out of her victim will confirm it.

Her pause gives me a moment to recover, and behind where she stands, I peripherally try to determine if we are still in the sector or not. Difficult to tell with no map and only a set of directions to go by; the area looks different up here, some of the marking tape is obscured by brush, and I can no longer be sure of our boundaries. Matt, twenty yards away, is also considering, but we don't have long to deliberate. Puzzle suddenly twitches, and she's off again, taking her chosen path west-southwest to a low valley while Matt and I, on intercepting courses, meet behind her. At the base of a hill, she leaps suddenly upward, taking in air with merry, greedy gulps, as though she's wading through a bowl of scent soup. She ignores paths and scrambles through low brush to the top, where a young woman is hidden beneath a camouflage tarp. Puzzle alerts, beaming at the victim, at me, at the victim, at me as I make it to the top.

Twenty-two minutes.

Matt calls in the find, and we all return to the place where Puzzle had first bounded away from our sweeps. We'll begin the sweeps again, working our way through the last third of the sector systematically, looking for evidence from Puzzle that someone else is there. This last area is the tough one, however, a right bastard third of an acre, the stuff of my misgivings. In we go. Even Puzzle feels it. She struggles to work her way through the thicket, and from feet away I can see bloody streaks on her haunches and another on her ear where thorns have caught her. Our pace slows as moving forward becomes a matter of kneeling, crawling, and cutting in some spots.

I am on my hands and knees working my way around a tree when Puzzle's head pops upward again, and I hear her thrashing in the brush as she shoulders her way to the hottest point of scent, about fifteen yards away from me. She's got someone, and I can hear the foliage rustle with her wiggling happiness, the beginnings of her victory croon. I blunder forward and a branch snags my glasses and twists them half off my head with enough torque that the frame bends and one of the lenses pops out. The offending branch swings back to pop me in the eye.

The timer ticks forward.

We're down a hat and a pair of glasses, but ahead, Puzzle has found a third victim: Sara, heavily camouflaged and trying not to giggle as Puzzle wriggles around her in a sort of happy orbit. When the dog cannot easily get to Sara beneath the tarp, she woofs twice in frustration, turns to me, and woofs again.

Thirty-seven minutes. Matt attempts to radio in the find, but in this low spot, there seems to be no clear signal, and we get no response. He tries to call a teammate on a cell phone, again getting no response. I feel the passage of time, and though we are well inside the test window, we've got further brush to clear. On the third attempt, the teammate answers and promises to relay the message.

We've connected to the team at forty-two minutes, and though I know the test parameters suggested no more than three victims, I give Puzzle the "Find more" command anyway, just to make sure. This is more than the test for us. In this wood, it's quite possible someone else — a hiker, or a parent and child out for a walk — is in here. If they're in here, I want Puzzle to find them. I want to report that we found every human in our sector, whether a part of the test or not.

No, she indicates. No one else. She is very sure. She pushes through the last small section of the sector with her head up and her tail swaying lazily, aware she's done a good job and that it's over. When she catches the scent of our teammates in the parking lot, she dashes to them with great show, wagging and circling and *wroo*ing. And hobbling. She's got something in her paw, and when I arrive to debrief, she grins up at Johnny while I kneel beside her to examine it. There's a broken thorn stuck deep in the largest pad. *When did she pick that up?* I wonder. *She never showed me.* I clean the wound, marveling at the power of adrenaline. My own arms and hands are crisscrossed with bloody scratches that, at the time of the search, I didn't even feel, but this thorn is large. I certainly would have felt it.

"Good dog," says Johnny.

"Good search," says Fleta.

"Nice hair," says Johnny, and the rest look at one another and laugh.

Yes, I can see in a car's rearview mirror, the hair has gone every which way, some of it braided with tiny leaves, some of it sticking straight up. And the branch that cost me my glasses also left a cut on my forehead that looks like a second eyebrow. When I smile in the mirror (and I can't help smiling — we passed!) the cut shifts upward a little, giving me a slightly demonic look of surprise.

Puzzle puts her soft muzzle in my hand. She's drunk some water and blown a few bubbles in the bowl. There are droplets across her nose and forehead. Never a tidy drinker, she dribbles across my palm. She's good on the hurt paw, but she's cut across the face, and one ear's a little ragged. As I clean her wounds, Puzzle seems content. She lies beside me, both paws extended across my leg as I disinfect the cut on her face. I see her ears pivot; she's aware that other dogs are working other sectors. At the sound of distant "Find!" commands, she looks up at me with sudden question, and her shoulders quiver. *Let's go! Let's go! I could do another sector easy!* her demeanor suggests, but this is our cooldown period, and whether she needs it or not, I do. My legs are shaky with fatigue.

One cert test down and two to go. We sit together at the edge of a clearing and listen for the sounds of other searches borne by intermittent wind.

21

CLEAR BUILDING

FOR THE FIRST TIME in twenty years, I dream of tornadoes again. Tornadoes and running and uncertain spaces in the dark. One week not long after the Wilderness test, I have a storm dream every night, dreams vivid enough to wake me straight up — not frightened, but breathless and full of wonder — like Alice with the Red Queen, running *Faster! Faster!*

These aren't the helpless nightmares of childhood. In these dreams, I have choices — this room or that one, leave the car to hide in a gulley or run downstairs to huddle over my dog. And I'm not alone. Puzzle is always with me. I love that she is with me. Sometimes the whole pack of Poms is with us too, their little hedgehog shapes racing over dark fields. I'm amazed how fast we move together. And in the same direction (that *is* the stuff of dreams).

"Wow," says a friend who loves to talk dream symbols. "Tornadoes mean upheaval, destruction, fear of separation." She waves a teaspoon at me. "Your life must be in a whole lot of turmoil right now."

No more than usual, I think. But it's spring, and the civil defense sirens have already sounded a couple of times. And then there is this coming thing with the search dog. We're all about tornadoes these days. We've got the Clear Building test on us soon.

The Clear Building test simulates search in structures damaged by explosion, or tornado, or flood — structures that may become rapidly unstable. Some call it the Triage search, which thrusts the implications upfront: In very little time, a dog and handler must determine where victims are located in a building or if an at-risk structure is "clear," which would allow responders to turn their attention to other places where victims may be trapped. This is urgent, accurate canine searching against the clock. There's a special command to start the search and a special reward at the end of it.

Sister to the Clear Building search is perhaps an even harder one — where dog and handler must circle an unstable building and make the victim/no victim call from outside it. In the catastrophic conditions following disaster, this means the difference between a building being shored, stabilized, and entered by first responders, or not. There are so many variables for dog teams here: Where are the open spaces that allow scent to escape? From where to where does the air move within the building? After storm or before another one oncoming, which way does the wind blow, if it blows at all? And in the dark and in the wind, if my dog makes a slight signal that indicates faint scent from some remote, internal part of a building, will I be able to see it?

These are the searches that wake handlers in the middle of the night. These are the searches that reset priorities in the weeks before a cert test — when the drive to succeed on a test can eclipse the greater duty to the work. The idea that my dog's signals and my subsequent call may be a life-and-death decision for victims and the first responders who serve them is chilling. The trick is to attend this responsibility without stressing over it. It's easy to feel too much, to think too hard — which for me are first-cousin behaviors to second-guessing and failing to trust my dog.

Puzzle doesn't carry the weight of such knowledge with her, and she'll work most efficiently if she gets no uncertainty from me.

Handlers say that if she really enjoys this training now, she'll commit to the job in situations where it is no longer fun. So on the Clear Building scenario I've got to ramp the dog up, let her do her job, and pay attention to her signals while she's doing it. I've got to be upbeat. She's got to be fast, confident, brief, clear. And we both have to be absolutely in sync.

We've got this, I think, the first time we try the exercise. Even in the dark, I'm better at sidestepping debris than untangling thorns. And Puzzle loves live finds. She loves to run.

Puzzle has never been that interested in treat rewards, but the other handlers tell me that zapped weenies really keep dogs motivated on Clear Building exercises. I have a brand-new bag of cut-up microwaved chicken wieners as a special reward for doing this fast, hard job. They are greasy, wizened, disgusting. But I'm suddenly very popular with every search dog I pass.

We take our first Clear Building practice session on so beautiful a day it is hard to imagine disaster is even possible. Puzzle quivers with excitement near the building we are to search. Part of the building simulates an apartment complex. Part of it simulates a warehouse. Part of it simulates a high-rise. There are a lot of rooms here, a lot of corridors and closets. In many rooms — debris. We'll be running from bright light into dim. I cup my hands around the edges of my eyes to make my eyes adjust.

Though my head is full of midgies I can't quite ignore — little flustered thoughts about light, and time, and the pair of us failing to find victims, the specter of a real search where failure could mean a death sentence for someone else — Puzzle seems assured. I wish again for a thirty-second sync to the workings of her mind at the edge of all of this. Standing here with my head bowed against the light, I know only that she seems ready to enjoy her work. She likes the wind-up. She sparks like a firecracker at the moment of command.

The instructor gives me the signal. "Search and find!" I shout to Puzzle with a quick unclip of her lead. She flashes quickly into and through the nearest room, disregarding its tumble of furniture, jumping over an overturned couch that half blocks the door. While I hopscotch after her, and Rob follows as FAS team in trail, Puzzle dashes into the next room. She finds Melody crouched in a corner beneath a desk. Quick work. A good start.

"Good girl!" I cry (*oh, we've so got this*), and hand her the brand-new high-value treat to eat on the run. "Find more!"

Except she doesn't eat on the run. For the first time in her search training history, Puzzle sits, and takes the zapped weenie, and rolls it around in her mouth, and drops it on the ground, and sniffs it and takes it again, where she chews it blissfully, passing the half-inch morsel from one cheek to another with her mouth open slightly, as though to catch every nuance of its taste across her tongue. She has her head tilted back and her eyes closed in a little where-have-you-been-all-my-life? squint of pleasure. It takes her six times as long to eat the treat as it did to find the first victim. Forty-seven seconds. I clock the treat time and groan.

"Find more!" I cry as she thoughtfully licks her lips. She bobs her head and canters out of the room to another warehouse area where Johnny is hiding behind a door. Johnny inspires a huge alert in triplicate, a *Johnny-Johnny-Johnny* ecstasy. They briefly connect; he gives her a scritch; I fumble for a smaller chunk of mini-weenie, the size of my littlest fingernail. Puzzle takes it with a modest smile and to my dismay sits down to enjoy it as the timer continues to tick. It's a small bit of wiener that one of the Poms would have downed in a gulp, but not Puzzle. She makes a full meal of the experience, tilts her head from side to side, working it. At one point, she seems to push her lips forward a little, as though to send the weenie's delicious scent up into the sweetest part of her palate. *Oh baby!* She seems to smile up at me afterward — *is this what searching really fast tastes like? A hard run and then canapés afterward!*

Twenty-eight seconds on the second treat.

"Find more!" I call again, and Puzzle springs up cheerfully, dashing down the stairs and through a first room, then a second, pivoting from her nose and leaping over an air tank to find Teresa crouched behind a coil of fire hose. The room is dim, but I can see Puzzle working her way into the corner. I see the wave of her blond tail and her dark eyes shining up at me when Teresa is revealed. Puzzle glances to the treat bag and sits with a give-the-doggy-her-due expectation. This is the last room. I tear apart a tiny bit of cocktail weiner and give it to her. It's portion-sized for a Barbie doll, but Puzzle seems prepared to savor it, finishing with a little sigh of pleasure.

We exit the building, me stumbling squint-eyed into the bright, at five minutes, twelve seconds. An early run, not a terrible time, but almost half of it was devoted to chicken wieners.

"How'd she do?" asks Terry.

"Was she motivated?" asks Deryl.

"She did well," says Rob, while I fumble for words to describe the quick finds coupled with the snail's-pace consumption of weenie. With characteristic understatement, Rob looks down at my dog and says, "But I think maybe she needs a treat she can eat a little faster."

What would that be exactly? Having set a high standard with the chicken wieners, I've painted myself into a corner as far as treats are concerned. Puzzle has quickly learned that this, her fastest duty ever, comes with one heckuva reward. But weenies are slow eating. When we run the Clear Building exercise again, I try a variety of smaller, crispier treats that the other dogs seem to inhale in motion. Puzzle takes the not-wieners, shoots me a look, then dribbles them to the ground — as if to suggest I'm just having an off day in the treats department — before she dashes off.

Treat or no treat, at least she dashes off, I think. Our times are improving. We're coming very close to the required three minutes or under. As her skills solidify here, I want to keep her motivation high. In time, Puzzle may not need any treat at all during this kind of work, but for now, I want the new activity associated with very good things.

Zapped wieners seem to be the reward of choice. She loves best what she loved first, but they are killing our time. One day, I cut them up into Chiclet-size morsels — quick for her to eat, but difficult for me to get hold of in the bag, I realize, when she's speedy to a find and I reach for a reward, coming up with nothing more than wiener grease on my fingers.

Which is enough, apparently. I make a little abracadabra movement over her head; Puzzle gives my fingertips a quick lick and races off again with the "Find more!" command. At the end of the three-minute drill, we come out with all victims in 2:52. I cheer and praise and feed her three legitimate pinches of shredded wiener during her mad samba among bystanders. She is very proud and has added a popping smack of the lips to her whole *woo-dig-me* vocabulary.

Success at last! We've worked out the routine. She runs and finds full tilt, and I pound through the building after her, one hand with a flashlight, the other in a bag fondling weenies.

By the time we take the Clear Building certification test, the vague scent of grease on my fingers is enough to reward Puzzle for the moment. On the test drill, she gallops through both floors of the building, chivvying out a victim in a stairwell, another behind a door, one in a wooden maze, and another beneath a stack of sawhorses, then canters outside and down the stairs and sits to wait for me, her head high (two floors, eleven rooms and a stairwell, four victims, 2:43). I follow cautiously, squinting and winking and feeling for steps down in the bright morning light.

I talk with the evaluator. Without requiring a command, Puzzle sits at my feet. I can feel her quivering there, barely able to contain her great joy. She is a grown-up, polite girl, but I have forgotten to reward her for this search well done. As the evaluator and I agree that all victims were found within the timeframe, Puzzle begins to nudge the treat bag hanging from my waist. I hear another handler laugh.

Rob says, "I think you better reward your dog."

I look down and she looks up. *Ah-roo-wow-wow-wow,* Puzzle says, smacking her lips with such vigor her bottom scoots a few inches in its required sit. The message is clear: *Good search. Quick search. Some fun was had by dog.* She noses the treat bag again and eyes me speculatively, as if to say, *But you, my dear, could be a little faster.*

22

TRUST THE DOG

TWO THINGS I THINK I know about the debris pile at this moment: 1) there's human scent but no human here, and 2) there are also no snakes in the rubble, warm from the sun of this midmorning in May. In these opening minutes of the most downwind point of our Urban/Disaster certification test at a fire training academy, Puzzle has circled the debris pile and climbed onto it with the confidence of a dog that has issued her own all-clear about the snakes. She moves quickly, her mouth open and her tongue already out sideways against the day's rising heat. Her tail, always a barometer of what she's sensing, sways with the rhythm of her movement. I've finally learned to decode the sway of tail that marks Puzzle wandering off-command and the sway of the tail that says she's working, and she is working here.

Rubble work is a curriculum all its own: a safety risk with its unstable surfaces, angry, fissured edges and twists of rebar, and a scent challenge due to its fitful air currents. In warm weather, heavy debris may double as a happy habitat for snakes. A tornado or hurricane can change neighborhoods into miles of such rubble, and genuine disaster adds additional problems for the work — the presence of hazardous materials within the debris, the potential that a poorly coordinated search can be fatal to the living victims trapped there.

With their lower center of gravity and the virtue of four feet, search dogs negotiate rubble much more swiftly than we do. I've tried to learn from them the virtues of staying low, distributing my weight widely, and climb-crawling rather than trying to walk upright over it. I cannot follow Puzzle step-for-step across the rubble, and part of the necessary skill requires working apart from the dog, decoding her indications from a distance, and moving closer only when careful size-up allows us to do so.

The debris pile here represents years of donated cement from torn-up street department projects. In addition to the jagged concrete, there are lengths of old pipe and an upright series of unearthed water department vaults that once would have contained switching devices. Standing in the center of the pile, the vaults — resting on their sides — look like the world's tiniest apartment high-rise. You can crawl in the ground floor, climb up through a hole in the ceiling to the second floor, then climb up through another hole to the third floor and the "roof," perhaps fifteen feet high. Scent works oddly in this small space, rising or falling and, in strong winds from the east, swifting around inside the little structure like a canned tornado, then pushing out the top to drift down on another part of the pile, yards away. It can be a good place to hide a victim and watch the dogs work out the tough find.

We are fortunate to have access to the pile, a constant challenge with its always changing configuration. Though we are able to work it fairly often, it's not a space to take for granted. One misstep or careless move can easily result in the rescuer also becoming a victim, a risk shared by the dogs. Though none of us have been seriously hurt on training debris or actual disaster sites, the possibility exists. Search dogs have been severely injured doing rubble work, and search dogs have died from it.

Puzzle is on task. She seems to enjoy working rubble. But she has always seemed to me to be aware of her small size and the risks here. I wonder what she makes of debris beneath her paws, with its uneasiness and the vibration of air funneling through its open spaces. Puzzle crosses the pile methodically now, moving over the fractured cement in a series of calculated jumps and scrambles. She has found volunteer victims here before and seems ready to do so again, but a first diagonal pass across it, and then a second in the other direction, have resulted in no locally hot scent. Or so it seems to me, watching her. Though Puzzle is definitely engaged here, she shows me nothing in the low spaces along the edge of the pile. The breeze is variable. I can't be sure how well air is moving across the rubble, so I gesture her around the debris a second time just to make sure. I instantly feel a conscience twitch about the failure to trust my dog the minute I tell her to do it. She circles obediently counterclockwise around the pile but makes no quickening movement there.

Nothing in the debris pile itself, but in three places she has scrambled upward to the highest spot on the upwind side and bobbed her nose appreciatively away from the pile, her little anticipatory gesture I associate with the scatter of faint scent. She doesn't bring her head down toward the rubble, and unhindered by me (this time), she moves away from the debris pile with the easy, dismissive movement of a dog who is certainly willing to find a human but is convinced there is no human here. She was a good girl to circle again when I asked her, but now she switches away from it with a bit of a priss to her step: *The debris pile is clear. Got it?*

We work across the area in wide sweeps, passing railway cars, a partly demolished box truck, a row of wrecked cars. She has no interest in any of them, but on the second sweep, upwind of the debris pile we have cleared, her head pops strongly, and I release her from the sweep to let her run. She dashes across thirty yards of turf to find her first victim, Rob, hidden in a propane gas training tank. Puzzle is ecstatic when he snakes his hand out to pet her; she is all wiggling and crooning, taking her praise as due and her treat as a politeness. She smiles as she takes the jerky, then drops it on the ground. I look back to the debris pile, directly downwind of us, a fair distance away. Was it Rob whose scent she had at the top of the rubble? The wind is blowing the right direction, and because it was funneling through the open tank over him, I think it's likely. Puzzle's proud of her find, but she isn't telling.

We return to the place we had abandoned our sweeps back and forth across the sector, and this time, alongside a railway tanker, Puzzle stiffens, turns her head to the ladder tower and lifts her nose. Again the narrowing of the eyes and the change in her breathing. It is the same gesture I saw earlier on the debris pile: *scent-but-not-scent-here.* I watch her work and note the direction of her nose. She is uninterested in the tanker, rejecting anything nearby, and when we turn to sweep back the other way, she abandons the sweep to head for the base of the ladder tower, where she has to make a choice: go in the enclosed first floor or climb the stairs for the open floors above? Puzzle puts her nose to a crack beneath the door, huffs, and turns away at once for the stairs.

The day has begun to warm, and she's panting heavily. I give her a quick drink from her portable water bowl before she heads upstairs. Puz is a sloppy drinker. Water has settled in the deep pockets of her jowls, and moving more quickly than I, she dribbles on me the whole way up, a 7 percent solution of dog spit and cold water. I get an unexpected charge from this and laugh, trotting upward faster. This is the same ladder tower I rappelled so badly while my twelve-week-old puppy watched. Today it feels a very different place beside her. Puzzle rejects the second floor and the third, not hesitating on the stairs but climbing to the very top, where she finds Teresa crouched in the northeast corner of the roof. We are all excited — Teresa is a perfect second victim. She has honed a lovely high shriek of congratulation that would give any prideful dog a boost, a *good dog!* of such an octave she makes Puzzle facewhip herself with her tail, a puppy behavior I thought she had long left behind.

This is a cert test, so we're not taking Teresa's pulse or offering her water or asking her if she knows what day it is. But we are not totally cavalier, either; we help Teresa to her feet (I lift and Puzzle supervises) — and then we're off again. Back down the stairs. Another drink of water and a return to our strategic sweeps. Puzzle dashes across the next two passes, and I get the sense that she has caught the strategy of this sector and that she would prefer to set the rhythm of it — especially now that I've relaxed a little and have remembered to trust her a lot. Her canter away from me is bright. I get an impression of proud head and flashing blond tail all the way to the brushy fence line, where her passage flushes a dithery bird she does not follow. She meets me coming back the other way.

The next sweep includes a peculiar little structure known as the "maze," for firefighter confined-space training. It looks like a horizontal series of ventilation shafts hooked together or stacked on top of one another. Doors and hatches here and there, a little ladder for access to a door on a second level. Puzzle is interested in the maze. She huffs at one door and rejects it, choosing to trot down the length of the plywood structure to a second door, where she *oofs* and wags and grins in such a way I think it must be one of three family members in there — Matt, or Johnny, or Cindi. And it is. How did I know that? Puzzle belly-crawls into the shaft to give Cindi a wag and a cold nose, and in some first stray flash I recognize that though her alert signals are consistent, Puzzle greets individuals with hellos as specific as a human would greet differently a neighbor, a colleague, and a friend from childhood. Puzzle buries her nose deep in Cindi's outstretched hand, coming up with a smile, gulping slightly, as though she'd just taken a long drink of favorite human and oh, that was nice.

We return to our sweep across the area, which this time includes the burn building. There's been a recent burn here; the interior is black with soot that licks the walls upward, and the building's scent of smoke and ash is strong enough on this warm day that my eyes water. It must be even stronger to the dog, but Puzzle moves through the building without any apparent distress. She sniffs at one pile of sooty, soggy hay before clearing the building of any human scent. Quick work in that dark space, and if Puzzle hadn't had so much experience in the thick air of that building, I might wonder how easy it was for her to distinguish human scent among all the other overpowering smells associated with the earlier fire. Would I smell a single wildflower in a room full of Limburger cheese? But she and the other dogs have literally grown up searching here. With few exceptions, *no* in the burn building means *no*.

Puzzle exits the building wearing stripes across her haunches and a grubby, speckled tail. This may be the first bonus of the day for her. My blond dog loves being dirty. She flashes me a grin as we head next for the multistory high-rise. Puzzle's having a good time. She is undeniably fresh.

I resist the urge to stop, bend over, put my hands to my knees, and take a breather. I'm exhausted without really being tired. I feel strong enough to push a car off a pedestrian, but my neck is tight. As Puzzle bounds into the high-rise, I am really, really glad I skipped the coffee this morning. Caffeine on top of today's nervousness would not have been a good thing. Supercharged with *yi!yi!yi!*, I would have moved like a wind-up chicken on speed, skittering after Puzzle in the dark. Not the best mindset for paying attention.

I flip on my flashlight as Puz takes her bearings in a large warehouse room on the first floor. It is full of ladders, barrels, and red fire mattresses, and it has a couple of closets behind steel doors at the end. Even to me, it is an environment rich with scent. In warm weather, the mattresses smell much like the gymnastics mats of my elementary days, but heavier somehow, and sweatier. Air can move oddly here, a strong current through the middle of the room created by the doors at either end, the stairwell at the north entrance, and windows with heavy metal shutters, while air in the corners can settle motionless behind objects.

Puzzle picks her way confidently to the center of the great

space, stepping over the rungs of ladders lying flat on the floor. She turns her head slowly, her nose lifted. A moment later, she moves to one corner and shrugs out of it, no scent, then trots along a clear space of floor to the back door. There she twitches at the bottom of the door with some interest. It is locked, and before we leave the room, I motion her to check the other corners, the cracks underneath the closet doors. She does so, dismissing them to return to the back door leading out of the building. That return gives me pause. I think of her earlier behavior on the debris pile, scenting Rob in the tank yards and yards away, and in this room we could again be downwind of human scent outside.

We leave the room and circle the building. A few clouds have passed over the sun, and the wind has risen slightly. At the back of the high-rise, Puzzle canters to the flashover bin, and at the moment I'm thinking we may have a victim in the bin, a bent elderly man comes around the corner of it and almost collides with me, Puzzle beside him at his knees. I'm startled. He holds his hands up as though he were being robbed and mumbles something I cannot understand.

Puzzle has found him, but he's not one of our volunteer victims. And he is somehow here but not here. When he speaks to me, his eyes don't connect and his words are unclear. He raises and lowers his hands as if to submit to something or to avoid my dog, but in another way he doesn't seem to recognize she's there. He takes out a card that indicates he is a patient in a care facility and has communication disabilities. He extends the card for me to read.

I am about to direct him to Max when a security guard drives up and with a kind word gently moves the elderly man to her vehicle. Puzzle and I watch her drive him away. He gazes straight forward, anticipation in his posture, as though this change was in his plans. I get the sense he has been picked up in other places and moved to somewhere else before. The last I see of him is the flash of white card as he flips it through his fingers.

"Good dog," I say to Puzzle, who has never seen one of her victims chauffeured away on a golf cart. "Find more!" We return to the cert test and to the high-rise, where there are other rooms to clear.

Don is probably the happiest of our volunteer victims to be found. He's at the farthest end of our sector, and he's been hidden in one of the stuffiest rooms of the high-rise, buried in old uniforms for quite a while, long enough to have sweat a little and spread his scent wide over the tumbled clothing that surrounds him. He is as obvious to Puzzle as a fly vibrating the strands of a spider's web. She snuffles in and finds him; he pushes himself up out of the pile, blinks into the light, and gives Puzzle a pat of congratulations. We watch him walk back to the group waiting at the academy.

Four official victims and one unofficial one; we have another half of the high-rise to clear. Puzzle has dropped her bottom on the cool cement with an air of finality. I give her another drink of water from the collapsible bowl, and when I tell her it's time to go back to work, she rises affably, but I get the sense that she knows the air moving through this building far better than I do, and really, though there's a lot to be interested in — *did you note the scatter graph of pigeon droppings in the farthest room?* — there's nothing to be urgent about; there are no other humans here.

Puzzle wanders through a central room full of lumber. I have always liked this room's fresh wood smell, but its narrow space and strange currents can give dogs trouble. Today, Puzzle pauses intently in one corner and, in a response I have never seen from her, does not alert but begins to paw at something that's caught her attention. She exposes some kind of weighted vest. I bend down to inspect it by flashlight, noting a quarter-size smear of what appears to be dried blood at the back of the neckline, as though the vest had once chafed a raw spot on the person who had worn it. Curious. I can't smell the blood, but I can smell sweat and something like grease. Two scents to the hundreds it must have collected as firefighter after firefighter wore it. Now that Puzzle has inspected the vest and knows that I have seen it, she shows no further interest. *It isn't live,* she seems to suggest, *but it certainly has a lot of human on it.*

We move quickly through the rest of the ground-floor rooms and up the stairs, where Puzzle dashes through the overturned furniture of three apartment rooms and then into the topmost warehouse area. Several plywood structures give it winding air patterns and curious crawlspaces. Puzzle has searched this room occasionally before, and some exciting thing about it always makes her race. She does so here again, her nose low as she gallops its circumference and around again to me, her expression bright. *Great room, terrific space,* she seems to be saying, *and thanks so much, but nada.*

The high-rise is clear. We exit the building, do a quick sweep of the lumber pile and the flashover bin, and with another toss of her head, Puzzle exits the sector. She pauses and turns back to me in a gesture of easy partnership, and something in her ease overrides every nervous urge I have to double- or triple-check the closest spaces we have cleared. I already regret my are-you-sures of the earlier debris pile. Puzzle flops down in the grass and begins to roll. She's happy and absolute, wiggling her hieroglyph across the turf: Trust the dog. Trust the dog. Trust the dog.

Right, I say to myself. *Enough.* We head back to the classroom building, the team, and the three evaluators standing there, ready to make our report.

An hour later, Puzzle's about to have grilled chicken and a kid's cup of ice cream on the patio of a favorite restaurant, and I'm planning on a mimosa — light on the orange juice, double the champagne. We're at a favorite local café that allows dogs. The porch is generous, with heavy cast-iron tables covered by umbrellas; the atmosphere is upbeat. My dog recognizes the scent of the place a block before we get there, and when we turn the corner that leads to the front door, her pace quickens. She's wearing her orange work vest, and those already seated make little comments as she passes, remarking about her size (petite), her coloring (blond), her leash behavior (beautifully improved). Some people remark with open curiosity about her job. They've missed SEARCH AND RESCUE printed on the side of the vest, and I see them bend together a bit as they try to figure her out.

We stand at the door and wait for a table. Puz cranes her head and weaves back and forth a bit as the door opens and closes, either hoping for the beautiful scent of chicken or to catch sight of favorite waitpersons who spoil her. After a long day of search work, there's nothing she likes better than to lounge under a café table and receive a nice grilled chicken breast with rosemary, a to-go carton full of cool water, and the general praise and admiration of young women she's known since puppyhood, young women who smell splendidly of fajitas, melted cheese, and ice cream. This looks to be a very good day.

A young man we don't know seats us at the only available table. I sit, Puzzle quietly lies at my feet, and heads turn to consider her thoughtfully. On the other side of us, a couple is curious. They glance over and put their heads together, then glance over again, as if hesitant to ask something. Their adolescent son, I notice, is pointedly not looking at the dog. It's a strange combination. As Mom and Dad slowly inch their chairs toward Puzzle and occasionally flick an inquisitive glance at me, the boy in perfect counterpoint inches away.

Finally, the father speaks. He says, "We are wondering about your dog. Does it really say 'Search' on her vest?"

When I nod, the son makes another five-inch hitch to the other side of their table.

"What does she look for?" his mother asks.

"Bombs?" asks the father.

"We were thinking criminals, but she doesn't look mean enough."

"I wondered if she might be a drug dog," the father continues. The boy gives another scoot to the left.

When I shake my head and say no, explaining that Puzzle

searches for lost people, the teenager at the table looks up for the first time. I point to the other side of her vest, where the embroidery more clearly reads SEARCH AND RESCUE. The boy relaxes so visibly that I expect his parents to notice, but they are all about the dog at the moment.

"Glad it's not bombs," says the father. "I hate to think of a sweet dog like yours in that kind of danger."

"Drug dogs come to your school, don't they, Cody?" they turn to their son and ask. He shrugs and nods, squinting up at the sun now shining down on him, and he scoots his chair back the way it came, just a little enough to be in the shade.

His mother explains, "They smell the lockers and the cars in the parking lot once a month."

"It's amazing," says the father, "how much dogs pick up on things we humans would otherwise miss."

For a while we eat in silence, then a young man brings his toddler daughter up to ask for a greet and a pet. As the little girl reaches down and says, "Lula, Lula, Lula," her father explains that they lost their Golden a month before to cancer. Lula was an eight-year-old "red dawg," as breed fanciers sometimes call them, a darker field Golden, but the child clearly recognizes the characteristic expression, shape of the head, and plume tail. "Lula," she says. She lifts Puzzle's ear and begins to whisper into it, and Puzzle's occasional wariness with children melts in the presence of this small dark-haired girl, who sits beside her quietly and strokes her shoulder with a forefinger. Her father says little, though he smiles when I compliment his daughter on her gentleness with my dog. He bends down to them both, Puzzle's tail thumps, and I get a sense of the missing dog who would once have completed their circle. When they leave us, the young father's shoulders sag. His daughter may have done the asking, but he apparently needed the contact with Puzzle too.

We go home to lie together on a lounge chair in the backyard. I stroke my newly certified Golden, who wastes no time going belly-up beside me in the deep shade of pecan trees. Any celebration worth doing is, apparently, worth doing upside down, unconscious, teeth bared.

"Mission Ready" is the term we apply to dogs that have trained and passed all initial air-scent tests for living victims — Wilderness, Urban/Disaster, and Clear Building. Puzzle is now ready to deploy on any land search involving potential live finds. The tests have been rigorous, but they have simulated many of the most common search conditions. And like all good tests, they have taught us something as well. Puzzle and I can go forward with a thorough understanding of the hard strategy behind canine search and with a confidence in our working partnership. *What's next?* I wonder, glad to have Puzzle next to me, glad to be ready at last.

But I am thoughtful too. We can take nothing for granted. This decade's unprecedented disasters — the 9/11 attacks, a levee's failure, and the loss of a space shuttle — have already scribbled new rules in the margins of canine search procedure. And the *Columbia* disaster continues to raise debate over what dogs offer this kind of recovery and how they may be changed by it. The shuttle's disintegration at 207,000 feet and at eighteen times the speed of sound still instructs us about fire, compression, exposure, and altitude, about the catastrophic transformation of human scent on the wind.

23

COLUMBIA

A YEAR BEFORE Puzzle was born, the space shuttle *Columbia* fell over Texas on a sunny winter morning already giving way to what seemed like an early spring. I first knew of the disaster when suddenly all my dogs began to bark, jerking me from sleep. The dogs — including deaf Scuppy — erupted as suddenly as though someone had kicked down the door, and seconds later I heard a resonant boom, and then a second one, fainter. I had grown up next to air force bases, and the sound of a sonic boom was familiar to me, though it had been decades since I heard one, supersonic flight being banned over the United States in the late sixties.

Unsure if I had heard a sonic boom or a sequence of explosions, I opened the back door. The dogs rushed out to the yard and there joined all the other barking dogs in the neighborhood. I could identify individual dogs in the uproar: the Wirehaired Terrier across the street, the Border Collie two houses down, the pair of senior German Shepherds a block away. While my dogs raced across the fence line, yapping frantically over something I couldn't perceive, I stood in the sunshine — a beautiful day remarkably similar to September 11, 2001 — and looked up at the sky, wondering if I had heard the first moments of another terrorist attack.

The sounds had seemed to come from the south, the general direction of downtown Dallas, and if something were happening there, the civil defense sirens might go off soon, I thought, or surely police and fire vehicles from all over town would begin their screaming course toward the area. I listened for sirens and heard none. A mystery.

The sounds had been so clear to me. *Boom.* And fainter, *boom.*

I turned on a radio outside and a television inside, where two voices from separate stations quickly broke in on regular programming to release early information. Communication with shuttle *Columbia* lost, the news said — then twenty minutes of deliberation over what that phrase, "communication lost," might mean. On television, there was a tight, curious friction between the official statements and the faces of the people reading them. Though nothing was confirmed, no one on the air seemed doubtful. No one seemed hopeful, either. *Columbia* was gone long before a NASA press release confirmed it. Homeward bound, the aircraft was presumed destroyed across the skies just west, and south, and east of us, the trouble beginning as far away as the Texas Panhandle, they said, and ending in Louisiana.

I looked at my pager, as search team personnel were probably doing across the country, and wondered if we would be called. The immediate question for canine teams would involve not rescue but human recovery, if such was even possible after a high-altitude, high-speed catastrophe of this kind. Unlike the low-altitude loss of the shuttle *Challenger*, where the aircraft itself remained somewhat intact when it fell into the Atlantic Ocean, *Columbia*'s breakup and its outcomes were a matter of great question, debated by every aerodynamics expert that newscasters could get on camera as the day progressed.

When the search team met for training later that morning, we still didn't know. Word had it that some pieces of the shuttle were still airborne, some still coming down, and that the lightest debris might be falling for weeks. Hard to imagine, looking up into a blue and seamless sky. We'd learned that federal agencies would join forces to collaborate on the recovery of the aircraft itself, but in those early hours, we had no word about plans for crew recovery and whether dog teams would be needed at all. Guesswork at this point was useless. We set up the day's training scenarios, and the dogs of the team headed out in the field to work.

Late the next afternoon, the pager went off, signaling deployment, followed by a rush of e-mail and faxes. Authorities believed the *Columbia* recovery would be a long one, and our team would deploy in stages, three dogs and human counterparts leaving the first day, another three dog teams to leave five days later as canine units were rotated in and out for rehab periods. The unspoken message suggested this would be a hard search — grueling physically, difficult emotionally, perhaps tough psychologically. Six of us left Dallas the next day in a tandem of cars at midnight, already girding up for a human recovery we could not imagine. We would snake a course through small towns in the five-hour drive southeast to Lufkin, where we would join search teams from across the country convening in the same place.

It was a long drive to begin at midnight after most of us had worked all day. There was a lot of time to think. We made our way out of the Metroplex down a major freeway as far as we could take it, then onto narrow state roads, darkness increasing as civilization gave way to stretches of ranchland and wide plains of undeveloped scruff. Too long a city dweller, I noticed how the night sky changed colors as we drove, shifting gradually from a hazy dark gray to an immense and star-flecked black that stretched from horizon to horizon. I had seen this sky before from my airplane, and beneath it I again felt small, puttering down the two-lane in my red PT Cruiser, insignificant beneath a velvet and diamond drum skin. Normally that anonymity was a comfort, but tonight the size of the sky and the size of the job ahead combined in such a way that I drove with both hands gripped on the wheel.

We drove with our FRS radios on, checking up on one another as the drive wore on and two, then three in the morning approached. A mistake: I'd bought coffee at an all-night gas station on our way out of town — scorched, tarlike coffee that seemed strong enough to melt the thin Styrofoam cup that held it and made my stomach burn as though I were sipping sulfuric acid. The coffee had enough jolt to keep me wide-eyed through Kemp, Mabank, and Eustace, but by Athens I was stiff and achy in the driver's seat, and horribly tired.

Ninety minutes out of Lufkin, I was in trouble. I was so impossibly sleepy that I began to slap myself to stay awake, sharp little pops on the face, the way they do in movies. I thought of Jimmy Stewart in *The Spirit of St. Louis*, playing Lindbergh on his transatlantic flight, dozing off while the plane made a steady descent down to the water, but I couldn't think of it long. This was not a time for thinking about sleepy people in the small hours.

Time to pull over. I was about to key the mike to tell Max I'd have to stop when suddenly something hit the side of my car with the force of a softball, exploding across my half-opened window and, through it, into my face and hair. I jumped, the car swerved, and immediately teammates began calling on the radio. Though they had not seen the object that hit the car, they saw the swerve and feared I'd fallen asleep at the wheel.

No, I had not, and I was certainly awake now. No need to slap further.

Coffee. I could smell coffee, artificial creamer, and the pungent smell of something else. My face was sticky, and the heat of the car and the wind whip from the open window had already begun to dry my hair into crisp, sugary twigs. Someone had thrown a full cup of liquid out of a vehicle going the other way, and whether intentionally or not, they'd broadsided my car — and me — with it. Lufkin was still miles away, but the night was creeping on, and since we were called to an early morning briefing there, this was no real time to stop. I poured a little bottled water into my hand and patted the gunk off my face and eyelashes, figuring I could manage a better wash-up at the Civic Center once we were there.

The road seemed to grow darker before Lufkin's lights pricked the horizon. Now there were occasional objects in the shadows at the edge of my headlights, objects on the side of the road, objects in the grass alongside it. The shapes weren't immediately recognizable as curls of tires or sheared bumpers or the frame of a chair fallen off the back of a truck. One violent twist of metal extended up from the grass like a rabbit on its hind legs, shiny in some places and dull in others. We were moving quickly, and I didn't stop to stare, but I wondered if we were seeing shuttle debris that previous drivers had moved from the road.

Two of the dogs worked me over thoroughly when we arrived and, once out of the car, they got a downwind whiff. Both dogs were busy peeing and shaking off the long sleep, but they weren't too busy to stretch up for the sleeve of my jacket, and when I bent down to them, to examine my face. Intently curious about the odd-smelling Susannah, neither of them attempted to lick the residue off my arm. I wondered about that until Hunter's interest in my splashed jacket was so profound that two of my teammates suspected the coffee-bomber had also taken a pee in the cup. One of them peered at the driver's side of the PT Cruiser and noted the precision of the impact and the wide spray of fluid extending to the back of the car. Huge and goopy, like the bird-splat of a pterodactyl doing a victory roll. Might be good, my teammate said, to find a drive-through car wash sometime soon and get whatever that was off the paint.

The parking lot at the Civic Center was already full. We were early for the briefing, but the area was in motion — a starburst trajectory of uniformed figures walking out and back to vehicles and a number of people moving the other way toward the door. A ring of television trucks circled the action in as close a press to the building as could be managed, bristling with antennae and dishes tilting toward the sky. A passing police officer gestured us in the direction we needed, and we walked into the building caught by a line of cameras marking the new day in the recovery of *Columbia*.

The agencies in charge were still getting established in separate areas of the main auditorium. We gathered to wait at the edge of a corridor, watching food vendors and the Salvation Army arrive to set up emergency support. As we passed, kindly staff offered Happy Meals, hot coffee, doughnuts, and foil-covered plastic cups of orange juice. I had eaten a day's worth of food on the drive, suspecting it might be a long time before I ate again, so I was too full to eat anything. One older woman looked so worried when I declined that I took a cup of orange juice to drink on the ride to wherever.

More movement in and out of the auditorium, then whole groups were ushered out of the main hall and into the corridor. I could hear the tinny whine of a loudspeaker. There was a pointed closing of the doors. We waited there more than an hour, taking turns checking on the dogs in the trucks, who had wisely decided on another nap in the pinkish-gray light of morning. I leaned against a wall and closed my eyes. The corridor was cold and fatigue had stretched my tired nerves to the point that every sensation seemed to leave a bruise.

"You okay?" asked a teammate, who was also a nurse.

"Just figuring out a way to get around the tired," I answered.

She sipped a cup of coffee and said, "I'm trying to tell myself that I've actually *had* a good night's sleep and that what I feel now is just a hard time waking up."

It sounded like a good idea. "How's that working for you?" I asked, cracking an eye open.

"Oh," she laughed, "votes won't be in until noon."

But she looked better than I did, and she'd been up a lot longer. I looked across at the vendors, on standby as they waited for the auditorium briefing to end. They were primed to serve, gazing back at me from behind coffeepots and big bowls full of ice and juice and bottled water. Inspired by self-deception, I returned to the woman who'd fussed over me as tenderly as a grandmother and tried my colleague's line: "I'm having a hard time waking up." She poured me a cup of coffee the way, she said, her husband the trucker drank it: five plastic thimbles of cream and three sugars. I thought of my earlier car bomb, and I felt my teeth curl, but I had to admit this hot coffee milkshake smelled delicious. The lady pressed me to take an iced-chocolate doughnut, and I did not refuse her, returning to the group charged with enough sugar and caffeine to make an elephant tap dance.

The auditorium doors opened. An intense young woman arrived to brief us, or rather, to brief Max while we stood in earshot. She identified the chain of command — who we should report to and who, in turn, would report our information upward. She described the small town we would stage from, told us to make certain we took no cameras into the field, and confirmed the place we would return to sleep. We should leave immediately, she said, and expect to be in search sectors by 10:00 A.M. We were to watch out for the media, to refuse to respond to reporters, and to refer them to the designated NASA and FBI spokespersons. As she moved away, she stopped and turned back briefly to look at the group of us. "And," she said, her expression somber as she nodded to the row of media vans outside, "no jokes. No jokes about *anything* at all." It was a comment out of nowhere, relayed downward perhaps from incident management and designed to forestall gallows humor, that desperate levity that sometimes shows up on searches.

Easy to comply. We weren't laughing and didn't have a joke between us, but we left Lufkin duly cautioned. Dawn had given way to another mild day in late winter, and we drove to the place of deployment on a gray ribbon of road beneath a dome of blue sky.

Shadow's ticked coat threw sparks in the sunlight as she moved confidently, person to person, introducing herself and petitioning for treats. We were standing outside a small-town meeting hall with our dogs and our gear amid a number of other canine teams. From a distance, the crowd of people, backpacks, and dogs on this bright day might have suggested a happier gathering. It would have seemed a good day for a group hike or a geocache expedition. But here where we stood, the dogs alone were lively among us. They had all had naps. They were experienced enough to recognize their handlers' gear and their own. Perhaps they smelled the surge of human scent each time the door to the meeting hall opened and someone pushed definitively through, as though an announcement were about to be made.

Search management personnel braided their way through the crowd, accounting for us as resources and prioritizing locations on the map where we should be sent. Something about the process seemed a little slippery. We'd been on standby for hours. We'd given our team IDs, our names, our dogs' names to a sequence of persons who have come out with clipboards to crosscheck how many of us were able to deploy. So far, we'd seen no canine teams move from the command post into sectors, but long standbys can be the rule on major searches. One police officer from a Houston suburb said that he and his dog sat here in the grass all day the day before, on standby to work but never sent out. *At least,* he said, *I'm getting paid for this.* I couldn't tell if he was grinning or gritting his teeth. He looked at two brothers who had taken vacation days from work to assist the search. *How much vacation you got?* he drawled.

The officer's story circulated, causing the occasional mild exclamation and a number of squared shoulders, drooping heads.

Many of us removed our packs and arranged them in lumps that doubled as pillows; some of us stretched out on the rolling slope of pale grass to make up for lost sleep. The rest stood and watched the dogs as they idly wound back and forth at the ends of long leads. One young man seemed particularly nervous about the TV cameras trained on the group from a distance. He repeatedly shifted to the middle of the group, borrowed a dark jacket to cover his bright shirt, and turned his back to the parking area across the street. He had called in sick to work from three states away and was worried his boss might see him on national television. One of his teammates suggested a temporary hair dye, pointing to a supermarket just across the street. She was only half-joking; she said their team rarely had the luxury of employer support. The camera-shy young man would have a hard time avoiding attention. He was tall and his lovely German Shepherd bitch was a stunner, a showy girl with dark eyes and an intelligent expression. Ready to go and sensitive to every change, she occasionally barked with excitement, causing her handler to speak sternly to her in a low voice, afraid her exuberance would turn cameras their way.

"A Husky," said one woman to Jerry. She had a Border Collie at her feet, a bright boy so keen to get on with it he seemed to crackle where he stood. She looked down at Shadow, who amiably returned the gaze. "I would have thought they are too much a one-person dog for search work."

Jerry shook his head. "Well," he said, "she only works for one person, me, but there's no question she wants to do it."

Shadow grinned upward and mumbled something in Husky that could have been *You betcha*. Shadow, the dog of many consonants and vowels.

Jerry's leadership and Shadow's commitment had made them a strong team in the field. I had watched their accord a long while. Though I had not seen Shadow evolve from puppyhood, I'd seen the working outcome. Theirs was a unique partnership managed differently from the Lab or German Shepherd pairs. Definitive, unforced, amicable. Jerry knew how to tell her what he needed from her, and he knew how to reward her for doing so. The woman appeared unconvinced, but she admitted she'd never seen a dog like Shadow work. Jerry was equally undisturbed. There are all kinds of breed biases in canine search-and-rescue. He gets the Husky comment a lot.

A helicopter descended into a clearing half a football field away. Its rotor continued to *woop-woop-woop* at a low RPM after it landed, suggesting this was just a short stop. But it sounded to all of us like progress, and the rotor-wash excited the dogs too as it stirred the border of low brush at the periphery of the clearing and scattered scent every which way. They raised their noses and wuffled. Some huffed and some bobbed their heads; some knitted their nostrils rapidly together and apart. One older Retriever seemed to just close his eyes and savor, like an aging vintner of scent, his mouth slightly open and his jaw working as though the smells were rich enough to chew. I could imagine the dogs happily sorting today's squirrel and yesterday's rabbits and the passage of a coyote ten days before — and all our human scents — greasy, tired, car uphol-stery-and-fried-chicken us. A row of dog ears perked. Two men with notebooks and dark jackets ducked out of the helicopter and dashed purposefully across the grass to the command post, disap-pearing inside.

Afternoon had raised a breeze, and the clear blue sky above had begun to give way to mare's tail cirrus. The pilots among us looked up. Our good weather was about to change; tomorrow would not be fair. Someone inside the command post with access to a fore-cast must have heard the same, because minutes later, two men were rigging an antenna, and five others were raising a tent. The command post itself suddenly seemed to stir. We could hear the clatter of chairs and the occasional bump against a wall.

"Is this it?" asked the young man with his back to the cameras. "Do you think we're about to go?"

"Believe it when your feet hit the sector," said a woman as she shredded the top of a hamburger bun into neat chunks and dropped them in a clean poop bag. She was obviously experienced at this, and we watched her with a sort of fascination as she shred-ded each piece almost identically to the one before and after, neat little cumulus puffs of hamburger bun, as though she were about to make bread pudding and was worried about the presentation. Dog treats? A field snack, maybe? Pigeons back at the motel? We watched without asking why. At this point, we were easily — and groggily — engaged by anything at all.

Later that day in the tent put up against forecast bad weather, I continued to wait to be deployed, sitting by a man called JD from a sheriff's department several states away. He'd arrived the day be-fore and was already a little grumpy with frustration. Between us, we counted seven roll sheets we'd signed in an eight-hour day of standby, all brought by different people saying, "Don't leave. Don't go anywhere, but be ready to deploy. And sign this so we know who's here."

"Obsessive-compulsiveness?" mused JD about the seven roll sheets. "Or incompetence?"

"Evolving situation, change of leadership maybe," I said. I was as eager to go to work as any of us, but I wondered how someone plans a large-scale search even as they recognize they don't really know what's out there. And how do you know what's really out there when things are still falling? This was catastrophe beyond known poses. I could imagine all the issues of combustion, trajectory, physics, and mundane things like personnel safety and jurisdiction. Man, I was impatient to get out there and search too, but I felt a certain sympathy for search management, many of whom were red-eyed and gray with fatigue.

"Did you search yesterday?" I asked JD.

"Nope," he said. He and the earlier police officer compared notes. JD's weary Coonhound had melted into the grass, now consoled himself this second day by worrying a hotspot on his forepaw and farting.

"It was like this, then?"

"A-yup."

Not long after that exchange, we were fitfully, finally deployed — with warnings about the media, the locals, and our own behavior ("no jokes, no press . . . no goddamn cameras in the field"). We loaded up our packs into cars and trucks and headed out, ten vehicles of dogs and searchers, and twenty minutes later, as we reached the edge of the sector we were about to search, we met the lead vehicle coming the other way.

"Back to base!" the driver called. "We've been called back." The cords of the driver's neck were tight. He mouthed something else and spat, screeching away with a chain of us behind him. JD was quiet in the seat next to me. His face darkened to a purplish red. *Believe it,* the woman among us had said, *when your feet hit the sector.*

While her handler and I watched, a search dog inspected human effects found in an area of dense, unpopulated wood. "Will she find more of this?" the NASA representative asked her handler as the dog worked her nose across several items he had offered. Her handler nodded, and after a brief discussion about direction, we were off. The dog's head was up. A gray and shining creature, she moved on long, muscular legs toward the deepest part of the wood.

"The question is," I heard one man say to another, "will she find it fast?"

She seemed to. We moved quickly — handler, assistant, and two agency representatives — behind the dog as she penetrated the wood, and after a series of passes across the sector, stiffened and paused in a clutch of young trees.

"There's interest," said her handler quietly, watching.

A light breeze threaded fitfully through the wood, and the dark gray dog began moving more rapidly across the small area, perhaps fifteen by twenty feet. She worked methodically at the periphery, her nose to the air, the trees, and the ground — clearly trying to isolate where scent began and where it ended and to find a cone to follow to the scent's source.

"What is this?" asked an agency representative quietly. He was a dark-haired, youngish man with his hands thrust deep into the pockets of his jacket, intently watching the dog move. She was all concentration, her body taut with focus.

"She's got something," said her handler, "and she's trying to narrow it down so she can give me a location."

The dog's circling became more rapid, and as the wind rose a little, I heard her mutter with frustration. She pawed at the turf, passed her nose along the brush, as though the source of the scent was elusive.

I looked up into a young tree next to where I stood and thought I saw a bright red and blue fleck of something in its topmost branches. Putting my hands to its supple trunk, I shook the tree once, then harder. The flitch of fabric fell and with it, apparently, fell a riot of scent. The dog grew frantic, circling haphazardly, stumbling now and colliding with trees, her mouth open as she huffed and ferreted for a source.

"Jesus," said the other man with us, who had been silent all the way from the command post.

After a dizzying few minutes the dog returned to her handler, dropped down to sit beside him, and moaned. It was an exhausted, anxious sound, as if to say she'd tried to show him something, but the scent was too much everywhere here.

"What she's got?" asked the second man.

"She's got a whole lot of scent, but it's not — coming from one place," said her handler. He spoke with confidence in his interpretation. "I don't know if there's anything here large enough to recover."

We stood a moment, then without a word crouched carefully where we'd been standing. I rolled cautiously onto my knees, spidered my fingers apart, and leaned forward on them, scanning the turf. The dog did not move but lay among us, panting rapidly as we studied the ground by inches, looking for anything we might be able to identify. The breeze now was both friend and adversary. The gentler gusts turned over the smallest leaves, revealing areas we were reluctant to touch, but the moving air seemed to worry the search dog. She didn't rise again but lay where she had dropped, her head between her paws, her expression tight.

"Nothing," said the dark-haired man.

The dog's handler shook his head also. He couldn't see anything either.

"Just this," said the second man, and he pointed to the ragged scrap of red and blue fabric the size of a tarot card that had fallen onto a patch of raw ground. They studied it together. One took out a recovery bag as his colleague unfurled a length of crime-scene tape. From my knees, I marked the spot with the GPS, jotted the coordinates in my notebook as backup, then pushed up awkwardly to stand.

The handler moved and his dog rose to follow. Waiting for a signal that I too could step free of where I stood, I watched the pair leave the area. I could hear her handler's praise, but the young dog's head and tail were down. Was there too much scent for her?

Did she think she had somehow failed? Her confident demeanor was gone. She seemed to have withdrawn even from her partner, moving stiffly away from us as though she were old.

Columbia fell over towns, farms, and forests. The developing search began to reveal just how great an area was affected. In the days we worked there, we heard the circulated stories of miraculous misses and amazing recoveries. Hot chunks of metal that had barely missed school buildings or wedding parties, heat tiles flung across a pasture like cards from a bad hand of poker. The debris field was generous.

At the command post, someone wondered if we would recover more than the shuttle in the deep woods we were searching. This area had its meth labs and its body dumps, we'd been told. There could be anything — or anyone — out there. We were to report all human finds, but it could well be that some of them would be entirely unrelated to the loss of *Columbia*. Someone else commented that there were probably some mighty anxious criminals straining forward on their barstools, watching the evening news in a state of wince, unprepared for the presence of thousands of search personnel across the woods of East Texas and Louisiana.

Perhaps due to the careful choices made by search management, perhaps because shuttle fragments were so widespread, every sector I searched beside canine units recovered something of *Columbia*. Though the dogs were charged with crew recovery, human colleagues also took GPS readings and noted the fall of the shuttle's physical debris for written reports when we returned to base. Some pieces were recognizable — straps, switch panels, or fragments of studded circuit board the size of a stamp. One great upended object resting against a tree in deep wood was, we were told, a toilet. Dogs had apparently shown great interest there the previous day, tugged their handlers a fair distance to arrive at the spot. Their handlers debated whether it was the ammonia in its cleaning solution or the associated human scent that had caused the dogs to respond so strongly.

Though I can't speak for everyone associated with the recovery of *Columbia*, the teams I worked with — my own and others from across the country — approached the work soberly. We made no jokes, took no cameras into the field. Sometimes a NASA representative, often an astronaut, accompanied us into sectors. We flagged mechanical debris with strips of brightly colored construction tape. When the dogs indicated human scent, our response to the finds was respectful: we alerted search management and remained beside the find until an official and a NASA representative could complete the recovery. Unlike the knots of pink, green, and orange construction tape that marked shuttle debris, areas with finds of the crew or personal effects were marked with yellow crime-scene tape. As the search extended over days, it became possible to read the recovery on the long roads leading through forest to new sectors, the tails of colored tape revealing the end result of *Columbia*'s fall.

That first day in the shadows of late afternoon, the sunlight filtering through the trees to land on charred or shining debris seemed a kind of blessing. "God light," said one of the searchers a little wryly. He was a student cinematographer from Georgia, less faithful than visual perhaps. But I was glad of the sun; we needed light sometimes in the private spaces where debris had landed.

This was a region of hardship. On some farms, we sidestepped thin, hungry livestock. We slip-slid past empty chicken coops, into slaughtering pits with our notebooks and our GPS units, wading through old blood and skin and feathers to mark a single shard of motherboard thrusting upward from the sludge. We found corkscrews of metal and tiny actuators from the shuttle deep in the woods, scattered across makeshift tent cities suggesting profound human poverty.

On one farm where debris had peppered the top of an aged mobile home, we were met at the end of a long dirt drive by a little boy in a suit and bow tie, scrubbed pink to the hairline. Skittish of the search dog, he appeared close to tears, uneasy and babbling. He was reluctant to lead us back to the house. At first he confused us, until we pieced together his conversation and realized he knew nothing about the space shuttle. But someone in his family must have learned that federal government representatives were in the area, without knowing why. This boy was the youngest son of a family of a dozen children. His mother had sent him down the twisting drive to assure federal agents that all the boys and girls got food on the farm. They did their school at home. They had clothes and shoes, and there was no real need to take her children away.

Another homeowner met three of us in her driveway. She was dressed for work, a coat folded over her arm, fidgeting with her car keys as she explained she had to leave and her small farm was ours to search. She had been out already, had seen some new damage on her roof. She'd found a few computer parts, she said, and something she thought looked like upholstery. She knew for a fact that the things she had seen hadn't been there long. She'd be glad if we'd move all of it as soon as possible. She said it was like living in the middle of a train wreck — all these strangers and all this stuff everywhere. The knowledge that it was even there made her uncomfortable on her own land, and very sad. She balanced her purse on her shoulder to gesture how far her farm reached, pointing down a graduated slope that led to a creek that was sometimes there and sometimes not.

And then she turned back, remembering to warn us about her dogs: five dogs out on chains, where they lived at the corners of her land and nearest the pens for the animals. They were lean dogs and half-wild, and they were there to keep the wild hogs and coyotes away from her stock. She said the chains were secure enough, but not to get too close. These dogs weren't hunt partners. These dogs weren't pets. They weren't dog-friendly. They weren't human-friendly, not even to her, except for feeding time. They didn't really have names.

"How long are the chains?" asked the handler, a colleague from another team, his pretty Border Collie sitting at his side.

The woman thought a minute. She couldn't be sure. The chains had been there since her grandfather's day, forty years or more. *So go*, she said. *But don't take your dog off that leash. And good luck.* Her voice was tired.

When she left, the handler said grimly, "This will be interesting." With his dog in a tight heel, we entered the land through a gate not far from the house. The farm was not a large one, but the land was difficult to see to the fence line, choked with standing farm equipment and old cars, dipping down as it did toward the creek bed. We could see two pens of goats and beside them a pair of dogs chained not far away, instantly aggressive, barking angrily—a female and a young male, much alike in their postures and voices, straining to get to us. I saw the Border Collie stiffen beside her handler. With a quiet word, her partner said to let it go.

Two dogs known and three unseen. The handler gave his girl her command, and as we headed for the most downwind point of the sector, out of nowhere another dog leaped out of the brush as though conjured, a roaring, rust red creature that seemed to be on us before he was checked by his chain. He missed the Border Collie by only feet. She froze, ears down and tail tucked, trembled as her handler pulled her in.

"Let it go," he repeated, his voice shaking with the nearness of this. While the chained dog raged, it took a moment for us to assess his tie-down, mentally calculating arc and just how possible it would be for us to get to the farthest point of the sector. We stood still, and the rust red dog also quieted—growling low, watching us with cold eyes. I had no doubt that if he broke free, it would be short work for him to maul two humans and kill the search dog.

A long, considered moment. A breeze rose as we stood there, and something in it made both dogs turn the same direction. The Border Collie woofed a shy single note, and her handler looked to her, then at me. The red dog's gaze turned back our direction.

"All right," said the handler. "We'd better get in there. And we'd better hope that chain holds."

He gave a command to his partner and she stepped forward, still trembling slightly, her head up and eyes forward despite the angry drone of the other dog. Moving down the slope, I walked behind them with an eye to that chain. It's a fine line, working past aggressive dogs in the field, whether fenced, chained, or held in check by a human: don't engage, don't provoke, get on with the work, but don't underestimate the situation either. We were still uneasy when we moved down the rise out of sightline. The back of my neck prickled. Red dog's absence was somehow scarier than his presence.

We sidestepped what appeared to be slaughtering ground with an acrid stench of its own — dried blood, remnants of skin, and bristly hair. Rounding a truck and battered trailer, on the other side of the creek bed, we could see chunks of raw metal and scorched circuitry in the thick brush ahead, a swatch of fabric, entwined strands of wire caught on a roll of old fencing. The search dog sprang forward with intention: from some artifact or another, human scent, whether *Columbia*'s or not.

"Ah," said her handler, looking at the brush, the wide scatter of debris. "God." And then he said quietly, "We're going to be here awhile."

Fine weather in the early days of the search gave way to rain, then freezing rain and sleet by Wednesday of the first week, changing the complexion of the recovery. Now I was assigned to a different group of searchers — a collection of personnel from three separate teams. We were covering areas already searched by others, perhaps hundreds of others, and yet there were still finds, all of them small. Tomorrow there would likely be more. One official said it might take months for any sector to be clean, that every gust of wind brought more of *Columbia* down.

We'd been out in the freezing rain since early morning, and in some cases individual searchers stood over human remains for an hour or more, waiting for the process of official recovery to occur. An astronaut and a handful of dogs worked among us, as well as a gridline of young men from a military school who walked the uneven terrain at arm's length from one another, their eyes on the ground. Two of them passed near me as I stood waiting for the recovery team. "Ma'am," they said politely, without looking up. They parted slightly around the tree where I stood, then came together again, their heads bowed, taking careful steps.

I now stood over a fragment of vertebra, tilted upward among the stones and leaves. Knobbed edges and an internal fretwork gave it a tiny, bony alien face. I had nearly missed it earlier. We had entered the sector in ice pellets and sleet, and though the ground was still too warm for much accumulation, parts of the ground rapidly crusted with ice. Rocks had grown slick. Somehow in the press forward, negotiating the terrain with my head bent against the sting, scanning, scanning, I had walked past it. I don't know what provoked me to turn around, but in the different light behind me the bone stood in sharp relief against the dull brown of old leaves. I called out the find.

"Yes," said the officer running the sector, bending down to look at it. "Call it in. And stay here."

I made the required phone call used for human finds and stood there a long while, slapping my gloved hands together and occasionally wiping a glaze of ice from my glasses. Though there were perhaps sixty of us working across that wood — some moving, some standing as I was, waiting for recovery teams — tucked deep into our coats we seemed isolated from one another, so quiet amid the *tic-tic-tic* of falling ice that I could hear both the ragged crunch of the cadets as they moved down slope and the individual snuffles of the dogs as they passed yards away.

The dogs' heads worked low today. Perhaps time, sleet, and cold, heavy air had pressed scent down. I could see their noses crossing back and forth, lifting occasionally a few inches from the turf. One sniffed thoughtfully at the boots of a nearby cadet, then lifted his head to his handler and barked. There was little energy in it. To keep the dogs encouraged, last night we'd arranged live finds for many of them by stepping out of our hotel rooms and hiding volunteers there. This dog had been in that group, but now he showed none of last night's exuberance.

"*Barrow,*" I heard a Bloodhound cry about another find some-where else in the wood. "*Barrow.*"

I crouched in place, arms wrapped around my knees. The offi-cer running the sector returned to verify that I'd called in the find. He said, "*You* look a little green."

"Just cold," I answered, and that was the truth of it, after days of disturbing human finds.

"There's counseling back at the command post when you need it."

Did I need it? I couldn't be sure if the numb I felt was cold or some kind of event saturation that made me feel little at all. No more horror, no longer deep, abiding grief. I had seen enough of *Columbia* that the vertebra before me provoked only a weary sense of inevitability. I watched the dogs and handlers make their small, tight sweeps, the dark dogs subdued, their backs frosted with ice. The ground around us was rapidly going white. Kneeling there, I cupped my hands above the little bone as though I could warm it. I felt the freezing rain stitch both of us down tight to the earth.

Days later, outbound along the same road we'd come in on, I led several other cars full of personnel who were also cycling off the search as new responders were due to arrive. We would drive in train until our paths diverged. Two cars would head west. One, northeast. I would drive back to Dallas. The other drivers put me in the lead, saying my red car was the easiest to see in bad weather. As we drove, I occasionally glanced back and could see dog heads in silhouette, sticking up from the back seats of the cars behind me. After a time, I could see only drivers. The dogs were no longer there. They were all tired, surrendering to the long drive and the rhythm of the cars. This had been a hard week.

Some dog teams had left the day before. There were circulating stories that this dog or that one had been overcome by the work. Not one of them physically injured, but several of them affected by the search. "Too many days of too much scent, none of it good," ex-plained one handler, speaking of his dog now curled in his crate, a normally outgoing German Shepherd, an experienced recovery dog that had stopped eating the day before and had withdrawn from play and affection. Was this illness, stress, field exhaustion, or a canine form of compassion fatigue? The handler shrugged. He said that when a dog gives signals like these, you pay attention. His German Shepherd had had enough.

The true nature of canine grief — if this was grief — was a mystery to me. I had listened to experienced handlers at this search, and opinions were strongly divided. Some said dogs didn't share grief in human terms, but that critical incident stress was as real for them as it was for their human partners. It could overwhelm a dog in the field, or it might take a while to surface. They said that handlers and dogs would need to proceed cautiously across the coming weeks. Easy, motivating practice searches for the dogs. Lots of play. Upbeat rewards. Pushing too hard could create an aversion to the work and shut a dog down from search for good. Perhaps some humans too — though none of us talked about that before we packed the cars to go.

We left East Texas in heavy rain that gradually tapered to drizzle, then ceased altogether beneath fringed clouds giving way to blue sky. The road lightened. The woods on either side of us were quiet, the hundreds of searchers who had penetrated them now gone. For a while we could see the twitch of colored tape among the trees: pink, green, orange, and the occasional curl of crime-scene yellow. Less and less of it as we drove free of the area, none at all for a long stretch — then suddenly two trees wreathed in pink, something of the shuttle far apart from everything else. We all slowed. At the base of the trees, a hand-painted sign read GOD-SPEED, COLUMBIA. Someone in our group keyed his radio, then thought better of it and left the call unsaid.

24

NO BAD NEWS

I'LL LET YOU get dressed," the nurse says as she leaves the small examining room where I've lain for an hour or so, staring alternately at a diagram of the eye and a video on cholesterol. The door clicks shut, but for a moment I am unable to move. The room is meticulously impersonal, like a public bathroom, its furniture all hard, slick sides made for wiping down the more embarrassing truths about being human. Though there's probably good news now and again, they are prepared for tears here. There's a box of tissues on the counter and another on a small cabinet near the examining table. It is the kind of room that hears the kind of news that warrants seatbelts on the single chair for family members and a roller coaster's pull-down, lock-tight bar over the space where patients wait for the sudden drop.

I haven't cried. Having lost a good friend to cancer nine months ago, I easily see that my own prognosis, while not wonderful, doesn't throw the long shadow that Erin's did. But as I step into jeans that once fit and turn my T-shirt inside-in, my fingertips are curiously numb. The clothes slide on easily, but I feel no connect with them, as though I'm dressing a mannequin using robotic arms while looking the wrong way through a telescope. Buttons are tough. Zippers hard to grasp. I am still finding buttonholes to account for the mismatched alignment of my blouse when the doctor returns.

He is a tall man with wiry brown hair that doesn't settle neatly around his ears. Glasses worsen the problem, so that sometimes he has sticky-uppy tufts protruding over the earpieces. He is young enough to have been my son if I'd been particularly enterprising, or maybe my much younger brother, and some remaining vulnerability in him makes me want to smooth down those tufts, pat the front of his lab coat, and say, "There." His expression is kind, but it is clear he gives this kind of information often enough that the lines of his face quickly settle into a kind of bad-news barrier, and that he speaks from behind that necessary distance. He is there, but not there, with his frequent glances to my medical record. He is compassionate in the way one might be at the sight of a car accident a block away. And he is brisk with his list of recommendations and protocols, clear about what the future might hold in a year. He says, "There will probably be days when you're going to feel very bad."

He's right. That's already happened. Some days, it's hard to make my feet move. Other days, I feel too weak to stand. And then an unexpected reprieve: I'll go for a few months feeling completely normal, with all the energy I had in my twenties.

I've had a while to prepare for this. The condition has been a known possibility since I was a toddler — a birth defect combined with factors of heredity have made it a question mark during my adolescence and young married life, which had seen a number of related infections. In short, I have lousy kidneys. I'd grown up with kidney infections that occurred so frequently I could sense the earliest symptoms when they were coming on, but in adulthood I'd decided I would strong-arm the condition and ignore it to the best of my ability. Eat the right things, yes. Avoid the wrong things, absolutely. See a doctor regularly. But other than that, I refused to think about two organs that could become old-lady kidneys even while I was relatively young.

For the most part, such optimistic thinking has worked. I responded well to medical intervention and found it easy to follow the suggested diet. I continued to fly, worked a few weeks as a deckhand on a tall ship a couple of summers in a row. But a bad episode at age forty seemed to be significant. Was the condition stepping up? My treatment reconfigured and I adapted to it, and when I joined the search team in 2001, I did so firmly believing that I could work despite the illness, planning to stand myself down from searches during the bad periods and deploy during the good ones. I must have done something right. I chugged liters of water and followed the medical protocol. I never failed to show for a search due to illness. Puzzle's chaotic arrival in 2004 seems now to have been such a bright point of distraction that, looking back, I can remember few bad days during her puppyhood.

Now I leave the office with a sheaf of papers in hand, heading out of the tinted-window gloom of the building into a summer day that has relented, this one time, and traded heat for heavy cumulus clouds and a breeze with the sound of thunder at its back. Any cool in a Texas summer feels like a gift. I don't want to outdrive the coming rain, so I get in the car and wait. I watch drops slide down the windshield and quiver one upon another above the wipers, stacked like circus acrobats waiting for a fall.

The dogs have known something was wrong for some time. Just weeks after Puzzle's certification tests, Jack and Puzzle were the first to behave differently in my presence, the first to begin to hover when I moved through the house. On bad days, I come home too exhausted to turn on the lights for evening. I throw my jacket over a chair and fall into bed fully clothed, shoes thumping to the floor. Jack has taken to pulling the jacket off the chair and curling up on it next to the bed. Puzzle leaps up on the bed to lie beside me, pressing her forehead to my cheek. Whether the scent of my changed chemistry or the altered homecoming have provoked this, I don't know, but this is the first time I have seen Jack and Puzzle consistently act in common accord. They follow me every evening to my bedroom, and there they stay until I get up again. In recent weeks,

Sprits'l too has joined the entourage, following the others as they trail me through the house. Sprits mutters and circles worriedly on the floor when I lie down.

For several evenings after work, I retreat to the semigloom of my bedroom, drinking ginger tea and considering the future. The dogs like this. Their natural response at the end of hot days is to lie still. They join me in everything but the tea, the Golden lying long across the bed and the Poms stretched wide, bellies to the breeze of the fan. My thoughts are as much on them as they are on illness. The most immediate concern is strength, which I'm told will come and go. It's mostly gone these days, and it isn't difficult to realize that right here, right now, managing the house and the dogs will be difficult. And right now I'm certainly not strong enough to work Puzzle in the field. As my doctor wrangles treatment protocol, this might improve in coming months. Or not.

Lying beside me on the bed, belly-up, the Golden is oblivious to my private debate. Extended strategically beneath the air-conditioning vent, she has her forepaws bent like a praying mantis and her back legs inelegantly splayed. Her ears extend outward like wings, and her mouth is open; the seed-pearl bottom teeth show. Some of her snores must tickle, because as they come out she gives them a final, unconscious chew with those bottom teeth, which makes a little dipthong of the snore. Or perhaps the chew means she is dreaming of doughnuts, which she nibbles in much the same way. Even in the heat of these late summer evenings, Puzzle presses close. She's my dog now, by choice, and we both know it.

A firefighter friend and I used to talk about the "tap on the shoulder" — the moment when emergency responders make a choice to put themselves at risk on behalf of another. There are taps and there are *taps*, he said to me once. The first tap tells a person she wants to become a firefighter, or a police officer, or — and he elbowed me — run after some dog in the dark. Another tap tells him to go into a burning structure when every natural impulse says no. At its most extreme, the "Courage Meets Oh Geez" moment, he called it and laughed, not wanting to claim that he is some kind of saint.

Now it occurs to me that in this working partnership with Puzzle, I might be the one to fail, and that the tap on the shoulder might instead be saying step aside. *Oh geez,* I say aloud the way my friend does through his nose, but there's little courage in it. The dogs twitch awake at the sound of me, stretching and grinning with an optimistic eye to the kitchen. *Treats?* they seem to ask. *Did you just say "Treats"?*

I can lie in the dark with a teacup only so long. I remember Erin, who ten weeks before she died was at Home Depot buying mulch. In the heat of the "meanest summer ever," as she put it (and 2005 was a right scorcher), she put in new flower beds full of moss roses and vinca. Fierce gardening for anyone in that vindictive heat, and though I thought it was Erin's sort of karmic make-peace with fate and an unkind universe, she shook her head. No, she said, she liked the bright colors, but her mind was on her aging mother, who would have to sell the house after she died. Theirs was a neighborhood full of foreclosures; Erin wanted her house competitive. She would dig for hours in the garden, then be too weak to stand for several days.

After she died, her two little Poms came to live with me. They remind me of her often this year after we lost her, and for some contrary reason on a day I'm feeling pretty good, I go to Home Depot to wander the garden department. I tweak a vinca or two and pat several bags of mulch in honor of my friend, before wandering takes me outside to a row of prefab storage sheds in architectural postures. There are red barns and log-cabin look-alikes, and one with a wrought-iron star on it has a distinctly Texas prairie feel. Why am I looking here? I don't need a storage shed, but I walk the row of them, anyway, stopping at the final example. It's not a storage shed at all, but a child's cottage playhouse, complete with porch, shutters, dormers on the roof, and window boxes. Unfinished on the inside, the exterior is already primed taupe and crimson. A sign promises that the primer will take any paint color, and that the whole thing can be delivered and built in a half-day or less.

SURPRISE YOUR CHILD, a sign on the cottage reads.

Inside, the scent of raw plywood smells like possibility. I ignore the adult-size side door and choose, instead, to walk through the little Dutch-door entrance. It's not a tiny playhouse. Six adults could stand up and have cocktails in here, if they were feeling friendly. I bend down to look out the four-over-four cottage windows. When another woman opens the door to come inside, I feel a little silly kneeling there. But she enters with a grin and bends to peer out the other window.

"I always wanted a playhouse," she says.

Me too. At forty-six and childless and on the trailing edge of bad news, there's no reason for me to want one now, but I do. I pull loose a free-take-one flyer and make a crazy-lady circle of it next to my head. My companion laughs and asks, "Are you gonna do it?" When I walk out of the little house and across the parking lot for a cashier, I can still see her in there. She's shifted to the other window and gives me a little wave, one elbow on the sill as she looks out at the world.

I convince myself that I'm building a *dog* house — a luxe little space to share with my crew and any doggy visitors. Friends are not convinced. "Uh huh," says one of them. "And where are you gonna put the dolls?"

The cottage arrives on a flatbed truck two weeks later. Two young men spread its sections out across the backyard in a sequence they understand, but which to me looks as though the little house has been felled by a particularly organized tornado. While inside the house the Poms are going nuts against every available window, the two men assemble the house with almost no conversation between them. Cinderblock foundation, floor, walls, roof, dormers, porch, doors, window boxes. They pause only when I come out with canned soft drinks and cups of ice. One shows me a manufacturer's metal tag that's supposed to be screwed onto the roofline of the cottage. He doesn't speak much English, but he holds the sign up where it should go, looks at me, and shakes his head.

"Ugly," he says.

"Ugly," I agree.

He points to the cottage's serial number for warranty's sake, then slides the little sign under the right edge of the front porch. He taps his forehead and then mine, as if to say *remember*. I lift a soda can in tribute.

The dogs rush out of the house when the cottage is finished. They stream to the fence to bark away the last remaining scent of the two men that still hovers across the yard, and without breaking a stride, they rush to the cottage to examine it. Though the adult- and child-size doors are open, they first dash around it in a circle, examining it on the fly. It's their old game of chase with a new objective. Puzzle is in the joyful lead, Sprits'l is already acting a little territorial, and I get the sense that Puz is much less interested in the cottage than she is in its current ability to provoke a chase from the Poms. She wheels around and play bows to Sprits'l, who takes the gesture as a challenge and an insult and begins to chase her around the cottage in earnest — *stay-away-from-this-thing-that's-now-mine* — her canter leading his furious hop-chop-chop of a gallop. The other little dogs pick up on the energy and follow, yapping and nattering at her heels.

Around and around the cottage they go, never once dashing inside until Sprits'l ducks through the adult door after Puzzle blazes around a corner ahead of him. Smart boy. She doesn't realize he isn't back there still chasing her; the other Poms are slathering behind her and haven't missed their ringleader, either. When Puz circles around the cottage again, Sprits'l leaps out from the door with a yap that sounds very like *hiiii-ya!* They collide, spin briefly together like Elmer Fudd and the Tasmanian Devil, then fall apart panting, a cue for the other dogs to collapse on the grass and look dazedly at the cottage and one another. One by one, they recover themselves and totter into the little house to claim it.

Friends insist that the cottage needs to have a name. In the days before its delivery, I have considered a few pretty, artful titles, but nothing seems to fit until the dogs' chase makes the house their own. Charlotte, a Canadian, suggests *La Folie des Chiots* — the madness of the pups — which seems completely right. The house is my folly, in the English architectural sense, a structure built for no reason other than pleasure, but it is also — yes — a place to share with the dogs. There is much to do to complete the cottage and integrate it into the garden. It needs a complete paint job over the primer, its window boxes planted, and walls, a floor, perhaps furniture on the inside. I imagine a faux-tin ceiling and a small electric heater that mimics a wood-burning fireplace. There can be no question that I'm about to play house for a while. What I don't understand is why the project seems necessary and why, from the moment I buy the first cans of paint to bring home, the future seems a little brighter, if not entirely clear.

Field assistant Ellen has never wanted to work a search dog, and she doesn't want to work one now. Not even Puzzle, though she has long collaborated on her training. It's a hard moment when I ask if she'd be willing to learn to run my dog in the event I can no longer do so. And it takes a while for her to respond. For her, it's not a matter of disliking dogs. She has dogs of her own. For Ellen, it's the question of vulnerability. She has seen a dozen dog-and-handler relationships and she's seen the environments where they work. She has never wanted to become a handler, because the risk of loving and losing a dog is too great, and she doesn't know that she'd be able to bear that loss. And, she says, knowing she would be working *my* dog makes all those concerns even greater.

Trouble is, all the team handlers have dogs of their own, many of them in their prime and far from retirement. If Ellen doesn't want to handle Puzzle, and if I get too sick to partner my dog, I'll need to decide what's better for her: leaving to work with another handler on another team, or living quietly with me as a pet. Either option makes my stomach twist. Puzzle seems to love her job, and she seems to love me. I cannot retire her before she's been on a single search. On good days, I refuse to think I'm going to have to make a choice. On bad days, I make a note to call her breeder to discuss this. Somehow word spreads to other handlers in other states and to strangers. I get an e-mail from Mike in Vermont titled *I will take your dog.*

Kindly meant, I'm sure. But I think, *The hell you will.*

That e-mail is a snap-to message. There are alternatives I can make peace with, and alternatives I cannot.

I ask Ellen again. It's a little easier when I tell her that learning to run with my dog is a backup plan, a what-if safety net. I don't want to think that the past two years of hard training and testing have been for nothing. And I also want to be fair to Puzzle. When she isn't working, she seems to watch and wait for some sign from me that we're heading out — the pager, the gathering of the search gear, the words, "Are you ready to go to work?" She's a good girl, young and motivated. I don't think she'd be happy as a housedog yet. And there are larger issues here: quite apart from our history together is the truth that she's a dog able to make a contribution. The job is still there to be done, with or without me in the search field beside her.

These are all arguments that make sense to Ellen. One day after training, she gives Puzzle's ear a tug and says she'll give it a shot.

Puzzle seems to know where she is the minute she hops out of the Jeep, bounding across the parking lot to the greenbelt beside the road, happily nosing through the brush. This is the same hiking area where she certified for wilderness search months ago. It is warmer today, humid and airless. Nevertheless, the winding trails, hilly terrain, and thick brush seem to excite her in ways that urban landscapes do not, reminding me that Goldens have a love of the field in their genes and that the crashing and bounding required here must feel very right to Puzzle. She has her head up now, and her tail waves a wide, happy flag as she greets dog friends and human colleagues alike. Johnny and Cindi with Labs Buster and Belle, Rob and Belgian Malinois Valkyrei. Deryl and Max with German Shepherds Sadie and Mercy. Birgit and Pit Bull Ali. Terry and Border Collie Hoss. Jerry and elegant Husky Shadow.

On a good day with three sectors working here, every dog on the team can get in four to five searches during a three-hour training session. We will take turns as victims or as FAS team if necessary, rotating the dogs in and out across the area so that all canine units get a chance to work and everyone also gets a chance for water and rehab on this hot day. While the dogs stretch their legs and socialize, revving up for the work, each of us organizes the backs of our vehicles for ready access to training records, water, scent articles for the dogs working scent discrimination, and medical supplies both for dogs and humans. I toy with gear in the back of the Jeep longer than I really have to, tidying and re-tidying my first-aid kit and breaking up training treats for Puzzle.

I look up to see Ellen standing beside the Jeep. She's been there a while, watching. When I have no more excuses to keep rearranging my pack, I close the back door to the Jeep and tug Puzzle's long lead, calling her to me. She trots over easily, her smile deep and her tongue already out sideways. I take up her backpack of gear and move to a stretch of grass where we will wait together.

"Puzzle's number four to go out," Ellen says. "I'm going to go hide for Val, and then I'll come back and get . . ." She can't say it. She gestures to Puzzle. We both know what she means. While we settle in the grass, Ellen heads out to hide in a sector. We watch her disappear up the winding curve that marks the entrance to the second trail. Puzzle's head is up. She tilts it a little and moans when Ellen disappears from sight, looking at me in the way she does when one of her supposed pack leaves the group and goes off solo. Puz has seen the process for a couple of years now, but she shoots me a look every time, as though I were pretty sloppy about pack maintenance and in just a few bounding steps she could fix that.

We watch Deryl and Sadie head out for a sector off the first trail, while Johnny and Buster take their places, waiting for word to search, at the head of trail number three. Rob and Val are also ready to go. As soon as Ellen is hidden deep in the sector, they will be off. And running. Belgian Malinois Val never takes things at a lope that would be much more fun at a gallop.

Puzzle lies beside me, but her posture is alert, and each time she hears a handler give the "Find!" command, she starts a little where she lies, the product of hundreds of searches bound in muscle memory. As the third handler disappears, she sighs but does not relax. Though she cannot see the dogs and handlers work each search, she seems to be able to follow their progress through scent and sound. We are down slope and downwind from two of the sectors, and as I watch her, I wonder how much she makes of all of this that totally escapes me. I see her head turn as though she were watching, but the bob of her nose and the delicate working of her nostrils suggest that even here where we sit together she has a good idea where dogs, handlers, and victims already are.

Johnny and Buster return quickly, two victims in tow. Val makes short work of finding Ellen. They also return in less than ten minutes. Rob is laughing and Val's bright dash around him suggests hers was a tight, efficient search. Ellen and Rob confer a minute at the edge of the wood; he glances over to the place where I sit in the grass with Puzzle. Then he puts Val in her crate, and after a word to two other teammates, Rob disappears up the third trail.

As Ellen approaches, I push awkwardly up to stand, and when I stand, Puzzle also rises, shaking herself and giving a little whimpering strain at the lead as if to say she's ready to run. Without comment, Ellen takes the treat bag from my hand and clips it on to her belt. I hand her Puzzle's lead. In a low voice, she asks Puzzle if she'd like a drink. Puzzle puts her nose to the bowl and takes a casual lap, but she isn't thirsty and she's eager to head out, and she isn't confused about the change of leadership until Ellen gives her lead a tug and asks if she's ready to go to work. The phrase is a familiar one, and at the sound of it Puzzle responds with a shiver of anticipation, but as they step away from me, she turns and looks at me with a bewildered expression on her face. I can't be sure what I'm seeing from her, and I wonder if what I do see is merely a reflection of my own feelings: confusion, hurt, and a hint of betrayal.

Ellen gives another command and urges Puzzle away. I watch the dog's reluctance shift to subdued obedience, the tension of her walk away from me giving way to a loose-lead trot. As they move to the edge of the sector and wait for word to begin, Puzzle stands quietly beside Ellen, her focus already deep in the woods. This is the first time I've seen Puzzle begin a search from a distance, and I'm struck by how my girl has grown up, and how rapidly. She is a different dog just in the five months since her certification, as though the tests had given her a sense of purpose that training had only hinted at.

Ellen seems anxious. I watch her gather and ungather the long lead in her hands, bunching it against her stomach and then dropping it free. She checks her watch and pushes the hair back from her face. She encourages Puzzle, the usual rev-up words. Puzzle flicks an ear and stands, as though she knows something about the sector before Ellen has had word of it. When Max, who has hidden Rob as victim, comes down the trail and gives Ellen the word, they are ready to search. Ellen glances at me once, then quickly away. She clicks Puzzle off-lead. When she shouts "Find!" to Puzzle, the dog springs forward to meet the woods. For a moment, I can see her flash through the green. She bounds quickly up the trail. She does not look back.

There are good days and there are bad days. On the good days, I train with Puzzle as I always have — a little slower, perhaps, and bathed in sweat and nausea, while she bounds ahead of me, alight. On the bad days, I stay out of sight while Puzzle runs with Ellen. Sometimes I wait in cars parked outside the buildings where we train, watching for the flick of my blond Golden Retriever running past a window, Ellen and FAS team assistant in trail. Sometimes I see her. Once, from a parking lot and through the glass of two windows, I witness the moment when Puzzle orients from faint scent to the location of her hidden victim. I watch her pivot on that upturned nose, a 90-degree change of direction so sudden that her back end spins out a little, the way it did in her puppy days, before she scrambles out of sight and into the room she has chosen.

"How's it going?" I ask Ellen of their work together, and she says, "Fine," but adds after a pause that Puzzle is different — she's doing the job, but completes the training searches without her usual joy. Refusing treats for the most part, shrugging away from praise.

"Not even *weenies?*" I ask, thinking this dog can surely be bought.

"Not even weenies," Ellen answers.

Returning from one training scenario, Puzzle spots me sitting half a football field away. She abandons Ellen and ignores nearby teammates and dashes across the turf, exuberant with success, colliding with me, wiggling the way she did as a puppy. *I-was-wonderful-you-are-wonderful-I-was-wonderful.*

"She'll do it for me," says Ellen, who has caught up with her, breathless, "but she wants to search with you."

Birgit is always acute about dog-human relationships. She says, "Susannah, you better get strong."

During the months while my strength boxes the compass, Puz and I train at every opportunity, large or small. Friends and teammates are generous. Some hide for us in the park a couple of blocks away; a few come over and hide in the house, the yard, the garage, or in cars for Puzzle: currency training that doesn't require as much stamina from me. On Labor Day weekend, one neighbor brings his own son and two little nieces, giving Puzzle the opportunity to find three giggling children wedged in small spaces. One friend gives me four pairs of old shoes for scent discrimination training, so that I can scent Puzzle on a single shoe and ask her to find its match amid the other ones. Having the Golden fetish for shoes in general, this is a game Puzzle enjoys. She puts her nose deep in the chosen shoe and huffs her bliss, then scrambles around the yard to find its mate.

"Oh," I cry out when she makes an accurate find, shrieking in a nasty, guttural voice that Puzzle has always loved, "she's FABU-LOUS." Puzzle tosses her head at that and begins to race through the yard, galloping a figure-eight around the cottage and the fire pit that I've come to call her "Folie 500." "FABULOUS," I shout again, throwing up my hands, and she races a little faster. Around and around again, until she stops, flopping down on the slate path and bobbing her head up to me with the *yo-babe!* expression I've come to associate with her own pride. "Good job. You're fabulous," I say, but softer, stroking her ears while she grins up like *I so am.*

On a particularly awful pair of bad days, I lie on the couch and fiddle with paint swatches and decide to paint *La Folie* candy-box colors — a bright green called "Picnic," and for the trim a butter yellow, a periwinkle blue, and a pearly white called "Marshmallow." Gerand once said that the right colors together inspire energy, and maybe I've stumbled onto a clutch of good ones, because one late-summer morning, I feel strong enough to lug the paint cans out into the yard, prizing them open and stirring the paint with fat sticks. That's my goal for the day: just to open the cans and stir the paint with fat sticks. But the paint smells fresh and good, and the row of bright cans is cheerful. And I think there are brushes in the garage, and what would it hurt to get a little of the base coat up?

This is a day I should feel lousy. Certainly my neighbors do, creeping like suspects from their cars into the artificial cool of their houses, where the central air has droned since June. I don't blame them. Even beneath the deep shade of pecan trees, the heat is palpable, roaring up from the street beside the house. There's a row of grackles on the lowest power lines, their mouths open wide in an attempt to cool.

Against all better wisdom, I let the dogs out in the yard, where they circle and yap the grackles and are immediately curious about the paint, putting their noses to the open cans and coming away with their dark whiskers tipped green and yellow. While I get pans and brushes and drop cloths, the Poms assume supervisory poses on the slate sidewalk, frog-legged to press their bellies against cool stone. Puzzle prefers to saunter into the garage and out of it beside me.

The day progresses, the heat rises, and by midafternoon, two-thirds of the cottage is green and all of the comfort-loving Poms are back inside the house, worshipping the central air, draped like roadkill across the tile beneath the ceiling fan. Puzzle alone has remained with me. She lies inside the cottage and watches me paint through the open doorway, panting lightly, her smile wide in easy camaraderie. When I head for the garage, she follows. When I take a break from the painting, she shares my water, then offers me a ball to toss or simply lies against my feet. We study the hummingbirds as they hover along the Turk's Cap, sometimes inches away from both of us.

At the end of the day, we both seem pleased. It's 102 degrees, and Puzzle and I look a little goofy as we stand admiring *La Folie* with our mouths open against the heat. I'm liberally smeared with green. Puzzle has somehow avoided the green, but in the process of inspecting the paint for the doors, she's acquired a spot of periwinkle on her muzzle, another smudge on her haunch, and the waving feathers of her tail are so liberally streaked blue on one side that when she wags, she appears to be waving a Go Team pennant.

"Whoa," says trainer Susan about the cottage later that afternoon. "You got a lot painted for a sick girl. Actually . . ." she amends, "you got a lot painted for a *well* girl." She looks down at my periwinkle-smeared Golden. "Puzzle in her blue period?"

She is. And across the coming weeks, she's in her yellow period. Her white period. And, at last, her green period, when I give a few sections of the cottage a second coat. Whatever the weather of the day and whatever my own strength directs, Puzzle seems deeply content beside me. Indoors or out. I look down at her and find it hard to remember the puppy that, two years ago, turned away from me with a shrug.

But it is not hard to remember the search dog. One afternoon the pager pips, and green-speckled Puzzle springs up to stand eagerly at the door while I scramble for the cell phone. It is a call to search, but it's a drowning call, an advanced water search that Puzzle has not yet certified to work. I am able to deploy. For a few anticipatory minutes, she seems sure she's heading out too, and it is as though the world is back in the greased grooves she remembers, but when I head for the door without her vest and long lead, her face falls. I am heading out to work, she is ready to go to work, *and I'm not taking her.* She huffs to the back of the couch muttering, clearly aware there's something very wrong with this system.

This summer was initially quiet with regard to search call-outs, and then in late July we began to get a series of drowning calls leading into August. Summer 2006 is a season of hard drought. The lakes are low, and our area is critically short of water, but for recreational enthusiasts it is also dangerous. Since only one Texas lake is natural and the rest are reservoirs, boats are now sitting just over the remnants of trees or other rubble that make up parts of manmade lake beds. When swimmers jump from the boats, they come to grief in the trees that once would have been fifteen to twenty feet below the surface.

This September call is a search for a middle-aged missing man who'd gone boating with his mother on a late Friday evening in the moonlight. At one point, he stood up in his boat and turned to speak to her, took a misstep, and pitched over the side of the boat and into the water. She threw him a life preserver, but she said he never reached for it. Down he went in a sort of tangle, a thrash and down out of sight, and he never came up again.

Fifteen hours later, we are out on the boats with the dogs. We've been briefed on the accident's history by the local sheriff's department, and the story of a drowning off a boat with two life preservers in it makes me grit my teeth a little with frustration. Every drowning we've had in the last three years has been someone off a boat with a life preserver in it, but no life preserver on the victim. You want to headbang a little after weeks of lost daughters, fathers, fiancés, and best friends.

At one point, after I've been out on a boat assisting another handler and his dog, I am walking back to the command post and stop to wipe my face next to a woman eating half a sub sandwich and gazing out to the water. I initially think she is one of the Red Cross volunteers, but she introduces herself and is, rather, the mother of the man who had drowned.

She says, "I'm so sorry you've had to give up a Saturday." She says she's always loved boats and water, and that this outing the evening before had been inspired by good intention: an evening with her boy after she'd had a serious illness. Neither could swim.

She speaks of a double mastectomy and a chemotherapy follow-up in May, and says her son had taken her out the night before because it was the first time she was well enough to go. The pressure of the life preserver was too painful for her to wear on her chest, so she did not, and because she couldn't, he chose not to wear his also. She is slight and pale beneath a large hat, her eyes shadowed with fatigue. But she is out in the heat, will stay out here until he's found. Her tired voice is laced with tenderness and respect as she speaks of her son — he was just trying to do something nice for her at the end of a very bad time. He said, "You need to have a little summer," and he took her out on the boat. It was a beautiful evening. The water was calm. The way he fell over the side, she says, makes her think he'd had a heart attack or something acute and unexpected. She wonders what he'd been about to say before he fell.

We stand for a time together, watching the other search boats go out, back and forth across the area, the dogs' noses up, then down to the water. From where we stand, a hundred yards away, their alerts are absolutely clear, and I wonder what it is like to be her, watching us debride that wound. She says that when she was diagnosed with cancer earlier in the year, a friend told her, *There is no bad news, only information.* She says she grew up with a dad who raised Labs. Now, when a dog on the boat tenses over the edge, his bark ringing across the water, she doesn't ask me what it means. She offers me half her turkey sandwich, and though I am a vegetarian, I take it. We sit in the grass and make our separate sense of what will happen next.

Summer's sullen heat gives way to the cooler temperatures of late autumn. By October, *La Folie* is painted and its window boxes planted, and most days its doors are thrown open wide for the dogs to enter and exit at will, while I sit inside reading *Cadaver Dog Handbook*. There are dog beds and a water bowl inside it, a white tin of dog biscuits on a little table just inside the front door. The tin has a lid that snaps tight over its contents for freshness, but one day I walk past one of *La Folie*'s open windows and see Puzzle sitting before the table, staring earnestly upward at the tin while Fo'c'sle Jack stands on his back legs and fantasizes about height and opposable thumbs. When I call the two dogs, they come out of the cottage, Puzzle immediately and Jack more sluggishly. He glances back and forth to the tin as though weighing the hazards of disobedience or the advantages of begging. He's a good boy, but only just, and I grin watching Jack's internal debate: "You . . . the treats . . . you . . . the treats . . . (sigh) . . . well, all right . . . you." With the Golden, there's no longer any doubt.

I feel stronger in the cool air — more up than down — able to work more training sessions with Puzzle, who at two and a half is physically changing also. I'm seeing the early shape of the mature dog. She is taller and sturdier. Her winter coat has begun to come in, a thatch of waves across her chest, her haunches deeply feathered and tail feathers thickened. On wilderness workdays, we're getting close to the 2:1 ratio Fleta used to joke about: for every hour searching, the handler of a long-coated dog spends two hours combing out the search.

Apart from training, we walk together daily. I try to be careful. Short walks some days. Longer on others. I have a tendency to push myself hard, and it rarely works out well. We add blocks and increase speed incrementally. On bad days, which sometimes still happen, we back everything down several notches. Puzzle, who two years before was determined to set the pace of every walk (*faster! faster!*) from a lead taut as a ski rope, now looks to me to set the standard. She's still showy and prideful. She is pleased to be out and about. But if I need to stop, we stop. If I want to jog a little, we jog. A little. As the holidays approach, I put on her red and white velvet jingle-bell collar, and Puzzle walks beside or ahead of me, depending on the command, the steady *jing-jing-jing* of her lope causing the neighbors to wave and lean over the fence to admire her. They shake their heads and smile, remembering the puppy that bucked and snorted and shot me the paw.

On a cool, foggy morning just after Thanksgiving, I decide to try the pace test required of all team members for Senior certification with the team: a circuit around the training academy campus that must be done with a forty-five-pound pack in fifteen minutes or under. I did the circuit successfully in January 2004 and again in summer 2005, but have not attempted it this year, and certainly not since I've been sick, when stamina newly emerged as an issue.

Puzzle stands next to me as I lean into the Jeep and rebalance the pack's contents. Something is up, and she knows it. I'm going to take her with me on the circuit, interested in what kind of time we'll make together. The sight of the pack excites her, and I briefly wonder if she'll be too wound up to keep pace beside me. It'll be a test for us both — and maybe an affirmation that things are looking up.

I give a nod to the timekeeper, say "With me" to Puzzle, and we head onto the track. We begin the circuit with a walk that slowly escalates to a jog and from there, halfway through it, to a run for a fifth of the distance. I haven't felt like running, haven't run at all in six months, and my feet seem awkward thumping over the track in thick-soled boots. The pack is heavy too, and maybe one strap's not quite right — there's a slight *galumph-galumph* against my left shoulder with every step. But the balance is good.

And this feels good and strong. For a little while.

Puzzle canters off-lead beside me, and I'm so intent on not falling and not failing at this that for a long period I'm aware only of the muffled sound of her tags jingling in the fog. But the track widens a little, and I catch better sight of her beside me, this former Dog Who Would Not Heel, her light coat curly in the thick air, up-down-up-down ears punctuating every step. A neighboring dog rushes the fence as we pass. From another direction, a car door slams and two voices raise from some disembodied distance. I hear the clink of metal and the word "alternator," but Puzzle ignores it all.

As the path curves down to a low point, I huff and wobble, nursing a stitch. The fog thickens, and the air through my open mouth feels thick enough to chew. We are passing a row of fire trucks now, and ambulances, and I'm thinking wryly of collapsing behind one of them when we make a last corner to the home stretch. Puzzle looks up at me, all snort and dance and challenge. She's still fresh, and I'm somewhere in the nether between dazed and brain-dead, but we are going on just this little last way.

The sun is moving high over us, and here in the thickest part of the fog, Puzzle is spectral in the filtered light. She is my dog but filtered somehow and unfamiliar, rendered in aquatint. We push for the end of the circuit and, at the end of it, flop down together. Now she is real again. I can smell her damp coat and her warm dog breath, and as the timekeeper calls "13:08," I hear the *thump-thump-thump* of Puzzle scratching a sweet spot behind her ear.

"13:08," I say to Puzzle, who I'm sure has no clue why that's a good thing. But she rolls over onto her back and wiggles across the damp grass and exposes her belly, and from where we lie, she tilts her head to my shoulder and looks at me, grinning. It's not the hardest push we've ever done, but it's a hint of what we were.

Good job, she seems to say of us. *Fabulous.*

25

JIMMY

IN THE HARD GLARE of headlights from a police car two houses away, Puzzle puts her nose to a single sock in a plastic bag on the ground, working thoughtfully over it a moment, then looking up for her release command.

"Ohhhh —" says a bystander from across the street. "Look at that."

All the dogs glow when they are backlit, and blond Puzzle shines silver in the light. Huffing frostily in the cold air, she looks like the dog angel one sees on condolence cards that come from the vet, but she's flexing her right paw a little, a characteristic gesture associated with scent and unease. Puzzle likes her space. She's a little uncertain about the ring of officers that leaned forward as she put her nose to the bag, watching her with fixed intensity. This is her *let's-go-let's-go* signal to me. She will flex that paw until I send her out to search. When a nearby officer drops a cup and coffee explodes across the cement, she quivers and shoots me a *can-we-get-on-with-it* look, and I do.

"Find *that*," I say to her. *That* is the scent she has taken from the article in the bag. Without hesitation (and with some suggestion of relief), she makes her immediate choice of direction: east not west. She lopes, then canters easily down the residential street away from the police cars and the crowd. I follow behind her; a young officer and Jerry working FAS team walk behind me. Puzzle is easy to see in the darkness. She moves confidently, her plume tail flicking across the beam of our flashlights.

This is her first official search, and she's running with me. Her job is clear: *find him if he's in this sector or communicate absolutely that he's not — and because this search is scent-specific, ignore any other human scent you find.* My job is to make sense of all she communicates.

We have seen photographs of the missing man. We can perhaps overtake and identify him if Puzzle and the other dogs isolate the direction he's walked tonight. Jimmy is a senior citizen of diminished capabilities, who hears well but cannot speak. He is described as friendly, outgoing, and childlike in his attraction to bright lights and sweets. The photo we have of him seems to verify the description. He has a long, narrow face and a thinning swath of hair combed neatly back over the top of his head. His face is ducked slightly as he looks into the camera, as though he isn't sure whether to trust the camera, the photographer, or both. In sync with his posture is a fixed, wide smile that reminds me of the grin of a shy dog about to roll over in submission.

Caregiver interviews describe a man who has had difficulties negotiating the everyday world from childhood, and his expression in the photograph suggests a long history of misunderstanding, coupled with a desperate, inextinguishable hope. He's a tractable man with those who know him, but he's got gumption too — an adventurous fellow with an eye to the main chance. Last night in warmer weather, he slipped out of his assisted-living residence and walked northwest a few hours before he was found by police officers, who took him to McDonald's for a milk shake before driving him home. Tonight he has walked away again after spying the unlocked front door to his house, perhaps bent on repeating the adventure of the night before.

Tonight, however, he has walked out in striped pajama bottoms and nothing else, and though the weather was warm earlier in the evening, a cold front has pushed through the area, dropping temperatures by thirty degrees with the promise of subfreezing temperatures by morning. His caregivers and local police searched for hours after he disappeared, and when Jimmy did not turn up at his previous haunts, the dog team was called.

The three of us move quickly behind Puzzle. We are bundled in winter jackets and hats against a bitter wind from the north. A few clouds scud across stars in the night sky, but rain is not in the forecast — a positive note. Jimmy is already at risk for hypothermia in his half-clothed state; falling precipitation would increase his risk, and quickly too. He has been out four and a half hours, and unless he's found shelter, he's been in the cold for two of those.

There are other potential harms. An approachable man like Jimmy is an easy target. Though his neighborhood is a quiet one, gang activity has been reported at its fringes. I saw the painted tags on Dumpsters and telephone poles driving in. Tonight much of Jimmy's safety depends on the direction of his travel and whether those whose paths he crossed were kind.

Still heading east, Puzzle elects to enter the driveway of an apartment complex. She sniffs thoughtfully at the curb, then lopes into the complex parking lot and turns left along the long row of cars beneath carports. Though it is late, there are a half-dozen residents in the lot — some getting into and out of cars, two talking with their heads bowed and their arms crossed, as though their subject is mutually uncomfortable. We pass a woman wearing scrubs and a sweater tied around her waist, carrying a sleepy child toward the door of an apartment. She has her boy on one arm and her purse slung over the other. She pauses at the sight of the search dog and the officer, but she doesn't stop to ask questions. Puzzle ignores her as she sweeps past and ignores every other person in the lot. *Good girl,* I think. *She's working a specific find, not a general one.*

At the fifth apartment, Puzzle turns back the way she came. Though something provoked her interest here, she's dismissed the area now, trotting out the driveway and eastward again. At the intersection of the street we are on and a busy road bordering our sector, we turn south. There's a moment's pause. Puzzle pulls briefly eastward again, perhaps interested in crossing the major road that forms the edge of our sector. It is a light tug from her rather than a hard, urgent pull, as though she has a little scent she'd like to eliminate, but the busy road separates one city from another here. The officer with us confirms it: to cross the road would be to pass out of the local jurisdiction and into a separate city requiring permission for us to search. After the slight tug of interest, Puzzle heads south again, then obediently turns west at the next intersection as we continue to sweep the streets for some indication that Jimmy has passed this way or that Jimmy is here.

A hundred places to hide in any one block of this street, and none of them warm. It could take a team of humans hours to visually search the same night sector a dog can clear in an hour. Puzzle works calmly, either unaware of her great responsibility or unafraid of it.

The houses are mostly dark. Here and there, a lamp for a walkway, but not too many of those. These are long, flat neo-Colonials or ranch houses built in the eighties, it appears — brick and siding, vinyl-clad windows and painted shutters that were never meant to shut. Mature trees throw long shadows across doorways; the streetlight that filters through their branches turns the pale winter grass a silvery blue.

There are vehicles parked on both sides of the street, I zigzag Puzzle back and forth as we pass along them. A single unlocked car or truck might be enough to shelter Jimmy, and from his caregivers' description, I think he might be enterprising enough to climb into an unfamiliar vehicle. I wonder also about him huddling in the darkened doorways of houses, but Jimmy's scent would be quickly apparent to Puzzle even if we couldn't see him.

Puzzle has no interest in any of the cars. She puts her nose to the edges of doors and beneath each one itself, but it's a trained check, not one provoked by the scent she remembers from Jimmy's sock twenty minutes ago. Behind us, the police officer flicks his flashlight into each car as we approach it, briefly revealing their interiors white-bright in sequence, as though each were caught by the flash of an intruder's camera. We see knobby seatback massagers, cardboard pine trees hanging from rearview mirrors, a stack of textbooks, and a mound of fast-food bags in a passenger seat. In one car, an adult magazine lies on the dashboard. Trotting ahead as the officer works behind us, Puzzle has already cleared the cars, and the officer also dismisses every vehicle on this street in turn.

We move briefly south at a cross street, then turn into an alley to work our way back east. Here are private spaces and a great deal more light than we found on the street. Whether fearing break-ins or not yet down for the night, the residents on either side of the alley have their garage lights on. We walk more slowly here as Puzzle threads her way behind each house. Some have motion-sensitive security lights; our passage causes a *click-click-click* and a sudden blaze to warn us away.

The cold front has thoroughly arrived; the wind is fitful and irregular around the fences and the boats, campers, and spare vehicles parked on driveways. No uninterrupted scent cones here. I try to frame this environment as Puzzle experiences it: I imagine human scent swifting between houses, slamming into the sides of campers, and parting there to wind around each side or slip underneath. I watch Puzzle raise her nose and circle slightly, maneuvering the odd spaces as she ferrets this human scent and that one — new, older, and oldest — dismissing all of them as irrelevant.

"What's she got?" asks the officer, watching the movement of her nose. He has never seen a dog work before.

"Looks like a lot of human scent. All of it old at this point. And none of it Jimmy."

Though the area is more brightly lit, the houses here seem more vulnerable from the alley. Not just vulnerable to theft, naked in the display of owners' private lives: the rusted car up on blocks over dark spots of old grease beside the speedboat carefully cocooned in its tarp. An open garage door reveals an aging Honda motorcycle next to an empty playpen and a set of four upside-down wooden chairs in various stages of sand and stain. Would any of these spaces appeal to Jimmy? Puzzle poises, nods in the direction of them all, but turns away. Behind one house, she bobs her head but also turns away from an elderly man in a bathrobe who sits in the lit doorway of a pop-up trailer, smoking a cigarette. His legs and feet are bare. He sits easily, as though he cannot feel the cold.

"Evening," he says to the officer.

"Sir," the officer responds. "Any chance you've seen a man about this tall" — he gestures — "wearing blue and white pajama pants?"

The man shakes his head and thumbs the filter of his cigarette. Ash falls, sparks bright on the cement, and slides away in the breeze.

We move on. Puzzle sets the pace, a quick trot in some places and a thoughtful walk in others, but I do not see the canter or the low stir of wuff-wuffling excitement I've come to recognize from her when desired scent is close on the wind. She is not difficult to follow on this urban search, and her light color makes her easy to read in the shadows. Jimmy isn't in this alley, and from what I can make of Puzzle's signals, he hasn't been here tonight.

From some dark place against a house, a pair of dogs rush a fence she passes, barking furiously, startling us all. Puzzle shudders and is about to spring away when she recognizes there's a barrier between them. She stands still, her tail waving faintly and her ears pushed forward, ready to pass them, but wary. Two mixed-breeds, both bigger than she is, one white, the other blotchy with liver-colored spots and a mouth so wide it would have a great grin if the dog weren't so busy savaging Puzzle through the fence three feet away.

Whether they are pissed at her for her proximity or pissed at her because she's with three unfamiliar humans in the night, I have no idea, but they are glad to make noise about it. The spotted dog is the shorter one, and he leaps up at the fence in a sort of competitive besting of the other, landing on the bigger dog's back a couple of times before the white dog shudders him free, no offense taken. We can hear the *ting-ting* of their nails catching on chain link.

This looks like a ritual. There's a raw spot in the dirt where they've done it before. The dogs are territorial and maybe a little jealous of her freedom of the alley. Certain now about the fence that separates them from her, Puzzle turns away pointedly, like a snub.

We pass out of the alley at the easternmost point, turning southward again. Puzzle seems more interested in this side of the sector, something I noticed before and, on the next sweep, will notice again. It is no more than slight interest, though, a small, subtle intensifying of body and quickening of step, but that's it. The more westward we move, the less interested she is in the sector. She has remained true to the designated scent. When a man gets out of a car upwind of us on a fourth street, Puzzle lifts her head in acknowledgment but doesn't quicken her pace. His is human scent, sure, but it is not the scent we want.

At the southernmost end of the sector, we find a bridge over a small creek bordered by a ravine and an elementary school. The school is surrounded by a wide, fenced yard with a playground, bare of trees, the turf immaculate. There is a long curl of black hose lying at the edge of a student garden. Puzzle steps over it without a hitch in her step.

Jimmy, like most victims, does not fall neatly into a lost-person classification, which means he also does not precisely fit one of the many lost-person behavior categories suggested by research. He does not have Alzheimer's or another diagnosed dementia. He is a senior citizen, but on the hardy end of that spectrum. He can hear, but he cannot speak. He isn't manic; he isn't depressed. He's not despondent or aggressive or angry. One of his caregivers suggests he is like a curious five-year-old with a toddler's emotional maturity in the body of a sixty-eight-year-old man.

Lost-person theory suggests that a majority of people, when wandering without a specific goal in mind, will turn right when they first set out to walk. Right-turnedness is linked to right-handedness, and right-handed Jimmy had, in fact, turned right when he headed out the night before. When he disappeared tonight, caregivers and officers searched the area he'd explored on Saturday, but he was not in those locations, nor had he been seen there again. The dogs confirmed this. Every dog scenting Jimmy's sock headed left — east — not right and westerly tonight.

Where Alzheimer's patients will follow travel aids like sidewalks or paths until they run out, or "go until they get stuck," Jimmy is less likely to have done so. His feet are bare, and he may well have chosen what surface to walk simply by what was most comfortable underfoot, but his processing capabilities are sound enough that when a sidewalk ran out, he could have easily crossed a street to find another.

Some walk aways, whether influenced by Alzheimer's or other dementias, will walk with a memory-driven goal in mind. They walk to pick up now-grown children from school; they head for a bus that would have taken them to work in another city forty years before. Jimmy is likely more aware of chronology than this. If he has a goal in mind, it may be similar to the goal a child would have — a high-value attraction frequently passed by car — a playground, creek, restaurant, video arcade, or store. Or something else he has seen and stored and wants badly to connect with that searchers might not recognize: a piñata hanging from the limb of a tree. A friendly cat with a bell sitting on a porch stoop. Because he does not speak, caregivers have not heard repeated themes from him: *Want this. Go there.* If Jimmy has given nonverbal clues about his interests, they have not passed them on to us.

As I pause to give Puzzle a drink, I look at Jimmy's photo again, aware that we work across two terrains here: the physical one and the unknowable territory of Jimmy's impulses. Where in the Venn diagram of his wandering would those two conditions intersect? I wonder how his priorities have shifted, if at all, in the almost five hours he's been gone. Would staying warm replace Jimmy's urge for a candy bar? Would he know not to approach unfriendly strangers for money or would he overlook risk in the pursuit of bubblegum?

Potential hypothermia adds another layer of question. Irrational behavior often occurs with severe hypothermias, including a condition called paradoxical undressing, where the victim receives false signals from the hypothalamus, believes he is warm, and sheds his clothes. *Keep your clothes on, Jimmy,* I think. *Get out of the wind.*

Puzzle finishes her water and I shake out the collapsible bowl, then fold and tuck it into a pocket. We are off again, across the bridge and into the ravine. The creek below is a shallow one, sparkling occasionally from a corner streetlight. Water is always relevant on missing persons searches: a perpetual fascination, a potential hotspot for children — even in the cold — and though Jimmy might also be attracted, Puzzle is into the creek bed and out of it in less than a minute. She loves water too, but she is clear about it. Nothing there.

We head into the schoolyard to begin sweeps across it. The school itself is perpendicular to the wind here, and because I can't know how scent might be distorted around its edges and deep side-door pockets, our sweeps are closer together than they need to be, perhaps. It's Puzzle's first formal search, and this new environment has made me cautious. We work across the schoolyard as the officer flashes light into its empty doorways.

When we move to the side of the school, Jerry suggests that I circle Puzzle around a Dumpster as we pass. She has little interest in the area, and when we circle the Dumpster, no interest at all, but there is precedent for Jerry's suggestion: Dumpsters are often the sad endpoint of searches, and scent there can be muddled through their heavy lids and slide-hatches or muffled when a victim has been wrapped in garbage bags. Puzzle moves away from the Dumpster as the officer verifies by peeking in, and I feel a little twitch of relief that Jimmy hasn't been discarded there. Whether he'd climb in one to keep warm is anyone's guess, but clearly he hasn't made that choice, either.

The schoolyard marks the end of our assigned area, and we return to the command post along the easternmost side of the sector. Puzzle has indicated interest, mild interest, only on the eastern side. I want to return the same way to see if that interest intensifies or goes away altogether. We move quickly north along the street we had previously used to head south, and twice Puzzle twitches eastward. Again, it's only a twitch, not the body shiver I've felt from her when desired scent was hot and close, nor the gathering to run that I associate with a very near alert. Jerry has reported this repeated interest to the search manager, and we move quietly back to the command post in the early hours of the morning.

We arrive to find the search manager bent over a map and in conference with the police officer coordinating the search. Fleta has tallied all indications from the responding dogs, and when asked what the next sectors might be, indicates that the wisest move would be new sectors to the east. Several dogs had interest that direction. She begins to mark the map while the officer in charge discusses the situation with police in the neighboring town.

Handlers full of hot coffee and the dogs now warm from a rehab period in cars, we are ready to go out again, waiting for authorization to head east. We've now been on-scene for a couple of hours. Jimmy has been missing for almost seven. Most of us have added a layer or two of clothing as night has deepened and the temperature has continued to drop. Even so, it doesn't take much exposure to the wind to feel cold again. An officer raises the question we all carry: would Jimmy be aware enough to seek shelter and come in from the cold, or would he regress as hypothermia advanced, losing the ability to walk, in time unable to stay awake as his brain and body began to shut down? If Jimmy made all the wrong choices three hours ago, he could have died soon after the front had passed.

I look down the line of teammates already in packs and ready to head out again. They stand queued and ready to receive second sectors, gloved hands in pockets, shoulders up and heads retracted into the collars of jackets. Quiet. Conserving energy. Most of them are due at work in a few hours. Those who can stay will stay until Jimmy is found, then go on to work second or third shift. This is not the first time any of us will have searched most of the night and gone straight to work afterward, a little punchy and disembodied. I can see the puffs of exhale that mark each of my colleagues — the slow, steady thought bubbles above those who have learned to rest standing, waiting; the erratic steam-engine puffs above those whose conversations I cannot hear.

Puzzle's little exhales are also visible as she stands knitting scent. I have draped one of my down vests over her back as we wait. She doesn't whine or bark or strain at the lead, but I can see the steam of deep breaths and small ones, the occasional round huff of her mouth as some new Not Jimmy person steps onto the scene. When I touch the back of her neck, I can feel the tension of her readiness for *Next*, whatever it is, whenever it comes.

We hear a burst of static and unintelligible words over a distant radio, and suddenly there is a rush of feet and a huddle of officers, and Fleta is eclipsed within a ring of taller men. The dogs pick up the changed energy and transmit it, dog to dog and rapidly, their ears perked and tails in new motion. We humans lean forward where we stand. We strain for a single clarifying word. "Found" would be a good one. "Alive" would be even better.

The word I think I hear is "chips," and I'm trying to make sense of that when information crackles down the line that Jimmy has been found, alive, and just a few blocks east of the road that separated his neighborhood from the next town. "East" a few murmur and look down at their dogs. Alerted to the search, police officers in the adjoining town quickly began to sweep nearby streets and had located Jimmy in an all-night fast-food restaurant.

For the second time in two nights, Jimmy returns in a police cruiser with lights blazing. His forehead presses against the window, and his eyes widen at the sight of the luminous, frosty dogs pacing beneath the street lamps. Jimmy is cold. He is small and huddled when he gets out of the car, barefoot still. His feet curl and he hops a little when he steps onto the chilly sidewalk. He is staccato there in the flash of emergency lights, *pop-pop-pop*, looking gleeful and impossibly young. He points to the dogs and smiles wide.

There have been some good Samaritans and possibly some scavenging in tonight's history. Jimmy wears a worn blanket like a shawl and struggles to hold it closed across his chest while managing his armful of prizes: a martial arts videotape, a half-empty bag of corn chips, a Twinkie, and what's left of a soda in a supersize cup. He seems a little chastened by tonight's experience, but as a huddle of people move him to the front door, he appears genuinely delighted over the light show, the gathered crowd, and the atmosphere of victory over his return.

Though Lassie and Rin Tin Tin have schooled the world to Hollywood dogs and Hollywood victories, Puzzle and I celebrate a much quieter one. Jimmy is alive. Puzzle did her job thoroughly. She did it well — no distractions, no abandonment, no false alerts. We ran pace for pace on this first official search of our partnership. She never once stopped, and I never once had to.

We return home wide awake, hungry, and renewed. Oatmeal and Milk Bones at three in the morning, e-mail at four, and at five I'm still up playing Tug-o-war with the Golden, who by now would gladly wind down if I would. The Poms have grumbled themselves off into deeper rooms of the house, their sleep disturbed by our late, late entrance that will not resolve. But Puzzle, who is also tired, is generous. She has shared a bit of the oatmeal, which she doesn't like much, and put her head on my boots while I read e-mail, and now she will tug as often as I drop the Booda rope before her, though I notice more and more often that she's tugging recumbent — giving me a little deadweight game while she hints that it might be time to let go of the search.

Which is one of her many gifts, this moving forward, this letting go.

I bend down to Puzzle and kiss her street-worn paws. These are early days in our career together, and there will be more stumbling places ahead, few easy lessons. "Good girl," I say without a referent, a generic thank you for the partnership and the history, for the anarchy, the instruction, and the solace of her. We go to bed at first light, and we leave the pager on.

EPILOGUE

Despite the amazing capabilities of new technology in the search field—the pinpoint GPS units, sidescan sonar, tiny cameras, and hypersensitive microphones—canine search-and-rescue continues. Law enforcement agencies recognize that for some search scenarios, there is no substitute for a well-trained dog with a gift of nose and a handler who can translate even the most subtle cues. Canine SAR teams exist worldwide, partnering other rescue resources, serving communities ravaged by natural or manmade disaster, and deploying with the same commitment to search for a single person gone lost. Many dogs and handlers give the best years of their lives to this service, retiring only when injury demands it, or when age and strength begin to fail. It is a quiet message in the long dialogue between partners: *enough*.

The dogs of MARK-9 remain beside us even after they retire, much-loved family members after their partnership days in the search sector are done. German Shepherd Hunter, a second-chance dog rescued himself just days before scheduled euthanasia, worked a long and distinguished career. Hunter retired in 2004 and died at home in 2007, his handler, Max, beside him. Rough-coat Collie Saber, another of MARK-9's foundation dogs and an AKC ACE Award recipient in 2004, took on the gentler job of bringing in the mail after retiring from the search field. Saber died at home just three weeks short of his sixteenth birthday in 2008. An off-duty injury forced brilliant Shadow into retirement from SAR, though she participated in the occasional training search and helped instruct the team's youngest dogs for as long as she was able. Shadow's heart surrendered in 2008. She was the last of the team's foundation dogs, whose ashes are jointly scattered across their favorite training spot.

At the time of this writing, Buster, Belle, and Hoss continue in the field, still driven, focused, successful — and opinionated. High-energy Valkyrei remains full of dash and go beside Rob. Max and Fleta continue to work beside their talented second partners, Mercy and Misty. Puzzle is no longer the puppy upstart: Jerry's second partner, the clever Aussie Shepherd Gypsy, certified in 2008. And youngsters have joined the team: Border Collie Pete recently certified with his partner, Sara, and Border Collie Scout is training hard with new handler Michele now.

Puzzle and I are still partners in the field. Puz is happy to be a part of any search, period, but wildly happy to bust brush in the wilderness. With her dog and human colleagues, Puzzle has participated in urban, wilderness, and weather-related disaster searches, once surprising a reporter hidden deep in a search sector with an unexpected *wroo!* In 2006, Puzzle and many of her canine teammates trained for and successfully challenged the certification test for Texas Task Force 2, a state disaster-response unit.

At home, Scuppy, Sophie, and Whisky died in successive years, rescues themselves who learned love and shared joy. The cats thrive. Fo'c'sle Jack and Mr. Sprits'l are very much alive and happy to tell you about it. And tell you about it. And tell you about it. The puppy discord when Puzzle first arrived is gone. Her affinity for fragile senior dogs continues. I'm aware how much we owe all the little dogs that came through the house in those early years, who taught and challenged Puzzle, from whom she learned the ways of canine compassion. She also learned how to *insist*. In 2007, Puzzle met an abandoned calico kitten she was determined to bring home. Enter: Thistle. Cat and Golden are inseparable playmates.

In the prime of her strength and drive, Puzzle is a joyful dog, a daily instruction. I like to think I have brought her something too, and that we achieve things together neither of us could have ever done alone. And I'm aware how thoroughly she is one of her own kind. At the end of a recent search for a child found unharmed, I watched Puzzle bob her nose with the other dogs as the boy stepped beneath a street lamp and his mother rushed to meet him. The tired, street-greasy search dogs came alive, nostrils working and tails in motion. "Yes," they seemed to huff happily in the second scent of him, "you're the one we're here for."

July 2009

ACKNOWLEDGMENTS

Behind lucky writers, there are good souls throwing sparks. I could not be more grateful to my agent, Jim Hornfischer, and editor, Susan Canavan, for their faith in this project and rigorous encouragement throughout.

A special thank-you to seven authors — Tony Broadbent, Lee Child, Cornelia Read, and Hallie Ephron for urging me to do this thing in the first place, and early readers Robin Hemley and Irene Prokop for showing me how to do it better. And to Michael Perry, that decent soul in Wisconsin whose work always resonates, and who was kind at a critical point — more kind than he probably knew. Thanks also to Mitch Land, George Getschow, and Ron Chrisman of the Mayborn Literary Nonfiction Conference, where this project received important critique and quite the jump-start!

To Devon Thomas Treadwell of Pollywog Naming and Branding, Minneapolis — thanks for so many things, including intuitive Googling and long-distance assistance on multiple searches, and for a working title here that made the cut! And to Marina Cing Hsieh, a fine woman of candor and unconditional love.

Thanks to Kim Cain, of Mystic Goldens, who brought Puzzle into the world, and to Susan Blatz, obedience instructor, who helped me teach my smart dog how to love a "Sit!" Special thanks to Manny Yzaguirre, DVM. Puz is in such good hands.

At Houghton Mifflin Harcourt, no writer could ask for better support than I have received from Carla Gray, Taryn Roeder, Meagan Stacey, Martha Kennedy, Bridget Marmion, Laurie Brown, Melissa Lotfy, Lisa Glover, Shuchi Saraswat, Mary Kate Maco, and Lori Glazer. Thanks also to copy editor Beth Burleigh Fuller and to photographers Debbie Bryant and Chris Moseley. Woot! and Yowza! I am so fortunate.

Thanks to the staff at Legal Grounds, Dallas, for a quiet place to write. (I recommend the grilled mozzarella sandwich.) And to Tom and Karen Watson at the Tartan Thistle Bed and Breakfast, McKinney, Texas, for weeks of safe haven and really good shortbread. More than half this book was written there. I am grateful, grateful to Elaine Harris, of PomRescue.com, who brought four-pound Pomeranian rescue Tupper into my life. From first draft to final edits, Tup was beside me every time I sat to write — a loving presence, my unfailing muse. Thank you to Megan Glunt of Borders, Lovers Lane, Dallas, who did a rescue of her own, helping me retrieve a third of this edited manuscript when it was caught by a thunderstorm and blown yards away. All kinds of gratitude to Chef Duff Goldman, Mary Alice Fallon Yeskey, Anna Ellison, and the staff of Charm City Cakes, Baltimore, for keeping a secret and making one *amazing* cake.

To my colleagues at MARK-9 Search and Rescue: bless you, thank you. Dog and human — you had me from the very first "Find!"

And in the largest sense, thank you to every officer, EMT, paramedic, and firefighter, to every dog and volunteer who goes out in the middle of the night on behalf of another.

BIBLIOGRAPHY

Ackerman, Diane. *A Natural History of the Senses*. New York: Vintage, 1995.

Bidner, Jen. *Dog Heroes: Saving Lives and Protecting America*. Guildford, CT: The Lyons Press, 2002.

Brown, Ali. *Scaredy Dog! Understanding and Rehabilitating Your Reactive Dog*. Allentown, PA: Tanacacia Press, 2004.

Coren, Stanley. *How Dogs Think: Understanding the Canine Mind*. New York: Free Press, 2004.

Ellman, Vikki. *Guide to Owning a Pomeranian*. Neptune City, NJ: TFH Publications, 1996.

Fischer, Cindy. *Our Pets Have a Story to Tell*. North Chelmsford, MA: BGB Publications, 1998.

Fleming, June. *Staying Found: The Complete Map and Compass Handbook*. 3rd ed. Seattle: The Mountaineers Press, 2001.

Kalnajs, Sarah. *The Language of Dogs*. DVD. Blue Dog Training and Behavior, 2007.

McConnell, Patricia. *The Other End of the Leash*. New York: Ballantine Books, 2002.

Rebmann, Andrew, Edward David, and Marcella H. Sorg. *Cadaver Dog Handbook: Forensic Training and Tactics for the Recovery of Human Remains*. Boca Raton: CRC Press, 2000.

Shojai, Amy D. *Complete Care for Your Aging Dog*. New York: New American Library, 2003.

Volhard, Jack, and Wendy Volhard. *The Canine Good Citizen: Every Dog Can Be One*. New York: Howell Book House, 1994.

Wood, Deborah. *Help for Your Shy Dog: Turning Your Terrified Dog into a Terrific Pet*. New York: Howell Book House, 1999.